Beginning Ubuntu LTS Server Administration

From Novice to Professional, Second Edition

Sander van Vugt

Apress®

Beginning Ubuntu LTS Server Administration: From Novice to Professional, Second Edition

Copyright © 2008 by Sander van Vugt

ISBN-13 (pbk): 978-1-4302-1082-5

ISBN-13 (electronic): 978-1-4302-1081-8

Printed and bound in the United States of America 9 8 7 6 5 4 3 2

Trademarked names may appear in this book. Rather than use a trademark symbol with every occurrence of a trademarked name, we use the names only in an editorial fashion and to the benefit of the trademark owner, with no intention of infringement of the trademark.

Java™ and all Java-based marks are trademarks or registered trademarks of Sun Microsystems, Inc., in the US and other countries. Apress, Inc., is not affiliated with Sun Microsystems, Inc., and this book was written without endorsement from Sun Microsystems, Inc.

Lead Editor: Frank Pohlmann
Technical Reviewers: Tim Hall, Samuel Cuella
Editorial Board: Clay Andres, Steve Anglin, Ewan Buckingham, Tony Campbell, Gary Cornell,
    Jonathan Gennick, Matthew Moodie, Joseph Ottinger, Jeffrey Pepper, Frank Pohlmann,
    Ben Renow-Clarke, Dominic Shakeshaft, Matt Wade, Tom Welsh
Project Manager: Beth Christmas
Copy Editor: Nancy Sixsmith
Associate Production Director: Kari Brooks-Copony
Production Editor: Liz Berry
Compositor: Dina Quan
Proofreader: Liz Welch
Indexer: Odessa&Cie
Cover Designer: Kurt Krames
Manufacturing Director: Tom Debolski

Distributed to the book trade worldwide by Springer-Verlag New York, Inc., 233 Spring Street, 6th Floor, New York, NY 10013. Phone 1-800-SPRINGER, fax 201-348-4505, e-mail orders-ny@springer-sbm.com, or visit http://www.springeronline.com.

For information on translations, please e-mail info@apress.com, or visit http://www.apress.com.

Apress and friends of ED books may be purchased in bulk for academic, corporate, or promotional use. eBook versions and licenses are also available for most titles. For more information, reference our Special Bulk Sales–eBook Licensing web page at http://www.apress.com/info/bulksales.

The source code for this book is available to readers at http://www.apress.com.

This book is dedicated to Florence.

Contents at a Glance

Contents

About the Author

 **SANDER VAN VUGT** is an independent trainer and consultant who lives in the Netherlands and works in the extended EMEA (Europe, Middle East, and Africa) area. He specializes in Linux high availability, storage solutions, and performance problems; and has successfully implemented Linux clusters across the globe. Sander has written several books about Linux-related subjects, including *The Definitive Guide to SUSE Linux Enterprise Server* (Apress, 2006).

Sander's articles can be found on several international web sites and in magazines such as *SearchEnterpriseLinux.com, Linux Journal*, and *Linux Magazine*. He works as a volunteer for the Linux Professional Institute (LPI), contributing topics for different certification levels. Most important, Sander is the father of Alex and Franck, and is the loving husband of Florence.

For more information, consult Sander's web site: www.sandervanvugt.com. Sander can be reached by email at mail@sandervanvugt.com.

About the Technical Reviewers

SAMUEL CUELLA was born in 1985. He is currently an IT student and also works as a Linux/Solaris trainer. Samuel taught the complete Mandriva certification program in China (JUST University) and also teaches Linux for LPI certification training.

TIM HALL currently provides front-line support for 64 Studio. He has also written newbie tutorials for *Linux User & Developer* magazine in between more mundane system admin and web authoring jobs. Tim has released albums and performed as a musician and songwriter, both solo and in collaboration with other artists. He has been further honored as the holder of the Bardic chair of Glastonbury between 2005 and 2007.

Introduction

*B*eginning Ubuntu LTS Server Administration: From Novice to Professional, Second Edition provides a complete introduction to Ubuntu Server. I wrote it for people who are new to Ubuntu Server administration but have a solid foundation in IT. The target readers are Windows administrators as well as people who are used to managing other flavors of Linux (or UNIX). It was the goal of this book to give a no-nonsense introduction to working with Ubuntu Server, so it provides all the basics that are needed to get you going. It also includes many useful tips that help you do your work in a more efficient manner.

Many books about Ubuntu are presently available, but you can't do Ubuntu Server justice by covering both the desktop and the server version in one book. The needs of a server administrator are vastly different from the needs of a desktop administrator. So I chose an approach that makes sense for the server administrator, and all topics are selected and organized to make sense for your day-to-day work as a server administrator.

Who This Book Is For

This book is written for Linux administrators, whether novice or experienced, who are looking for a quick, thorough, and authoritative introduction to daily Ubuntu Server management.

How This Book Is Structured

The book starts by describing Ubuntu Server, with a special focus on storage configuration, which is an especially important concern when dealing with server environments. You'll then find a quick introduction to driving Ubuntu Server from the command line, in case you haven't done this before. The third chapter tackles some of the common generic tasks of a server administrator, including managing software packages and configuring a graphical user interface. Next are chapters about file system management, Ubuntu Server security, managing processes, and the boot procedure. The last chapter, which deals with stand-alone server functionality, explains Bash shell scripting—in fewer than 30 pages, you'll learn everything you ever need to know about this complex topic.

The second part of the book teaches you all about network services. First, you'll learn how to configure and troubleshoot a network interface. Next, you'll read how to set up infrastructure services such as time services, name services, and DHCP. The following chapters discuss managing file services, the Apache web server (including performance tuning hints and a section on virtual hosts), and related packages such as MySQL. Finally, the last chapter provides an overview of the approaches to running virtualization on Ubuntu Server.

Prerequisites

To get the most out of this book, you should have a computer that you can use to install Ubuntu Server. Any Pentium-based system with 128 MB of RAM and a hard disk with at least 2 GB of free space will do fine. You also need the Ubuntu Server software, which you can download from www.ubuntu.com. Apart from these simple elements, there are no further prerequisites. This book assumes no preliminary knowledge of Linux or Ubuntu.

Downloading the Code

The source code for this book is available at www.apress.com in the Downloads section of this book's home page. Please feel free to visit the Apress web site and download all the code there. You can also check for errata and find related Apress titles.

Contacting the Author

The author can be reached via his web site (www.sandervanvugt.com) and by mail at mail@sandervanvugt.com.

■■■

## CHAPTER 1

Installing Ubuntu Server

You probably chose Ubuntu as a server solution because of either your gratifying experience using it on the desktop or the raves you've heard from others about its user-friendly approach. Accordingly, you might expect the general Ubuntu Server installation process to be fairly easy, and indeed it is. Nevertheless, because your ultimate goal is to deploy the server in a production environment, it's a good idea to follow some key aspects of the installation process with rigor, and this chapter is intended to help you do exactly that.

To keep things as simple as possible, you'll read how to complete the installation on a real server, with no virtualization involved. You'll explore the different options presented to you while installing Ubuntu, as well as the best choice to make to ensure that your installation is successful.

Preparing for the Installation

Before starting the installation, you have to do a bit of preparation. First, you must make sure that the required hardware is available. At the most basic, any PC will do, but, if you are interested in putting a real server to work, I recommend using server-grade hardware because that kind of hardware is optimized for the tasks that servers typically perform. On such hardware, you can install Ubuntu directly or virtualized. If you don't have server-grade hardware available, a standard PC is fine. In the end, it all depends on what you plan to do with your Ubuntu Server. An Apache web server at home does have some other requirements—as a corporate database server, for example.

In this chapter you won't learn how to install Ubuntu Server on a computer that already has some Windows installation. The reason for this is simple: on a real server you want only your server operating system and nothing else. Creating a dual-boot machine is cool for a desktop operating system, but you just don't want that for a production server. Because your Ubuntu Server probably has to be available at all times, it won't have any time to run anything but Ubuntu Server. So at this point, make sure that you have the hardware available to start the installation of a dedicated server.

Also make sure that you have the installation CD, which can be downloaded from www.ubuntu.com. (Make sure that you select the server version of Ubuntu.) In this book, I'm working with Ubuntu Server 8.04 LTS. The letters *LTS* stand for Long Term Support, which means that this version of Ubuntu Server will have five years of support. That makes it a perfect server operating system to run in an enterprise environment, in which support is of the highest importance.

Are you looking for the latest that Ubuntu Server has to offer? You can download the latest version of Ubuntu Server from www.ubuntu.com.

Starting the Ubuntu Server Installation Process

Have everything ready? Time to go! I assume that you already found the CD image at www.ubuntu.com and burned it as an image to a CD. Insert the installation CD in your server's optical drive and boot your server. Make sure the server boots from the CD-ROM and follow these steps to complete the installation.

1. In the installation menu that appears once the CD spins up, specify what you want to do. Often, it will be enough to select Install to the hard disk, but in certain cases other options are required as well. This is especially the case if you want to install in a language other than English and you're using a keyboard different from a US keyboard. If this is the case, use the F2 and the F3 keys to specify your language settings. The other options are rarely used, although the F6 key hides an option that some will like: Free software only in this menu ensures that no commercial packages are installed on your server. Make sure that you have everything you need, select Install Ubuntu Server, as shown in Figure 1-1, and then press the Enter key to start the installation.

Figure 1-1. *In many situations, you just have to press the Enter key to start the installation.*

■**Note** If your graphical hardware doesn't support displaying the full graphical menu, you might get an installation screen that looks a little different. In that case, press F1 to see the options that are mentioned before.

2. The next screen shows a menu-driven interface. Ubuntu Server does not have a graphical user interface (GUI) by default because it runs on servers that are hidden in a data center, anyway. Using a GUI would be a waste of precious system resources, so the installation procedure itself is also text-based. In case you did not choose your installation language in the first step of this procedure, you get another chance in the second screen. In this book we'll use English; if you want to install in another language, select it from the menu that you see in Figure 1-2.

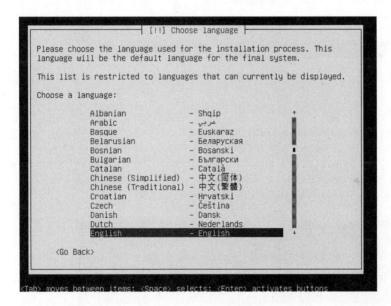

Figure 1-2. *If you did not specify the installation language in the boot screen, you have another chance of selecting the language here.*

3. Based on the language that you selected, you'll see a list of countries (see Figure 1-3). Select your country to make sure that other local settings are applied automatically. If your country is not in the default list, browse to the bottom of the list and select Other, which supplies a larger list.

■**Tip** Ubuntu Server makes some choices for you automatically. If you want to make these choices your-self, use the Go Back button that appears in almost every screen of the installer. This will display a more detailed list of options that are relevant to that particular stage of the installation, and you can choose what you want to do yourself.

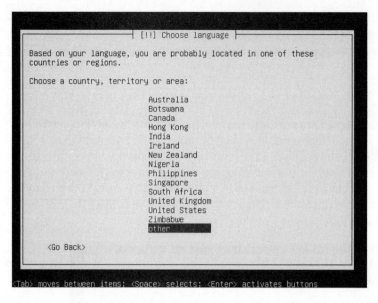

Figure 1-3. *If your country doesn't appear in the default list of countries, select Other to choose from a larger list of countries.*

4. Next, you can have the installer automatically detect the keyboard that you are using. After selecting this option, the installer will ask you to use some keys on your keyboard; based on the keys you use, the installer will determine the correct keyboard setting. If you don't want to use this feature, click No from the screen that you see in Figure 1-4, and select your keyboard type from the list displayed next.

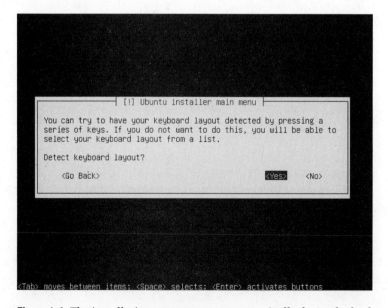

Figure 1-4. *The installation program can automatically detect the keyboard layout that you are using.*

5. If you want the program to detect the keyboard automatically, select Yes. Next, the installer will ask you to hit a specified key (see Figure 1-5), by which it can detect the right keyboard layout in a matter of seconds. If you don't want to do the automatic detection, that's fine. You can just select the keyboard from a list of keyboards.

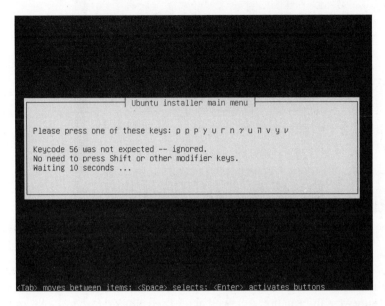

Figure 1-5. *Based on the keys that you pressed, the installation program will quickly detect the proper keyboard layout.*

6. After the keyboard is configured, most hardware is detected and configured automatically. Some hardware—such as WiFi network cards or graphical adapters—may require later configuration. Among the most important settings is the network configuration. If a DHCP server is available in the network to automatically assign IP addresses, your server will be provided with an IP address and ask you only for a name for the server; you'll see nothing that is related to the configuration of the network board at all! If you don't have a DHCP server, the network configuration program will start automatically. For a server, it is always a good idea to work with a fixed IP address, because you wouldn't want your services to suddenly switch to a different IP address suddenly. To start the manual network configuration, use the Go Back button now and manually configure the network card. You'll see a list of the available options. In the next step, you manually configure the IP address of your server.

7. After selecting the Go back option, move your cursor to Configure network manually (see Figure 1-6) and press Enter.

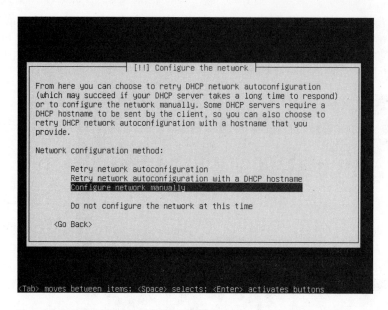

```
                    ┤ [!!] Configure the network ├
  From here you can choose to retry DHCP network autoconfiguration
  (which may succeed if your DHCP server takes a long time to respond)
  or to configure the network manually. Some DHCP servers require a
  DHCP hostname to be sent by the client, so you can also choose to
  retry DHCP network autoconfiguration with a hostname that you
  provide.

  Network configuration method:

          Retry network autoconfiguration
          Retry network autoconfiguration with a DHCP hostname
          Configure network manually

          Do not configure the network at this time

      <Go Back>
```

  `<Tab> moves between items; <Space> selects; <Enter> activates buttons`

Figure 1-6. *If you don't use the Go Back option, you can't configure your network manually.*

8. Enter the IP address that you want to use for your server, select Continue, and press Enter. Not sure what information you need here? Then either return to step 6 and have DHCP automatically assign an IP address, or ask your service provider or network administrator for the proper address configuration.

9. Every IP address needs a netmask that explains to your server what network it is in. Most IP addresses can use the netmask that is assigned to them by default. If this doesn't work in your situation, enter the proper netmask in the screen shown in Figure 1-7, select Continue, and press Enter.

10. Now you're asked to enter the IP address of the default gateway. This is the IP address of the router that is connected to the rest of the Internet. If you don't know what to enter, ask your network administrator what to use here and then proceed to the next step.

11. Enter the IP address of the DNS server that you want to use (see Figure 1-8). This server allows you to reach other computers on the Internet by their names instead of their IP addresses. If you are on a small network, this is probably the address of a server at your Internet service provider. If you are on a larger network, the network administrator may have configured a separate DNS server. Ask what IP address you should use and then proceed to the next step. You would normally enter two IP addresses for DNS name servers to ensure that names will still be resolved if the first DNS server is down. To enter a second IP address for a DNS server, just enter the address with a space as the separator between the two addresses. Use the actual IP addresses here, not names (because using names requires a means for them to be resolved, and setting up that mechanism is just what you're doing here).

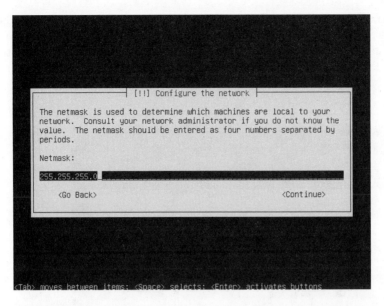

Figure 1-7. *On most networks, the default netmask can be used.*

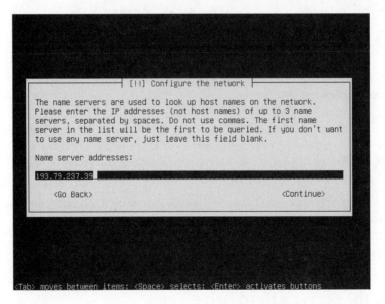

Figure 1-8. *The IP address of the DNS server is necessary to contact other computers on the Internet by their names instead of their IP addresses.*

12. Now you are asked for the name you want to use for your computer. By default, the installer assigns a host name automatically (depending on the hardware configuration you're using, it will usually be Ubuntu). There's nothing wrong with using this assigned name, but you may want to use a name that provides a little more information or individuality. Also, the name typically has to conform to the naming scheme of your network.

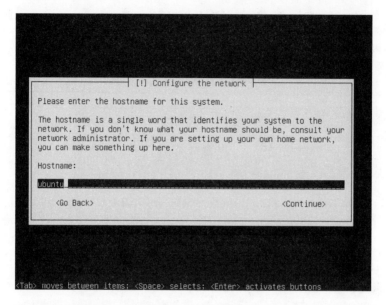

Figure 1-9. *The default host name is set to Ubuntu. You may want to change that to something that provides more information.*

13. As the last part of the network configuration, you have to enter a domain name now. If there's a DHCP server on your network, you'll see that a domain name was entered automatically. (You're free to change that automatically assigned name to any other name if it doesn't fit what you want to do with your server.)

14. Now you have to select your server's time zone. It is based on the country that you selected earlier, so if you don't see the time zone you want to use, go back and change the country that you selected or change the time zone after your server has been installed completely.

Configuring the Server's Hard Drive

You've now completed the first part of the installation, but basically nothing has changed on your computer yet. So, if you want to stop the installation of Ubuntu Server and install Windows NT anyway, you can. If you want to continue, it's time to do some thinking. The installer is going to ask you how you want to lay out your server's hard drive. You have a couple of choices here, and you'd better make them now because they'll be very difficult to change later. So wait before you press Enter and read this section first.

The first choice you have to make is between using just one partition or volume to install your server, or using several of them. Using more than one storage unit can make your server more flexible and more secure. If, for example, you put all data on one large storage unit (like one root partition), a user or a process can fill that partition completely by accident, thus making your server completely unusable. It's useful to use more than one storage unit for the following reasons, as well:

- Working with more than one partition or logical volume makes it possible to mount them with different properties while mounting. For example, a partition where things normally wouldn't change can be mounted as read-only, thus increasing the security of your server.

- Using more than one partition makes it easier to work with external storage like a storage area network (SAN). For example, you could put all the system data on the server's local hard drive, and all the user data could reside on the SAN.

- Working with more than one partition is necessary in some situations. For example, to make sure that your server will always be able to start up, you could create a separate partition to boot from.

Next, you have to decide between using logical volumes or partitions. *Partitions* are fixed-size slices of disk space. It is very hard (although not impossible) to change them later. *Logical volumes* from the Logical Volume Manager (LVM) system are much more flexible. It's very easy to resize them, and they offer some other cool advanced features as well (about which you'll read in Chapter 4 of this book). In the next subsections you'll learn more about partitions and volumes.

Working with Traditional Partitions

Partitions have been used to divide server hard disks in several usable slices since the very first days of the personal computer. To create partitions, you use the partition table in the master boot record of your server's hard disk. Because this partition table is only 64 bytes, you can create only four partitions here. Originally, these were so-called primary partitions. In some cases, four is not enough, and that's what the extended partition was invented for. A *primary partition* can contain a file system directly. This is not the case for extended partitions. An *extended partition* functions like an empty box that allows you to create logical partitions inside of it. So the only purpose of extended partitions is to allow you to create logical partitions. No logical partitions without extended partitions. The number of logical partitions that can be created depends on the hardware and software that you are using, but it is never more than 16. So, using the traditional partitioning scheme, a maximum of 20 partitions can be created. This number may seem enough, but in some situations it isn't.

The next characteristic of a traditional partition is that it is not very flexible. If, after some time, you learn that one of the partitions is almost full, it is very difficult in a traditional partitioning scheme to increase the size of one partition while decreasing the size of another partition. It can be done, but the work is really best left to the experts, because you could lose all data on all partitions involved.

■**Caution** You think you're an expert? Okay. Here's how it works: first shrink the size of the file system in the partition (check Chapter 4 for more information). After that, delete the partition you want to reduce in size and create it again, using the same start cylinder and the new size you want to use for the partition. But remember when you do this, you're only one small step away from destroying all files on your partition, so be careful and don't blame me if it goes wrong. Better wait until you read Chapter 4 before you try to perform a potentially dangerous action like this.

Advantages of Logical Volumes

The LVM system can be used to avoid the disadvantages of traditional partitions. If you use an LVM layout, you format the logical volumes instead of the partitions. The logical volume has more or less the same functionality as the partition, but LVMs have some important benefits:

- You can create as many as 256 LVM logical volumes.

- Logical volumes are very easy to resize.

- A logical volume does not have a one-to-one relationship with the storage device that it's created on. Thus, it's possible to create a logical volume that uses three hard disks at the same time. (Although this process is certainly not recommended because if you lost one hard disk, you would lose your complete volume, but it's cool that you can do it, and there are ways of coping with hard disk failure.)

- Logical volumes support working with snapshots. A *snapshot* allows you to freeze the state of a volume at a given point in time, which makes backing up data on a logical volume very convenient. This is done in a very clever way, so that the snapshot uses only a fraction of the disk space of the original volume.

■**Note** Really want to understand how LVM is working? The LVM-HOWTO at `http://tldp.org/HOWTO/` `LVM-HOWTO` has some good in-depth information. Chapter 4 has some more information as well.

Apart from all the good news, LVMs have one drawback: it is very hard to boot from a logical volume. Therefore, even if you're using LVMs, you'll always need at least one traditional partition to boot your server.

Creating an Efficient Hard Disk Layout on the Server

When installing a Linux server, it's common not to put all files on one huge partition or logical volume for the reasons just discussed. Because Linux servers normally contain many different files, it is a good idea to create some partitions or volumes to store these files. Each of these partitions or volumes is assigned to (mounted on) a specific directory. Of course, you can put everything on one partition only, but you may run into troubles later, such as if a user completely fills this partition. Before starting the actual installation of your server, you should decide on the most appropriate way to use your hard drive.

Tip You don't want to go for the complicated setup straight away—just a simple Ubuntu Server? Use the first Guided partitioning option from the menu in Figure 1-10 (in the section "Using the Guided Partitioning Procedure") and press Enter. In that case, you can also skip the next couple of pages of this chapter. Want to have not just a Ubuntu Server but also a well-performing Ubuntu Server? Read on, please.

It is a good idea to give the directories their own partition or logical volume on your server.

- /boot: Because the information in the /boot directory is needed to start a server, it's a rather important directory. For that reason and especially to protect it from everything else that is used on your server, /boot often has its own partition. This directory cannot be on a logical volume because booting from logical volumes is currently not supported out of the box. Because this directory is the first thing that is needed when booting a server, it's a very good idea to put it at the beginning of your server's hard drive. Doing so will prevent time-out issues while booting the server. It will also make troubleshooting a lot easier. And if these reasons are not enough, it is a good idea to have a separated /boot partition if working on a server with an older BIOS because it should be at the beginning of your hard disk. Typically, it is more than enough to allocate the /boot directory to a 100 MB partition.

- /: The root directory of the file system always has its own file system, which is also referred to as the root file system. The *root file system* is rather simple: it contains everything that hasn't been split off to another partition. If no data files are stored here, 8 GB is typically large enough.

- /var: The /var directory is used by lots of processes that need to create files on your server dynamically (such as printer spool files or the cache that is created by your proxy cache server). However, because the /var directory is so very dynamic, it has an increased chance of problems. So it's always a good idea to put it on its own partition. In a normal environment, 4 GB is a reasonable amount of disk space to assign to this partition, but in some specific environments, you'll need lots more.

Caution A badly configured log system can eat up available disk space very fast. So don't just create a /var volume and never look at it again; make sure that you tune your logging services as well. (More on that in Chapter 3.)

- /home: The /home directory belongs to the user and is where he or she will normally store files if the server is a file server. Because it also is very dynamic, and users are accessing it all the time, make sure that it also has its own partition. The amount of disk space you reserve for this partition depends on how much space you want to grant to your users.

- /srv: The /srv directory is used by servers such as the Apache web server and the FTP server to store data. Because files in this directory can be accessed by users that make a connection from the Internet, it should have some extra security. A simple way to do this is to place it in its own partition or volume. The amount of disk space on this partition depends on how you are going to use your server. If it is a public FTP server, assign it the maximum space; if your servers serve web or FTP files only occasionally, you can keep the disk space in this directory quite moderate.

File Systems

Because it's a Linux server, Ubuntu offers a choice from many file systems. When creating disk partitions or volumes, you have to tell the partitioning utility what type of file system you want to use on that volume. The following file systems are available for Ubuntu Server:

- *Ext3*: This is the default file system on almost all Linux distributions. Although it is a very stable file system with many debug tools available, there is a major drawback: Ext3 isn't the best file system to handle many files on one volume. It also isn't the fastest if you have to write many small files to your volume.

- *Ext2*: Ext2 and Ext3 are largely the same, except that Ext3 uses a journal to make it easier to recover a corrupted file system. This isn't the case for Ext2. Despite the absence of a journal, Ext2 is still a good choice for small volumes where the services of a journal aren't necessarily needed (because, for example, the files are not supposed to be opened for writing anyway). For instance, if you create a 100 MB /boot partition, the Ext2 file system is an excellent choice for it.

- *ReiserFS*: ReiserFS is a very advanced file system with great features. These features include journaling, advanced indexing, and many others. ReiserFS is particularly strong if many small files have to be written. However, it has two drawbacks: its main developer is currently facing myriad legal issues, and the file system is not particularly known for its stability and active community support. Use it if you want to write intensively or if you want to store many files in one directory, but make sure that you make a good backup at the same time. Want something that offers the same functionality but is more stable? Better use XFS.

- *XFS*: XFS was developed by SGI as a special-purpose open source file system. It is especially meant to be used when the server will see lots of usage or when the files are very large. So use it if you want to stream lots of media files or if you have an FTP server with multiple terabytes of data. In its most recent versions, XFS offers a good alternative for ReiserFS.

- *Ext4*: As you can probably guess from its name, Ext4 is the next generation of the Ext file systems. At the time of this writing, the first code was just available and it was far from being a usable file system. It is not in Ubuntu Server 8.04, but you will probably see it soon in future releases of Ubuntu Server.

- *FAT*: FAT vfat and NTFS file systems allow you to create a multiboot environment for a computer on which both Windows and Linux are installed. The purpose of these file systems is to access files stored in Windows partitions. Because there's no Windows on your Ubuntu Server, you don't need it there.

Continuing the Installation of Ubuntu Server

Now that you know some more about the choices that are offered when installing Ubuntu Server, let's continue. You now have to specify how you want to partition your server's hard disk. Because the partitioning of a hard disk is one of the most important parts of the server installation process, we will cover all choices. The choices are divided into three main categories:

- *Guided - use entire disk*: This is the easiest option. It offers a guided installation of your hard disk, based on traditional partitions. If you want to keep the partitions that already are on your server's hard drive, use Guided – resize instead. This option will shrink any installed operation system and use the space that is freed for installing Ubuntu Server. There is also an option that allows you to use the largest continuous free space, but this option is usable only if you have some free, unpartitioned disk space on your server's hard drive. Because the last of these two options is useful only for multiboot configurations, it is not covered in this chapter.

- *Guided - use entire disk and set up LVM*: This configuration option is a bit more complex. It offers you a wizard that allows you to create an LVM-based disk configuration. If you want to put up a well-secured environment, you can even choose to set up encrypted LVM instead. This is a good idea if you want to be sure that unauthorized people will never be able to access the data on your volume. Be aware, though, that an encrypted LVM volume will never be accessible if the related user credentials get lost. Also, there is a performance price for using encrypted volumes, so make sure that you really want them before applying them.

- *Manual*: Use this procedure if you're sure you know what you are doing and you don't need the help of any wizard.

Using the Guided Partitioning Procedure

Let's first talk about the guided procedure to set up a server hard disk. Your starting point is the screen shown in Figure 1-10. (At least, something that looks like it because the exact offering depends on what you already have on your server's hard drive.)

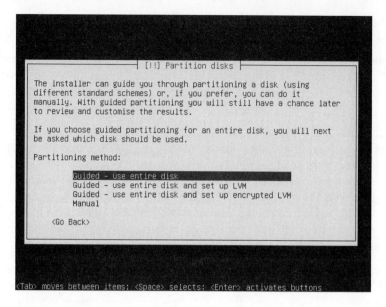

Figure 1-10. *You have several choices for configuring your server's hard disk.*

1. From the screen shown in Figure 1-10, select Guided - use entire disk.

2. The installation shows an overview of all the available hard disks (see Figure 1-11). Choose the disk that you want to use and press the Enter key.

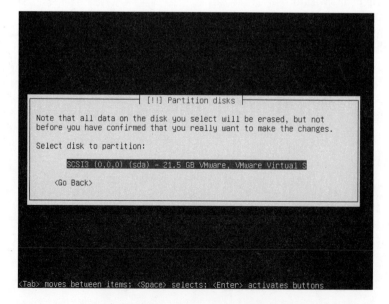

Figure 1-11. *Choose the hard disk that you want to partition.*

3. Now the installation program shows you what it intends to do with your server's hard disk (see Figure 1-12). The program isn't very verbose about this, as it just shows that it wants to create a swap partition and an Ext3 partition. But you probably don't care because this option is meant to offer a simple partitioning for your server. So select Yes and then press Enter to continue.

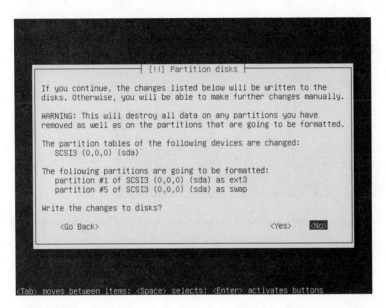

Figure 1-12. *The default partitioning scheme is rather basic.*

Using the Guided LVM-Based Setup

The procedure for an LVM-based disk layout is a lot like the simple guided disk setup. Choosing the guided LVM-based setup also brings you to a screen from which you can select the disk or disks that you want to use. Press Enter to select your disk. The partitioning program next tells you that it wants to write a basic partitioning scheme to disk before it can continue (see Figure 1-13). This is needed because an LVM environment is created on top of a traditional partition. Be aware that this is the point of no return; after you've written this basic partitioning scheme to hard disk, you can't undo your installation.

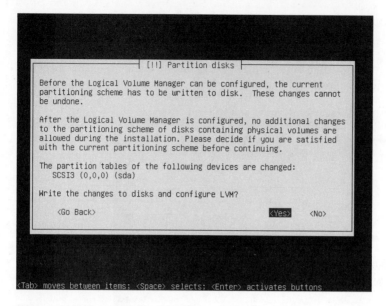

Figure 1-13. *Before the logical volumes can be created, some traditional partition setup has to be written to disk.*

Once the default partitioning has been set up, the installation program makes a proposition for two logical partitions that are set up on top of that (see Figure 1-14). By default, this is a root partition, formatted as Ext3 and a swap partition. Select Finish partitioning and write changes to disk and press Enter to continue with the installation.

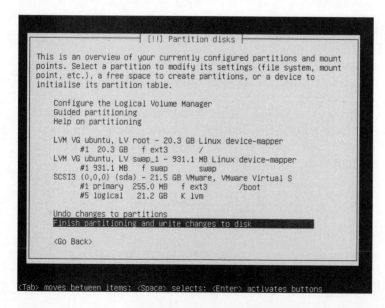

Figure 1-14. *By default, two logical volumes are created on top of the partitions.*

Manually Setting Up Your Hard Drive

If you want to set up your server's hard drive manually, that's perfectly fine, but you need to do some thinking before you start. First, you need to decide if you want to use LVM or traditional partitions only. Once you have made this decision, you need to choose between the different file systems that are available for Linux. I recommend making a small overview like the one in Table 1-1. While making such an overview, don't forget to assign some swap space as well. In Linux, swapping happens to a partition or volume, so you must consider it while setting up your server. In general, there is no need to make your swap space larger than 1 GB, with the exception of servers with special applications such as Oracle. If that is the case for your environment, consult your application documentation to find out what amount of swap space is reasonable for your situation.

Table 1-1. *Hard Disk Configuration Overview*

Directory	Type	File System	Size
/boot	Primary partition	Ext2	100 MB
/var	LVM	XFS	4 GB
/home	LVM	XFS	200 GB
/	LVM	Ext3	50 GB
swap	LVM	Swap	1 GB

Once you have made up your mind about the hard disk usage, follow these steps to apply your decision.

1. From the Partition disks interface, select Manual.

2. You now see a screen like the one in Figure 1-15. In this screen, select the hard disk that you want to configure first.

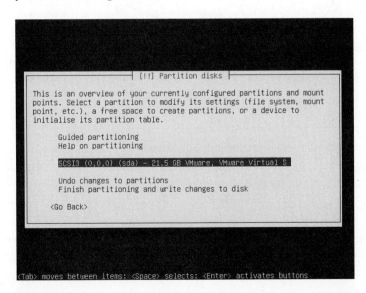

Figure 1-15. *Select the hard disk on which you want to create partitions and volumes.*

3. Because you have just selected an entire hard disk to configure, the installation program warns you, stating that continuing will remove all existing partitions on the hard drive. If you are sure you want to do this, select Yes and press the Enter key. If there's more than one hard disk on which you want to create partitions, select this additional hard disk and repeat these steps.

4. You now see an overview of all available unconfigured disk space on the selected hard drive (see Figure 1-16). Select this free space and press Enter.

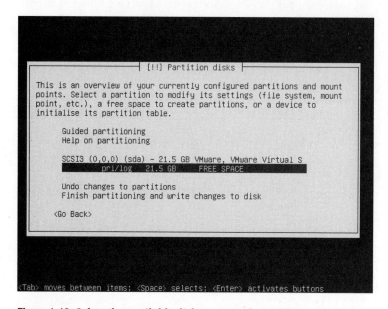

Figure 1-16. *Select the available disk space and press Enter.*

5. Now the installer asks how to use the available disk space. To create the setup detailed in Table 1-1, you first have to set up two partitions. One of them will be used by the /boot partition, and the other will contain all available disk space on the hard drive. This second partition is used to create a partition of the type 0x8e (LVM), which will be used to set up logical volumes later. To set up the /boot partition first, select Create a new partition (see Figure 1-17) and press Enter.

■**Note** Partition types are written as hexadecimal numbers. You know that they are hexadecimal numbers because you can often see them as *0x8e* (the *0x* indicates that it is a hexadecimal number). In most cases, however, there is no problem in omitting this *0x*, so *0x8e* and *8e* can both be used to refer to the partition ID.

---

6. Next, enter the size that you want to assign to the partition. You can enter a percentage of disk space that you want to use or just type **max** if you want to use the maximum available size. Next, select Continue and press the Enter key.

7. Now you have to enter the type of partition you need, and the installation program offers a choice between a primary and a logical partition. If you choose a logical partition, the program will automatically create the necessary extended partition. Because you need only two partitions in this scenario, you can choose the primary partition type for both of the partitions.

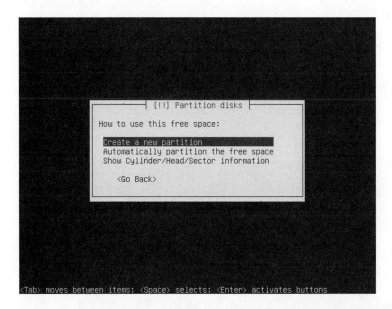

Figure 1-17. *You first have to create two traditional partitions, even if you want to create an LVM-based setup.*

8. Now specify where the new partition should start. Choose Beginning to create the partition at the beginning of the available disk space, or choose End to create it at the end of the available disk space. It makes sense to create the first partition at the beginning, so select Beginning and then press the Enter key.

9. Next, you see a screen that contains all the default properties for the new partition (see Figure 1-18). Assuming that this really is the partition that you want to use for /boot, make sure you enter the following values, select Done setting up the partition, and press the Enter key to continue.

- *Use as*: Ext2 file system. You are going to create a very small file system with files that will rarely change, so it doesn't make sense to use a journaling file system here.

- *Mount point*: /boot

- *Mount options*: Use the options that are selected by default

- *Label*: none

- *Reserved blocks*: 5%

- *Typical usage*: standard

- *Bootable flag*: off

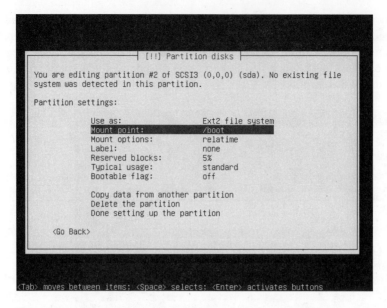

Figure 1-18. *Make sure your boot partition uses these settings.*

10. In the screen shown in Figure 1-19, select the available free space to create the LVM partition.

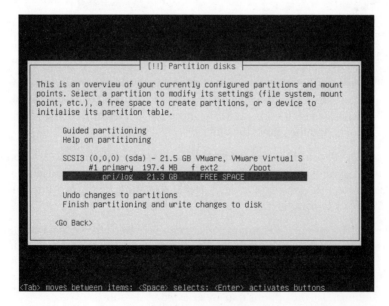

Figure 1-19. *Select the available free space again to create the LVM partition.*

11. Select Create a new partition and accept the default in which all available disk space is assigned to the new partition. Then specify that the new partition should be a primary partition. Next, in the screen with the partition settings, make sure you set the following options as shown:

  • *Use as*: physical volume for LVM

  • *Bootable flag*: off

■**Tip** Did something not work out the way it should have? Take a look at the syslog screen. You'll be able to see exactly what the installation program is trying to do and whether it succeeds. You can access the syslog screen by using Alt+F4. To return to the main installation screen, use Alt+F1.

---

12. Now select Done setting up the partition, and press Enter.

13. Once back in the main screen (see Figure 1-20), select Configure the Logical Volume Manager and press Enter.

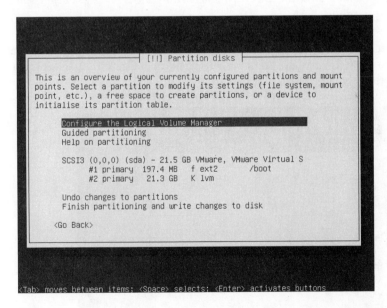

Figure 1-20. *After setting up the partitions, you must create the LVM environment.*

14. You'll now get a message (see Figure 1-21) that the current partitioning scheme has to be written to disk before setting up LVM. Select Yes and press Enter.

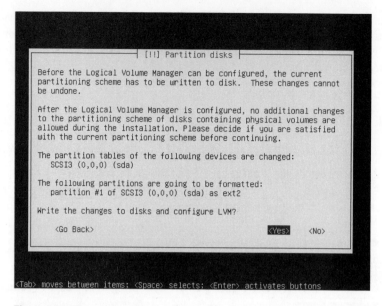

Figure 1-21. *You must write the changes in the partitioning to hard disk before you can create logical volumes.*

15. As the first step in the setup of an LVM environment, you must now assign all usable disk space to a volume group. From the screen shown in Figure 1-22, select Create volume group.

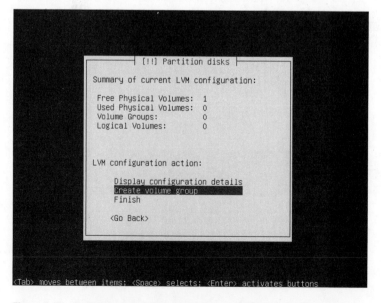

Figure 1-22. *An LVM setup is based on one or more volume groups.*

16. Next, enter a name for the volume group. In this example setup, I'll use "system". After specifying the name, select Continue and press Enter. You next see a list of all devices that are available for the LVM environment, which in this case is just one device that probably has the name /dev/sda2 (see Figure 1-23). Select the device and select Continue once more to return to the main screen of the LVM setup program.

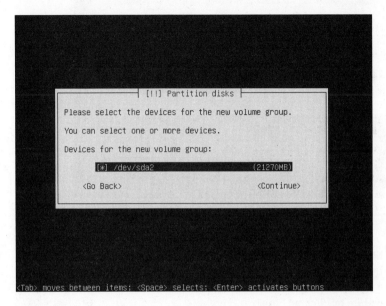

Figure 1-23. *In most situations, you'll select the device /dev/sda2 to be used by the Logical Volume Manager.*

17. From the LVM main screen, select Create logical volume. Next, select the volume group that you have just created and enter a name for the first logical volume that you want to use (see Figure 1-24). I recommend using the name of the file system you are going to mount on the logical volume, so *root* is a decent name for the root file system, *var* is good if you are going to mount the /var directory on it, and so on. I'll show you how to create the root logical volume in this and the following step. Make sure to repeat these steps for all other volumes that you want to create.

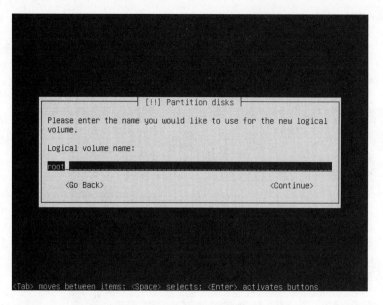

Figure 1-24. *Every logical volume needs a unique name.*

18. Now enter the size that you want to assign to the logical volume. Even if logical volumes are quite flexible, you should try to specify a realistic size here. Next, specify the file system sizes that you want to use on your logical volumes and finalize the LVM setup procedure by clicking Finish.

■**Tip** If you run into problems while writing the new partitioning scheme to disk, this is probably due to a conflict with some already existing setup. In this case, it may be a good idea to wipe your server's master boot record (MBR). From the installation program, use Alt+F2 to display a console window. Press Enter to activate the console and enter the following command: `dd if=/dev/zero of=/dev/sda bs=512 count=1`. This will wipe your server's MBR so that you can start all over again. You'll have to restart the installation as well.

---

19. Back in the main partitioning screen, you now see a list of all the logical volumes that you have created; they're just on top of the list (see Figure 1-25). You now have to put a file system on every one of them. To do that, select the logical volume from the list and press Enter.

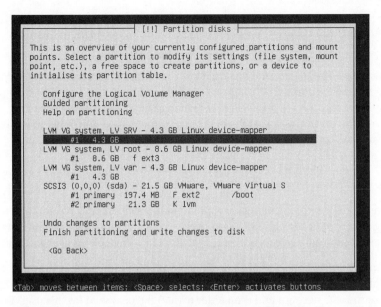

Figure 1-25. *Select the logical volume you want to format and press Enter to put a file system on it.*

20. You now see the Partition Settings screen, in which the option Use as shows do not use. Select this option and press Enter. Now from the list of available file systems, select the file system that you want to use on this volume; for example, Ext3 if this is the root volume (see Figure 1-26).

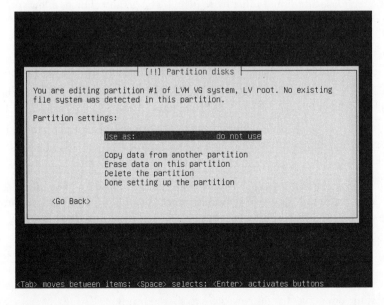

Figure 1-26. *Select Use as to specify the file system that you want to use on your logical volume.*

21. Select the Mount Point option and select the directory to which you want to assign this volume (/ for the root volume). Select any specific options you want to use on this file system as well and then select Done setting up the partition.

22. Repeat this procedure to put a file system on all the remaining logical volumes. When finished, from the Partition disks main screen (refer to Figure 1-25), select Finish partitioning and write changes to disk. Select Yes when asked if you want to write the changes to disk. This brings you to the next stage of the installation, in which all relevant software packages are copied to your server.

Completing the Installation

Now that you have created the partitioning scheme for your server's hard drive, it's time to finalize the installation of your server. In this part of the installation, you enter some generic properties (like some user information), and you specify what software packages to install.

1. Next, the installer asks you to create a user account. This is the user account that you will normally be working with, instead of using the root user account by default. Enter the name of the user account and then enter (twice) the password for this user. The installation of the base system now begins. In this phase, some basic packages that are needed at all times are copied to your server. Hang on because this can take a couple of minutes.

2. After the core system is installed, the installer asks if you want to use an HTTP proxy. If this is the case, enter its details now, or leave the information bar empty and select Continue to go on.

3. Next, you can choose additional software to install. The default choices allow you to select between some of the most important server tasks (see Figure 1-27):

   - *DNS server*: A DNS server allows your server to participate in the DNS hierarchy and translate computer names into IP addresses.

   - *LAMP* server: Selecting the LAMP (*Linux*, *Apache*, *My*SQL, and *PHP* server) option will set up a versatile web server for you.

   - *Mail server*: Want to set up your server as an MTA? Select this option to make it a mail server that allows you to send and receive e-mail messages for all users in your company.

   - *OpenSSH server*: This is the option you'll want to use in almost all situations. It allows you to access your server remotely, which is very useful for doing maintenance work on it.

   - *PostgreSQL*: Use this option if you want to install your server as an application server, hosting a PostgreSQL database.

   - *Print server*: This option installs the Common UNIX Print System (CUPS). Select it if you want your server to control access to shared printers.

- *Samba File server*: Need a server to offer shared files to the Windows users in your network? Check this option. The Samba file server offers the best-performing CIFS-based file server in the world, and it even is a good solution if you want to offer shared files to Linux and Apple users!

That's it for installation choices! If you need additional software to be started on your server, you need to install that software later. See Chapter 3 for more details on that.

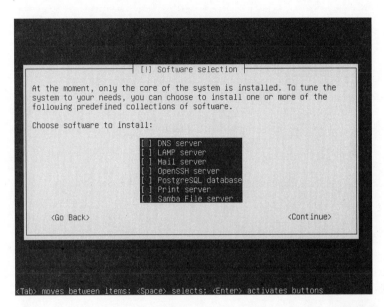

Figure 1-27. *The installation program lets you choose between different server profiles.*

4. Once all software packages have been copied to your server, the system is ready for use. You just have to press the Enter key once more to restart the server, and it will be usable.

Once the server has been restarted, you will see the text-based login prompt of your server. You are supposed to enter your user name and password here. A *text-based* prompt? Yes, this is a server, and a server is generally locked behind doors in an air-conditioned room. Therefore, there is no need to set up a graphical user environment in most cases. But because many people consider a GUI quite useful anyway, you'll learn how to set it up in Chapter 3. For now, though, you'll learn in Chapter 2 how to manage Ubuntu Server from the command line.

Summary

You learned in this chapter how to set up Ubuntu Server. Because the file system layout is a very important part of a server configuration, special attention was paid to configuring your server's file system with LVM or traditional partitions. At the end of this chapter, you ended up with a text-based console that's not so user friendly. In Chapter 2, you will learn to work with the most important commands needed for Linux server administration.

CHAPTER 2

■■■

Getting the Most from the Command Line

You may know the workstation versions of Ubuntu as very accessible graphical desktops. This is not the case, however, for Ubuntu Server! You can't manage a server properly without using the command line, so it's absolutely necessary that you can find your way around the Bash interface. Once you have mastered the command line, you will find it so much more powerful and flexible that you may not miss the graphical interface at all. For command-line newbies, this chapter offers an introduction.

Working As root?

By default, every Linux system installation creates a user with the name *root*. Many Linux distributions ask you to enter a password for this user during the installation. Ubuntu Server doesn't, and it instead takes a radically different approach to performing privileged tasks.

Ubuntu Server takes a different approach for several good reasons. The powers of the user root are limitless within the confines of that operating system. As root, you can bypass all system security and do anything at all. And you will not be given a warning screen if, for instance, you log in as root and then mistakenly type in a command that destroys all the files.

This is why Ubuntu Server handles privileged access in a different way. By default, the user root does not have a password, so you cannot log in and work as root in the conventional way, but you still need to perform many tasks that require root privileges. For this purpose, Ubuntu offers the sudo mechanism, which is explained in detail in Chapter 5. With sudo, normal users can perform tasks that require root privileges. And it's very simple: for every command that needs root permissions, you type **sudo** first. For example, whereas user root could just type **passwd linda** to change the password of user linda, a normal user enters **sudo passwd linda**.

■**Note** Want to work as root? Use the command sudo su, and you'll be root. Alternatively, you can change the password of user root as well, which allows you to log in as user root directly. Don't ever want the possibility to log in as root? In that case, you should change the default shell for this user to /bin/false. In Chapter 5, you'll read how to do that.

In a default installation, any user can use sudo to perform tasks as root. As you can guess, this doesn't make for a very secure situation. So you should limit this privilege. In Chapter 5, you can read how to do that. Before you do this, however, you need more understanding of Linux commands.

■**Tip** You don't like sudo and want to work as root anyway? You can do that, but you need to first set a password for user root. To give root a password, as a normal user, use the command sudo passwd root. Next, you can enter the new password that you want to set for the user root.

Working with the Shell

Ubuntu Server uses the kernel to address and control the machine's hardware. The kernel can be considered the heart of the Linux operating system. Ubuntu Server gives users the shell interface to tell this kernel and the services running on top of it what they should do. Typically, the shell is a command-line interface in which users can enter their commands. This interface interprets the commands that users type and translates them to machine code.

Several shells are available. The very first shell that was ever created for UNIX, back in the 1970s, was the Bourne shell. In Ubuntu Server you also have /bin/sh, but it's not the real original sh; it's just a link to the /bin/dash shell. Another popular shell is Bash (short for the Bourne Again Shell). The Bash shell is completely compatible with the original Bourne shell, but it has many enhancements. Most system scripts on your server are executed with dash as well; dash is used as the default shell for all users. The user root, however, has Bash as its default shell.*
Some people prefer using other shells, three of which follow:

- *tcsh*: A shell with a scripting language that works like the C programming language (and is thus fairly popular with C programmers).

- *zsh*: A shell that is based on the Bash shell, but offers more features. Because of these additional features, you can run Bash scripts in zsh, but you can't run zsh scripts in a Bash environment.

- *sash*: The standalone shell. This is a very minimal shell that runs in almost all environments. It is thus very well suited for troubleshooting systems.

Using Bash to Best Effect

Basically, in the Bash environment, an administrator is working with text commands. An example of such a command is ls, which can be used to display a list of files in a directory. Bash has some useful features to make working with these line commands as easy as possible.

---

* Because it has many more features and ensures better compatibility, I prefer working with Bash. For that reason, I'll focus on discussing Bash rather than dash features in this book. When administering your server as root, you will be working with Bash anyway.

Some shells offer the option to complete a command automatically. Bash has this feature, but it does more than just complete commands. Bash can complete almost *everything*: not just commands, but also file names and shell variables.

Using Automatic Command Completion

Using this feature is as simple as pressing the Tab key. For example, the cat line command is used to display the contents of an ASCII text file. The name of this file, which is in the current directory, is this_is_a_file. So, to open this file, the user can type **cat thi** and then press the Tab key. If the directory has only one file that starts with the letters t-h-i, Bash automatically completes the name of the file. If the directory has other files that start with the same letters, Bash completes the name of the file as far as possible. For example, let's say that there is a file in the current directory with the name this_is_a_text_file and another named thisAlsoIsAFile. Because both files start with the text this, Bash will complete only up to this and no further. To display a list of possibilities, you then press the Tab key again. This allows you to manually enter more information. Of course, you can then use the Tab key again to use the completion feature once more.

■**Tip** Working with the Tab key really makes the command-line interface much easier. Imagine that you need to manage logical volumes on your server and you remember only that the command for that starts with lv. In this case, you can type **lv** and press the Tab key twice. The result will be a nice list of all commands that start with lv, from which you'll probably recognize the command that you need.

Working with Variables

A *variable* is simply a common value that is used often enough by the shell that it is stored with a name. An example of such a variable is PATH, which stores a list of directories that should be searched when a user enters a command. To refer to the contents of a variable, prefix a $ sign before the name of the variable. For example, the command echo $PATH displays the content of the current search path that Bash is using.

On any Linux system, you'll get quite a few variables automatically. For an overview of all of them, you can use the env (short for *environment*) command. Listing 2-1 shows the result of this command.

Listing 2-1. *The* env *Command Shows All Variables That Are Defined in Your Shell Environment*

```
root@RNA:~# env
TERM=xterm
SHELL=/bin/bash
SSH_CLIENT=192.168.1.71 1625 22
SSH_TTY=/dev/pts/1
USER=root
LS_COLORS=no=00:fi=00:di=01;34:ln=01;36:pi=40;33:so=01;35:do=01;35:bd=40;33;01:cd\
=40;33;01:
or=40;31;01:su=37;41:sg=30;43:tw=30;42:ow=34;42:st=37;44:ex=01;32:*.tar=01;31:*.tgz\
```

```
=01;31:*.arj=0
1;31:*.taz=01;31:*.lzh=01;31:*.zip=01;31:*.z=01;31:*.Z=01;31:*.gz=01;31:*.bz2=01;\
31:*.deb=01;31:*.
rpm=01;31:*.jar=01;31:*.jpg=01;35:*.jpeg=01;35:*.gif=01;35:*.bmp=01;35:*.pbm=01;\
35:*.pgm=01;35:
*.ppm=01;35:*.tga=01;35:*.xbm=01;35:*.xpm=01;35:*.tif=01;35:*.tiff=01;35:*.png=01;\
35:*.mov=01;3
5:*.mpg=01;35:*.mpeg=01;35:*.avi=01;35:*.fli=01;35:*.gl=01;35:*.dl=01;35:*.xcf=01;\
35:*.xwd=01;35:
*.flac=01;35:*.mp3=01;35:*.mpc=01;35:*.ogg=01;35:*.wav=01;35:
MAIL=/var/mail/root
PATH=/usr/local/sbin:/usr/local/bin:/usr/sbin:/usr/bin:/sbin:/bin:/usr/games
PWD=/root
LANG=en_US.UTF-8
SHLVL=1
HOME=/root
LOGNAME=root
VISUAL=vi
SSH_CONNECTION=192.168.1.71 1625 192.168.1.70 22
LESSOPEN=| /usr/bin/lesspipe %s
LESSCLOSE=/usr/bin/lesspipe %s %s
_=/usr/bin/env
```

Normally, as a user, you'll get your variables automatically when logging in to the system. The most important source of new variables is the /etc/profile file, a script that is processed for every user who logs in to the system. Want to add a new variable? Add it to the bottom of the /etc/profile file to make sure it is available for all users. If you have some code that you want to apply to /etc/profile, you can put it in a separate file and put that file in the /etc/profile.d directory as well. The master script /etc/profile will make sure that these commands also are executed automatically. Don't worry about naming conventions for this file because there are none. The only requirement is that the script you put in here contains valid shell code.

Working with Bash History

Another useful feature of the Bash shell is the history feature, which remembers and lets you reuse commands you have recently used. By default, the last 1,000 commands are remembered. This feature is useful for sessions beyond even the current one. A file named .bash_history is created in the home directory of every user, and this file records the last 1,000 commands that the user has entered. You can see an overview of these commands by typing **history** at the Bash prompt. Listing 2-2 is an example of this list.

■**Note** In addition to the history command, you can also use the up/down arrow keys, page up/down keys, and Ctrl+p/Ctrl+n to browse the history.

Listing 2-2. *The* history *Command Shows a List of All Commands That You Recently Used*

```
sander@RNA:~$ history
    1  clear
    2  dpkg -l "*" | grep ^un
    3  aptitude search xen
    4  aptitude show xen-source
    5  aptitude show xen-source-2.6.16
    6  exit
    7  apt-get install xen
    8  sudo apt-get install xen
```

This is where the history feature becomes especially useful because you can reissue any command from this list without typing it all over again. If you want to run any of the listed (and numbered) commands again, simply type its number preceded by an exclamation mark. In this example, typing **!5** would run aptitude show xen-source-2.6.16 again.

Users can also erase their history by using the history command. The most important option offered by this Bash internal command is the option -c, which clears the history list for that user. This is especially useful because everything that a user types at the command line— such as passwords—is recorded. So use history -c to make sure your history is cleared if you'd rather not have others knowing what you've been up to. Once using this option, however, you can't use the up arrow key to access previous commands because those commands are all erased.

Because everything you enter from the command line is saved, I recommend never typing a plain-text password in the first place, even if you regularly erase the history. Most commands that do require you to enter a password will prompt you anyway if you don't enter one right away.

Managing Bash with Key Sequences

Sometimes, you'll enter a command from the Bash command line and either nothing happens at all or else something totally unexpected happens. In such an event, it's good to know that some key sequences are available to perform basic Bash management tasks. Here are some of the most useful key sequences:

- *Ctrl+C*: Use this key sequence to quit a command that is not responding (or simply takes too long to complete). This key sequence works in most scenarios where the command is operational and producing output to the screen. In general, Ctrl+C is also a good choice if you absolutely don't have a clue as to what's happening and you just want to terminate the command that's running in your shell. If used in the shell itself, it will close the shell as well.

- *Ctrl+D*: This key sequence is used to send the end of file (EOF) signal to a command. Use this sequence when the command is waiting for more input, which is indicated by the secondary prompt (>). You can also use this key sequence to close a shell session.

- *Ctrl+R*: This is the reversed search feature. It will open the "reversed I-search" prompt, which helps you locate commands that you used previously. The Ctrl+R key sequence searches the Bash history, and the feature is especially useful when working with longer commands. As before, type the first characters of the command and you will see the last command you've used that started with the same characters.

- *Ctrl+Z*: Some people use Ctrl+Z to stop a command that is running interactively on the console (in the foreground). Although it does stop the command, it does not *terminate* it. A command that is stopped with Ctrl+Z is merely paused, so that you can easily start it in the background using the bg command or in the foreground again with the fg command. To start the command again, you need to refer to the job number that the program is using. You can see a list of these job numbers using the jobs command.

Performing Basic File System Management Tasks

On a Linux system such as Ubuntu, everything is treated as a file. Even a device like your hard disk is addressed by pointing to a file (which, for your information, has the name /dev/sda in most cases). Therefore, working with files is the most important task when administering Linux. In this section, you'll learn the basics of managing a file system. The following subjects are covered:

- Working with directories

- Working with files

- Viewing text files

- Creating empty files

Working with Directories

Because files are normally organized in directories, it is important that you know how to handle these directories. This involves a few commands:

- cd: This command changes the current working directory. When using cd, make sure to use the proper syntax. First, names of commands and directories are case sensitive; therefore, /bin is not the same as /BIN. Next, you should be aware that Linux uses a forward slash instead of a backslash for directory paths. So use cd /bin and not cd \bin to change the current directory to /bin.

Tip Switching between directories? Use cd - to return to the last directory you were in.

- pwd: The pwd command stands for *print working directory*. Although you can usually see the directory you are currently in from the command-line prompt (this is a Bash shell setting), sometimes you can't. If this is the case, pwd offers help.

- mkdir: If you need to create a new directory, use mkdir. With mkdir you can create a complete directory structure in one command as well, which is something you can't do on other operating systems. For example, the command mkdir /some/directory will fail if /some does not already exist. In that case, you can force mkdir to create /some as well: do this by using the mkdir -p /some/directory command.

- rmdir: The rmdir command is used to remove directories. However, this isn't the most useful command because it works only on directories that are already empty. If the directory still has files and/or subdirectories in it, use rm -r or (eveb better) rm -rf, which makes sure that you'll never get a prompt for confirmation. You should be sure that you know what you're doing when using this option.

Working with Files

An important task from the command line is managing the files in the directories. Four important commands are used for this purpose:

- ls lists files.

- rm removes files.

- cp copies files.

- mv moves files.

Listing Files with ls

Before you can manage files on your server, you must first know what files are there; to do that you can use the ls command. If you just use ls to show the contents of a given directory, it displays a list of files. Of course, these files have properties as well, such as a user who is the owner of the file, some permissions, and the size of the file. To list all the files along with their properties, use ls -l. See Listing 2-3 for an example.

Listing 2-3. *Example Output of* ls -l

```
root@RNA:/boot# ls -l
total 10032
-rw-r--r-- 1    root root    414210 2007-04-15 02:19 abi-2.6.20-15-server
-rw-r--r-- 1    root root     83298 2007-04-15 00:33 config-2.6.20-15-server
drwxr-xr-x 2    root root      4096 2007-07-29 02:51 grub
-rw-r--r-- 1    root root   6805645 2007-06-05 04:15 initrd.img-2.6.20-15-server
-rw-r--r-- 1    root root     94600 2006-10-20 05:44 memtest86+.bin
-rw-r--r-- 1    root root    812139 2007-04-15 02:20 System.map-2.6.20-15-server
-rw-r--r-- 1    root root   1763308 2007-04-15 02:19 vmlinuz-2.6.20-15-server
-rw-r--r-- 1    root root    240567 2007-03-24 10:03 xen-3.0-i386.gz
```

Apart from the option -l, ls has many other options as well. An especially useful one is the -d option, and the following example shows why. When working with the ls command, wildcards can be used. So, ls * will show a list of all files in the current directory, ls /etc/*a.*

will show a list of all files in the directory /etc that have an "a" followed by a dot somewhere in the file name, and ls [abc]* will show a list of all files whose names start with either an "a," "b," or "c" in the current directory. But something strange happens without the option -d. If a directory matches the wildcard pattern, the entire contents of that directory are displayed as well. This doesn't really have any useful application, so you should always use the -d option with ls when using wildcards.

■**Tip** If you really are sure that you want to use a given option every time you issue a certain command, you can redefine the command by making an alias for it. If you put the definition of this alias in the system generic "login script" /etc/profile, it will be available to all users after they log in. To do this, open the profile file for editing with a command like sudo vi /etc/profile. Next, use the o command to open a new line and enter **alias ls='ls -d'** on that line. Now press Esc to return to Vi command mode and use the :wq! command to save your changes. The redefined ls command will now be available to all users who log in at your server. If the alias is intended for only one user, you can also make sure that it is executed when logging in by including it in the file .bash_profile in the user's home directory.

One last thing you should be aware of when using ls is that it will normally not show any hidden files. If you want to see hidden files as well, use the -a option.

■**Note** A *hidden file* is a file whose name starts with a period. Most configuration files that are stored in user home directories are created as hidden files to prevent the user from deleting the files by accident.

Removing Files with rm

Cleaning up the file system is another task that needs to be performed regularly, and for this you'll use the rm command. For example, rm /tmp/somefile removes somefile from the /tmp directory. If you are root or if you have all the proper permissions on the file, you will succeed without any problem. (See Chapter 5 for more on permissions.) Removing files can be a delicate operation (imagine removing the wrong files), so it may be necessary to push the rm command a little to convince it that it really has to remove everything. You can do this by using the -f (force) switch (but only if you really are *quite* sure). For example, use rm -f somefile if the command complains that somefile cannot be removed for some reason. Conversely, to stay on the safe side, you can also use the -i option to rm, which makes the command interactive. When using this option, rm will ask for every file that it is about to remove if you really want to remove it.

The rm command can be used to wipe entire directory structures as well; in this case the -r option has to be used. If this option is combined with the -f option, the command will become very powerful and even dangerous. For example, use rm -rf /somedir to clear out the entire content of /somedir, including the directory /somedir itself.

Obviously, you should be very careful when using rm this way, especially because a small typing mistake can have serious consequences. Imagine, for example, that you type rm -rf / somedir (with a space between / and **somedir**) instead of **rm -rf /somedir**. The rm command will first remove everything in /. When the rm command is finished with /, it will remove somedir as well. Hopefully you understand that the second part of the command is no longer required once the first part of the command has completed.

■**Caution** Be *very* careful using potentially destructive commands like rm. There is no good undelete mechanism for the Linux command line, and, if you ask Linux to do something, it doesn't ask whether you are sure (unless you use the -i option).

Copying Files with cp

If you need to copy files from one location in the file system to another, use the cp command. This command is straightforward and easy to use; for example, use cp ~/* /tmp to copy all files from your home directory to the /tmp directory. As you can see, in this example I introduced a new item: the tilde (~). The shell interprets that as a way to refer to the current user's home directory (normally /home/username for ordinary users and /root for the user root. If subdirectories and their contents need to be included in the copy command as well, use the option -r.

You should, however, be aware that cp normally does not copy hidden files. If you need to copy hidden files as well, make sure to use a pattern that starts with a dot; for example, use cp ~/.* /tmp to copy all files whose names start with a dot from your home directory to the /tmp directory.

Moving Files with mv

As an alternative to copying files, you can move them. This means that the file is removed from its source location and placed in the target location, so you end up with just one copy instead of two. For example, use mv ~/somefile /tmp/otherfile to move the somefile file to /tmp.

If a subdirectory with the name otherfile already exists in the /tmp directory, somefile will be created in this subdirectory. If /tmp has no directory with this name, the command will save the contents of the original somefile under its new name otherfile in the /tmp directory.

The mv command also does more than just move files. You can use it to rename files or directories, regardless of whether there are any files in those directories. If, for example, you need to rename the directory /somedir to /somethingelse, use mv /somedir /somethingelse.

Viewing the Content of Text Files

When administering your server, you will find that you often need to modify configuration files, which take the form of ASCII text files. Therefore, it's very important to be able to browse the content of these files. You have several ways of doing this:

- cat: Displays the contents of a file

- tac: Does the same as cat, but displays the contents in an inverse order

- `tail`: Shows just the last lines of a text file

- `head`: Displays the first lines of a file

- `less`: Opens an advanced file viewer

- `more`: Like `less`, but not as advanced

First is the `cat` command. This command just dumps the contents of a file on the screen (see Listing 2-4). This can be useful, but if the contents of the file do not fit on the screen, you'll see some text scrolling by and, when it stops, you'll only see the last lines of the file displayed on the screen. As an alternative to `cat`, you can use `tac` as well. Not only is its name opposite to `cat`, its result is, too. This command will dump the contents of a file to the screen, but with the last line first and the first line last.

Listing 2-4. *The* `cat` *Command Is Used to Display the Contents of a Text File*

```
root@RNA:/boot# cat /etc/hosts
127.0.0.1        localhost
127.0.1.1        RNA.lan RNA

# The following lines are desirable for IPv6 capable hosts
::1      ip6-localhost ip6-loopback
fe00::0 ip6-localnet
ff00::0 ip6-mcastprefix
ff02::1 ip6-allnodes
ff02::2 ip6-allrouters
ff02::3 ip6-allhosts
```

Another very useful command is `tail`. If no options are used, this command will show the last ten lines of a text file. The command can also be modified to show any number of lines on the bottom of a file; for example, `tail -2 /etc/passwd` will display the last two lines of the configuration file in which user names are stored. Also very useful for monitoring what happens on your system is the option to keep `tail` open on a given log file. For example, if you use `tail -f /var/log/messages`, the most generic log file on your system is opened, and, when a new line is written to the bottom of that file, you will see it immediately. Use Ctrl+C to stop viewing the file that you opened using `tail -f`. The opposite of `tail` is the `head` command, which displays the top lines of a text file.

The last two files used to view the contents of text files are `less` and `more`. The most important thing you need to remember about them is that you can do more with `less`. Contrary to common sense, the `less` command is actually the improved version of `more`. Both commands will open your text file in a viewer, as you can see in Listing 2-5. In this viewer you can browse down in the file by using the Page Down key or the spacebar. Only `less` offers the option to browse up as well. Also, both commands have a search facility. If the `less` utility is open and displays the content of your file, use `/sometext` from within the `less` viewer to locate `sometext` in the file. To quit both utilities, use the `q` command.

Listing 2-5. *The* less *Command Can be Used as a Viewer to View File Contents*

```
127.0.0.1       localhost
127.0.1.1       RNA.lan RNA

# The following lines are desirable for IPv6 capable hosts
::1     ip6-localhost ip6-loopback
fe00::0 ip6-localnet
ff00::0 ip6-mcastprefix
ff02::1 ip6-allnodes
ff02::2 ip6-allrouters
ff02::3 ip6-allhosts
/etc/hosts (END)
```

Finding Files That Contain Specific Text

As a Linux administrator, you'll sometimes need to search for a specific file by some word or phrase within the file. Because most configuration files created on your server are ASCII text files (in the /etc directory or one of its subdirectories), it is rather easy to search for text within them using the grep utility, which is one of Linux's most useful utilities. Let's start with a rather basic example, in which you want to get a list of all files that contain the text "linda" in /etc. You can just use grep linda /etc/* and if you want to make sure that you can search files that are readable for root only, use sudo grep linda /etc/*. Notice that the grep command is case sensitive. If you want it to be case insensitive, you should include the -i option: grep -i linda /etc/*. This command produces a list of file names, followed by the line in which the text you were looking for is shown; see Listing 2-6.

Listing 2-6. *The* grep *Utility Is Useful for Searching Files That Contain a Certain Word or Phrase*

```
sander@RNA:~$ sudo grep linda /etc/*
/etc/group:linda:x:1001:
/etc/gshadow:linda:!::
/etc/passwd:linda:x:1001:1001::/home/linda:/bin/sh
/etc/shadow:linda:!:13671:0:99999:7:::
```

If the output gets a little longer, you may find it confusing to see the lines that contain the text you were looking for as well. If that's the case, use the -l (list) option. You'll see only file names when using this option. Another disadvantage is that grep does not search subdirectories by default, but you can tell it to do so by using the -r option. If, however, you want fast results, be careful with the -r option because searching an entire directory tree structure for the occurrence of some word in a file is very labor intensive.

Using Regular Expressions

When you get more experience with grep, you'll find that it is a very powerful and versatile command. Particularly useful is the option to work with advanced regular expressions, which let you search for very specific text patterns in a file. Imagine, for example, that you want to find files that contain the text string "nds", but only if that string occurs as a separate word.

You wouldn't want to retrieve all files that contain the word "commands", for instance. So you would use regular expressions, and they offer a wide range of options. Four of them, which are also known as *anchors*, are particularly useful:

- `^text` searches for text at the beginning of a line.

- `text$` searches for text at the end of a line.

- `\<text` searches for text at the beginning of a word.

- `text\>` searches for text at the end of a word.

When using any of these regular expressions, it is always a good idea to put the search pattern between single quotes. The single quotes tell the shell not to interpret anything in the regular expression, so that grep can do the interpretation. So use `grep '\<linda' *` and not `grep \<linda *`. Let's examine some examples. To show how it works, consider the name poem file in Listing 2-7.

Listing 2-7. *Example Text File*

```
blah ra dala ma na
na blahra dala ma nana
narablah naka dala ma
ka ka radalamanablah
```

Listing 2-8 shows the result of the different regular expressions.

Listing 2-8. *Example of Regular Expression Usage*

```
sander@RNA:~$ grep '^blah' poem
blah ra dala ma na
sander@RNA:~$ grep 'blah$' poem
ka ka radalamanablah
sander@RNA:~$ grep '\<blah' poem
blah ra dala ma na
na blahra dala ma nana
sander@RNA:~$ grep 'blah\>' poem
blah ra dala ma na
narablah naka dala ma
ka ka radalamanablah
sander@RNA:~$ grep '\<blah\>' poem
blah ra dala ma na
```

As you can see, in the first example line (grep '^blah' poem), grep locates only those lines that start with the text "blah", which produces one match only. Next, grep 'blah$' poem is used to find lines that end with the text "blah". Following that, grep '\<blah' poem is used to find all lines that contain a word that starts with the string "blah". Next, you can see that grep 'blah\>' poem finds all words that end with the poem string. Finally, the command grep '\<blah\>' poem finds only those lines in which "blah" occurs as a word on its own.

Creating Empty Files

The last file management task discussed in this section is the option to create empty files, which can be very useful for testing purposes when you need a file to exist but without necessarily having any contents. The touch command will do just that. For example, touch somefile will create a zero-byte file with the name somefile in the current directory.

   You should be aware that it was never the purpose of touch to create empty files. The main purpose of the command is to open a file so that the last access date and time of the file that are displayed with ls are modified to the current time. For example, touch * will set this time stamp to the present date and time on all files in the current directory. If, however, touch is used with the name of a file that doesn't exist as its argument, it will create this file as an empty file.

Piping and Redirection

Piping and redirection are some of the most powerful features of the Linux command line. *Piping* sends the result of a command to another command, and *redirection* sends the output of a command to a file. You can also use redirection to send the contents of a file to a command. The file doesn't have to be a regular file; for example, it can be a device file. So you can send output directly to a device, as you will see in the following examples.

■**Note** Every device present on your server is represented by a device file. One of the cool things of Linux is that you can talk to these device files directly. Try the command cat /dev/sda, for example. It will show you the binary contents of your server's hard drive. Pretty cool, isn't it? You may want to use Ctrl+C to get out of this stream of data; you can also use the reset command to get the normal appearance of your terminal back.

Piping

The goal of piping is to execute one command and send its output to a second command so that the second command can do something with it. For instance, a common scenario is when the output of a command doesn't fit on the screen, in which case the command can be piped to less, thus allowing you to browse the output of the first command screen by screen. This is useful when working with ls -lR, which normally displays a list of files with all properties as well as all subdirectories of the current directory. To view the output of this command screen by screen, you can use ls -lR | less to send the output from the first command (ls -lR) to the second command (less).

   Another very useful command that can be used in a pipe construction is grep. You've already seen grep as a way of searching files for a given string, but it can also be used to filter information. This technique is often used to find out whether a given process is running or to check that a certain network port is offered by your server. For example, the command sudo ps aux | grep http will show you all lines in the output of the command ps aux (which produces a list of all processes active at your server) that contain the text "http". Another example is sudo netstat -tulpen | grep 22, in which the output of netstat -tulpen (which produces a list of all processes that are offering network connections on your server) is examined for the occurrence of the number 22 (the SSH port). You can see what this looks like in Listing 2-9.

Listing 2-9. *Filtering Command Output by Piping to* grep

```
sander@RNA:~$ sudo netstat -tulpen | grep 22
tcp6     0      0 :::22     :::*      LISTEN     0   15332    4321/sshd
```

Redirection

Although piping sends the result of a command to another command, redirection sends the result of a command to a file or the contents of a file to a command. As I mentioned, this file can be a text file, but it can also be a special file like a device file. An easy example of redirection is shown in the command ls -l > list_of_files. In this command, the redirector (>) sign will make sure that the result of the ls -l command is redirected to the file list_of_files. If list_of_files doesn't exist yet, this command creates it. If it already exists, this command overwrites it.

If you don't want to overwrite the content of existing files, you should use the double redirector sign (>>) instead of the single redirector sign (>). For example, who > myfile will put the result of the who command (which displays a list of users currently logged in) in the file myfile. If you want to append the result of the free command (which shows information about memory usage on your system) to the same file (myfile), then use free >> myfile.

Apart from redirecting output of commands to files, the inverse is also possible when using redirection. In this case, you are redirecting the content of a text file to a command that will use that content as its input. For example, the command mail -s "Hi there" root < . sends a mail to root with the subject line "Hi there". Because the mail command always needs a dot at a separate line to indicate the end of the message, in this command the construction < . is used to feed a dot to the mail command.

■**Tip** The mail command is a very useful command to send messages to users on your system. I also use it a lot in shell scripts to send a message to the user root if something goes wrong. To see a list of the messages that you've received this way, just type **mail** on the command line. Once you stop viewing your e-mail, press the q key to get out of the list.

When using redirection, you should be aware that you can do more than redirect output (technically referred to as STDOUT). Commands may produce error output as well, as in the following example, in which I deliberately made an error (no files that start with a* existed in the current directory):

```
ls -l a*
ls: cannot access a*: No such file or directory
```

This error output is technically referred to as STDERR. It is possible to redirect STDERR as well; and you can do this with the 2> construction, which indicates that you are interested in redirecting only error output. For example, the command grep root * 2> err.txt would have the `grep` command find the text root in all files in the current directory. Now the redirector `2>` `err.txt` will make sure that all error output is redirected to the file `err.txt` that will be created for this purpose, whereas STDOUT will be written to the console where the user has issued this command.

■Note The STDIN, STDOUT, and STDERR can be referred to by numbers as well; STDIN = 0, STDOUT = 1, and STDERR = 2.

That's also the reason why you are using `2>` to redirect error output. Similarly, you could use `1>` to redirect the standard output instead of `>` (in the following line in the example).

It's also possible to redirect both STDOUT as STDERR. This would happen if you use the command `grep root * 2> somefile > someotherfile`. In this command, `2>` is used to redirect all error output to `somefile`; `>` is then used to redirect all standard output to `someotherfile`.

As I mentioned previously, one of the interesting features of redirection is that you can use it to redirect output to regular files, and you can also redirect output to device files. One of the nice features of a Linux system is that any device connected to your system can be addressed by addressing a file. Before discussing how this works, take a look at this short and incomplete list of some important device files that can be used:

- `/dev/null`: The null device is a special software routine that helps with testing. It throws away all data written to it (while reporting success) and immediately returns EOF when read from. Use this device to redirect to "nowhere".

- `/dev/zero`: This is your friendly zero generator. Use this device before selling your old hard drive online; `cat /dev/zero > /dev/sda` will erase all data on your hard drive and put zeroes there instead. Want to make sure that no one can ever reconstruct data on your hard drive? Make sure to run this command several times.

- `/dev/ttyS0`: The first serial port.

- `/dev/lp0`: The first legacy LPT printer port.

- `/dev/hda`: The master IDE device on IDE interface 0 (typically your hard drive).

- `/dev/hdb`: The slave IDE device on IDE interface 0 (not always in use).

- `/dev/hdc`: The master device on IDE interface 1 (typically your optical drive).

- `/dev/sda`: The first SCSI or serial ATA device in your computer.

- `/dev/sdb`: The second SCSI or serial ATA device in your computer.

- `/dev/sda1`: The first partition on the first SCSI or serial ATA device in your computer.

- `/dev/tty1`: The name of the first text-based console that is active on your computer (from tty1 up to tty12).

- `/dev/fd0`: If available: the diskette drive in your PC.

One way of using redirection together with a device name is to redirect error output of a given command to the null device. You would use a command like grep root * 2> /dev/null to do this. Of course, there's always the risk that your command is not working properly because it's been prevented, and for a good reason. In this case, use (for example) the command grep root * 2> /dev/tty12, which would log all error output to tty12. This can also be activated with the key sequence Alt+F12 (use Ctrl+Alt+F12 if you are working from a graphical environment).

Another cool feature you can use with redirection is to send the output from one device to another device. To understand how this works, let's first look at what happens when you are using cat on a device, as in cat /dev/sda. This command would display the complete content of the sda device on the standard output.

When displaying the contents of a storage device like this, the interesting thing is that you can redirect it. Imagine a situation in which you have a /dev/sdb as well, and this sdb device is at least as large as /dev/sda and is empty at the moment. You can clone the disk just by using cat /dev/sda > /dev/sdb! However, this redirecting to devices can be very dangerous. Imagine what would happen if you were foolish enough to issue the command cat /etc/passwd > /dev/sda; it would just dump the content of the passwd file to the beginning of the /dev/sda device. And because you're working on the raw device here, no file system information is used, and this command would overwrite all important administrative information that is stored at the beginning of the device that is mentioned. And you would never be able to boot the device again! (If you're not an expert in Linux troubleshooting, that is. If you are, it can usually be repaired.) In Chapter 4, you will learn about the dd command, which can be used to copy data from one device to another in a way that is much more secure.

Finding Files

Another useful task you should be able to perform on your server is to find files, and find is the most powerful command to use to do that. The find command helps you find files based upon any property a file can have. For starters, you can find a file by its name; the access, creation, or modification date; the user who created the file; or the permissions set on the file. If you want to find all files whose name begins with hosts, use sudo find / -name "hosts*". I recommend always putting the string that refers to the file you are looking for between quotes because doing so ensures that find knows where the argument starts and where it stops.

■**Note** When analyzing a command, the shell parses the command to see what exactly you want to do. While doing this, it will interpret signs that have a special meaning for the shell (such as *, which is used to refer to all files in the current directory). To prevent the shell from doing this (so that the special character can be interpreted by something else; by the command you are using, for example), you should tell the shell not to interpret the special characters. You can do this by *escaping* them using any of three methods. If it is just one character that you don't want interpreted, put a \ in front of it. If it is a series of characters that you don't want interpreted, put them between single quotes. If it is a string that contains certain elements that you do want to be interpreted, use double quotes. Between double quotes, many special signs such as * and $ are still interpreted. Chapter 7 deals with shell scripting, and you'll find more details there.

Another way of locating files is by the name of the user who created the file. The command find / -user "alex" will find all files created by user alex. The fun thing about find is that you can execute a command on the result of the find command by using the -exec option (for example, if you want to copy all files of user alex to the directory /groups/sales, use find / -user "alex" -exec cp {} /groups/sales \;). In such a command, you should pay attention to two specific elements. First is the {} construction, which is used to refer to the result of the find command that you started with. Next is the \; element, which is used to tell find that this is the end of the part that began with -exec.

To illustrate how this rather complex construction works, let's have a look at another example. In this example, you want to search all files owned by user susan to check if the word "root" occurs in it. So the first thing you need to do is find all files that are owned by user susan; you can do this by typing find / -user "susan". Next, you need to search these files to see if they contain the word "root". To do this, you need a construction like grep root *. However, that construction is not the right way of doing it because the grep command would search all files in the current directory. Therefore, you first need to combine the two commands using -exec. Next, you need to replace the * from the grep root * example by {}, which refers to the result of the find command. So the final construction would be find / -user susan -exec grep root {} \;. If this command gives you too much information, you can pipe the result through the less command to read the output screen by screen. In that case, the command would be find / -user susan -exec grep root {} \; | less.

Working with an Editor

For your day-to-day management tasks from the command line, you'll often need a text editor to change ASCII text files. Although many editors are available for Linux, Vi is still the best and most popular because of its power and versatility. It is a rather complicated editor, however, and Ubuntu Server fortunately includes Vim, which is Vi Improved, the user-friendly version of Vi. To make sure that you use Vim and not Vi, use the following command: echo alias vi=vim >> /etc/profile. When talking about Vi in this book, I assume that you are using Vim.

Every Linux administrator should be capable of working with Vi. Why? You'll find it on every Linux distribution and every version of UNIX. Another important reason why you should get used to working with Vi is that some other commands are based on it. For example, to edit quota for the users on your server, you would use edquota, which is just a macro built on Vi. If you want to set permissions for the sudo command, use visudo which, as you likely guessed, is another macro that is built on top of Vi.

■**Tip** If you'd rather work with an editor that is simple, doesn't have too many options, and just does the job, you can use nano instead. This editor doesn't really require much further explanation.

In this section, I'll provide the bare minimum of information that is needed to work with Vi. The goal here is just to get you started. You'll learn more about Vi if you really start working with it on a daily basis.

Vi Modes

One of the hardest things to get used to when working with Vi is that it uses two modes: the command mode that is used to enter new commands and the insert mode (also referred to as the input mode) that is used to enter text. Before being able to enter text, you need to enter insert mode because, as its name suggests, command mode will just allow you to enter commands. Notice that these commands also include cursor movement. The nice thing about Vi is that it offers you many choices. For example, you can use many methods to enter insert mode. I'll list just four of them:

- Press i to insert text at the current position of the cursor.

- Use a to append text after the current position of the cursor.

- Use o to open a new line under the current position of the cursor (my favorite option).

- Use O to open a new line above the current position of the cursor.

After entering insert mode, you can enter text and Vi will work just like any other editor. Now if you want to save your work, you should get back to command mode and use the appropriate commands. The magic key to return to command mode from insert mode is Escape.

Tip When starting Vi, always give as an argument the name of the file you want to create with it, or the name of an existing file you would like to modify. If you don't do that, Vi will display help text, and you will have the problem of finding out how to get out of this help text. Of course, you can always just read the entire help text to find out how that works (or just type **:q** to stop viewing help).

Saving and Quitting

After activating command mode, you can use commands to save your work. The most common method is to use the :wq! command, which performs several tasks at once. First, a colon is used, just because it is part of the command. Then, w is used to save the text you have typed so far. Because no file name is specified after the w, the text will be saved under the same file name that was used when opening the file. If you want to save it under a new file name, just enter the new name after the w command. Next in the :wq! command is q, which makes sure that the editor is quit as well. Finally, the exclamation mark tells Vi that it shouldn't complain, but just do its work. Vi has a tendency to get smart with remarks like "a file with this name already exists", so you are probably going to like the exclamation mark. After all, this is Linux, and you want your Linux system to do as you tell it, not to second-guess you all the time.

As you have just learned, you can use :wq! to write and quit Vi. You can also use the parts of this command separately. For example, use :w if you just want to write the changes while working on a file without quitting it, or use :q! to quit the file without writing changes. The latter option is a nice panic key if something has happened that you absolutely don't want to store on your system. This is useful because Vi will sometimes work magic with the content of your file when you hit the wrong keys. Alternatively, you can recover by using the u command to undo the most recent changes you made to the file.

Cut, Copy, and Paste

You don't need a graphical interface to use cut, copy, and paste features; Vi could do this back in the seventies. But you have two ways of using cut, copy, and paste: the easy way and the hard way. If you want to do it the easy way, you can use the v command to enter the visual mode, from which you can select a block of text by using the arrow keys. After selecting the block, you can cut, copy, and paste it.

- Use d to cut the selection. This will remove the selection and place it in a buffer.

- Use y to copy the selection to the area designated for that purpose in your server's memory.

- Use p to paste the selection. This will copy the selection you have just placed in the reserved area of your server's memory back into your document. It will always paste the selection at the cursor's current position.

Deleting Text

Deleting text is another process you'll have to do often when working with Vi, and you can use many different methods to delete text. The easiest, however, is from insert mode: just use the Delete key to delete any text. This works in the exact same way as in a word processor. As usual, you have some options from Vi command mode as well:

- Use x to delete a single character. This has the same effect as using the Delete key while in insert mode.

- Use dw to delete the rest of the word. That is, dw will delete everything from the cursor's current position of the end of the word.

- Use dd to delete a complete line. This is a very useful option that you will probably like a lot.

That's enough of Vi for now because I don't want to bother you with any more obscure commands. Let me show you how to get help next.

Getting Help

Linux offers many ways to get help. Let's start with a short overview:

- The man command offers documentation for most commands that are available on your system.

- Almost all commands accept the --help argument. Using it will display a short overview of available options that can be used with the command.

- For Bash internal commands, you can use the help command. This command can be used with the name of the Bash internal command that you want to know more about. For example, use help for to get more information about the Bash internal command for.

■**Note** An internal command is a command that is a part of the shell and does not exist as a program file on disk. To get an overview of all available internal commands, just type **help** on the command line.

- The directory /usr/share/doc/ has extensive documentation for almost all programs installed on your server.

Using man to Get Help

The most important source of information about commands on your Linux system is man, which is short for the System Programmers Manual. In the early days, they were nine different volumes that documented every aspect of the UNIX operating system. This structure of separate books (nowadays called *sections*) is still present in the man command. Here is a list of the available sections and the type of help you can find in these sections:

0 Section 0. Contains information about header files. These are files that are typically in /usr/include and contain generic code that can be used by your programs.

1 Executable programs or shell commands. For the user, this is the most important section because it normally documents all commands that can be used.

2 System calls. As an administrator you will not use this section on a frequent basis. The system calls are functions that are provided by the kernel. It's all very interesting if you are a kernel debugger, but normal administrators won't need this information.

3 Library calls. A *library* is a piece of shared code that can be used by several different programs. Typically, a system administrator won't need the information here.

4 Special files. In here, the device files in the directory /dev are documented. This section can be useful to learn more about the working of specific devices.

5 Configuration files. Here you'll find the proper format you can use for most configuration files on your server. If, for example, you want to know more about the way /etc/passwd is organized, use the entry for passwd in this section by issuing the command man 5 passwd.

6 Games. On a modern Linux system, this section contains hardly any information.

7 Miscellaneous. This section contains some information on macro packages used on your server.

8 System administration commands. This section does contain important information about the commands you will use on a frequent basis as a system administrator.

9 Kernel routines. This is documentation that isn't even installed standard and optionally contains information about kernel routines.

So the information that matters to you as a system administrator is in sections 1, 5, and 8. Mostly you don't need to know anything about the other sections, but sometimes an entry can be found in more than one section. For example, information on an item called passwd is found in section 1 as well as section 5. If you just type **man passwd**, you'll see the content of the first entry that man finds. If you want to make sure that all the information you need is displayed, use man -a <yourcommand>. This makes sure that man browses all sections to see if it can find anything about <yourcommand>. If you know what section to look in, specify the section number as well, as in man 5 passwd, which will open the passwd item from section 5 directly.

The basic structure for using man is to type **man** followed by the command you want information about. For example, type **man passwd** to get more information about the passwd item. You'll then see a page displayed by the less pager, as can be seen in Listing 2-10.

Listing 2-10. *Example of a* man *Page*

```
PASSWD(1)                      User Commands                      PASSWD(1)

NAME
       passwd - change user password

SYNOPSIS
       passwd [options] [LOGIN]

DESCRIPTION
       passwd changes passwords for user accounts. A normal user
       may only change the password for his/her own account, while
       the super user may change the password for any account.
       passwd also changes account information, such as the full
       name of the user, the user's login shell, or his/her
       password expiry date and interval.

   Password Changes
 Manual page passwd(1) line 1
```

Each man page consists of the following elements:

- *Name*: This is the name of the command. It describes in one or two lines what the command is used for.

- *Synopsis*: Here you can find short usage information about the command. It will show all available options and indicate whether an option is optional (shown between square brackets) or mandatory (not between brackets).

- *Description*: The description gives the long description of what the command is doing. Read it to get a clear and complete picture of the purpose of the command.

- *Options*: This is a complete list of all options that are available, and it documents the use of them all.

- *Files*: If it exists, this section provides a brief list of files that are related to the command you want more information about.

- *See also*: A list of related commands.

- *Author*: The author and also the mail address of the person who wrote the man page.

Now man is a very useful system to get more information on how to use a given command. On its own, however, it is useful only if you know the name of the command you want to read about. If you don't have that information and need to locate the proper command, you will like man -k. The -k option allows you to locate the command you need by looking at keywords. This option often produces a very long list of commands from all sections of the man pages, and in most cases you don't need to see all that information; the commands that are relevant for the system administrator are in sections 1 and 8. Sometimes, when you are looking for a configuration file, section 5 should be browsed as well. Therefore, it's good to pipe the output of man -k through the grep utility that can be used for filtering. For example, use man -k time | grep 1 to show only lines from man section 1 that have the word "time" in the description.

■**Tip** Sometimes man -k provides only a message stating that there is nothing appropriate. If this is the case, run the mandb command. This will create the database that is necessary to search the man indexes.

Using the --help Option

The --help option is pretty straightforward. Most commands accept this option, although not all commands recognize it. But the nice thing is that if your command doesn't recognize the option, it will give you a short summary on how to use the command anyway because it doesn't understand what you want it to do. You should be aware that although the purpose of the command is to provide a short overview of the way it should be used, the information is very often still too long to fit on one screen. If this is the case, pipe it through less to view the information page by page.

Getting Information on Installed Packages

Another nice source for information that is often overlooked is the documentation that is installed for most software packages in the directory /usr/share/doc/. Beneath this directory you'll find a long list of subdirectories that all contain some usage information. In some cases, the information is really short and not very good, but in other cases, thorough and helpful information is available. Often this information is available in ASCII text format and can be viewed with less or any other utility that is capable of handling clear text.

In many cases, the information in /usr/share/doc is stored in a compressed format. You can recognize this format by the extension .gz. To read files in this format, you can use zcat and pipe the output of that to less, which allows you to browse through it page by page. For example, if you see a file with the name changelog.gz, use zcat changelog.gz | less to read it.

In other cases, you will find the documentation in HTML format, which can only be displayed properly with a browser. If this is the case, it is good to know that you don't necessarily need to start a graphical environment to see the contents of the HTML file because Ubuntu Server comes with the w3m browser, which is designed to run from a nongraphical environment. In w3m you can use the arrow keys to browse between hyperlinks. To quit the w3m utility, use the q command.

Summary

This chapter has prepared you for the work you will be doing at the command line. Because even a modern Linux distribution like Ubuntu Server still relies heavily on its configuration files and the commands to manage them, this is important information. The real work, though, starts in Chapter 3, where you'll learn how to perform some of the most important administration tasks.

CHAPTER 3

■■■

Performing Essential System Administration Tasks

So you have your server up and running, and you've just learned how to get your work done from the command line. This is where the real work starts! Next, you need to learn how to tune your server so it does exactly what you want it to. First, you need to know how to manage software. Next, even if many in the Linux community will flame you for it, you may want to work with a graphical interface on your server to accomplish common tasks. Even if Ubuntu Server is a command line–oriented server, in some situations the graphical interface just makes things much easier. So I'll explain how to install that at your server. Once the server starts to take shape, you'll want to make sure that it is properly backed up. And finally, if something goes wrong, you'll need logging to find out what happened. All these are considered essential system administration tasks, and you'll learn about them in this chapter.

Software Management

As on any other computer, you'll need to install software on Ubuntu Server on a regular basis. You can approach software installations in two ways. First and most important are the software packages containing programs that are ready to install and integrate easily with Ubuntu Server. The server keeps a list of all software packages that are installed, which makes managing them much easier. The second approach to software installation is the tarball, which is basically just an archive that contains files. (For more information about archives, see the section titled "Creating Backups" later in this chapter.) These files can be really anything (for example, a backup of your server's data is stored in a tarball), but the tarball can also be used to deliver software to install.

You should be aware of two important differences between the two methods of software installation. One is that your server keeps track of everything that is installed only if that software is installed from a package. Software installed from tarballs is not tracked. The second difference between tarballs and packages is that some software needs other software to be present before it can be installed. (This is called a *dependency*.) An example of such a dependency is an application that would need a graphical user interface (GUI) to be present before you can use it. Both the tarball and the software package have installation programs that can check if all dependencies have been met, but only the software package interacts via the package manager software with a database of packages that are installed and packages that are available at your server. Because of this interaction, the package manager can install missing dependencies for you automatically, and this is why software packages are preferred over tarballs on modern Linux distributions.

From the preceding information, you may have guessed which way of managing software is best: use packages and a decent package manager if they're available; use tarballs only if such a solution is not present for the software you want to install.

For Ubuntu Server, the package manager to use is apt-get. This package manager is focused on the Debian (.deb) package format. These packages can be managed perfectly with the apt-get package manager.

Software Repositories and Package Databases

To understand a Linux package manager, you need to know about software repositories. A *software repository* can be considered a source of installation for software. On your server, a list of all these installation sources is kept in the file /etc/apt/sources.list. As an administrator, it is important to be aware of this list. Although the most important software repositories are added to this file automatically, you may occasionally want to add other software repositories to this list.

In all repositories, you'll always find the following five package categories:

- *main*: The main category portion of the software repository contains software that is officially supported by Canonical, the company behind Ubuntu. The software that is normally installed to your server is in this category. By working with only this software, you can make sure that your system remains as stable as possible and—very important for an enterprise environment—that you can get support for it at all times.

- *restricted*: The restricted category is basically for supported software that uses a license that is not freely available, such as drivers for specific hardware components that use a specific license agreement or software that you have to purchase. You'll typically find restricted software in a specific subdirectory on the installation media.

- *universe*: The universe category contains free software that is not officially supported. You can use it, and it is likely to work without problems, but you won't be able to get support from Canonical for software components in this category.

- *multiverse*: The multiverse component contains unsupported software that falls under license restrictions that are not considered free.

- *backports*: In this category, you'll find bleeding-edge software. If you really need to work with the latest software available, you should definitely get it here. Never use it if your goal is to install a stable server.

When installing software with the apt-get utility, it will look for installation sources in the configuration file /etc/apt/sources.list. Listing 3-1 shows a part of its contents.

Listing 3-1. *Definition of Installation Sources in* sources.list

```
deb http://security.ubuntu.com/ubuntu hardy-security main restricted
deb-src http://security.ubuntu.com/ubuntu hardy-security main restricted
deb http://security.ubuntu.com/ubuntu hardy-security universe
deb-src http://security.ubuntu.com/ubuntu hardy-security universe
```

```
deb http://security.ubuntu.com/ubuntu hardy-security multiverse
deb-src http://security.ubuntu.com/ubuntu hardy-security multiverse
```

As you can see, the same format is used in all lines of the sources.list file. The first field in these lines specifies the package format to be used. Two different package formats are used by default: deb for binary packages (basically precompiled program files) and deb-src for packages in source file format. Next, the Universal Resource Identifier (URI) is mentioned. This typically is an HTTP or FTP URL, but it can be something else as well. For instance, it can refer to installation files that you have on an installation CD or in a directory on your server. After that you'll see the name of the Ubuntu Server distribution that is used, and you'll always see the current server version there. Last, every line refers to the available package categories. As you can see, most package categories are in the list by default. Only installation sources for security patches have been included in the partial listing of sources in Listing 3-1. For a complete overview, take a look at the configuration file itself.

Now that you understand how the sources.list file is organized, it follows almost automatically what should happen if you want to add some additional installation sources to this list: make sure that all required components are specified on the same line and add as many lines as you want to include additional installation sources. Once an additional installation source has been added, it will be automatically checked when working on software packages. For example, if you should use the apt-get update command to update the current state of your system, the package manager will check your new installation sources as well.

A second important management component used by package managers on your server is the package database. The most fundamental package database is the dpkg database, which is managed by the Debian utility dpkg. On Ubuntu, however, the Advanced Packaging Tools (apt) set is used for package management. These tools add functionality to package management that the traditional dpkg approach typically cannot offer. Because of this added functionality, the apt tools use their own database, which is stored in /var/lib/apt. By communicating with this database, the package manager can query the system for installed software, and this enables your server to automatically solve package-dependency problems.

Every time a package is installed, a list of all installed files is added to the package database. By using this database, the package manager can even see whether certain configuration files have been changed, which is very important if you want to update packages at your server!

■**Caution** Because working with two different package management databases can be confusing, I suggest you choose the package management system that you want to work with and stick to it. In this book, I will cover only the apt utilities.

Package Management Utilities

You can use any of several package management utilities on Ubuntu Server. The most important of these interact directly with the package database in /var/lib/apt. You would typically use the apt-get command for installation, updates, and removal of packages, so you'll find yourself working with that utility most of the time. You should also know about the aptitude utility, which works in two ways. You can use aptitude as a command-line utility to query your server for installed packages, but aptitude also has a menu-driven interface that offers an intuitive way to manage packages. If this still isn't easy enough, you can use the graphical utility Synaptic as an alternative. Both aptitude and Synaptic are front-end utilities for apt. Before you can use Synaptic, however, you need to install a GUI, and I don't recommend doing that. You can read more about that later in this chapter.

Understanding apt

Before you start working on packages on Ubuntu Server, it is a good idea to decide what tool you want to use. It's a good idea because many tools are available for Ubuntu Server, and each of them uses its own database to keep track of everything installed. To prevent inconsistencies in software packages, it's best to choose your favorite utility and stick to that. In this book I'll focus on the apt-get utility, which keeps its database in the /var/lib/apt directory. This is my favorite utility because you can run apt-get as a very easy and convenient tool from the command line to perform tasks very quickly. The apt-get utility works with commands that are used as its argument, such as sudo apt-get install something. In this example, install is the command you use to tell apt-get what you really want to do. Likewise, you can use some other apt-get commands. The following four commands are the most important building blocks when working with apt-get:

- update: This is the first command you want to use when working with apt-get. It updates the list of packages that are available for installation. Use it to make sure that you install the most recent version of a package.

- upgrade: Use this command to perform an upgrade of your server's software packages.

- install: This is the command to use every time you want to install a specific software package. It's rather intuitive. For example, if you want to install the Xen software package, you would just type apt-get install xen.

- remove: You've probably guessed already, but you'll use this one to remove installed packages from your server.

■**Note** To work with apt-get, you need root privileges. So make sure to use sudo for all apt-get commands.

Showing a List of Installed Packages

Before you start managing packages on Ubuntu Server, you probably want to know what packages are already installed, and you can do this by issuing the dpkg -l command. It will generate a long list of installed packages. Listing 3-2 shows a partial result of this command.

■Note The `apt-get` utility is not the most appropriate way to list installed packages because it can see only those packages that are installed with `apt`. If you have installed a package with `dpkg` (which I do not recommend), you won't see it with `apt-get`. So to make sure that you don't miss any packages, I recommend using `dpkg -l` to get a list of all installed packages.

Listing 3-2. *The* `dpkg -l` *Command Shows Information About Installed Packages*

```
$ dpkg -l
ii  xvidtune     1.0.1-0ubuntu1 X client - xvidtune
ii  xvinfo        1.0.1-0ubuntu1 XVideo information
ii  xwd           1.0.1-0ubuntu1 X client - xwd
ii  xwininfo     1.0.1-0ubuntu1 X client - xwininfo
ii  xwud          1.0.1-0ubuntu1 X client - xwud
ii  yelp             2.18.1-0ubuntu Help browser for GNOME 2
ii  zenity           2.18.1-0ubuntu Display graphical dialog boxes from shell sc
ii  zip              2.32-1          Archiver for .zip files
ii  zlib1g          1.2.3-13ubuntu compression library - runtime
ii  zlib1g-dev   1.2.3-13ubuntu compression library - development
```

The result of the `dpkg` command shows information about packages and their status. The first character of the package shows the desired status for a package, and this status indicates what should happen to the package. The following status indicators are used:

- i: You'll see this option in most cases, indicating that the package will be installed.

- h: This option (for "hold") indicates that the package cannot be modified.

- p: This option indicates that the package will be purged.

- r: This option indicates that the package will be removed without removing associated configuration files.

- u: This option indicates that the current desired status is unknown.

The second character reveals the actual state of the package. You'll find the following options:

- I: The package is installed.

- c: Configuration files of the package are installed, but the package itself is not.

- f: The package is not guaranteed to be correctly installed.

- h: The package is partially installed.

- n: The package is not installed.

- u: The package did install, but the installation was not finalized because the configuration script was not successfully completed.

The third character indicates any known error state associated with the package. In most cases you'll just see a space (so basically you don't see anything at all), indicating that nothing is wrong. Other options are as follows:

- H: The package is put on hold by the package management system. This means that dependency problems were encountered, in which case some required packages are not installed.

- R: Reinstallation of the package is required.

- X: The package requires reinstallation and has been put on hold.

The dpkg command can be used to show a list of packages that are already installed in your system, but you can also use it to display a list of packages that are available to your system. The only difference is that you have to provide some information about the package. For example, the command dpkg -l "samba*" would provide information about the current installation status of the Samba package. Listing 3-3 shows the result of this command.

Listing 3-3. Dpkg *Can Be Used to Display a List of Packages That Are Available*

```
sander@mel:~$ dpkg -l "samba*"
Desired=Unknown/Install/Remove/Purge/Hold
| Status=Not/Installed/Config-files/Unpacked/Failed-config/Half-installed
|/ Err?=(none)/Hold/Reinst-required/X=both-problems (Status,Err: uppercase=bad)
||/ Name            Version        Description
+++-==============-==============-============================================
un  samba-common   <none>         (no description available)
```

As you can see in the output that is provided for each package, the first two positions show that the package status is currently unknown. In combination with some smart use of the grep command, you can even use this construction to find out what packages are available for installation on your server. In the command dpkg -l "*" | grep ^un, the grep command is used to filter out all packages that show a result that starts with the letters "un," which is very typical for a package that is not installed.

You can also use the dpkg utility to find out what package owns a certain file. This is very useful information. Imagine that a file is broken and you need to refresh the package's installation. To find out what package owns a file, use dpkg --seach /your/file. The command will immediately return the name of the package that owns this file.

Using aptitude

On Ubuntu, a few solutions are available for package management. One of these is aptitude. The major benefit of this solution is that it is somewhat more user friendly because it can work with *keywords*, which are words that occur somewhere in the description of the package. For example, to get a list of all packages that have "xen" (the name of the well-known Linux virtualization product) in their description, you would use aptitude search samba. Listing 3-4 shows the result of this command.

Listing 3-4. *Showing Package Status Based on Keywords*

```
sander@mel:~$ aptitude search samba
[sudo] password for sander:
p   dpsyco-samba                - Automate administration of access to samba
p   ebox-samba                  - ebox - File sharing
p   egroupware-sambaadmin - eGroupWare Samba administration application
p   gsambad                     - GTK+ configuration tool for samba
p   samba                       - a LanManager-like file and printer server
v   samba-client                -
p   samba-common             - Samba common files used by both the server
p   samba-dbg                   - Samba debugging symbols
p   samba-doc                   - Samba documentation
p   samba-doc-pdf             - Samba documentation (PDF format)
p   system-config-samba     - GUI for managing samba shares and users
```

Once you have found a package using the aptitude command, you can also use it to show information about the package. To do this, you'll use the show argument. For example, aptitude show samba | less will show you exactly what the package samba is all about (see Listing 3-5). As you can see, in some cases very useful information is displayed.

Listing 3-5. *The* aptitude show *Command Shows What Is Offered by a Package*

```
sander@mel:~$ aptitude show samba
Package: samba
State: not installed
Version: 3.0.28a-1ubuntu4
Priority: optional
Section: net
Maintainer: Ubuntu Core Developers <ubuntu-devel-discuss@lists.ubuntu.com>
Uncompressed Size: 9425k
Depends: adduser, debconf (>= 0.5) | debconf-2.0, libacl1 (>= 2.2.11-1),
        libattr1 (>= 2.4.4-1), libc6 (>= 2.7-1), libcomerr2 (>= 1.33-3),
        libcupsys2 (>= 1.3.4), libgnutls13 (>= 2.0.4-0), libkrb53 (>=
        1.6.dfsg.2), libldap-2.4-2 (>= 2.4.7), libpam-modules, libpam-runtime
        (>= 0.76-13.1), libpam0g (>= 0.99.7.1), libpopt0 (>= 1.10), logrotate,
        lsb-base (>= 3.0-6), procps, samba-common (= 3.0.28a-1ubuntu4),
        update-inetd, zlib1g (>= 1:1.2.3.3.dfsg-1)
Suggests: openbsd-inetd | inet-superserver, smbldap-tools
Replaces: samba-common (<= 2.0.5a-2)
Description: a LanManager-like file and printer server for Unix
 The Samba software suite is a collection of programs that implements the
 SMB/CIFS protocol for unix systems, allowing you to serve files and printers to
 Windows, NT, OS/2 and DOS clients. This protocol is sometimes also referred to
 as the LanManager or NetBIOS protocol.

 This package contains all the components necessary to turn your Debian
 GNU/Linux box into a powerful file and printer server.
```

Currently, the Samba Debian packages consist of the following:

samba - LanManager-like file and printer server for Unix.
samba-common - Samba common files used by both the server and the client.
smbclient - LanManager-like simple client for Unix.
swat - Samba Web Administration Tool
samba-doc - Samba documentation.
samba-doc-pdf - Samba documentation in PDF format.
smbfs - Mount and umount commands for the smbfs (kernels 2.2.x and above).
libpam-smbpass - pluggable authentication module for SMB/CIFS password
                 database
libsmbclient - Shared library that allows applications to talk to SMB/CIFS
               servers
libsmbclient-dev - libsmbclient shared libraries
winbind - Service to resolve user and group information from Windows NT
          servers

It is possible to install a subset of these packages depending on your particular needs. For example, to access other SMB/CIFS servers you should only need the smbclient and samba-common packages.

http://www.samba.org/

Adding and Removing Software with `apt-get`

The best tool to perform package management from the command line is apt-get. It provides a very convenient way to install, update, or remove software packages on your machine. It requires root permissions, so you should always start the command with sudo.

Before you do anything with apt-get, you should always use the apt-get update command first. Because apt-get gets most software packages online, it should always know about the latest available versions of those packages. The apt-get update command makes sure of this, and it caches a list of the most recent version of packages that are available on your server. Once the update is performed, you can use apt-get to install and remove software. Installation is rather easy: to install the package blah, use apt-get install blah. The advantage of the apt-get command is that it really tries to understand what you are doing. This is shown in Listing 3-6, where the apt-get command is used to install the Samba server software.

Listing 3-6. *The* apt-get *Command Tries to Understand What You Want to Do*

```
sander@mel:~$ sudo apt-get install samba
Reading package lists... Done
Building dependency tree
Reading state information... Done
The following extra packages will be installed:
  libcupsys2 samba-common
Suggested packages:
  cupsys-common openbsd-inetd inet-superserver smbldap-tools
```

```
The following NEW packages will be installed:
  libcupsys2 samba samba-common
0 upgraded, 3 newly installed, 0 to remove and 0 not upgraded.
Need to get 6849kB of archives.
After this operation, 16.8MB of additional disk space will be used.
Do you want to continue [Y/n]? y
Get:1 http://us.archive.ubuntu.com hardy/main libcupsys2 1.3.7-1ubuntu3 [174kB]
1% [1 libcupsys2 99595/174kB 57%]
```

In the example from Listing 3-6, everything went all right because a package with the name *samba* exists. In some cases, you'll see that apt-get doesn't understand what you want it to do. If that happens, it sometimes gives a hint about the package that you need to install instead. If that doesn't happen either, try to search the appropriate package first, using the aptitude search command.

You can also use apt-get to remove software, upgrade your system, and much more. The following list provides an overview of the most important functions of the apt-get command. Be aware that you should always run the command with root permissions, so use sudo to start apt-get (or set a root password and work as root directly).

- *Install software*: Use sudo apt-get install package. If you have problems installing the packages, use sudo apt-get -f install. It will force installation of the packages and not halt on errors.

- *Remove software*: Use sudo apt-get remove package. This option does not remove configuration files. If you need to remove those as well, use sudo apt-get remove --purge package.

- *Upgrade software*: To upgrade your complete operating system, use sudo apt-get update first so that you're sure that apt-get is aware of the most recent version of the packages. Then use sudo apt-get dist-upgrade.

Making Software Management Easy with Synaptic

I know, Ubuntu Server is not supposed to be a graphical operating system, but, as you'll see later in this chapter, it is perfectly possible to install a graphical system. A GUI makes administering your Ubuntu Server a lot easier. One of the tools that come with the graphical interface is the Synaptic package manager. As you can see in Figure 3-1, it offers a very intuitive interface to help you install and manage software packages. It isn't installed by default, however, so use sudo apt-get install synaptic first to install it. Make sure to do this only after you have installed X, as described in the next section of this chapter.

In Synaptic, the Sections button is a good starting point because clicking it allows you to see all available software, organized by software category. To see what's inside a category, click it; a list of available packages will be displayed in the right part of the Synaptic window. Clicking an individual package will provide a description of the package, allowing you to see exactly what is in it. Next, select the Mark for Installation option and click Apply. You'll then see the window in Figure 3-2, asking you if you really want to install this package. Click Apply to start the installation.

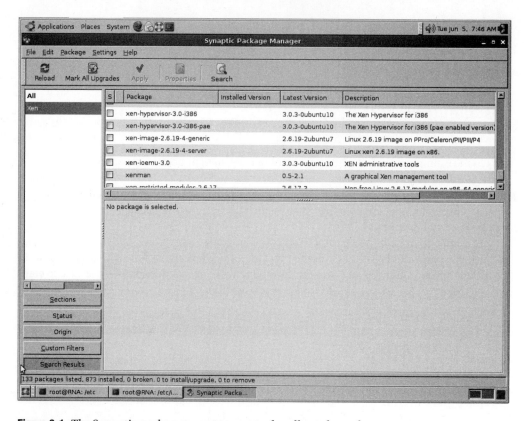

Figure 3-1. *The Synaptic package management tool really makes software management easy.*

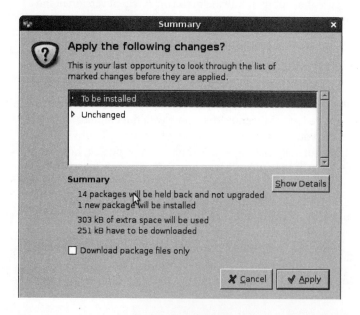

Figure 3-2. *Click Apply to start installation of the selected package.*

Another very useful option from the Synaptic interface is the Search feature. Click Search and select the software you are looking for from the window that's displayed. Click Search again and you'll see a list with all matching packages. If you want to use these packages, mark these for installation and click Apply.

Installing Software from Tarballs

Most software for Ubuntu is available from the normal Ubuntu installation channels. Sometimes, however, you'll encounter software in other formats, such as source files that are delivered in the .tar.gz format. These packages have been archived with the tar utility and then compressed with gzip, so they're known as *tarballs*.

Before doing anything with the files in a tarball, you need to extract them. For instance, the tarball blah.tar would be extracted using tar -xf blah.tar. Extraction will reveal that the tarball contains one of two types of files: source files and binary files. You will recognize the source files by their extension; if you see many files that have the extension .c, you are definitely dealing with source files. If the tarball contains binary files, it's normally enough to run the installation program and install them. This installation program will normally be included in the archive. The best way to find it is to look at the names of the files you've just extracted. In many cases, you will see files with a name such as setup or install, and if you don't see anything that looks like an installation program, see if there is a file with the name readme that contains a clue about how to install your software. If the tarball contains source files, you first have to compile them.

Before starting to install software by compiling its source files, you need to be aware of something. Although you'll probably end up with perfectly working software, all the software that you install in this way is *unmanaged*. This means that it will not be updated when you update everything else on your server, simply because the software is not in the databases maintained by software management programs such as apt-get. Therefore, I always recommend that you try to install software using the regular Ubuntu software installation methods first. If that doesn't work (and only then), use the method described next.

■**Caution** The procedure described here works in many cases, but it doesn't work all the time for the simple reason that it is all dependent on the person who created the package. I always recommend that you read the readme file that comes with most source files to see if the software installation has any specific instructions or requirements.

---

1. Before starting to compile the source files, you need to make sure that the required compiler is installed on your server. The command dpkg -l | grep gcc is an excellent choice to do that because most (although not all) software is written in the C programming language, which uses gcc as its compiler. If you don't see the gcc compiler, use apt-get install gcc to install it before you proceed.

■Tip To describe this procedure, I've downloaded the latest version of nmap from `http://insecure.`
`org/nmap/download.html`. If you want to follow this procedure, download this file as well.

---

2. Once you have downloaded the software you want to install into your home directory, use `ls -l` to check how the file is compressed. If the file has the `.bz2` extension, it has been compressed with the `bzip2` utility. To uncompress it, you need the `tar` command-line switch `-j`. If the file has the `.gz` extension, it has been compressed with the `gzip` utility, and the `tar` utility needs the `-z` switch to extract it. Our example file is compressed with `bzip2`, so run the `tar -jxvf nmap*` command to extract the archive. In this command, the option `x` is used to extract the `tar` archive, the option `v` does that in a verbose way so that you'll see what happens, and the option `f nmap*` specifies that the name of the file you want to extract is anything that starts with "nmap." This creates a subdirectory in your current directory in which all source files are installed. Now activate this subdirectory with the `cd` command.

3. From the directory that was created while extracting the tarball, run the `./configure` command. This command will verify that everything required to install the selected software is present on your server. If the utility fails, it is usually because some required software component was not installed. If this is the case, you'll see an error message stating what exactly is missing. Read what software component that is, and install it before you proceed. When `./configure` runs without errors, continue with the next step.

4. Compiling software is a lot of work and involves very complex commands. However, the `make` utility is available to make the compiling process easier. This utility reads a file with the name `Makefile` that has to be present in the directory with the source files; based on the instructions in that file, it compiles the software. Depending on the software that you want to install, the compiling process can take a long time. Once it's finished, though, continue with the next step.

5. You should now have all the program files that you need. But you're not quite done because you still have to make sure that these files are copied to the appropriate paths on your server. To do this, you must run the `make install` command as root. Type **sudo make install** and press Enter. This completes the installation of the source files for your machine, and they're ready for use.

Configuring a Graphical User Interface

I'll make this clear from the start: you shouldn't be reading this section, and I shouldn't have written it. Installing a GUI on Ubuntu Server is not a good idea for several reasons:

- You'll make your server more vulnerable.

- You don't get the full five years of support on the graphical elements.

- Valuable system resources are required to run the GUI.

- Most essential tasks cannot be performed from a graphical interface. You'll still have to create and configure text configuration files, anyway.

Despite all the objections, doing everything at the command line can be quite a chore if you have no Linux experience. Personally, I believe in freedom of choice. You want to use a graphical interface to get familiar with Ubuntu Server? That's fine with me. However, if you are an experienced Linux server administrator and you don't want to waste system resources on a useless graphical interface, please skip ahead to the section called "Creating Backups." That's fine with me as well. Are you still hesitant about whether or not to install a GUI? If so, Table 3-1 lists some advantages and disadvantages for you to consider.

Table 3-1. *GUI Advantages and Disadvantages*

Advantages	Disadvantages
Makes administration easier	Security risks
	Slows down your server
	GUIs are often rather limited

Are you still with me? Okay, that means you want to install a GUI. As you saw in the preceding section, installing software is easy with Ubuntu Server. When installing a graphical interface, however, you need to make some choices, the first of which is the kind of graphical interface you want to use. You basically have two different options: the window manager and the desktop environment.

In general, a *window manager* is a program that manages graphical program windows and other graphical elements on your server. A *desktop environment* is a complete graphical workspace that also offers a wide range of applications. If you have worked with Ubuntu on the desktop, you are probably familiar with the GNOME desktop manager, which is the default graphical user environment for the desktop. Besides window managers and desktop environments, you can also choose to install graphical tools that help you do remote administration of your server. In the next subsections you'll learn how to install these three components. I'll also explain how to turn Ubuntu Server into something very similar to Ubuntu Desktop by installing the complete Ubuntu Desktop graphical interface.

Installing the GNOME Desktop Manager

Because you probably want to install a graphical desktop to make managing Ubuntu Server easier, in this section you'll learn how to set up the GNOME desktop. I chose GNOME because it is the most complete graphical desktop environment available for Linux. Installing it is rather easy with apt-get; you just have to know what to install. To install everything that is needed, enter the following command:

```
sudo apt-get install xserver-xorg xfonts* gnome gdm
```

This command makes sure that all required software is copied to your system. Some of the software has to be downloaded from the Internet, and it can take awhile before everything is installed. After that, reboot and you will have a complete graphical user environment, like the one shown in Figure 3-3.

Figure 3-3. *It doesn't come by default, but you certainly can manage Ubuntu Server from a graphical interface.*

■**Note** Even if the graphical interface that you have just enabled makes system administration a lot easier, installing it doesn't make Ubuntu Server a graphical system. At some points, it makes sense to use a graphical interface, such as if you need a browser to look up some information on the Internet or if you want to install software packages using the Synaptic package management program. In essence, however, system administration on Ubuntu Server happens from the command line. Where relevant, though, I'll indicate which graphical programs can make administration tasks easier for you.

Installing a Lightweight Graphical Environment

Let's face it. GNOME is pretty, but it's also a rather heavy graphical environment. If you want to work with a GUI anyway, it may be a better idea to install a lightweight window manager instead, such as openbox. To install it, use the following command:

```
sudo apt-get install xserver-xorg x-window-system-core openbox
```

You can now start the graphical user environment by running the startx command.

Installing a Full-Scale Graphical Desktop

You really should not do this because it will turn your Ubuntu Server into a Ubuntu Desktop with all server programs installed; but because some people like to know how to do it, you can install the complete graphical desktop on Ubuntu Server. Before doing so, make sure that you *really* want to do it because support for your server will be a problem. For example, if there is a conflict between a package that is used by both a core server element and a core desktop element, there is a risk that the desktop element will break server functionality. If you have a support contract with Canonical, it can't help you because the graphical desktop is not supported on Ubuntu Server. You'll also find that not many people on the Internet can help you, either, because very few people want to use this unsupported method.

Some people just want to run everything on one computer and instead of running it on Windows, they want to make it an all-Ubuntu computer. One of the cool things about Linux is that you can use it any way you want. To install the full-scale graphical desktop on Ubuntu Server, use the following command:

```
apt-get install ubuntu-desktop
```

■**Caution** It may look useful to work with a GUI on your server, but you won't get support if you do. So it's better to avoid it altogether!

Managing Your Server Remotely with eBox

The new eBox utility offers a way to manage your server remotely from a web interface. So if you want graphical management options without installing the complete GUI, use eBox. eBox is modular, which means that there are different modules for different services. You can just install the complete package by using the following:

```
sudo apt-get install ebox
```

You can choose to install the bare minimum as well. To find out what that is, you first need an overview of all eBox modules that are available. Use the following command to get that information:

```
apt-cache rdepends ebox | uniq
```

While installing eBox, you'll be asked to supply a password for the eBox user. Remember this password and keep it in a safe place; you'll need it to access eBox from the web browser later. Once installed, you can access the eBox web interface from https://yourserver/ebox. Figure 3-4 shows you what its interface looks like.

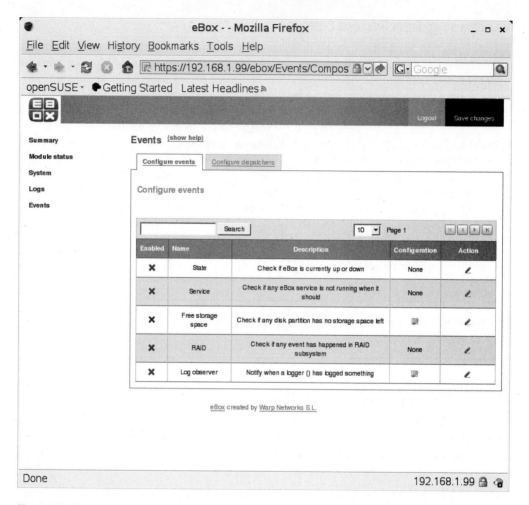

Figure 3-4. *If you want graphical management, but not the graphical interface on your server,* eBox *offers a decent web-based administration platform.*

When installing eBox, normally only the default modules are installed. Although these modules fit in most situations, sometimes a module that you need is not installed. If that happens too often, install the eBox-all package as well. From this package you'll find several modules, such as the network module that allows you to change network configuration, the firewall module that makes configuring a firewall a lot easier, and even a CA module that helps you set up a Certificate Authority for your server. So it might be a good idea to install the eBox-all package in all situations by using sudo apt-get install ebox-all.

After installing the modules, you can't use them immediately. This makes sense because you don't want to enable a module that manages a server that's not installed on your server. So you have to enable a module before you can use it. To enable a disabled module, click Module status. Next, click all modules that you want to enable and then click Save to apply the changes.

You'll find that working with eBox is rather easy. Just remember one vital thing: everything you change from the eBox interface has to be saved. For most modules, you'll find a Save changes link in the upper-right corner; click it to make sure that your changes are applied to your server.

Creating Backups

One thing always seems to be true about computers: one day they'll fail. If the computer in question is a server, the failure can cause huge problems. Companies have gone bankrupt because their vital data was lost. Therefore, making decent backups of your data is essential. In this section, I'll cover two different methods of creating backups, all of which are native Linux solutions. Apart from these solutions, quite a few commercial backup solutions are available that fit into the backup infrastructure that is often used at the enterprise level in a company. Those solutions are very specific, and I do not include them in this book. I'll discuss two backup solutions: making file backups with tar and making device backups using dd.

Making File Backups with tar

The command-line utility tar is probably the most popular Linux backup utility. It functions as a standalone utility to write backups to an archive. This archive can be tape (hence the name *tar*, which stands for *tape archiver*), but it can also be anything else. For instance, tar-based backups are often written to a file instead of a tape, and if this file is compressed with a compression utility like bzip2 or gzip, you'll get the famous tarball, which is a common method to deliver software installation archives. In this section, you'll learn how to create tar archives and how to extract files from them. I'll also provide some tips and tricks to help you get the most out of the tar utility.

■**Note** The tar command is not only used for backup and restore; on the Internet you'll find many tar packaged software archives as well. Even when working in an environment in which a package manager is used, you'll find that occasionally you need to unpack tar archives as well. In the section "Installing Software from Tarballs," you'll find more information.

Creating an Archive File

In its most basic form, tar is used to create an archive file. The typical command to do so is tar -cvf somefile /somedirectory. This tar command has a few arguments. First, you need to indicate what you want to do with the tar command. In this case, you want to create an archive. (That's why the option c is used; the "c" stands for *create*.)

After that, I used the option v (*verbose*). Although it's not required, it often comes in handy because verbose output lets you see what the tar command is actually doing. I recommend always using this option because sometimes a tar job can take a really long time. (For instance, imagine creating a complete archive of everything that's on your hard drive.) In cases such as these, it's nice to be able to monitor what exactly happens and that's what the option v is meant to do.

Next, you need to specify where you want the tar command to send its output. If you don't specify anything here, tar defaults to the standard output (STDOUT). In other words, it simply dumps all the data to your server's console. This doesn't accomplish much, so you should use the option f (file) to specify what file or device the output should be written to.

In this example, I've written the output to a file, but, alternatively, you can write output to a device file as well. For example, the command tar -cvf /dev/mt0 /somedir will write the result of the tar command to the /dev/mt0 device, which typically is your tape drive.

The last part of the tar command specifies exactly what you want to put into your tar archive. In the example, the directory /somedir is archived. It's easy to forget this option, but if you do, tar will complain that it is "cowardly refusing to create an empty archive."

And you should know a couple of other things about tar. First, the order of arguments *does* matter. So there is a difference between tar -cvf /somefile /somedir and, for example, tar -f /somefile -vc /somedir. The order is wrong in the last part, and tar won't know what you want it to do. So, in all cases, first specify what you want tar to do. In most cases, it's either c (to create an archive), x (to extract an archive), or t (to list the contents of the archive). Then specify how you want tar to do that; for example, you can use v to tell tar that it should be verbose. Next, use the f option to indicate where you want tar to write the backup, and then specify what exactly you want to back up.

Creating an archive with tar is useful, but you should be aware that tar doesn't compress one single bit of your archive. This is because tar was originally conceived as a tape streaming utility. It streams data to a file or (typically) a tape device. If you want tar to compress the contents of an archive as well, you must tell it to do so. And so tar has two options to compress the archive file:

- z: Use this option to compress the tar file with the gzip utility. This is the most popular compression utility because it has a pretty decent compression ratio and it doesn't take too long to create a compressed file.

- j: Use this option to compress the tar file with the bzip2 utility. This utility compresses 10 to 20 percent better than gzip2, but at a cost: it takes as twice as long.

So, if you want to create a compressed archive of the directory /home and write that backup to a file with the name home.tar.gz, you would use the following command:

```
tar -czvf home.tar.gz /home
```

■**Note** Of course, you can use the bzip2 and gzip utilities from the command line as well. Use gzip file.tar to compress file.tar. This command produces file.tar.gz as its result. To decompress that file, use gunzip file.tar.gz, which gives you the original file.tar back. If you want to do the same with bzip2, use bzip2 file.tar to create the compressed file. This creates a file with the name file.tar.bz2, which you can decompress using the command bunzip2 file.tar.bz2.

Extracting an Archive File

Now that you know how to create an archive file, it's rather easy to extract it. Basically, the command-line options that you use to extract an archive file look a lot like the ones you needed to create it in the first place. The important difference is that, to extract a file, you need the option x (extract), instead of c (create). Here are some examples:

- `tar -xvf /file.tar`: Extracts the contents of `file.tar` to the current directory

- `tar -zxvf /file.tar.gz`: Extracts the contents of the compressed `file.tar` to the current directory

- `tar -xvf /file.tar C /somedir`: Extracts the contents of `/file.tar` to a directory with the name `/somedir`

Moving a Complete Directory

Most of the time, `tar` is used to write a backup of one or more directories to a file. Because of its excellent handling of special files (such as stale files that are used quite often in databases), `tar` is also quite often used to move the contents of one directory to another. Some people perform this task by first creating a temporary file and then extracting the temporary file into the new directory. This is not the easiest way because you need twice the disk space taken by the directory whose contents you want to move: the size of the original directory plus the space needed for the temporary file. The good news is that you don't have to do it this way. Use a pipe and you can directly blow the contents of one directory to another directory.

To understand how this works, first try the command `tar -cC /var ..` In this command, the option c is used to tell `tar` that it should create an archive. The option C is used to archive the contents of the directory /var, not the complete directory. This means that in the archive itself, you won't see the original directory name /var. So, if there's a file called /var/blah, you will see blah in the archive, not var/blah, which would have been the case if you omitted the option C (a leading / is always stripped from the pathname in a `tar` archive). Now, as you may have noticed, in the `tar -cC /var` example, the option `f /somefile.tar` isn't used to specify where the output goes, so all the output is sent to STDOUT, which is your console. Don't forget the dot at the end of the command line; it tells the `tar` command what it has to archive. If you forget it, `tar` won't archive anything and just give you the error message "cowardly refusing to create an empty archive".

So that's the first half of the command, and you ended up with a lot of output dumped on the console. Now, in the second part of the command, you'll use a pipe to redirect all that output to another command, which is `tar -xC /newvar`. This command will capture the `tar` archive from STDOUT and extract it to the directory /newvar (make sure that newvar exists before you run this command). You'll see that this method allows you to create a perfect copy of one directory to another. So the complete command that you need in this case looks like this:

```
tar -cC /var . | tar -vxC /newvar
```

Creating Incremental Backups

Based on the information in the previous section, you can probably see how to create a backup of one or more directories. For instance, the `tar -cvf /backup.tar /var /home /srv` command creates a backup of three directories: /home, /var, and /srv. Depending on the size of these directories, this command may take some time. Because such large backups can take so long, it's often useful to make incremental backups, which is a backup in which the only files that get written to the backup are those that have changed since the last backup. To do this, you need the option g to create a snapshot file.

An incremental backup always follows a full backup, so you have to create the full backup first. In this full backup, you should create a snapshot file, which contains a list of all files that have been written to the backup. The following command would do that for you (make sure that the directory /backup exists before running the command):

```
tar -czvg /backup/snapshot-file -f /backup/full-backup.tar.gz /home
```

The interesting thing about the snapshot file is that it contains a list of all files that have been written to the backup. If, two days after the full backup, you want to make a backup of only the files that have been changed in those two days, you can repeat essentially the same command. This time, the command will check the snapshot file to find out what files have changed since the last full backup, and it'll back up only those changed files. So your Monday backup would be created by the following command:

```
tar -czvg /backup/snapshot-file -f /backup/monday-backup.tar.gz /home
```

These two commands created two files: a small file that contains the incremental backup, and a large file that contains the full backup. In an incremental backup scheme, you'll need to make sure that at some point a full backup is created. To do this, just remove the `snapshot-file` that was used in the preceding example. Because `tar` doesn't find a snapshot file, it will assume that you need to make a full backup and create the new snapshot file for you.

If you want to restore all files from an incremental backup, you need to restore every single file, starting with the first file that was created (typically the full backup) and ending with the last incremental backup. So, in this example, the following two commands would restore the file system back to the status at the time that the last incremental backup was created:

```
tar -xzvf /backup/full-backup.tar.gz
tar -xzvf /backup/monday-backup.tar.gz
```

Making Device Backups Using dd

You won't find a more versatile utility than `tar` to create a file system–based backup. In some cases, however, you don't need a backup based on a file system; instead, you want to create a backup of a complete device or parts of it. This is where the `dd` command comes in handy. The basic use of the `dd` command is rather easy because it takes just two arguments: `if=` to specify the input file and `of=` to specify the output file. The arguments to those options can be either files or block devices. So, the command `dd if=/etc/hosts of=/home/somefile` can be used as a complicated way to copy a file.

■**Note** dd is, strangely enough, short for "convert and copy." Unfortunately, the cc command was already being used by something else, and the developers choose to use dd instead.

More interesting is the use of dd to copy a complete device. For example, consider the command dd if=/dev/cdrom of=/mycd.iso. It would help you create an ISO file of the CD-ROM that's in the drive at that moment.

You may wonder why you shouldn't just copy the contents of your CD-ROM to a file with the name /mycd.iso. Well, the reason is that a CD-ROM, like most other devices, typically contains information that cannot be copied by a mere file copy. For example, how would you handle the boot sector of a CD-ROM? You can't find that as a file on the device because it's just the first sector. Because dd copies sector by sector, on the other hand, it will copy that information as well.

■**Tip** Did you know that it's easy to mount an ISO file created with dd? You only need to know that you have to use the -o loop option, which allows you to mount a file like any normal device. So to mount /mycd.iso on the /mnt directory, you would need sudo mount -o loop /mycd.iso /mnt. Check Chapter 4 for more information about the mount command.

Making a backup of a CD-ROM with dd is one option. And any other similar device can be copied as well. How would you go about making a complete copy of your entire hard disk? It's easy, but I recommend that you first boot your server using the rescue option that you can find on the installation CD-ROM. Doing this gives you a complete Linux system that doesn't use any of the files on your server's hard disk, which ensures that no files are in use at that moment. As an alternative, you can boot your server from any live CD-ROM or DVD. A Knoppix CD-ROM would work, for example. Before you start, make sure that you know what device is used by your server's hard drive. The best way to find out is by using the sudo fdisk -l command, which provides a list of all partitions found on your server, with the local hard disk coming first.

In most cases, the name of your hard drive will be /dev/sda, but it may be /dev/hda or something completely different. Let's assume that your server's hard drive is /dev/sda, and you now have to attach a second hard drive to your server. Typically, this second drive would be known as /dev/sdb. Next, you can use the dd command to clone everything from /dev/sda to /dev/sdb: dd if=/dev/sda of=/dev/sdb. This command takes quite some time to complete, and it also wipes everything that currently exists on /dev/sdb, replacing it with the contents of /dev/sda. Unfortunately, it often takes several hours to dd everything from one hard disk to another.

Configuring Logging

The last essential system administration task covered in this chapter is *logging*. It's obviously very important to understand where certain information is recorded on your server. Knowing this helps you troubleshoot when something doesn't work out the way you expect. Also, understanding how logging works may help prevent your entire server from filling up with log files. On Ubuntu Server, syslog is used to configure logging. You'll learn now how to configure it and where its associated log files are written.

Configuring syslog

Logging on to Ubuntu Server is handled by the syslogd process. The process reads its configuration file /etc/syslog.conf and based on the instructions it finds there, it determines what information is logged to what location. You can even define different destinations for different logs. For example, information can be logged to files or a terminal, or (if it is very important) a message can be written to one or more users who are logged in at that moment. Listing 3-7 shows the default contents of /etc/syslog.conf.

Listing 3-7. *Contents of* syslog.conf

```
root@RNA:~# cat /etc/syslog.conf
#  /etc/syslog.conf    Configuration file for syslogd.
#
#                      For more information see syslog.conf(5)
#                      manpage.


#
# First some standard logfiles.  Log by facility.
#

auth,authpriv.*              /var/log/auth.log
*.*;auth,authpriv.none    -/var/log/syslog
#cron.*                       /var/log/cron.log
daemon.*                     -/var/log/daemon.log
kern.*                       -/var/log/kern.log
lpr.*                        -/var/log/lpr.log
mail.*                       -/var/log/mail.log
user.*                       -/var/log/user.log
uucp.*                       /var/log/uucp.log


#
# Logging for the mail system.  Split it up so that
# it is easy to write scripts to parse these files.
#
mail.info                    -/var/log/mail.info
mail.warn                    -/var/log/mail.warn
mail.err                     /var/log/mail.err


# Logging for INN news system
#
```

```
news.crit                       /var/log/news/news.crit
news.err                        /var/log/news/news.err
news.notice                     -/var/log/news/news.notice


#
# Some 'catch-all' logfiles.
#
*.=debug;\
        auth,authpriv.none;\
        news.none;mail.none     -/var/log/debug
*.=info;*.=notice;*.=warn;\
        auth,authpriv.none;\
        cron,daemon.none;\
        mail,news.none          -/var/log/messages


#
# Emergencies are sent to everybody logged in.
#
*.emerg                         *


#
# I like to have messages displayed on the console, but only on a virtual
# console I usually leave idle.
#
#daemon,mail.*;\
#       news.=crit;news.=err;news.=notice;\
#       *.=debug;*.=info;\
#       *.=notice;*.=warn       /dev/tty8


# The named pipe /dev/xconsole is for the 'xconsole' utility.  To use it,
# you must invoke 'xconsole' with the '-file' option:
#
#    $ xconsole -file /dev/xconsole [...]
#
# NOTE: adjust the list below, or you'll go crazy if you have a reasonably
#       busy site..
#
daemon.*;mail.*;\
        news.crit;news.err;news.notice;\
        *.=debug;*.=info;\
        *.=notice;*.=warn       |/dev/xconsole
```

You can see from this listing that different rules are specified to define logging, and each of these rules has different parts. The first part of a log definition is the *facility*, which provides a basic idea of what part of the system the log message came from. The following available facilities are predefined:

- *auth*: Generic information, related to the authentication process. This is the process in which users log in and get access to system resources.

- *authpriv*: See auth.

- *cron*: Information that is related to the crond and atd processes. Both are processes that can be used to schedule processes to run at a specific time in the future.

- *daemon*: Generic information used by different system processes (daemons) that don't have a log facility of their own.

- *kern*: Everything that is related to the kernel. To log this information, a helper process named klogd is used. This process makes sure that information generated during the boot procedure is also logged.

- *lpr*: Information related to the printing subsystem.

- *mail*: Everything related to the mail system. Pay special attention to this because a misconfigured log line for the mail facility may cause lots and lots of information to be logged.

- *mark*: This is a marker that can be periodically written to the log files automatically. Using them makes it easier to read log files.

- *news*: All events related to a news server (if such a server is used).

- *syslog*: Internally used by the syslogd process.

- *user*: Generic facility that can be used for user-related events.

- *uucp*: Messages that are related to the legacy UUCP system. In the old days of UNIX, this was a way of exchanging information between UNIX systems (hence its name, which stands for UNIX to UNIX copy). Because UUCP is rather insecure, almost no one uses it anymore.

- *local0-7*: Local log facilities available for customized use. This facility can be used to assign a log facility to specific processes.

Apart from these specific facilities, a * can also be used to refer to all facilities. You can see an example of this in the last line of Listing 3-7, in which *=warn is used to handle warnings that are generated by whatever service.

For each facility, a priority is used to specify the severity of an event. Apart from *, which refers to all priorities, the following priorities can be used:

- *none*: Use this to ensure that no information related to a given facility is logged.

- *debug*: This priority is used only for troubleshooting purposes. It logs as much information as it can and is therefore very verbose. (Don't ever switch it on as a default setting.)

- *info*: This priority logs messages that are categorized as informational. Don't use this one as a default setting, either, because it generates lots of information.

- *notice*: Use this priority to log normal system events. This priority keeps you up to date about what specific services are doing.

- *warning*: This priority should be switched on by default for most services. It logs warnings related to your services.

- *err*: Use this priority to log serious errors that disrupt the process functionality.

- *crit*: This priority is used to log critical information that is related to programs. This category of error relates to critical errors that may disrupt your server's availability.

- *alert*: Use this priority to log information that requires immediate action to keep the system running.

- *emerg*: This priority is used in situations in which the system is no longer usable.

These priorities are shown in increasing order of severity. The first real priority (debug) relates to the least important events, whereas the emerg priority should be reserved for the most important. If a certain priority is specified, as in *.warn, all priorities with a higher importance are automatically included as well. If you want to refer to a specific priority, you should use the = sign, as in *.=warn. Using the = sign allows you to log events with a specific priority to specific destinations only. This happens for the mail process, for example, which by default has a log file for warnings, both for errors and for informational purposes.

The last part of the syslog configuration is the specification of the log destination. Most processes log to a file by default, but other possibilities exist:

- To log to a file, specify the name of the file. If you anticipate large numbers of log messages, it's a good idea to prepend the name of the file with a -, as in news.* -/var/log/news. Using the hyphen ensures that messages are cached before they are written to a log file. This decreases the workload caused by logging information. If the system crashes and the cache isn't written to disk, messages will be lost.

- To log to a device, just specify the name of the device that you want to log to. As can be seen from the example log file in Listing 3-7, important messages are logged to /dev/xconsole by default. It may also be a good idea to log important messages, such as those that have a priority of warn and higher, to an unused tty.

- To send alerts to users who are logged in, just specify the name of the user. In the example *.alert root,linda, all messages with at least an alert priority are written to the tty in which users linda and root are logged in at that moment.

- To send log messages to a specific log server, include the name of the server, preceded by an @. This server has to be configured as a log server by starting the log process with the -r option.

- For the most serious situations, use * to ensure that a message is written to all users who are logged in at that moment.

By default, syslog writes log messages to log files in the /var/log directory, in which you can find log information that is created in many different ways. One of the most important log files that you'll find in this directory is /var/log/messages. Listing 3-8 shows some lines from this file.

Listing 3-8. *Some Lines from* /var/log/messages

```
Jun  7 03:14:58 RNA gconfd (root-5150): Resolved address "xml:readwrite:/root/.gconf
" to a writable configuration source at position 1
Jun  7 03:14:58 RNA gconfd (root-5150): Resolved address "xml:readonly:/etc/gconf/gc
onf.xml.defaults" to a read-only configuration source at position 2
Jun  7 03:14:58 RNA gconfd (root-5150): Resolved address "xml:readonly:/var/lib/gcon
f/debian.defaults" to a read-only configuration source at position 3
```

All lines in /var/log/messages are structured in the same way. First, you see the date and time that the message was logged. Next, you see the name of the server that the message comes from. In the example lines in Listing 3-8, you can see that the three log messages all come from the same server (RNA), and you can see the name of the process that generated the message. This process name is followed by the unique process ID and the user who runs the process. Finally, the message itself is written.

The files that are created on your server really depend on the services that are installed. Here's a list of some of the important ones:

- apache2: This subdirectory contains the access log and error log for your Apache web server.

- auth.log: Here you'll find a list of events that relate to the login procedure. Typically, you'll see when user root has authenticated to the server.

- dmesg: This file has a list of messages generated by the kernel. Typically, it's quite helpful when analyzing what has happened at the kernel level when booting your server.

- faillog: This is a binary file that contains messages about login failures that have occurred. Use the faillog command to check its contents.

- mail.*: These files contain information on what happened on the mail service that may be running at your server. These logs can become quite big if your server is a mail server because all mail activity will be logged by default.

- udev: In this file you can see all the events that have been generated by the hardware plug-and-play manager udev (see Chapter 6 for more information about this). The information in this file can be very useful when troubleshooting hardware problems.

Logging in Other Ways

Many processes are configured to work with syslog, but some important services have their own log configuration. For example, the Apache web server handles its own logs by specifying the names of the files that information has to be logged to in the Apache configuration files. And many other similar services don't use syslog, so, as an administrator, you always have to take a careful look at how logging is handled for each specific service.

■**Tip** If you need logging from shell scripts, you can use the `logger` command, which writes log messages directly to the `syslog` procedure. It's a useful way to write a failure in a shell script to a log file. For example, use `logger this script completed successfully` if you want to write to the log files that a script has completed successfully.

Rotating Log Files

Logging is good, but, if your system writes too many log files, it all can become rather problematic. Log files grow quite large and can rapidly fill your server's hard drive. As a solution to this, you can configure the `logrotate` service. This runs as a daily `cron` job, which means that it is started automatically and checks its configuration files to see whether any rotation has to occur. In these configuration files, you can configure when a new log file should be opened and, if so, what exactly should happen to the old log file: should it be compressed or just deleted? And if it is compressed, how many versions of the old file should be kept?

You can use `logrotate` with two different kinds of configuration files. The main configuration file is `/etc/logrotate.conf`. In this file, generic settings are defined to tune how `logrotate` should do its work. Listing 3-9 shows the contents.

Listing 3-9. *Contents of the* `logrotate.conf` *Configuration File*

```
# see "man logrotate" for details
# rotate log files weekly
weekly

# keep 4 weeks worth of backlogs
rotate 4

# create new (empty) log files after rotating old ones
create

# uncomment this if you want your log files compressed
#compress

# uncomment these to switch compression to bzip2
compresscmd /usr/bin/bzip2
uncompresscmd /usr/bin/bunzip2

# former versions had to have the compress command set accordingly
#compressext .bz2

# RPM packages drop log rotation information into this directory
include /etc/logrotate.d
```

```
# no packages own wtmp -- we'll rotate them here
#/var/log/wtmp {
#       monthly
#       create 0664 root utmp
#       rotate 1
#}

# system-specific logs may be also be configured here.
```

In this example, some important keywords are used, and Table 3-2 describes them.

Table 3-2. *Options for* logrotate

Option	Description
weekly	This option specifies that the log files should be created on a weekly basis.
rotate 4	This option makes sure that the four previous rotations of the file are saved. If the rotate option is not used, old files are deleted.
create	The old file is saved under a new name (for instance, Xorg.0.log would be changed to Xorg.0.log.old), and a new file is created.
compress	Use this option to make sure that the old log files are compressed.
compresscmd	This option specifies the command to be used for creating the compressed log files.
uncompresscmd	Use this command to specify what command to use to uncompress compressed log files.
include	This important option makes sure that the content of the directory /etc/logrotate.d is included. In this directory, files exist that specify how to handle some individual log files.

As you have seen, the logrotate.conf configuration file includes some very generic code to specify how log files should be handled. In addition to that, most log files have a specific logrotate configuration file in /etc/logrotate.d/.

The content of the service-specific configuration files in /etc/logrotate.d is generally more specific than the content of the generic logrotate.conf. Listing 3-10 shows the configuration script for files that are written by Apache to /var/log/apache2/.

Listing 3-10. *Example of the* logrotate *Configuration for Apache*

```
/var/log/apache2/*.log {
        weekly
        missingok
        rotate 52
        compress
        delaycompress
        notifempty
        create 640 root adm
        sharedscripts
        postrotate
                if [ -f /var/run/apache2.pid ]; then
```

```
                    /etc/init.d/apache2 restart > /dev/null
            fi
        endscript
}
```

This example uses some more important options. Table 3-3 provides a description of these options.

Table 3-3. *Options in Service-Specific* logrotate *Files*

Option	Description
dateext	Uses the date as an extension for old versions of the log files.
maxage	Specifies the number of days after which old log files should be removed.
rotate	Used to specify the number of times a log file should be rotated before being removed or mailed to the address specified in the mail directive.
size	The size limit of a log file is specified here.
notifempty	Do not rotate the log file when it is empty.
missingok	If the log file does not exist, go on to the next one without issuing an error message.
copytruncate	Truncate the old log file in place after creating a copy, instead of moving the old file and creating a new one. This is useful for services that cannot be told to close their log files.
postrotate	Use this option to specify some commands that should be executed after performing the logrotate on the file.
endscript	This option denotes the end of the configuration file.

Like the previous example for the Apache log file, all other log files can have their own logrotate file. Some more options are available when creating such a logrotate file. Check the man pages for a complete overview.

Summary

As the administrator of a Linux server, you will be doing certain tasks on a regular basis. In this chapter you read about the most important of these tasks: managing software, creating backups, scheduling services to start automatically, and configuring logging. In Chapter 4, you'll learn how to manage your file systems on Ubuntu Server.

CHAPTER 4

■■■

Performing File System Management Tasks

In Chapter 2, you learned how to perform basic management tasks related to the file system of your server. For example, you read about file copying and navigating between directories. In this chapter, you'll learn about some more elementary file system management tasks. The concept of a mount will be discussed, and you will find out how to perform mounts automatically by using the /etc/fstab configuration file. You'll learn about the purpose of hard and symbolic links and how you can create them. Last but not least, you'll understand more about how the most important file systems, such as Ext3 and XFS, are organized; and how knowledge of that organization may come in handy, using advanced tools such as dd.

Mounting Disks

On a Linux server such as Ubuntu Server, devices are not always mounted automatically. They are if you're using the GUI, but otherwise you must know how to mount a device manually. Before you can access a device, you have to mount it, and in this section you'll learn everything you need to work with this command.

Using the mount Command

To mount devices manually, you use the mount command. The structure of this command is easy to understand: mount /what /where. For the "what" part, you specify a device name; for the "where" part, you provide a directory. In principle, any directory can be used, but it doesn't make sense to mount a device (for example on /usr) because doing so will temporarily make all other files in that directory unavailable.

Therefore, on Ubuntu Server, two directories are created as default mount points. These are the directories that you would typically use to mount devices. The first of these is the directory /mnt. This is typically the directory that you would use for a mount that happens only occasionally, such as if you want to test whether some device is really mountable. The second of these directories is /media, in which you would mount devices that are connected on a more regular basis. You would mount a CD-ROM or DVD in that directory with the command mount /dev/cdrom /media/cdrom. To make life easier for some of the veterans who aren't used to a /media directory in which a CD-ROM is mounted, a third directory is available, /cdrom, which is really just a symbolic link (a kind of shortcut) to /media/cdrom.

The mount command lets you mount devices like CD-ROMs or DVDs, but network shares can also be mounted with this command. You just have to be more specific. If, for example, you want to mount a share named myshare that is offered by a Windows computer named lor, you would use the command mount -t cifs -o username=yourname //lor/myshare /mnt.

You'll notice in the last example that some extra information is specified. First, the file system to be used is mentioned. The mount command is perfectly capable of determining the file system for local devices by looking at the superblock that contains a short description of the file system and exists in the beginning of every file system. But if you're using a network device, it is a good idea to avoid confusion and specify the file system type because the mount command needs to know what type of file system it is before being able to access it. The command does quite a good job guessing the right file system on the network, but you may want to avoid confusion by adding the file system type to be used as an option to mount.

In the example of the share on a Windows machine, the cifs file system type is used because you want to mount on a Windows file system. You also can use this file system type to access shares on a Samba server. Next, the name of the user who performs the mount must be specified. This must be the name of a valid user account on the other system. Then the name of the share is given. In the prior example, a computer name (lor) is used, but if your system has problems working with computer names, an IP address can be used just as easily. The computer name is followed by the name of the share. Finally, the name of the directory where the mount has to be created is given. In this example, I've mounted it on /mnt, because this is a mount that you would perform only occasionally. If it were a mount you used on a more regular basis, you would create a subdirectory under /media (/media/lor would make sense here) and create the mount in that subdirectory.

In Table 4-1, you can see a list of some of the most popular devices that you typically want to mount on a regular basis.

Table 4-1. *Mounting Popular Devices*

Device	Address as	Remarks
Floppy disk	/dev/fd0	Because modern servers rarely have more than one floppy device drive, the floppy drive (if present) will be fd0. If more than one drive is available, use fd1, and so on.
USB drive	/dev/sdX	USB drives (including USB keys) appear on the SCSI bus. Typically, you'll see them as "the next" SCSI disk. So, if you already have an sda, the USB device will appear as sdb.
Optical drive	/dev/sr0, /dev/hdX	If the optical drive is installed on the IDE interface, it is typically /dev/hda or /dev/hdc, depending on other IDE devices already present. On modern servers, you'll find the optical drive more often as /dev/sr0.
Hard drive	/dev/hdX, /dev/sdX	Depending on the bus the hard drive is installed on, you will see it as /dev/hdX (IDE) or /dev/sdX (SCSI and SATA). X is replaced by "a" for the first drive, "b" for the second drive, and so on. Notice that normally you don't mount a complete hard drive, but a file system on a partition on the hard drive. The partition on the drive is referred to by a number: /dev/sda1 for the first partition on an SCSI hard drive, and so on.

Device	Address as	Remarks
Tape drive	/dev/st0	Typically, a tape drive is installed at the SCSI bus and can be mounted as /dev/st0.
Windows Share	//server/share	Use // followed by the server name, followed by the share. Additional options are required, such as -t cifs to indicate the type of file system to be used and -o username=yourusername to specify the name of the user account that you want to use.
NFS Share	server:/share	Add -t nfs to indicate that it is an NFS server.

Options for the mount Command

The mount command offers many options, and some of them are rather advanced. For example, to perform the mount using the backup of the superblock that normally sits on block 8193, you can use the command mount -o sb=8193 /dev/somefilesystem /somedirectory. Why would you want to do this? Because mounting a file system using the backup superblock may be very useful if some problem is preventing you from mounting it normally.

Note The superblock is where all administrative data of a file system is kept. On an Ext2/Ext3 file system, a superblock is stored at the beginning of the file system, but some backup superblocks are created automatically as well. You'll learn more about this later in the chapter.

Although these are options you would use only in an emergency, some of the more advanced options are really useful. For example, when troubleshooting your server, you may find that the root file system is automatically booted read-only. When the system is mounted read-only, you cannot change anything, so after successfully starting in read-only mode, you would want to mount read/write as soon as possible. To do that, use the command mount -o remount,rw / to make your root file system readable/writeable without disconnecting the device first. In fact, the -o remount option allows you to change any parameter of a mounted file system without unmounting it first. It's very useful to change a parameter without losing your connection to the file system.

One of the most important options for mount is the -t option, which specifies the file system type you want to use. Your server normally would detect what file system to use by itself, but sometimes you need to help it because this file system self-check isn't working properly. Table 4-2 lists some file systems that you may encounter on your server (or other Linux systems).

Table 4-2. *Linux File System Types*

Type	Description
Minix	This is the mother of all Linux file systems (it was used in the earliest Linux version). Because it has some serious limitations, like the inability to work with partitions greater than 32 MB, it isn't used much anymore. Occasionally, it can still be seen on very small media, like boot diskettes.
Ext2	This system has been the default Linux file system for a very long time (it was first developed in the early 1990s). The Ext2 file system is a completely POSIX-compliant file system, which means it supports all the properties of a typical UNIX environment. However, it has one serious drawback: it doesn't support journaling and therefore is being replaced by journaling file systems like Ext3 and ReiserFS.
Ext3	Basically, Ext3 is Ext2 with a journal added to it. The major advantage of Ext3 is that it is completely backward-compatible with Ext2. Its major disadvantage is that it is based on Ext2, an elderly file system that was never designed for a world in which partitions of several hundreds of gigabytes are used. For instance, it does have problems with directories that contain more than about 5,000 files. It is, however, the most stable file system we have today and therefore is used as the default file system on Ubuntu Server.
ReiserFS	ReiserFS is another journaling file system. It was developed by Hans Reiser as a completely new file system in the late 1990s. ReiserFS was used only as the default file system on SUSE Linux, but even SUSE has changed to Ext3 as its default because there just isn't enough community support for ReiserFS.
Ext4	Ext4 is the successor to Ext3 and will fix some of the most important shortcomings of Ext3. For example, Ext4 will use a strong indexing system that helps you work with lots of files in one single directory. At the time of writing, Ext4 is still experimental, so I will not discuss it in this book.
XFS	The XFS file system was created as an open source file system by supercomputer manufacturer SGI. It has some excellent tuning options, which makes it a very good file system to store data. You'll read some more about this file system and its options later in this chapter.
msdos	If, for example, you need to read a floppy disk with files on it that were created on a computer using MS-DOS, you can mount it with the msdos file system type. This system is something of a legacy file system that has been replaced with vfat, however.
vfat	The vfat file system is used for all Windows and DOS file systems that use a FAT file system. Use it for accessing files from a Windows-formatted diskette or optical media.
ntfs	On Windows systems, NTFS is now the default file system. However, it is possible to read from an NTFS file system. To do this, mount the medium with the ntfs file system type. Some people even trust it to write files as well, but there have been problems with that, so I wouldn't recommend it. Anyway, there's no reason to use it on a server.
iso9660	This is the file system that is used to mount CD-ROMs. Normally, you don't need to specify that you want to use this file system as it will be detected automatically when you insert a CD-ROM.
cifs	When working on a network, the cifs file system is very important. This file system allows you to make a connection over the network to a share that is offered by a Windows server, as in the previous example. In the past, the smbfs file system type was used to do the same, but because cifs offers a better solution, it has replaced smbfs on modern Linux distributions. In case mounting a Samba share doesn't work with cifs, try smbfs.
nfs	This system is used to make connections between UNIX computers.

Apart from -t, the mount command has many other options as well, which can be prefixed by using the -o option. Most of these options are file system–dependent, so no generic list of these options is provided here. You'll find information that is specific for your file system in the man page of the mount command.

Tip More than just partitions and external media can be mounted. For example, it's also possible to mount an ISO file. To do this, use the command mount -t iso9660 -o loop nameofyouriso.iso /mnt. This will mount the ISO file on the directory /mnt, which allows you to work on it like you work on real optical media. Because normally you can mount devices but not files, in this command the loop kernel module is used. This module makes it possible to mount a file as if it were a device.

The last option that might interest you when using the mount command is the rather advanced -o bind option. Its purpose? It allows you to mount a directory on another directory. You can't do that using the loop option, so if you ever need to mount a directory on another directory, use mount -o bind /somedir /someotherdir. I use it when troubleshooting a Linux server with the chroot command, for example. I first boot my server that has problems from a Linux live CD-ROM. Next, I mount my server's root file system in a temporary directory (in /mnt, for example). Because some utilities don't expect their configuration files to be in /mnt/etc but in /etc instead, I next use chroot /mnt to make /mnt my new fake root directory. There is one problem, though. Because the /proc and /dev directories are generated automatically, they will not be available in the chroot environment. The solution? I use mount -o bind before using chroot. The following steps show the proper command sequence to mount your Linux distribution completely using chroot and mount -o bind:

1. Boot your server from a live CD-ROM, such as Knoppix, or use the rescue system boot option that you'll find on your Ubuntu Server installation CD-ROM. This procedure will generate the directories /proc and /dev.

2. Mount your root partition on /mnt. You'll see that the directories /mnt/proc and /mnt/dev are almost empty.

3. Use the command mount -o bind /dev /mnt/dev and next mount -o bind /proc /mnt/proc to make sure that complete /proc and /dev directories are available in the chroot environment.

4. Use chroot /mnt to make /mnt your new root environment and do your troubleshooting. You'll see that everything works neatly now.

5. When finished doing the troubleshooting, use exit to escape from the chroot environment and then reboot your server.

Getting an Overview of Mounted Devices

Every device that is mounted is recorded in the configuration file /etc/mtab. You can browse the content of this file with a utility like cat or less. You can also use the mount command to get an overview of file systems that are currently mounted. If this command is used without any other parameters, it reads the contents of /etc/mtab and displays a list of all mounted file systems that it can find, as seen in Listing 4-1.

Listing 4-1. *The* mount *Command Gives an Overview of All Devices Currently Mounted*

```
sander@ubuntu:~$ mount
/dev/mapper/ubuntu-root on / type ext3 (rw,errors=remount-ro)
proc on /proc type proc (rw,noexec,nosuid,nodev)
/sys on /sys type sysfs (rw,noexec,nosuid,nodev)
varrun on /var/run type tmpfs (rw,noexec,nosuid,nodev,mode=0755)
varlock on /var/lock type tmpfs (rw,noexec,nosuid,nodev,mode=1777)
procbususb on /proc/bus/usb type usbfs (rw)
udev on /dev type tmpfs (rw,mode=0755)
devshm on /dev/shm type tmpfs (rw)
devpts on /dev/pts type devpts (rw,gid=5,mode=620)
/dev/sda1 on /boot type ext3 (rw)
```

Unmounting Devices

On a Linux system, a device not only has to be mounted, but, when you want to disconnect the device from your computer, you have to unmount it first. Unmounting devices ensures that all the data that is still in cache and has not yet been written to the device is written to the file system before it is disconnected. You'll use the umount command to do this. The command can take two arguments: either the name of the device or the name of the directory where the device is mounted. So umount /dev/cdrom and umount /media/cdrom will both work.

When using the umount command, you may get the message "Device is busy" and the dismount will fail. This is likely because a file on the device is open, and the reason you're not allowed to disconnect the device is probably obvious: disconnecting a mounted device may lead to data loss. So first make sure that the device has no open files. The solution is sometimes simple: if you want to dismount a CD-ROM, but you are currently in the directory /media/cdrom, it is not possible to disconnect the device. Browse to another directory and try again. Sometimes, however, the situation can be more complex, and you need to first find out which processes are currently using the device.

To do this, you can use the fuser command. This command displays the Process IDs (PIDs) of processes using specified files or file systems. For example, fuser -m /media/cdrom displays a list of all processes that currently have open files in /media/cdrom. The fuser command also allows you to kill the processes that have these files open automatically. For open files on /media/cdrom, use fuser -km /media/cdrom. Be careful when using the option: if you are root, it may blindly kill important processes and make your server unreadable.

As an alternative to the fuser command, you can use lsof as well. This also provides a list of all processes that currently are using files on a given file system, but it provides more information about these processes. Whereas fuser just gives the PID of a process, lsof also gives information like the name of the process and the user who owns the process.

After using fuser with the -k switch to kill active processes, you should always make sure that the process is really terminated by using fuser -m /var again because this will show you whether there are still processes with open files.

Another way of forcing the umount command to do its work is to use the -f option. You can force an umount with umount -f /somemount. This option is especially intended for use on an NFS or a Samba network mount that has become unreachable, and does not work on other file systems. So you will not have much success if you try it on a local file system. Another nice option, especially if you don't like to hurry, is the -l option, which performs a "lazy umount" by detaching the file system from the file system hierarchy and cleaning up all references to the file system as soon as it is no longer busy. Using this option lets you do an umount right away, even if the file system is busy. But it may take some time to complete.

■**Tip** The eject command is a very easy way to dismount and eject optical media. This command will open the CD or DVD drive and eject the optical media that is currently in the drive. All you have to do is remove it. And then you can use eject -t to close the optical drive drawer.

Automating Mounts with /etc/fstab

When starting your server, some mounts need to be issued automatically. For this purpose, Ubuntu Server uses the /etc/fstab file to specify how and where these file systems must be mounted. This file contains a list of all mounts that have to occur on a regular basis. In /etc/fstab, you can state per mount if it has to happen automatically when your system starts. Listing 4-2 shows the contents of the /etc/fstab file on a test server that uses LVM.

In the listing, you can see that it is not only real file systems that are specified in /etc/fstab. The /proc file system is defined here as well. This file system offers an interface to the kernel from the file system. You can read more about this in Chapter 6.

■**Note** The /etc/fstab file is used at system boot, but you can also use it from the command line: enter the mount -a command to mount all file systems in /etc/fstab that are currently not mounted and have the option set to mount them automatically. Also, if a device is defined in /etc/fstab with its most common mount options, you don't need to specify all mount options on the command line. For example, if the /dev/cdrom device is in /etc/fstab, you can mount it by using a shortened mount /dev/cdrom (or mount /media/cdrom) command instead of the complete mount /dev/cdrom /media/cdrom command.

Listing 4-2. *The* /etc/fstab *File Makes Sure That File Systems Are Mounted During System Boot*

```
sander@ubuntu:~$ cat /etc/fstab
# /etc/fstab: static file system information.
#
# <file system> <mount point>   <type>  <options>        <dump>  <pass>
proc            /proc           proc    defaults         0       0
/dev/mapper/ubuntu-root /              ext3    defaults,errors=remount-ro 0       1
# /dev/sda1
UUID=62ec320f-491f-44cb-a395-1c0ee5c4afb2 /boot   ext3  defaults  0    2
```

```
/dev/mapper/ubuntu-swap_1 none              swap    sw              0       0
/dev/hda        /media/cdrom0   udf,iso9660 user,noauto     0       0
/dev/fd0        /media/floppy0  auto        rw,user,noauto  0       0
```

In fstab, each file system is described on a separate line, and the fields in these lines are separated by tabs or spaces. The following fields are always present:

- fs_spec: This first field describes the device or the remote file system to be mounted. Typically, you will see names like /dev/sda1 or server:/mount on this line. As you can see in the example, some /dev/mapper devicenames are used. These refer to the LVM logical volumes that have been created on this system (you'll find more information on logical volumes later in this chapter). You can also see that the device /dev/sda1, which is mounted on the directory /boot, uses its Universal Unique ID (UUID). Every disk device has a UUID, and the advantage of using it instead of a device name is that the UUID always remains the same, whereas the device name itself may change, especially in a SAN environment. UUIDs are generated automatically. In the directory /dev/disk/by-uuid you can see the names of all existing UUIDs. If you use the ls -l command from this directory (shown in Listing 4-3), you can see to what device a certain UUID relates. The server used in Listing 4-3 uses two LVM logical volumes as well as a normal sda1 device.

Listing 4-3. *In the Directory* /dev/disk/by-uuid, *You Can See What Device a UUID Relates To*

```
sander@ubuntu:/dev/disk/by-uuid$ ls -l
total 0
lrwxrwxrwx 1 root root 26 2007-07-01 23:23 2ec482ed-2046-4e99-9a4d
-583db1f31ef4 -> ../../mapper/ubuntu-swap_1
lrwxrwxrwx 1 root root 10 2007-07-01 23:23 62ec320f-491f-44cb-a395
-1c0ee5c4afb2 -> ../../sda1
lrwxrwxrwx 1 root root 24 2007-07-01 23:23 901533ec-95d5-45d7-80f2
-9f6948e227d2 -> ../../mapper/ubuntu-root
```

■**Tip** On most file systems, the device name can be replaced with a label like "ROOT". On an Ext2 or Ext3 file system, these labels can be created with the tune2fs -L command or with xfs_admin on an XFS system. Using labels makes the system more robust and avoids the situation in which adding a SCSI disk adds all the device names. Labels are static and are not changed automatically when a disk is added. Although labels are more obvious than the UUIDs generated by the system, you should consider working with UUIDs anyway because a UUID is in the device itself, and a label is in the file system. Therefore, a UUID is more direct and used by most modern Linux distributions.

- fs_file: The second field is used to describe the mount point for the file system. This is normally a directory in which the file system must be mounted. Some file systems (such as the swap file system) don't work with a specific directory as their mount point. In the case of swap partitions, just swap is used as the mount point instead.

■**Note** For special devices that are mounted from `/etc/fstab`, the specification of the file system type and mount point aren't really necessary. For instance, you can mount the swap device also using `none` or `foo` as a placeholder instead of the word `swap`.

- `fs_vfstype`: The third field is used to specify the file system type you can use. As seen previously, many file systems are available for use on Linux. No specific kernel configuration is needed to use them, as most file systems can be activated as a kernel module that is loaded automatically when needed. Instead of the name of a file system, you can also use `ignore` in this field. This is useful to show a disk partition that is currently not in use. To determine the file system type automatically, use the option `auto`. This is what you want to use on removable media like CD-ROMs and diskettes. Don't use it, however, on fixed media like partitions and logical volumes because it may lead to a failure in mounting the file system when booting your server.

- `fs_mntops`: The fourth field is used to specify the options that should be used when mounting the file system. Many options are available and of these, many are file system–specific. For most file systems, the option `default` is used, which makes sure the file system is mounted automatically when the server boots and normal users are not allowed to disconnect the mount. Also, the options `rw`, `suid`, `dev`, `exec`, and `async` are used. The following list contains some of the most-used options:

    - `async`: Does not write to the file system synchronously, but through the write cache mechanism. This ensures that file writes are performed in the most efficient way, but you risk losing data if contact with the file system is suddenly lost.

    - `dev`: Treats block and character devices on the file system as devices, not as regular files. For security reasons, it's a good idea to avoid using this option on devices that can be mounted by ordinary users.

    - `exec`: Permits execution of binary files.

    - `hotplug`: Do not report errors for this device if it does not currently exist. This makes sense for hot-pluggable devices like USB media.

    - `noatime`: Do not update the access times on this file system every time a file is opened. This option makes your file system somewhat faster if many reads are performed on it.

    - `noauto`: The file system will not be mounted automatically when the system boots or if a user uses the `mount -a` command to mount everything in `/etc/fstab` automatically.

    - `mode`: Used to set a permission mode (see Chapter 5) for new files that are created on the file system.

    - `remount`: Remounts a file system that is already mounted. It only makes sense to use this option from the command line.

- user: Allows a user to mount the file system. This option is normally used only for removable devices like diskettes and CD-ROMs.

- sync: Makes sure the content of the file system is synchronized with the medium before the device is dismounted.

- fs_freq: This field is for use of the dump command, which is a way of making backups of your file system. The field determines which file systems need to be dumped when the dump command is called. If the value of this field is set to 0, it will not be dumped; if set to 1, it will be dumped when dump is invoked. Make sure that the value is set to 0 on all file systems that contain important data that should always be included when making backups with dump.

■Note Although you might not ever use the dump command to create backups, some backup utilities do. So if you want to make sure that your backup utilities are successful, give all file systems that contain important data the value 1 in this column.

- fs_passno: This last field in fstab determines how a file system needs to be checked with the fsck command. At boot time, the kernel will always see whether a file system has to be checked with fsck or not. If this is the case, the root file system must always be checked first, and therefore has the value 1. Other file systems should have the value 2. If the file systems have the same fsck number, they will be checked sequentially. If the files are on different drives, they can be checked in parallel. If the value is set to 0, no automatic check will occur.

Checking File System Integrity

When a system crashes unexpectedly, any file systems that are open can be damaged, which might prevent you from using these file systems in a normal way. If this happens, the consistency of these file systems needs to be checked; you do this with the fsck command for most file systems. XFS has some other commands, which you'll read about later in this chapter. You can start this command with the name of the device you want to check as its argument: for example, use fsck /dev/hda1 to check files on /dev/hda1. If you run the command without any options, fsck will check the file systems in /etc/fstab serially, according to the setting in the fs_passno field in /etc/fstab. Normally, this will always happen when booting your system.

Nowadays, a system administrator does not have to regularly use fsck because most modern file systems are journaling file systems. If a journaling file system gets damaged, the journal is checked, and all incomplete transactions can easily be rolled back. To offer some protection regardless, an Ext2 or Ext3 file system is checked automatically every once in awhile.

■Tip On a non-journaling file system, the `fsck` command can take a very long time to complete. In that case, the `-C` option can be used when performing a manual check. This option displays a progress bar . . . which doesn't, of course, make it go any faster, but it at least lets you know how long you still have to wait for the process to complete. Currently, the `-C` option is supported only on Ext2 and Ext3 file systems.

Working with Links

A very useful option—although one that is often misunderstood—is the link. A link can be compared to a shortcut: it's basically a pointer to another file. On Linux (as on any UNIX system), two different kinds of links are supported: the hard link and the symbolic link.

Why Use Links?

Basically, a link makes it easier to find files you need. Links can be created for the operating system and program files that are used on that operating system, and they can be used to make life easier for users as well. Imagine that some users belong to the group `account` and you want the group members to create files that are readable by all other group members in the directory `/home/groups/account`. To do this, you can ask the users to change to the proper directory every time they want to save a file. Or you can create a link for each user in his or her home directory. Such a link can have the name `account` and can be placed in the home directory of all users who need to save work in the shared directory for the group account, and it's easy to see how this link makes it a lot easier for the users to save their files to the proper location.

Another example of why links can be useful comes from the world of FHS, the Filesystem Hierarchy Standard. This standard prescribes in which directory a Linux system should store files of a particular kind. In the old days, the X Windowing System had all its binaries installed in the `/usr/X11` directory. Later, the name of the directory where the X Windowing System stored its configuration files was changed to `/usr/X11R6`. Now imagine what would happen if an application referred to the `/usr/X11` directory after this change. It would naturally fail because that directory no longer exists. A link is the solution here as well. If the administrator just creates a link with the name `/usr/X11` that points to the `/usr/X11R6` directory, all applications that still refer to `/usr/X11` can still be used.

On a Linux system, links are everywhere. After Ubuntu Server is installed, several links already exist, and as an administrator, it's easy for you to add new ones. To do so, you should understand the difference between a symbolic link and a hard link, which is explained in the next two sections: "Working with Symbolic Links" and "Working with Hard Links."

Working with Symbolic Links

A link can refer to two different things. A symbolic link is a link that refers to the name of a file. Its most important advantage is that it can be used to refer to a file that is anywhere, even on a server on the other side of the world. The symbolic link will still work. However, the biggest disadvantage is that the symbolic link is naturally dependent on the original file. If the original file is removed, the symbolic link will no longer work.

To create a symbolic link, use the `ln` command with the option `-s`. When using the `ln` command, make sure that you first refer to the name of the original file and then to the name of the link you want to create. If, for example, you want to create a symbolic link with the name `computers` in your home directory that refers to the file `/etc/hosts`, use the command `ln -s /etc/hosts ~/computers`. As a result, a shortcut with the name `~/computers` will be created in your home directory. This shortcut refers to `/etc/hosts`. Therefore, any time you open the `~/computers` file, you would really be working in the `/etc/hosts` file.

Understanding Inodes

To understand the difference between a hard link and a symbolic link, you should understand the role of inodes on a Linux file system. Every Linux file or directory (from a technical point of view, there's no real difference between them) has an inode, and this inode contains all the file's metadata (that is, all the administrative data needed to read a file is stored in its inode). For example, the inode contains a list of all the blocks in which a file is stored, the owner information for that file, permissions, and all other attributes that are set for the file. In a sense, you could say that a file really *is* the inode, and names are attached to these inodes to make it easier for humans to work with them.

If you want to have a look at inodes, on an Ext2 or Ext3 file system you can use the (potentially dangerous!) command `debugfs`. This opens a low-level file system debugger from which you can issue advanced repair commands. You can also just check the properties of the file system and files that are used in it (which is not dangerous at all). The following procedure shows how to display the inode for a given file using this file system debugger on Ext2 or Ext3:

■**Note** Only the Ext2/Ext3 command `debugfs` offers you the possibility to show inodes. The fact that this file system has powerful utilities like this one helps to make it a very popular file system.

---

1. Use the command `ls -il` to find the inode number of the file `/etc/hosts`. As you can see in Listing 4-4, the inode number is the first item mentioned in the output of this command.

   Listing 4-4. *The Command* `ls -il` *Shows the Inode Number of a File*

   ```
   sander@ubuntu:/$ ls -il /etc/hosts
   15024138 -rw-r--r-- 1 root root 253 2007-06-05 00:20 /etc/hosts
   ```

2. Using root permissions, open the file system debugger. While starting it, use as an argument the name of the Ext2 or Ext3 file system on which your file resides. For example, our example file `/etc/hosts` is on a logical volume with the name `/dev/ubuntu/root`, so the command would be `sudo debugfs /dev/ubuntu/root`. This opens the `debugfs` interactive prompt.

3. Now use the `debugfs` command `stat` to display the contents of the inode that you want to examine. For example, in this case you would type **stat <15024138>**. The result of this command is similar to what you see in Listing 4-5.

Listing 4-5. *Showing the Contents of an Inode*

```
Inode: 13   Type: regular    Mode:  0644    Flags: 0x0    Generation: 5
84821287
User:     0   Group:     0    Size: 1763308
File ACL: 0    Directory ACL: 0
Links: 1   Blockcount: 3460
Fragment:  Address: 0     Number: 0     Size: 0
ctime: 0x4664e51e -- Tue Jun  5 00:22:54 2007
atime: 0x4664e51e -- Tue Jun  5 00:22:54 2007
mtime: 0x4621e007 -- Sun Apr 15 04:19:19 2007
BLOCKS:
(0-11):5716-5727, (IND):5728, (12-267):5729-5984, (DIND):5985, (IND):
5986, (268-523):5987-6242, (IND):6243, (524-779):6244-6499, (IND):650
0, (780-1035):6501-6756, (IND):6757, (1036-1291):6758-7013, (IND):701
4, (1292-1547):7015-7270, (IND):7271, (1548-1721):7272-7445
TOTAL: 1730

(END)
```

4. Use the `quit` command to close the `debugfs` interface.

Understanding the Differences Between Hard and Symbolic Links

When comparing the symbolic link and the original file, you will notice a clear difference between them (see Listing 4-6). First, the symbolic link and the original file have different inodes: the original file is just a name that is connected directly to the inode, and the symbolic link refers to the name. The latter can be seen from the `ls -il` (`-i` displays the inode number) output: after the name of the symbolic link, an arrow is used to indicate what file you are really working on. Also you can see that the size of the symbolic link is significantly different from the size of the real file. The size of the symbolic link is the number of bytes in the name of the file it refers to because no other information is available in the symbolic link. Also, you can see that the permissions on the symbolic link are completely open because the permissions are not managed here, but on the original file instead. Finally, you can see that the file type of the symbolic link is set to l, which indicates that it is a symbolic link.

Listing 4-6. *Showing the Differences Between Symbolic and Hard Links*

```
root@ubuntu:~# ln -s /etc/hosts symhosts
root@ubuntu:~# ln /etc/hosts hardhosts
root@ubuntu:~# ls -il /etc/hosts hardhosts symhosts
15024138 -rw-r--r-- 2 root root 253 2007-06-05 00:20 /etc/hosts
15024138 -rw-r--r-- 2 root root 253 2007-06-05 00:20 hardhosts
13500422 lrwxrwxrwx 1 root root 10 2007-07-02 05:45 symhosts -> /etc/hosts
```

You may ask what happens to the symbolic link when the original file is removed. Well, that isn't hard to predict! The symbolic link fails. Ubuntu Server will show this when displaying file properties with the `ls` command; you'll get a "File not found" error message when you try to open it.

Working with Hard Links

Every file on a Linux file system has an inode. As explained earlier, all of a file's administrative data is kept in its inode. Your computer actually works entirely with inodes, and the file names are only a convenience for people who are not too good at remembering numbers. Every name that is connected to an inode can be considered a hard link. So when you create a hard link for a file, all you really do is add a new name to an inode. To do this, use the ln command without any options; ln /etc/hosts ~/computers will create such a hard link.

The interesting thing about hard links is that there is no difference between the original file and the link—they are just two names connected to the same inode. The disadvantage of using them is that hard links must exist on the same device, which is rather limiting. If possible, you should always create a hard link instead of a symbolic link because they are faster and they don't waste an inode. Figure 4-1 shows an overview of the relationship of hard links, inodes, and blocks.

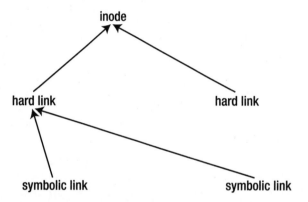

Figure 4-1. *Relationship of Inodes, Hard Links, and Symbolic Links*

Configuring Storage

At the beginning of this chapter, you learned how to perform some of the most common file system management tasks. However, there's more to managing storage on your server. In Chapter 1, you saw how to install your server using LVM and how to use different file systems for your server. I will now go into more depth with regard to these subjects. First, differences between file system types will be discussed in depth. Then you will learn about the creation of file systems, which involves creating and formatting partitions and logical volumes.

Comparing File Systems

An important goal of this chapter is to learn about setting up the best file storage for your server. Because everything on Linux is available as a file, setting up file storage space is one of the most important tasks on a Linux server. This goes for programs and regular text files, but also for more advanced things such as devices. Your server is probably going to host lots of different applications that all create their own files: some will create a few huge files; others will require the fastest possible access to no matter what files; and others may be something like a mail server, creating thousands and thousands of small files. Ubuntu Server provides you the flexibility to choose the best file system for all these different needs because many file systems are supported right out of the box. Before diving in to the details that are needed to create the partitions hosting the different file systems, let's first compare the most important file systems that you can use. The next subsections will cover the following file systems:

- Ext2
- Ext3
- ReiserFS
- FAT
- XFS

Ext2

Version 2 of the Extended File System has been the de facto standard for Linux for many years. It was the first stable file system that had all elements of a POSIX file system. The only reason why it doesn't see much use anymore is because it doesn't offer journaling.

■Note POSIX stands for Portable Operating System Interface, and its aim is to provide a standard level of UNIX compatibility. If any element running on Linux or any other UNIX version is POSIX-compliant, it will run without problems on any flavor of UNIX. The POSIX standard is not just limited to Linux and UNIX operating systems; most versions of Windows based on the NT kernel (up to and including Vista) are POSIX-compliant.

For modern file systems, journaling is an important option. In a journal, all transactions on open files can be tracked. The advantage is that if anything goes wrong while working with a system, all you have to do to repair damage to the file system is to do a roll-back based upon the information in the journal. Ext2 doesn't have a journal, and therefore it isn't a good choice for very large volumes: larger volumes will always take longer to check if no journal is present. If a small (less than 500 MB) volume is created, Ext2 is still a good choice, however. The first reason is that it doesn't make sense to create a journal on a small file system because the journal itself will occupy space (an average journal can be about 40 MB). Other good reasons to use Ext2 include the facts that it is a very mature file system, everyone knows how it works, it works on many distributions, and many utilities are available for management of an Ext2 file system. Some advanced utilities are available for tuning and troubleshooting as well. A short overview of some of them is provided next. You should notice that these commands are all available for Ext3 (Ext2's successor) as well.

- e2fsck: This utility is run automatically when an administrator issues the fsck command. It has some options that are specific for an Ext2 file system, one of which is the -b option that allows you to repair the file system in case the first sectors are damaged. In an Ext2 file system, the critical information about the file system is written to the superblock. A backup superblock is always present, and its exact location depends on the block size that is used. If 1 KB blocks are used, the backup superblock is in block 8193; if 2 KB blocks are used, it is in 16384; and, if 4 KB blocks are used, you can find it in 32768. By running the e2fsck -s 8193 command, for example, you may be able to repair a file system that can't be mounted any more by using its backup superblock. Another very interesting use is e2fsck -D, which causes e2fsck to optimize directories. It can do this by trying to index them, to compress them, or by using other optimization techniques.

- tune2fs: The Ext2 file system has some tunable parameters. For example, there is the maximum mount count option (which can be set using the -C option). By using this option, you can force e2fsck to run automatically every once in awhile by forcing an integrity check. This option may sound good, but on a server in which a file system is sometimes rarely remounted, it can make more sense to use the -i option to set an interval defined as a time period. For example, tune2fs -i 2m will force an e2fsck on your Ext2 file system every two months. The options to check the consistency of your Ext2 file system automatically are not the only options you can use with tune2fs. For example, the option -l will list all information from the file system's superblock. Another interesting option is -L label, which allows you to set a volume label. This can be very useful if device names on your system do change on a regular basis: by using volume names, you can use the name of the volume when mounting the file system in /etc/fstab instead of the name of the device where the file system was created. The last interesting option is -m, which you can use to set a percentage of reserved blocks for your Ext2 file system. By default, the last 5 percent of available disk space is always reserved for the user root to prevent users from filling up the file system by accident. Use the e2fsck -m 2 command to decrease the amount of reserved disk space.

- dumpe2fs: Every file system maintains a lot of administrative information, and Ext2 stores this in the file system superblock. Also, in Ext2, the block groups that are used as groups of data files can be administered as one entity. If you need to see the information about this file system administration, use dumpe2fs followed by the name you want to dump the administrative information for. Listing 4-7 shows the result of this command.

■**Note** When using a tool like dumpe2fs, you will see information about available inodes. Every file on every POSIX-compliant file system needs an inode to store its administrative information. On Ext2 and Ext3, inodes are created only when you are creating the file system. Normally one inode is created for about every four data blocks. If, however, you create many very small files, you can run into a situation in which free disk blocks are still available, but there are no more available inodes. This will make it impossible to create new files. As an administrator, you can use the dumpe2fs command to get an overview of available inodes on your Ext2 file system.

Listing 4-7. *The* dumpe2fs *Command Displays Properties of the Ext2 File System*

```
root@ubuntu:~# dumpe2fs /dev/sad1
dumpe2fs 1.40-WIP (14-Nov-2006)
dumpe2fs: No such file or directory while trying to open /dev/sad1
Couldn't find valid filesystem superblock.
root@ubuntu:~# dumpe2fs /dev/sda1
dumpe2fs 1.40-WIP (14-Nov-2006)
Filesystem volume name:    <none>
Last mounted on:           <not available>
Filesystem UUID:           62ec320f-491f-44cb-a395-1c0ee5c4afb2
Filesystem magic number:   0xEF53
Filesystem revision #:     1 (dynamic)
Filesystem features:       has_journal resize_inode dir_index filetype
 needs_recovery sparse_super
Filesystem flags:          signed directory hash
Default mount options:     (none)
Filesystem state:          clean
Errors behavior:           Continue
Filesystem OS type:        Linux
Inode count:               62248
Block count:               248976
Reserved block count:      12448
Free blocks:               224527
Free inodes:               62218
First block:               1
Block size:                1024
Fragment size:             1024
Reserved GDT blocks:       256
Blocks per group:          8192
Fragments per group:       8192
Inodes per group:          2008
Inode blocks per group:    251
Filesystem created:        Mon Jun  4 22:56:35 2007
Last mount time:           Mon Jul  2 03:22:21 2007
Last write time:           Mon Jul  2 03:22:21 2007
Mount count:               3
Maximum mount count:       26
Last checked:              Mon Jun  4 22:56:35 2007
Check interval:            15552000 (6 months)
Next check after:          Sat Dec  1 21:56:35 2007
Reserved blocks uid:       0 (user root)
Reserved blocks gid:       0 (group root)
First inode:               11
Inode size:                128
Journal inode:             8
Default directory hash:    tea
Directory Hash Seed:       0f4e7f5e-c83c-491b-85ca-a83d7c06f1b5
```

```
Journal backup:          inode blocks
Journal size:            4114k


Group 0: (Blocks 1-8192)
  Primary superblock at 1, Group descriptors at 2-2
  Reserved GDT blocks at 3-258
  Block bitmap at 259 (+258), Inode bitmap at 260 (+259)
  Inode table at 261-511 (+260)
  993 free blocks, 1993 free inodes, 2 directories
  Free blocks: 4640-5632
  Free inodes: 16-2008
Group 1: (Blocks 8193-16384)
  Backup superblock at 8193, Group descriptors at 8194-8194
  Reserved GDT blocks at 8195-8450
  Block bitmap at 8451 (+258), Inode bitmap at 8452 (+259)
  Inode table at 8453-8703 (+260)
  7221 free blocks, 2008 free inodes, 0 directories
  Free blocks: 9164-16384
  Free inodes: 2009-4016
```

- debugfs: The debugfs utility allows you to open the Ext2 file system debugger, from which you can perform powerful tasks. These tasks are performed using the special debugfs commands that can be started from the debugfs interactive shell. One of them is the lsdel command, which lists files that were recently deleted from your file system. After finding the inodes of these recently deleted files, you can use the debugfs dump command (not to be confused with the generic Linux dump command), followed by the number of the inode. For example, use dump <17468> /somefile to dump everything the inode refers to in the file /somefile that is created automatically. However, be aware that this works only if you are acting very fast: when a file is removed on any Linux file system, the inode and blocks that were used by the file are flagged as available, and the next time data is written to the volume, the inode and blocks can be overwritten. You should also be aware of the primary disadvantage of the debugfs method: it doesn't know anything about file or directory names. Therefore, you can see the inode number of a deleted file but not its name, and that can make recovery rather difficult. Currently, however, it is the only way to recover deleted files from an Ext2 or Ext3 file system.

To summarize Ext2, it offers some advantages and disadvantages. It is the file system to use for small volumes. If the size of a volume grows up to several gigabytes, though, it's best not to use Ext2 because it can take ages to complete a file system check.

Ext3

The Ext3 file system is just Ext2 with a journal added to it—nothing more, nothing less. Therefore, Ext3 is completely compatible with Ext2. As compared with other journaling file systems, however, Ext3 has some important disadvantages, most of which are based on the fact that Ext3 uses tables for storage of information about the files and not a B-tree database, as is the case in ReiserFS and XFS file systems. Because these tables have to be created and are accessed in a linear way, Ext3 is slow when dealing with large volumes or large amounts of data. Here are the most important disadvantages of using Ext3:

- It takes a relatively long time to create a large Ext3 file system.

- Ext3 isn't good in handling large numbers of small files in the same directory.

- Ext3 has no option to create new inodes after the file system has been created. This leaves a possibility in which disk space is still available but cannot be used because no inodes are available to address that disk space.

And, on the other hand, Ext3 has two important advantages. Most important, it is a very stable file system that has wide community support. Also, it is easy to convert an existing Ext2 file system to a journaling file system. The following procedure describes how to do this:

1. Make a complete backup of the file system you want to convert.

2. Use the tune2fs program to add a journal to a mounted or an unmounted Ext2 file system. If you want to do this on /dev/sdb1, use tune2fs -j /dev/sdb1. After creating the journal, a file with the name .journal will be created on the mounted file system. This file indicates that the conversion was successful.

3. Change the entry in /etc/fstab where your file system is mounted. Normally, it would be set to the Ext2 file system type, so change the type to Ext3.

4. Reboot your server and verify that the file system was mounted successfully.

The journal is the most important item in an Ext3 file system, and this journal can be configured in different ways. These journaling options are specified when mounting the file system, so you have to put them in /etc/fstab.

Before discussing the different journaling options, you need to know how data is written to a hard drive. In each file-write operation, two different kinds of information need to be written: the data blocks themselves and then the metadata of a file. This includes all administrative information about the file. You can basically think of the file metadata as the information that is displayed when using the ls -l command (but some more information is added as well).

When tuning the use of an Ext3 journal, you can specify whether both metadata and blocks need to be written to the journal, or just the metadata. Two options are available to you: activate them by using mount -t ext3 -o data=xxxx /yourdevice /yourmountpoint or put the data=xxxx option in fstab:

- data=journal: In this option, both the data and metadata of the file that is written are written to the journal. This is the safest option, but it's also the slowest.

- data=ordered: In this option, only the file's metadata is journaled. However, before updating the metadata with information about the changed file, a data write is forced. This ensures consistency within the file system with minimal performance impact. This is the default option when creating an Ext3 file system on Ubuntu Server.

- data=writeback: This option ensures that only metadata is written to the journal and that nothing happens to the data blocks themselves. This is a rather insecure option with a serious risk of corruption of the file system.

ReiserFS

Hans Reiser developed the ReiserFS file system in the late 1990s as a completely new file system, no longer based on file system tables but on a balanced tree database structure. This database makes locating files very fast as compared with older file systems like Ext2 and Ext3. And ReiserFS offers other advantages as well, one of which is that it has a better disk utilization. This is because it is capable of using disk suballocation, in which it is not necessary to use a complete block when writing a very small file. More than one small file can be written to the same disk block, using one leaf node in the B-tree database. Therefore, ReiserFS is more efficient in writing many small files.

ReiserFS is also more flexible because it allows for dynamic inode allocation: if a file system runs out of available inodes, new inodes can be created dynamically. Because small files are stored with their metadata in the same database record, ReiserFS is fast in handling small files. Of course, ReiserFS has some minor disadvantages as well: it's relatively slow in heavy write environments and it also gets slow if it is more than 90 percent full.

Unfortunately, ReiserFS has one hugely important disadvantage: the lack of community support. It was because of this that Novell—traditionally the most important Linux distribution that uses ReiserFS—decided to drop ReiserFS as the default file system and turned to Ext3 instead. In the long term, this doesn't bode well for ReiserFS, nor does the fact that Hans Reiser is currently in jail, facing some serious charges. Therefore, even if ReiserFS has some nice technical features, you should not depend on it too much. Better to use the XFS file system instead.

Like Ext2 and Ext3, ReiserFS also has some management utilities. Here's a short description of these tools, including some of the most interesting options:

- `reiserfsck`: The `reiserfsck` tool is used to check the consistency of a Reiser file system, and it has some powerful repair options. One of them is `--rebuild-sb`, which stands for *rebuild superblock*. Use this option when you get the error "read super_block: can't find a reiserfs file system". Another option is the `--rebuild-tree` option, which hopefully you won't see too often. This option is required when `reiserfsck` wasn't able to repair the file system automatically because it found some serious tree inconsistencies. Basically, the `--rebuild-tree` option will rebuild the complete B-tree database. Before using this option, always make a backup of the complete partition where you are running it and never interrupt the command; doing so will definitely leave you with an inaccessible file system.

- `reiserfstune`: The `reiserfstune` command can be used for several purposes. Basically, you use it to tune options with regard to the Reiser journal, but you can also use it to set a UUID and a label that allow you to mount the file system without being dependent on the name of the device where it resides. This command has some interesting options as well. One of them is the `-j` option that allows you to specify the journal device you want to use. This option makes it possible to separate the Reiser journal from the actual file system; it's a very useful option if you want to avoid a situation where a single-point failure can render your system inaccessible. Another interesting option that can be used with `reiserfstune` is the option `-l` that allows you to specify a label for the file system. This label can be used when mounting the file system and thus increases your flexibility when working on the file system.

- resize_reiserfs: As its name suggests, the resize_reiserfs utility is used to resize a Reiser file system. You should be aware that resizing a file system involves two steps: you first need to resize the device where the file system is created, and only then can you resize the file system itself. There'll be more on resizing devices later in this chapter. And using resize_reiserfs is rather simple: for example, use resize_reiserfs -s /dev/sdb2 to resize the Reiser file system on sdb2 so that it fills this device completely. Alternatively, you can specify the size to resize it with in kilobytes (-K), megabytes (-M), or gigabytes (-G). If you want to shrink a file system by 500 MB, use resize_reiserfs -M 500 /dev/sdb2. Be aware, however, that it is not fully supported; things could go wrong when shrinking a ReiserFS file system.

Tip If you want to shrink a ReiserFS file system, make sure to run reiserfsck immediately after the shrinking process to limit the risk of things going wrong.

- debugreiserfs: The debugreiserfs command allows you to dive into the ReiserFS administrative information to see if all is set according to your expectations. If you run it without options, you'll just get an overview of the superblock. Several options are available to tune its workings. For example, debugreiserfs -j /dev/sdb2 prints the contents of the journal. It's also possible to dive into specific blocks when using the -l option, which takes as its argument the block you want to see the contents of. Using this option can be useful if you want to do a block-by-block reconstruction of a file that was destroyed by accident.

Summarized, ReiserFS is a robust file system that offers many advantages. Because of its current lack of support and the unpredictable future of the company, it's not a very good idea to depend too heavily on it.

XFS

For very large environments, the XFS file system is probably the best choice. It was, after all, developed by SGI for use on supercomputers. Like ReiserFS, it is a full 64-bit file system, and its major benefit is that it works great on very large files. One of the key factors of XFS is that it uses allocation groups, which are like file systems in a file system. The advantage of using these allocation groups is that the kernel can address more than one group at the same time, and each group has its own administration of inodes and free disk space. Of course, XFS is capable of creating new inodes dynamically when this is needed. All of this makes the XFS file system very flexible and robust.

The XFS file system consists of three different sections: data, log, and real-time. User data and metadata are written in the data section. The log section contains the journaling information for XFS, and the real-time section is used to store real-time files. These files are updated immediately. Each XFS file system is identified by a UUID, which is stored in the header of each allocation group and helps you distinguish one XFS file system from the other. For this reason, never use a block-copying program like dd to copy data from one XFS volume to another XFS volume; use xfsdump and xfsrestore instead.

A unique feature of XFS is its delayed allocation, which makes sure that a pending write is not written to hard disk immediately, but to RAM first. The decision to write is delayed to the last minute. The advantage is that, when the file doesn't need to be written after all, it isn't written. In this way, XFS reduces file system fragmentation and simultaneously increases write performance. Another great feature of XFS is preallocation, which makes sure that space is reserved before the data blocks are actually written. This feature increases the chances that a complete file can be written to a series of consecutive blocks and thus avoids fragmentation. When creating an XFS file system with the mkfs.xfs command, some specific options are available:

- *Block size in bytes*: This option allows you to set the block size you want to use. By default, the block size is set to 4,096 bytes, but you can also set it to 512, 1,024, or 2,048.

- *Inode size*: Use this option to specify the size of inodes you want to create on the file system. This option is needed only if you have to do very specific things on your file system, like working with files that have lots of extended attributes.

- *Percentage of inode space*: If so required, you can limit the percentage of the file system that can be used for storage of inodes. By default, there is no maximum setting.

- *Inode aligned*: Make sure this option is always set to "yes" so it will ensure that no fragmentation occurs in the inode table.

Like all other file systems, XFS also has its own management tools, and, because it's a rather complex file system, many utilities are available. Here's an overview of these utilities with a short description:

- xfs_admin: Changes the parameters of an XFS file system.

- xfs_logprint: Prints the log (journal) of an XFS file system.

- xfs_db: Serves as the XFS file system debugger.

- xfs_growfs: Expands the XFS file system.

- xfs_repair: Repairs an XFS file system.

- xfs_copy: Copies the content of an XFS file system while preserving all its attributes. The main advantage of using xfs_copy instead of normal cp is that it will copy data in parallel and thus will work much faster than a normal copy command.

- xfs_info: Shows generic administrative information on XFS.

- xfs_rtcp: Copies files by placing them in the real-time section of the XFS file system, which makes sure that they will be updated immediately.

- xfs_check: Checks the consistency of an XFS file system.

- xfs_quota: Allows you to work with quotas on an XFS file system.

- xfs_io: Debugs the input/output path of an XFS file system.

- xfs_bmap: Prints block mapping for an XFS file system. The command allows you to see exactly what extents are used by a file.

■**Note** An *extent* is a group of blocks. Working with extents speeds up administration and file handling on file systems that work with large files. Also, because every file is initially written to its own extent, working with extents prevents fragmentation of your file system.

- `xfs_ncheck`: Generates pathnames for inode numbers for XFS. Basically, it displays a list of all inodes on the XFS file system and the path to where the file with the given inode number is stored.

- `xfs_mkfile`: Creates an XFS file. This command is used to create files of a fixed size to an XFS file system. By default, these files are filled with zeroes.

Summarized, XFS is the most feature-rich file system of all. Because of its flexibility, it is probably the best choice to store your company data, so use it for Samba shares, for example. Because you can also tune the size of the allocation unit, XFS is also a very efficient file system when writing very large files. Upon creation, make sure that you specify a large allocation unit to be used and you will get great performance.

Creating File Systems

You probably have an idea now as to what file system best fits the needs of your application. The next step is to create these file systems, which involves two steps. First, you need to create the device in which you want to store the files. This can be a partition, but it can also be an LVM logical volume. After creating the device, you can use the mkfs command to create the file system of your choice. I'll first explain how to create the devices in which you want to store your files.

Creating Traditional Partitions

You can use many utilities to create partitions on a server, but one utility can be considered the mother of all other utilities: fdisk. In this section, you'll learn how to use fdisk to create partitions on your disk.

1. From the command line as root, use the fdisk command followed by the name of the device in which you want to create the partition. If you want to create a partition on /dev/sdb, use fdisk /dev/sdb to open the partitioning utility.

2. The fdisk utility now opens its prompt. It may complain about the number of cylinders being greater than 1,024, but this dates from when many boot loaders were not able to handle hard drives with more than 1,024 cylinders, so you can ignore this message. A good start is to press the m (menu) key to tell fdisk to show a menu with all available options (see Listing 4-8).

Listing 4-8. *Working with* fdisk

```
root@ubuntu:~# fdisk /dev/sdb

The number of cylinders for this disk is set to 36483.
There is nothing wrong with that, but this is larger than 1024,
and could in certain setups cause problems with:
1) software that runs at boot time (e.g., old versions of LILO)
2) booting and partitioning software from other OSs
   (e.g., DOS FDISK, OS/2 FDISK)

Command (m for help): m
Command action
   a   toggle a bootable flag
   b   edit bsd disklabel
   c   toggle the dos compatibility flag
   d   delete a partition
   l   list known partition types
   m   print this menu
   n   add a new partition
   o   create a new empty DOS partition table
   p   print the partition table
   q   quit without saving changes
   s   create a new empty Sun disklabel
   t   change a partition's system id
   u   change display/entry units
   v   verify the partition table
   w   write table to disk and exit
   x   extra functionality (experts only)

Command (m for help):
```

3. Press the p key to print the current partition table, which will provide an overview of the size of your disk in cylinders, the size of a cylinder, and all partitions that exist on that disk. Then fdisk asks again what you want to do. Press the n key on your keyboard to create a new partition.

Listing 4-9. *When Working with* fdisk, *Use the p Key Often So That You Can See the Current Partitioning*

```
Command (m for help): p

Disk /dev/sdb: 300.0 GB, 300090728448 bytes
255 heads, 63 sectors/track, 36483 cylinders
Units = cylinders of 16065 * 512 = 8225280 bytes

   Device Boot      Start         End      Blocks   Id  System
```

4. After pressing n to create a new partition, fdisk will ask what kind of partition you want to create. On a hard disk you can create a maximum of four primary partitions. If you need more than four, you have to create one extended partition in which logical partitions can be created. In this example, I'll show you how to create an extended partition, so press the e key to start the interface that helps you create an extended partition.

5. The utility now asks what partition number you want to use. It will also show the numbers that are available.

6. Now you have to enter the first cylinder. By default, fdisk offers you the first cylinder that is still available. It's often a good idea to accept this choice, so press Enter.

7. Next, fdisk asks for the last cylinder that you want to use for your partition. Instead of entering a cylinder number, you can also enter a size in megabytes or gigabytes. However, because this is an extended partition that serves only as a repository where logical partitions are created, you can press Enter to accept the default value that will use all available disk space to create the partition. Listing 4-10 is an overview of what has happened so far.

Listing 4-10. *Creating an Extended Partition with* fdisk

```
Command (m for help): n
Command action
   e   extended
   p   primary partition (1-4)
e
Partition number (1-4): 1
First cylinder (1-36483, default 1):
Using default value 1
Last cylinder or +size or +sizeM or +sizeK (1-36483, default 36483):
Using default value 36483

Command (m for help):
```

8. The extended partition is now created. By itself, an extended partition is useless; it's just an empty box that you can use to create logical partitions. Use the n key again to create a logical partition in the extended partition. The partition number of any logical partition is always 5 or greater, regardless of whether lower partition numbers are already in use. You can follow the same guidelines for creating logical partitions as the ones you followed for creating the extended partition. When finished, press p to print the partition table you have created so far.

■**Note** When creating a partition, Linux fdisk will flag the partition as a Linux partition with ID 83 automatically. If you are planning on doing something else with it, you can press the t key to change the partition ID of your partition. A list of all available partition types is displayed by using the l key from the fdisk menu.

---

9. Until now, nothing has really been written to the partition table. If you want to back out, you can still do that by pressing the q key. If you are sure that you are happy with what you have done, press w to write the changes to the partition table on disk and exit the partitioning utility.

10. The partition table has now been updated, but your kernel currently does not know about it; you can see that by comparing the result of the command fdisk -l /dev/sdb (which shows the current contents of the partition table) with the file /proc/partitions (which shows the partitions that the kernel currently sees). To update the kernel with this new information, as root type **partprobe /dev/sdb**.

Now that you have created a new partition, the next step is to create a file system on it. This isn't too hard if you know what file system you want to create. You just have to create the file system with the proper utility, and fsck is a perfect wrapper utility to create any type of file system. Just remember to use the -t option to specify the type of file system you want to create. Before explaining how to create a file system, let's first take a look at logical volume management.

Working with Logical Volumes

There's one major disadvantage when working with fixed-size partitions. Imagine a system with multiple partitions, and you are running out of available disk space on one partition but there's more than enough disk space available on another partition. When using fixed-size partitions, there's really nothing you can do.

■**Note** "There's really nothing you can do?" Well, that's not completely true. You can do *something*: delete and re-create the partitions from the partition table and resize the file systems that are in use on them, but this is a difficult procedure in which you risk losing all data. Alternatively, you can use utilities like Partition Magic or the parted utility (which is a common Ubuntu utility), but partitions were never meant for easy resizing, which means that things might go wrong when trying to do it. Therefore, if you want to be able to resize partitions in an easy way, use logical volumes.

If logical volumes are used, you can easily resize them and their file systems to make some more space. Another advantage of using logical volumes is that you can create snapshot volumes of them. These snapshot volumes allow you to create backups in a flexible way, and I'll explain how it works later in this chapter. Therefore, for a flexible environment, it's best to work with logical volumes.

In a system that uses logical volumes, all available disk space is assigned to one or more volume groups (basically pools from which volumes can be created). The advantage of working with volume groups is that a volume group can include several storage devices and is therefore not limited to one physical device. Even better, if you run out of disk space in a volume group, you can just simply add a new device to it to increase the amount of usable disk space.

Currently, two systems are available for working with logical volumes. The first is Logical Volume Manager (LVM). It's been around for some time and can be considered mature technology. The other option is Enterprise Volume Manager System (EVMS), a volume manager that was created by IBM and then open sourced. Although LVM is the more mature volume manager, EVMS functions better in a cluster environment in which volumes have to swap over from one node to another (because volumes can be marked as shareable). Although the perfect volume manager system for such a system, EVMS is not very common on Ubuntu Server, so I'll focus on working with LVM in the rest of this chapter.

Creating LVM Volumes

Creating LVM logical volumes is a simple procedure that can be performed by using a few different commands. If you understand the way an LVM environment is organized, creating logical volumes from the command line is not difficult. The bottom layer of the LVM setup is the layer of the physical volumes (pv). These include complete hard disks, or partitions that were created with the partition type 0x8e. Based on the physical volumes, a volume (vg) group is created. From there, one or more logical volumes (lv) are created. Figure 4-2 shows how all components in an LVM setup relate to each other. To work with LVM, the lvm-binaries package must be installed, so run apt-get install lvm-binaries before you start.

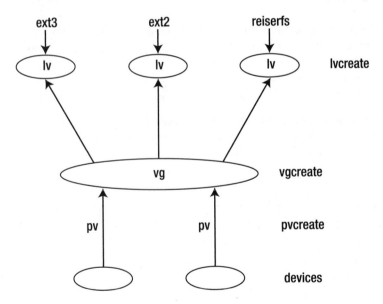

Figure 4-2. *Schematic of LVM structure*

■**Tip** If you understand the role of pv, vg, and lv, the rest is peanuts. All relevant commands start with either pv, vg, or lv and are followed by the specific task you want to perform. For example, if you want to create a pv, a vg, or an lv, use pvcreate, vgcreate, or lvcreate. If you want to extend them, use vgextend or lvextend (a pv cannot be extended). You want to show the current setup? Display it with pvdisplay, vgdisplay, or lvdisplay. More commands are also involved, and a good way of getting to know them all is to type the first two letters of the command that you are interested in at the Bash prompt; for example, type **vg**. Then press the Tab key twice. The automatic command-completion feature displays a list of all commands that start with "vg", which makes it rather easy to pick the right one.

---

1. Before you start, you have to decide what exactly you want to do. If you want to use a complete hard drive, no extra preparation is required. However, if you want only to add a partition to an LVM setup, create the partition with the partition type 0x8e and make sure not to format it.

2. Use the pvcreate command to mark the devices that you want to use in an LVM environment. For example, use pvcreate /dev/sd{b,c,d} to assign devices sdb, sdc, and sdd to be used by LVM.

3. Next, create the volume group. If you have used pvcreate before to assign the physical volumes, you can now use vgcreate to create the volume group. For example, use the command vgcreate somegroup /dev/sd{b,c,d} to create the volume group. Note that in this command, somegroup is the name of the volume group that is created. When making volumes from the volume group, you have to refer to this volume group name.

4. Now use lvcreate to create the logical volumes. For example, lvcreate -n somevol -L150M somegroup will create the volume somevol as a new volume with a size of 150 MB from logical volume group somegroup.

■**Tip** If you want to include a complete hard disk in a volume group, no partition table can be present on that hard disk. To wipe an existing partition table, use the command dd if=/dev/zero of=/dev/sdx bs=1k count=1, after which the hard disk will be ready for use by LVM.

Managing LVM

After you've created logical volumes in this manner, you'll manage them with their associated commands. For example, you can add new devices to the volume group after the device has been installed in your computer. If you have created a physical volume /dev/sde, use vgextend somegroup /dev/sde to add the /dev/sde device to the somegroup volume group.

As long as the physical volume media is not in use, you can remove it from the volume group as well by using the vgreduce command. For example, vgreduce somegroup /dev/sde would remove sde from the volume group again. Be aware that you risk losing data if you issue this command on a disk that currently is in use. Another important task is to monitor the status of the volume group or the volume. Use the vgdisplay somegroup command to display the properties of the volume group, and if you want to show properties of a logical volume, use lvdisplay somevol instead. It speaks for itself that somegroup is the name of the volume group you want to monitor the properties of, and somevol is the name of the volume you want to inspect. Listing 4-11 shows what the result of the vgdisplay command looks like.

Listing 4-11. *Use the* vgdisplay *Command to Show the Properties of a Volume Group*

```
root@ubuntu:~# vgdisplay
  --- Volume group ---
  VG Name               ubuntu
  System ID
  Format                lvm2
  Metadata Areas        1
  Metadata Sequence No 3
  VG Access             read/write
  VG Status             resizable
  MAX LV                0
  Cur LV                2
  Open LV               2
  Max PV                0
  Cur PV                1
  Act PV                1
  VG Size               279.23 GB
  PE Size               4.00 MB
  Total PE              71484
  Alloc PE / Size       71484 / 279.23 GB
  Free  PE / Size       0 / 0
  VG UUID               kl3o4T-T8Qx-gQiE-b8So-1LWo-SfiP-ctS6z1
```

Depending on what you're looking for, vgdisplay gives useful information. For example, if you were thinking about creating another logical volume, you would first have to be sure that some physical extents (the building blocks of both vg and lv) are available. As you can see in the example in Listing 4-11, this is not the case, so you have to add a physical volume first before you can proceed.

Using Advanced LVM Features

You can easily resize existing volumes in an LVM environment. It's also possible to create a snapshot of a volume. Let's explore how to do that.

Resizing Logical Volumes

When resizing logical volumes, you should be aware that the procedure always involves two steps: you need to resize both the volume as well as the file system that is used on the volume. Of all the different file systems, ReiserFS and Ext3 support resizing with the fewest problems. The following procedure details how the volume is first brought offline and then the file system that sits on the volume is resized. It is presumed that the volume you want to shrink is called data and that it uses an Ext3 file system. It is mounted on the directory /data.

■Caution Online resizing of a file system is possible in some cases. For example, the command `ext2online` makes it possible to resize a live file system. However, because resizing file systems is very labor intensive, I wouldn't recommend doing it this way. There's always a risk that it won't work out simply because all of the work that has to be done. So, to stay on the safe side, `umount` your volume before resizing it.

---

1. Use `umount /data` to unmount the volume from the directory `/data`.

2. Before shrinking the volume itself, you must shrink the file system used on it. Use `resize2fs /dev/system/data 2G` to make it a 2 GB file system.

3. Now you have to resize the volume itself: use `lvreduce -L -1G /dev/system/data`.

4. Finally, you can mount the volume again. Use `mount /dev/system/data /data`.

5. Use the `df -h` command to show the current size of the file system. It should be a giga-byte smaller than it was before.

In this procedure, you learned how to shrink a volume, and of course you can also increase its size. When increasing a volume, you just have to invert the order of the steps. First, you need to extend the size of the volume, and *then* the size of the file system can be increased as well. After dismounting the volume, this is a two-step procedure:

1. Use `lvextend -L+10G /dev/system/data` to add 10 GB of available disk space from the volume group to the volume.

2. Next, use `resize_reiserfs -f /dev/system/data`. This command will automatically increase the Reiser file system that is sitting in the volume to the maximum amount of available disk space.

You now know how to resize a volume with a Reiser file system in it. Of course, you can resize Ext3 and Ext2 as well. To increase the size of an Ext3 file system, you would use `resize2fs -f /dev/system/data`.

Creating LVM Snapshots

One of the best features of LVM is the possibility to make snapshots. A *snapshot* is a new block device that functions as a complete copy of the original volume. This works without a com-plete copy being made; only changes are written to the snapshot, and therefore a snapshot can be very efficient in its use of disk space.

A snapshot captures the file system metadata that is used to provide an overview of all existing files on a device and the blocks on a device that are occupied or free. So initially, the snapshot records only administrative information that is used to tell what file is at what loca-tion. Because of the close relation between the original device and its snapshot, all reads to the snapshot device are redirected to the original device.

When writing anything to the original device, a backup of the old data is written to the snapshot device. Therefore, the snapshot volume will contain the original status, whereas the original volume will always include the changed status. The advantage of this technique is that it requires a very limited amount of disk space. For example, if you create a snapshot of a 100 GB volume to exist only for an hour, it must be large enough to keep the file system's metadata as well as all data that is changed within that hour. In most cases, this means that a 5 GB snapshot is more than enough. If, however, your snapshot has to exist for a longer period, the amount of disk space that is used by the snapshot will be larger.

Using snapshot technology can also be very convenient for making backups of volumes that cannot be closed. Imagine, for example, the data volume of a mail server: you cannot just take the mail server down for a couple of hours to make a backup. The solution then is to make a snapshot of the original volume, back up the snapshot volume (which contains the frozen state of the logical volume at the moment the snapshot was made) and, when the backup is finished, remove the snapshot again. This is even something that you can put in a shell script and configure with `cron` so that it runs automatically every night. The procedure described next shows you how to create a snapshot of an existing LVM volume.

1. In the first step, you are using the `lvcreate` command to make a snapshot volume for the original volume `/dev/system/data`. The snapshot gets the name `databackup`. Because the original volume is in the system volume group, the snapshot will be created from that group as well. Do this by using the command `lvcreate -L500M -s -n databackup /dev/system/data`. Here, the option `-L500M` makes the snapshot 500 MB, `-s` makes it a snapshot volume, and `-n` uses the name `databackup`. Finally, `/dev/system/data` refers to the original volume that will be captured in the snapshot.

■**Tip** Problems creating the snapshot volume? Make sure that the kernel `module dm_snapshot` is loaded! Check this with the `lsmod` command; if it isn't loaded, load it manually with `modprobe dm_snapshot`.

---

2. If next you want to create a backup of the volume, first mount it. Do this the same way that you would mount any other volume, such as with `mount /dev/system/databackup /somewhere`.

3. To create a backup from the snapshot volume, use your regular backup (or `tar`, for example). To write a backup to a rewindable tape device, you would use `tar -cvf /dev/rmt0 /somewhere`.

4. Finished making the backup? Then you can remove the snapshot with `lvremove /dev/system/databackup`. Of course, this works only after you have unmounted the snapshot device.

Doing Magic on Your File Systems with dd

In your life as a system administrator, it is often necessary to copy data around. If it's ordinary data, an ordinary command like `cp` works well enough. But if the data is not ordinary, `cp` just isn't powerful enough. We'll now discuss some of the options that the `dd` command has to offer.

■**Caution** If the file system metadata contains important information, like a UUID that makes it possible for you to uniquely identify a file system, dd can cause some unpredicted results. If you are using dd to copy the complete file system, you will copy information like the UUID as well, so you can't differentiate the old file system from the new one.

Speaking in generic terms, the nice thing about the dd command is that it doesn't just copy files; it can copy blocks as well. As a simple example, I'll show you how to clone your complete hard drive. Assuming that /dev/sda is the drive that you want to clone, and /dev/sdb is an empty drive that can be used as the target, the dd command is rather easy: dd if=/dev/sda of=/dev/sdb. In this example, dd is used with two parameters only: if is used to specify an input file, and of is used to specify the output file (both of which are device files in this case). Next, wait until the command is finished, and you will end up with an exact copy of the original hard drive.

In this example, the contents of one device were copied to another device. A slight variation is the way that dd is used to clone a DVD or CD-ROM and write it to an ISO file. To do that, in case your optical drive can be accessed via /dev/cdrom, you can clone the optical disk using dd if=/dev/cdrom of=/tmp/cdrom.iso. And, of course, you can mount that ISO file as well using mount -o loop /tmp/cdrom.iso /mnt. Next, you can access the files in the ISO file from the directory where the ISO is mounted.

So far we have used dd only to do things that can be done with other utilities as well. It becomes really interesting if we go beyond that. What do you think of the following example, in which a backup of the master boot record (MBR) is created? Just make sure that the first 512 bytes of your hard drive, which contains the MBR, is copied to some file, as in dd if=/dev/sda of=/boot/mbr_backup bs=512 count=1. In this example, two new parameters are used. First, the parameter bs=512 specifies that the block should be 512 bytes. Next, the parameter count=1 indicates that only one such block has to be copied. Without this parameter, you would copy your entire hard drive, which I don't recommend. The backup copy of your MBR may be useful if some day you can't boot your server anymore because of a problem in the MBR. If this happens, just boot from a rescue disk and use the command dd if=/boot/mbr_backup of=/dev/sda bs=446 count=1. As you notice, in this restore command, only 446 bytes are written back because you may have changed the partition table since you created the backup. By writing back only the first 446 bytes of your backup file, you don't overwrite the original partition table which is between bytes 447 and 511.

Now I'll show you how to extend your swap space by adding a swap file. This is useful if you get an alert in the middle of the night that your server is almost running completely out of memory because of a memory leak you hadn't discovered so far. All you have to do is to create an empty file and specify that it should be added to the swap space. Creating this empty file is an excellent task for the dd command. In the following command, you are using dd to create a file that is filled with zeros completely by using the /dev/zero device: dd if=/dev/zero of=/swapfile bs=1024 count=1000000. This would write a file of 1 GB that can be added to the swap space using mkswap /swapfile and swapon /swapfile.

In the next example of the marvelous things you can do with dd, let's use it to recover the superblock on an Ext2 or Ext3 file system. To access a file system, you need the superblock, which is a 1 KB block that contains all metadata about the file system. It normally is the second 1 KB block on an Ext3 file system. In Listing 4-12, you can see a part of the contents of the superblock as displayed with the debugfs utility.

Listing 4-12. *Partial Contents of the Superblock*

```
Filesystem volume name:    <none>
Last mounted on:           <not available>
Filesystem UUID:           09979101-96e0-4533-a7f3-0a2db9b07a03
Filesystem magic number:   0xEF53
Filesystem revision #:     1 (dynamic)
Filesystem features:       has_journal ext_attr filetype needs_recovery
 sparse_super large_file
Default mount options:     (none)
Filesystem state:          clean
Errors behavior:           Continue
Filesystem OS type:        Linux
Inode count:               5248992
Block count:               10486428
Reserved block count:      524321
Free blocks:               3888202
Free inodes:               4825213
First block:               0
Block size:                4096
Fragment size:             4096
Blocks per group:          32768
Fragments per group:       32768
Inodes per group:          16352
Inode blocks per group:    511
```

If the superblock isn't accessible anymore because of an error, you have a serious challenge. Fortunately, some backup copies of the superblock are written on the Ext3 file system by default. Using these backup copies, you can still mount a file system that you may have otherwise considered lost. And, as you can guess, the dd command is an excellent help.

The actual position on disk of the first backup of the superblock depends on the size of the file system. On modern large file systems, you will always find it at block 32768. To see if it really works, you can mount from it directly using the mount option -o sb. The issue, however, is that mount expects you to specify the position of the superblock in 1,024 byte blocks, whereas the default block size for a modern Ext3 volume or partition is often 4,096 bytes. (Use dumpe2fs if you want to be sure about that.) Therefore, to tell the mount command where it can find the superblock, you have to multiply the position of the superblock by 4, which in most cases results in a block value 131072. If, for example, your /dev/sda5 file system should have a problem, you can try mounting it with the command mount -o sb=131072 /dev/hda5 / somewhere.

Did the file system mount successfully? If so, the problem really was in the superblock. So let's fix that problem by copying the backup superblock back to the location of the old superblock. You can do this using dd if=/dev/hda5 of=/dev/hda5 bs=1024 skip=131072 count=1 seek=1. Once finished, your file system is accessible again, just as it was before.

Summary

In this chapter, you learned about the most important file system management tasks. In the first part of the chapter, you read how to mount and unmount file systems. You also learned how links can make your life easier. The second part of this chapter concerned the organization of a file system. You learned how to use partitions or logical volumes to set up a file system, and you read how to use the dd command to perform some advanced file system management tasks. In Chapter 5, you'll find out how to secure your server with user and group accounts, permissions, sudo, and many more.

CHAPTER 5

■■■

Configuring Your Server for Security

No matter what you want to use your server for, it'll be useless if it isn't secure. In this chapter, you'll learn about the different security-related items that you'll encounter when setting up your server. First I'll talk about the configuration of users and groups because most of the security you'll be using on your server will be bound to users and groups. Next, I'll cover the Linux permissions that you can use to restrict access to your server's file system. Following that, I'll discuss some security mechanisms that aren't so obvious, like the sudo mechanism and the system of pluggable authentication modules (PAMs).

■Note In this section you'll learn all about securing services on your server, but also know that none of your software skills will do you any good unless your hardware—and I mean the server itself—is *physically* secured. So, before you start securing your server, make sure that it is locked in a restricted-access room.

Setting Up User Accounts

You have two approaches when creating users from a command-line environment: you can use the useradd command, or you can add users to the relevant configuration files by manually editing these files. Although this second approach—editing the configuration files—may be useful in an environment in which users are added from a custom-made shell script, it generally is not recommended. The reason for this is probably obvious: an error in the main user configuration files might make it impossible for *every* user to log in to the server. In this section, I'll discuss how to manage users from the command line using useradd and other related commands such as usermod and userdel. You can edit related configuration files to make creating users easier.

Commands for User Management

If you want to add users from the command line, useradd is just the ticket. And the other commands for user management are just as convenient:

- `useradd`: Adds users to the local authentication system

- `usermod`: Modifies properties for users

- `userdel`: Deletes users properly from a system

- `passwd`: Modifies passwords for users

Using `useradd` is simple. In its easiest form, it just takes the name of a user as its argument; thus, `sudo useradd zeina` creates a user called "zeina" to the system. However, you should also use the `-m` option because if you don't, that user will be without a home directory. In most cases, a user should have a home directory because it allows that person to store files somewhere. Unfortunately, if you create a user without a home directory, there's really no easy way to correct this problem later (but see the following tip for the not-so-easy way).

■Tip Did you forget to create a home directory for user zeina and want to create one now? First, use `mkdir /home/zeina` to make the directory itself. Then use `cd /etc/skel` to activate the directory that contains all files that normally need to be present in a user's home directory. Use `tar cv . | tar xvC /home/zeina` to copy all files, including hidden files from this directory to the user's home directory. Next, use `chown -R zeina:users /home/zeina` to set proper file ownership for all these files. You've now created a home directory, but wouldn't it have been easier just to use `-m`?

You have a few options with the `useradd` command. If an option isn't specified, `useradd` will read its configuration file in `/etc/default/useradd`, where it finds some default values such as what groups the user should become a member of and where to create the user's home directory. But let's take a look at the most important options, which are listed next. (For a complete list of available options, use `man useradd` or `useradd --help` for a summary.)

- `-c comment`: Allows you to enter a comment field to the user. Information set this way can be requested with the `finger` command, and this comment field typically is used for the user's name.

- `-e date`: Sets the expiration date for the user. Use this option to automatically disable the user's account on the specified date. This can be entered in the *YYYY-MM-DD* format or as the number of days since January 1, 1970. You'll probably prefer to specify the date.

- `-G groups`: Makes the user a member of some additional groups. By default, the user becomes a member of only those groups listed in `/etc/default/useradd`.

- `-g gid`: Sets the primary group of a user (see the section called "Group Membership" later in this chapter for more details).

- `-m`: Creates a home directory automatically.

When setting up user accounts, the user is added to two configuration files: `/etc/passwd` and `/etc/shadow`. The `/etc/passwd` file contains generic user-related information, such as the groups the user belongs to and the unique ID assigned to the user. The `/etc/shadow` file contains password-related information about the user. In the following subsections, you'll find information about the properties used in these files.

UID

The user ID (UID) is another major piece of information when creating a user. For your server, this is the only way to identify a user; user names are just a convenience for humans (who can't quite handle numbers as well as a computer does). In general, all users need a unique UID. Ubuntu Server starts generating UIDs for local users at 1000, and a total of 16 bits is available for creating UIDs. This means that the highest available UID is 65535, so that's also the maximum number of local users that your server will support. If you exceed this limit, you'll need a directory server such as OpenLDAP. Typically, UIDs below 500 are reserved for system accounts that are needed to start services. The UID 0 is also a special one: the user with it has complete administrative permissions to the server. UID 0 is typically reserved for the user root.

That said, you may want to give the same ID to more than one user in one situation: to create a backup root user. If you want to do this with useradd, use the options -o and -u 0. For example, to make user stacey a backup root user, use useradd -o -u 0 stacey.

■**Tip** Want to use some specific settings for all users that you are creating on your server? If so, you might be interested in the /etc/default/useradd file, which contains default settings that are used all the time when using useradd. Check the other files in this directory as well; many commands read configuration files from it.

Group Membership

In any Linux environment, a user can be a member of two different kinds of groups. First, there's the primary group, which every user has. (If a user doesn't have a primary group setting, he won't be able to log in.) The primary group is the group that is specified in the /etc/passwd file. By default, on an Ubuntu Linux system, all users get their own private groups as their primary groups, and this private group has the same name as the user. A user can be a member of more than just the primary group and will automatically inherit the rights granted to these other groups. The most important difference between a primary group and other groups is that the primary group will automatically become group owner of any new file that a user creates. Because every user has his or her own private group, this won't be a great challenge for your server's security settings (because the user is the only member). I'll discuss file permissions and ownership in detail later in this chapter, but I'll provide an example just to give you an idea of how it works.

Imagine that user zeina is a member of the private group zeina and also of the group sales. Now user zeina wants to create a file to which only members of the group sales have access. If she does nothing to change her primary group and creates a file, the default group zeina will become group owner of the file, and all users who are members of this group (in other words, just zeina) will have access to the file.

One solution is to use the newgrp command to set the primary group to sales on a *temporary* basis. If user zeina creates the file after using newgrp sales, the group sales will be owner of that file and all other files that the user creates until she uses `newgrp zeina` to switch the primary group setting back to users. This is just one way of using groups, and I discuss other methods later in the chapter.

As you can see, group membership in a stand-alone Linux file system environment isn't that sophisticated. The method sounds primitive, but it hardly ever causes problems because permissions are just set at another level, such as when the user is accessing the server through a Samba share. (See Chapter 10 for more on that.)

You now know some more about the relation between the primary group and the other groups that a user belongs to. In the sections about group management later in this chapter, you'll learn how to apply this knowledge.

Shell

Any user who needs to log in to your server needs a shell. (Conversely, users who don't need to work on your server directly generally don't need a shell; they just need a connection.) The shell will enable the user's commands to be interpreted. The default shell in Ubuntu is `/bin/ bash`, a shell that offers many features.

However, you should know that not every user needs a shell. A user with a shell is allowed to log in locally to your system and access any files and directories stored on that system. If you're using your system as a mail server (and so all that your users need is to access their mail boxes with the POP protocol), it makes no sense at all to give them a login shell. Therefore, you could choose to specify an alternative command to be used as the shell. For example, use `/bin/false` if you don't want to allow the user any local interaction with your system. Any other command will do as well. If, for example, you want the Midnight Commander (a clone of the once very popular Norton Commander) to be started automatically when a user logs in to your system, make sure that `/usr/bin/mc` is specified as the shell for that user.

■**Tip** Make sure that you include the complete path to the command you want to execute as the shell environment for a user. If you don't know the complete path for your favorite command, use the `which` command. For example, `which mc` shows the exact location of the program file you're looking for. Not installed yet? Use `sudo apt-get install mc` to install it now.

Managing Passwords

If your user really needs to do something on your system, she needs a password. By default, login for the users you create is denied, and no password is supplied. Basically, your freshly created user does not have any permissions on your server. However, the simple `passwd` command will let her get to work. If the user uses the command to change her password, she will be prompted for the old password and then the new one. It's also possible for the root user to change passwords as well. Only root can add the name of a user, for whom root wants to change a password, as an argument to the `passwd` command. For example, root can use the command `passwd linda` to change the password for user linda, which is always useful in case of forgotten user passwords.

The `passwd` command can be used in three generic ways. First, you can use it for password maintenance (such as changing a password, as you have just seen). Second, it can also be used to set an expiration date for the password. Third, the `passwd` command can be used for account maintenance. For example, an administrator can use it to lock a user's account so that login is temporarily disabled. In the next subsection, you'll learn more about password management.

Performing Account Maintenance with `passwd`

In an environment in which many users use the same server, it's crucial that you perform some basic account maintenance. These tasks include locking accounts when they are unneeded for a longer time, unlocking an account, and reporting password status. Also, an administrator can force a user to change his password after he logs in for the first time. To perform these tasks, the `passwd` command has the following options:

- `-l`: Enables an administrator to lock an account (for example, `passwd -l jeroen` locks the account for user jeroen)

- `-u`: Unlocks a previously locked account

- `-S`: Reports the status of the password for a given account

- `-e`: Forces the user to change his or her password upon next login

Managing Password Expiration

Although not many people are aware of this feature, it allows you to manage the maximum number of days that a user can use the same password. The `passwd` command has four options to manage expirations:

- `-n min`: This option is applied to set the minimum number of days that a user must use his password. If this option is not used, the user can change his password any time he wants. This option can be useful if you want to apply a password policy that forces users to change their passwords on a regular basis. Using a minimum number of days prevents users from changing a password and then immediately changing it back to the old password.

- `-x max`: With this option, you can set the maximum number of days that the user can use his password without changing it.

- `-c warn`: Use this option to send a warning to the user when his password is about to expire. The argument of this option specifies how many days the user is warned before his password expires.

- `-i inact`: Use this option to make an account expire automatically if it hasn't been used for a given period. The argument of this option specifies the exact duration in days of this period.

■**Caution** By default, a password can be used for 99,999 days. So, if you do nothing, a user may use his password for 273 years without changing it. If you don't want that, make sure you use the -x option.

Modifying and Deleting User Accounts

If you know how to create a user, modifying an existing user account is no big deal, and the usermod command has many options that are exactly the same as those used with useradd. For example, use usermod -g 101 linda to set the new primary group of user linda to the group with the unique ID 101. For a complete overview of the options that usermod shares with useradd, consult the man page of usermod, but some of the useful and unique options are listed here:

- -a, --append: Adds the user to some new groups. This option is followed by the group ID of the groups you want to add the user to.

- -L, --lock: Disables the account temporarily.

- -U, --unlock: Unlocks an account.

Another command that you'll occasionally need is userdel, which you'll use to delete user accounts from your server. Basically, userdel is a very simple command: userdel lynette deletes user lynette from your system. However, if used this way, userdel leaves the home directory of your user untouched. This may be desired (such as to ensure that your company still has access to the work a user has done), but you may just as well wish to delete the user's home directory. For this purpose, you can use the option -r; for example, userdel -r lynette deletes the home directory of user lynette. However, if the home directory of user lynette contains files that are not owned by user lynette, userdel can't remove the home directory. In this case, use the option -f, which removes every file from the home directory, even those not owned by the given user. So, to make sure that user lynette and all the files in her home directory are removed, use userdel -rf lynette.

You now know how to remove a user along with all the files in his home directory. But what about other files the user may have created in other directories on your system? The userdel command won't automatically find and remove these. In such a case, the find command is very useful. You can use find to search for and remove all files owned by a given user. To locate and remove all files on your system that are created by user lynette, you can use find / -user "lynette" -exec rm {} \;. However, this may lead to problems on your server in some circumstances. Let's say lynette was a very active user of the group sales and created many important files in the directory /home/sales that are used by other members of the group. So instead of immediately removing the files, it'd be better to copy them to a safe place instead. If no one has complained after a couple of months, you can remove them safely. To move all files owned by user lynette to a directory called /trash/lynette (that you must create beforehand), use find / -user lynette -exec mv {} /trash/lynette \;.

Behind the Commands: Configuration Files

In the previous section, you learned about the commands to manage users from a console environment. All these commands put the user-related information into what are known as configuration files, and a configuration file is also used for default settings that are applied when managing the user environment. The aim of this section is to give you some insight into the following configuration files:

- /etc/passwd

- /etc/shadow

- /etc/login.defs

/etc/passwd

The first and probably most important of all user-related configuration files is /etc/passwd, which is the primary database for user information: everything except the user password is stored in this file. Listing 5-1 should give you an impression of what the fields in this file look like.

Listing 5-1. *Contents of the User Database file* /etc/passwd

```
root@RNA:~# cat /etc/passwd
root:x:0:0:root:/root:/bin/bash
daemon:x:1:1:daemon:/usr/sbin:/bin/sh
bin:x:2:2:bin:/bin:/bin/sh
sys:x:3:3:sys:/dev:/bin/sh
sync:x:4:65534:sync:/bin:/bin/sync
games:x:5:60:games:/usr/games:/bin/sh
man:x:6:12:man:/var/cache/man:/bin/sh
lp:x:7:7:lp:/var/spool/lpd:/bin/sh
mail:x:8:8:mail:/var/mail:/bin/sh
news:x:9:9:news:/var/spool/news:/bin/sh
uucp:x:10:10:uucp:/var/spool/uucp:/bin/sh
proxy:x:13:13:proxy:/bin:/bin/sh
www-data:x:33:33:www-data:/var/www:/bin/sh
backup:x:34:34:backup:/var/backups:/bin/sh
list:x:38:38:Mailing List Manager:/var/list:/bin/sh
irc:x:39:39:ircd:/var/run/ircd:/bin/sh
gnats:x:41:41:Gnats Bug-Reporting System (admin):/var/lib/gnats:/bin/sh
nobody:x:65534:65534:nobody:/nonexistent:/bin/sh
dhcp:x:100:101::/nonexistent:/bin/false
syslog:x:101:102::/home/syslog:/bin/false
klog:x:102:103::/home/klog:/bin/false
mysql:x:103:106:MySQL Server,,,:/var/lib/mysql:/bin/false
bind:x:104:109::/var/cache/bind:/bin/false
sander:x:1000:1000:sander,,,:/home/sander:/bin/bash
messagebus:x:105:112::/var/run/dbus:/bin/false
haldaemon:x:106:113:Hardware abstraction layer,,,:/home/haldaemon:/bin/false
gdm:x:107:115:Gnome Display Manager:/var/lib/gdm:/bin/false
sshd:x:108:65534::/var/run/sshd:/usr/sbin/nologin
linda:x:1001:1001::/home/linda:/bin/sh
zeina:x:1002:1002::/home/zeina:/bin/sh
```

You can see that /etc/passwd uses different fields, and they all are separated with a colon. Here's a short explanation of these fields:

- *Loginname*: This is the first field and it stores the user's login name. In older UNIX versions, the field was limited to eight characters. Fortunately, Ubuntu Server does not have this limitation.

- *Password*: In the old days of UNIX, this file stored the encrypted passwords. The only problem was that everyone—including an intruder—was allowed to read the /etc/passwd file. This poses an obvious security risk, so passwords are now stored in the configuration file /etc/shadow, which is discussed in the next section. The "x" in the password field denotes the use of shadow passwords.

- *UID*: As you already learned, every user has a unique user ID. Ubuntu Server starts numbering local user IDs at 1000 and typically the highest number that should be used is 65535.

- *GID*: As discussed in the previous section, every user has a primary group, and its group ID (GID) is listed here. This is the numeric ID of the group that the user uses as his primary group. For ordinary users, the GID defaults to 100 (which belongs to the group users).

- *GECOS*: The General Electric Comprehensive Operating System (GECOS) field is used to include some comment to make it easier for the administrator to identify the user. However, the GECOS field is optional, and it's often not used at all.

- *Home directory*: This is a reference to the directory that serves as the user's home directory; it is typically the location in which a user stores files. Note that it is only a reference and has nothing to do with the real directory; just because you see a directory listed here doesn't mean that it actually exists.

- *Shell*: The last field in /etc/passwd refers to the program that should be started automatically when a user logs in. Most often, it's /bin/bash, but, as discussed in the preceding section, every binary program can be referred to here as long as the complete pathname is used.

As an administrator, you can manually edit /etc/passwd and the related /etc/shadow. If you intend to do this, however, don't use any editor; use vipw instead. This tailored version of the Vi editor is specifically designed for editing these critical files. Any error can have serious consequences, such as no one being able to log in. Therefore, if you make manual changes to any of these files, you should check their integrity. Besides vipw, another way to do this is to use the pwck command, which you can run without any options to see whether there are any problems you need to fix.

/etc/shadow

Encrypted user passwords are stored in the /etc/shadow file. The file also stores information about password expiration. Listing 5-2 shows an example of its contents.

Listing 5-2. *Example Contents of the* /etc/shadow *File*

```
root:$1$15CyWuRM$g72U2o58j67LUW1oPtDS7/:13669:0:99999:7:::
daemon:*:13669:0:99999:7:::
bin:*:13669:0:99999:7:::
sys:*:13669:0:99999:7:::
sync:*:13669:0:99999:7:::
games:*:13669:0:99999:7:::
man:*:13669:0:99999:7:::
lp:*:13669:0:99999:7:::
mail:*:13669:0:99999:7:::
news:*:13669:0:99999:7:::
uucp:*:13669:0:99999:7:::
proxy:*:13669:0:99999:7:::
www-data:*:13669:0:99999:7:::
backup:*:13669:0:99999:7:::
list:*:13669:0:99999:7:::
irc:*:13669:0:99999:7:::
gnats:*:13669:0:99999:7:::
nobody:*:13669:0:99999:7:::
dhcp:!:13669:0:99999:7:::
syslog:!:13669:0:99999:7:::
klog:!:13669:0:99999:7:::
mysql:!:13669:0:99999:7:::
bind:!:13669:0:99999:7:::
sander:$1$QqnOp2NN$L7W9uL3mweqBa2ggrBhTBO:13669:0:99999:7:::
messagebus:!:13669:0:99999:7:::
haldaemon:!:13669:0:99999:7:::
gdm:!:13669:0:99999:7:::
sshd:!:13669:0:99999:7:::
linda:!:13671:0:99999:7:::
zeina:!:13722:0:99999:7:::
```

Just as in /etc/passwd, the lines in /etc/shadow are divided into several fields as well, but only the first two fields matter for the typical administrator. The first field stores the name of the user, and the second field stores the encrypted password. Note that, in the encrypted password field, the ! and * characters can be used as well. The ! character denotes that login is currently disabled, and * denotes a system account that can be used to start services but that is not allowed for interactive shell login. Also note that an encrypted password is stored here by default, but it's perfectly possible to store an unencrypted password as well. The /etc/shadow file uses the following fields:

- Login name

- Encrypted password

- Days between January 1, 1970 and the date when the password was last changed

- Days before password may be changed (this is the minimum amount of time that a user must use the same password)

- Days after which password must be changed (this is the maximum amount of time that a user may use the same password)

- Days before password expiration that user is warned

- Days after password expiration that account is disabled (if this happens, administrator intervention is required to unlock the password)

- Days between January 1, 1970 and the date when the account was disabled

- Reserved field (this field is currently not used)

/etc/login.defs

The /etc/login.defs file is a configuration file that relates to the user environment, but is used only in the background. This file defines some generic settings that determine all kinds of things relating to user login. The login.defs file is a readable configuration file that contains variables. The variable relates to logging in or to the way in which certain commands are used. This file must exist on every system because you would otherwise experience unexpected behavior. The following list contains some of the more interesting variables that can be used in the login.defs file (for a complete overview, consult man 5 login.defs):

- DEFAULT_HOME: By default, a user will be allowed to log in, even if his home directory does not exist. If you don't want that, change this parameter's default value of 1 to the Boolean value 0.

- ENV_PATH: This variable contains the default search path that's applied for all users who do not have UID 0.

- ENV_ROOTPATH: This variable works in the same manner as ENV_PATH, but for root.

- FAIL_DELAY: After a login failure, it will take a few seconds before a new login prompt is generated. This variable, set to 3 by default, specifies how many seconds it takes.

- GID_MAX and GID_MIN: Specify the minimum and maximum GID used by the groupadd command (see "Commands for Group Management" in the next section).

- LASTLOG_ENAB: If enabled by setting the Boolean value to 1, LASTLOG_ENAB specifies that all successful logins must be logged to the file /var/log/lastlog. This works only if the lastlog file also exists. (If it doesn't, create it by using touch /var/log/lastlog.)

- PASS_MIN_LEN: This is the minimum number of characters that must be used for new passwords.

- UID_MAX and UID_MIN: These are the minimum and maximum UIDs to be used when adding users with the useradd command.

Creating Groups

As you've already learned, all users require group membership. You've read about the differences between the primary group and the other groups, so let's have a look at how to create these groups. We'll discuss the commands that you can run from the shell and the related configuration files.

Commands for Group Management

Basically, you manage the groups in your environment with three commands: groupadd, groupdel, and groupmod. So, as you can see, group management follows the same patterns as user management. The basic structure for the groupadd command is simple: groupadd *somegroup*, where *somegroup* is the name of the group you want to create. Also, the options are largely self-explanatory: it probably doesn't surprise you that the option -g gid can be used to specify the unique GID number you want to use for this group.

Behind the Commands: /etc/group

When a group is created with groupadd, the information entered needs to be stored somewhere, and that's the /etc/group file. As seen in Listing 5-3, this is a rather simple file that has just two fields for each group definition.

Listing 5-3. *Content of* /etc/group

```
plugdev:x:46:sander,haldaemon
staff:x:50:
games:x:60:
users:x:100:
nogroup:x:65534:
dhcp:x:101:
syslog:x:102:
klog:x:103:
scanner:x:104:sander
nvram:x:105:
mysql:x:106:
crontab:x:107:
ssh:x:108:
bind:x:109:
sander:x:1000:
lpadmin:x:110:sander
admin:x:111:sander
messagebus:x:112:
haldaemon:x:113:
powerdev:x:114:haldaemon
gdm:x:115:
linda:x:1001:
zeina:x:1002:
```

The first field in /etc/group is reserved for the name of the group. The second field stores the password for the group (a ! character signifies that no password is allowed for this group). You can see that most groups have an "x" in the password field, and this refers to the /etc/gshadow file, in which you can store encrypted group passwords. However, this feature isn't used very often because it is very rare to work with group passwords. The third field of /etc/group provides a unique GID, and the last field presents the names of the members of the group. These names are required only for users for whom this is not the primary group; primary group membership itself is managed from the /etc/passwd configuration file. However, if you want to make sure that a user is added to an additional group, you have to do it here.

Using Group Passwords

Although not many administrators use group passwords, what can they be used for? In all cases, a user has a primary group. When the user creates a file, the primary group is assigned as the group owner automatically. If a user wants to create files that have a group owner different from the primary group, the user can use the newgrp command. For example, newgrp sales would set the primary group of a user to the group sales. Using this command would work without any questions if the user is a member of the group sales. If the user is not a member of that group, however, the shell would prompt the user to enter a password. This password is the password that needs to be assigned to that group. You can change it using the gpasswd command.

Managing the User's Shell Environment

As a system administrator of a server that users access directly, you have to do more than just create users and make them members of the appropriate groups. You also have to give them login environments. Without going into detail about specific shell commands, this section provides an overview of what is needed for that. I'll first explain about the files that can be used as login scripts for the user, and next you'll learn about files that are used to display messages for users logging in to your system.

■Note The task described as follows makes sense on a server in which users log in directly. If your server is used as a mail server or file server, and users don't log in directly, it doesn't make sense to tune it by using these commands.

Creating Shell Login Scripts

When a user logs in to a system, the /etc/profile configuration file is used. This generic shell script (which can be considered a login script) defines environment settings for users. Also, commands can be included that need to be issued when the user first logs in to a server. The /etc/profile file is a generic file processed by all users logging in to the system. It also has a user-specific version (~/.profile) that can be created in the home directory of the user. The user-specific ~/.profile of the shell login script is executed last, so if there is a conflict in settings between the two files, the settings that are user-specific will always be used. In general, it isn't a good idea to give a login file to too many individual users; instead, work it all out in /etc/profile. This makes configuring settings for your users as easy as possible.

The /etc/profile file is not the only file that can be processed when starting a shell. If a user starts a subshell from a current environment, such as by executing a command or by using the command /bin/sh again, the administrator may choose to define additional settings for that. The name of this configuration file is /etc/bashrc, and it also has a user-specific version, ~/.bashrc (the tilde in the file name means that the file is located in the user's home directory).

Displaying Messages to Users Logging In

As an administrator, it's sometimes necessary to display messages to users logging in to your server. Two files can be used for this: /etc/issue and /etc/motd. The first, /etc/issue, is a text file whose content is displayed to users before they log in. To process this file, the /sbin/getty program, which is responsible for creating login terminals, reads it and displays the content. You may, for example, use the file to display a message instructing users how to log in to your system, or include a message if login has been disabled on a temporary basis. Related to this file is /etc/motd, which can be used to display messages to users after they have logged in. Typically, this file can be used to display messages related to day-to-day system maintenance.

Configuring Permissions

At first glance, it seems easy to manage permissions in a Linux environment: instead of the many permissions some other operating systems work with, Linux has just three. However, upon closer examination, you'll see that the system that was invented somewhere in the 1970s is only the foundation for a system that can be pretty complex. The following subsections are overviews of all subjects relevant to permission management.

Read, Write, and Execute: The Three Basic Linux Permissions

The three elementary permissions—read (r), write (w), and execute (x)—are the foundation to working with permissions in a Linux system. The use of these permissions is not hard to understand: read allows a user to read the file or the contents of the directory the permission is applied to, write allows the user to change an existing file if applied to a file and to create or remove files in a directory it is applied to, and execute is used to allow a file to execute executable code. If applied to a directory, it allows a user to access that directory with a command like cd. Therefore, the execute permission is applied as a default permission to all directories on a Linux system. Table 5-1 summarizes the workings of these three basic permissions.

Table 5-1. *Overview of Linux Basic Permissions*

Permission	Applied to Files	Applied to Directories
read	Read contents of a file	See files existing in a directory by using the ls command
write	Modify existing files and their properties	Create or delete files from a directory
execute	Execute files that contain executable code	Activate a subdirectory with the cd command

Permissions and the Concept of Ownership

To determine the permissions that a given user has on a file or directory, Linux works with the concept of ownership. Ownership is set on every file and on every directory, so when working with the three basic Linux permissions, there's no such thing as "inheritance," as there is with some other operating systems.

■Note In fact, on Linux, inheritance can be applied when working with Set Group ID (SGID) permissions and access control lists (ACLs), both of which I'll cover later in this chapter.

Linux works with three entities that can be set as the owner of a file or directory. First is the user who is owner. By default, the user who creates a file becomes the owner of that file (but an administrator can change ownership later using the chown command). Next is the group owner. By default, the primary group of the user who is owner of a file will also become the group owner of that file.

■Note When in this section I refer to a file, I also refer to a directory, unless stated otherwise. From a file-system point of view, a directory is just a special kind of file.

Last is the others entity. Typically, this entity refers to the rest of the world; permissions granted to the others entity apply to everyone who is able to access the given file. The ownership of files and the permissions that are set for the three different file owners can be reviewed with the ls -l command, as seen in the following line:

```
-rw-rw-r--  1  linda users  145906 2006-03-08 09:21 somefile
```

In this output, the name of the file is somefile. The first character refers to the type of file. In this case, it's just an ordinary file, therefore the - character is displayed. The next three groups of three characters refer to the permissions applied to the user, group, and others, respectively. As you can see, the user has read and write permissions, the group has read as well and write permissions, and all others just have read permission. The next important pieces of data in the preceding line are the names linda and users; they refer to user linda (who is owner) and the group users (which is group owner). Note that in the basic Linux permission scheme, just one user and just one group can be assigned as owner of a file. If you want more, you need to use ACLs.

With regards to Linux rights, ownership is the only thing that really matters. An example shows why this is important; imagine the home directory of user linda. Typically, the permissions on a home directory are set, as in the following output line of the ls command:

```
-rwxr-xr-x 1 linda users 1024   2006-03-08 09:28 linda
```

■**Note** In the examples shown here, the users are all members of the group user, which has GID 100. Although this is not default behavior on Ubuntu, it can be useful if you want to help users share information. If you want all new users created with useradd to automatically become members of this group 100 (which is actually the GID for the group user), make sure that you have the line GROUP=100 in the /etc/default/ useradd file.

Ownership is naturally very important when determining what a user can do to a file. Imagine that a file is created by the user root in the user linda home directory and that the permissions on this file are set as follows:

```
-r--r----- 1  root root 1 537   2006-03-08 10:15 rootsfile
```

The big question is what user linda can do to this file. The answer is simple, but there is a caveat. Because user linda is not the owner of the file and is not a member of the group that owns the file, she has no permissions at all to this file. The fact that the file is in her home directory doesn't mean much because Linux doesn't support inheritance of permissions by default. However, user linda has the write permissions in her home directory, so she can remove the file from her home directory. This is not inheritance; write permissions in a directory apply to the things that a user can do to files in that directory. What you should remember from this example is that to determine what a user can do to a file, the most important question to ask is "Is the user also the owner of the file?" The fact that a file is in the user's directory isn't relevant here; it's ownership that counts.

Changing File Ownership

To change the ownership of a file, use the chown command. The structure of this command is as follows:

```
chown {user|:group} file
```

For example, to make user linda owner of rootsfile, the command chown linda rootsfile must be used. To change the group owner of somefile to the group sales, the chown .sales somefile command is used. Note that for changing group ownership, the chgrp command can be used as an alternative. Therefore, chown .sales somefile does the same thing as chgrp sales somefile. When using chgrp, the name of the group does not need to be preceded by a dot.

By default, chown and chgrp apply only to the file or directory on which they are used. However, you can use the commands to work recursively as well: chown -R linda somedir makes user linda owner of all files in somedir and all subdirectories of it.

Group Ownership

When working with group ownership, you should be aware of how group ownership is handled. By default, the primary group of the user who creates a new file becomes the group owner of that file. If, however, the user is a member of more than one group, this default setting can be manipulated. When a user issues the newgrp command, he can change the primary group setting on a temporary basis. The following steps show what happens next:

1. Log in as some normal user on your computer. Then use the `groups` command from a console window to get an overview of all groups that you are currently a member of. The primary group is listed first. If you haven't modified anything for this user, it will have the same name as your user account. Listing 5-4 is an example of this output.

Listing 5-4. *The* groups *Command Always Shows Your Primary Group First*

```
sander@RNA:~$ groups
sander adm dialout cdrom floppy audio dip video plugdev scanner lpadmin admin
```

2. From the console window, issue the `touch newfile` command to create a new file with the name `newfile`. Then use `ls -l newfile` to display the ownership information for `newfile`. You will see that the primary group is set as the owner of the file (see Listing 5-5).

Listing 5-5. *The User's Primary Group Is Always Set As Its Owner*

```
sander@RNA:~$ ls -l newfile
-rw-r--r-- 1 sander sander  0 2007-07-28  10:05 newfile
```

3. Use `su` to become root. Then use `groupadd` to create a new group (for example, use `groupadd -g 901 sales` to create a group with the name `sales` and group ID 901). Next, as root, use `usermod -g 901 youruser` to make `youruser` (the user you used in step 1) a member of that group. After changing this group information, use `exit` to close the `su` session and become the normal user account again.

4. As the normal user, use `groups` again to get an overview of all groups you are currently a member of. The new group should appear now, probably as the last group in the list.

5. As the normal user, use `newgrp yournewgroup` to set the primary group to your new group on a temporary basis. You can use the `groups` command to check this; the new group should now be listed first. You'll also see that if you create a new file (use `touch somenewfile`), the new group will be group owner of the new file. This ensures that all users who are members of the same group can do the same thing to this file.

Working with Advanced Linux Permissions

Until now, I've covered just the three basic Linux permissions. But there are more. To start with, Linux has a set of advanced permissions, and this section describes the working of these permissions. Before diving into detail, the following list provides a short overview of the advanced permissions and the way they're used:

- *SUID*: If this permission is applied to an executable file (also known as "Set User ID" and "setuid"), the user who executes that file will have the permissions of the owner of the file while he is executing it. You can see that SUID is a very dangerous permission that, if wrongly applied, creates serious back doors on your server. On the other hand, some applications—/usr/bin/passwd, for example—can't function without it because these applications need the permissions of their owner root to be able to do their job.

- *SGID*: This permission is also known as the Set Group ID (also commonly known as "setgid") permission. It is applied in two ways. First, if applied to executable files, the user who executes the file will get the permissions of the group who is owner of the file upon execution. Next, the permission can be used to set the default group owner of files created in a given directory. If applied to a directory, all files and directories created in this directory, and even in its subdirectories, will get the group owner of the directory as its group owner. Imagine that all members of the group sales normally save the files they create in /data/salesfiles. In that case, you would want all files created in that directory to be owned by the group sales as well. This goal can be accomplished when setting sales as the group owner for salesfiles and next applying the SGID permission bit to this directory.

- *Sticky bit*: If the sticky bit is used on a directory; users can remove files only if one of the following conditions is met:

  - The user has write permissions on the file.

  - The file is in a directory of which the user is owner.

  - The user is owner of the file.

  The sticky bit permission is especially useful in a shared data directory. Suppose that user linda creates a file in the directory /data/sales. She wouldn't want her coworkers from the group sales who also have write permissions in that directory to remove her file by accident (normally they'd be able to because they have the write permission on the directory). If the sticky bit is applied, however, other users can remove the file only if one of those listed conditions has been met.

Some comments on these permissions may be helpful. First, you should realize the dangers of the SUID and SGID permissions if they are applied improperly. Imagine, for example, that a given application has a security issue that allows users with the right knowledge to access a shell environment, and at the same time the user root owns this application. This would make the user misusing the security issue root and give him permissions on your entire system! So you should be extremely careful when applying SUID or SGID to files. On the other hand, you may notice that some files have SUID set by default. For example, the program file /usr/bin/passwd cannot work without it. This is because a user who changes his password needs to write information to the /etc/shadow file. Only the user root can write data to this file, and normal users cannot even read its contents. The operating system solves this problem by applying the SUID permission to /usr/bin/passwd, which temporarily grants users root permissions to change their passwords.

Tip Someone using a back door to get access to your server may use SUID on some obscure file to get access the next time as well. As an administrator, you should regularly check your server for any occurrence of the SUID permission on unexpected files. You can do this by running find / -perm +4000, which will display all files that have the SUID permissions set.

The SGID permission has a dangerous side because it gives the user who runs a command that has this permission the same permissions as the group owner of the command. However, the SGID permission can be very useful. You may apply it on directories in which members of some user group need to share data with each other. The advantage of the SGID permission, if it is applied to a directory, is that all files created in that directory will get the same group owner. This allows all members of that group to read the file. Even if the group just has read rights on files that are created in this directory, the SGID permission may create a workable situation by allowing a user who is a member of the group to read the original file. Without the write permission she cannot change its contents, but she can save the file with a new name in the same directory. With the SGID permission applied to the directory, all files created in the complete tree structure under this directory will get the same group as owner, so the file will always be accessible for all members of the group. Thus, all users can work together in a shared group-data directory in an efficient way.

However, in the scenario I've just described, there is still the problem that one user can remove the files created by another user who is a member of the same group; both have write permissions in the directory, and that's enough to remove files. This can be prevented by applying the sticky bit as well. When this permission is set, a user can't remove a file if he has only write permissions to the directory the file is in, without being the owner of the file.

Setting Permissions

Okay, that's enough about how the permissions can be used. It's time to set them. You'll use two commands to set and manipulate permissions: the chmod command to initially set permissions and the umask command to set default permissions.

Using chmod to Change Permissions

The chmod command is used to set permissions on existing files. The user root or the owner of a file can use this command to change permissions of files or directories. It can be used in either an absolute or a relative mode. When using chmod in a relative way, the entity (user, group, or others) to which permissions are granted is specified, followed by the + (add), ? (remove), or = (set) operator, and then followed by the permissions you want to apply. In the absolute mode, a numeric value is used to grant the permissions.

Using chmod in Relative Mode

If working in relative mode, the following values have to be used for the permissions that are available:

- *read*: r

- *write*: w

- *execute*: x

- *SUID*: u+s

- *SGID*: g+s

- *Sticky bit*: t

The relative mode is useful when you want to add or remove one permission in an easy and convenient way. For example, you can easily make a script file executable by using chmod +x myscript. Because no u, g, or o is used in this command to refer to the entity the permissions are applied for, the file will be made executable for everyone. You can, however, be more specific and just remove the write permission for the other entity by using chmod o-w somefile, for example.

As for the special permissions, SUID is set with u+s, and SGID is set with g+s. As the result, you will see the SUID permission at the position of the x for users and the SGID permission at the position of the x for groups. Listing 5-6 shows where the first file has SUID applied, and the second file has SGID applied. Both permissions really make sense only in combination with the execute permission, so I won't discuss the hypothetical situation in which a file has SUID applied but not executed for the owner, or has SGID applied but not executed for the group.

Listing 5-6. *Displaying SUID and SIGD with* ls -l

```
-rwsr-xr-x  2  root root 48782 2006-03-09 11:47 somefile-withSUID
-rwxr-sr-x  2  root root 21763 2006-03-09 11:48 someotherfile-withSGID
```

Using chmod in Absolute Mode

Although the chmod relative mode is easy to work with if you just want to set or change one permission, it can get complicated if you need to change more than that. In such a case, the absolute mode is more useful because it offers a short and convenient way to refer to the permissions that you want to set. In the absolute mode, you work with numeric values to refer to the permissions that you want to set. For example, chmod 1764 somefile can be used to change the permissions on a given file. Of these four digits, the first refers to the special permissions, the second indicates permissions for the user, the third refers to the group permissions, and the last refers to permissions for others.

Of the four digits that are used in absolute mode, the first can be omitted in most instances. If you do that, no special permissions are set for this file. When working with chmod in absolute mode, you have to be aware of the values for the permissions you are working with:

- *Read*: 4

- *Write*: 2

- *Execute*: 1

- *SUID*: 4

- *SGID*: 2

- *Sticky bit*: 1

For example, to set permissions to read, write, and execute for others; to read and execute for group; and to do nothing for others, you would use chmod 750 somefile. In this example, the digit 7 refers to the user permissions. Because 7 is equal to 4 + 2 + 1, the user has read, write, and execute permission. The group has 5, which equals 4 + 1. The others have no permissions.

As an alternative, you can use the command but with a 0 preceding the value (chmod 0750 somefile). However, it makes no sense in this case to use the initial 0 because no special permissions are used here.

Using umask to Set Default Permissions for New Files

You have probably noticed that default permissions are set when creating a new file, and these permissions are determined by the umask setting. This is a shell setting that is set for all users when logging in to the system. The default umask makes sure that all users have read access to all new files. Because this isn't very secure, it makes sense to restrict the default umask a little.

A numeric value is used in the umask setting, and this value is subtracted from the maximum permissions that can be set automatically; the maximum settings are 666 for files and 777 for directories. Of course, some exceptions to this rule make it all quite hard to understand, but you can find a complete overview of umask settings in Table 5-2.

Of the digits used in the umask, as with the numeric arguments for the chmod command, the first digit refers to user permissions, the second digit refers to the group permissions, and the last digit refers to the default permissions for others. The default umask setting of 022 gives 644 for all new files and 755 for all new directories that are created on your server.

Table 5-2. umask *Values and Their Results*

Value	Applied to Files	Applied to Directories
0	read and write	everything
1	read and write	read and write
2	read	read and execute
3	read	read
4	write	write and execute
5	write	write
6	nothing	execute
7	nothing	nothing

You can change the umask setting for all users or for individual users. If you want to set the umask for all users, you must make sure the umask setting is entered in the /etc/profile configuration file. If the umask is changed in this file, it applies to all users logging in to your server.

An alternative to setting the umask in /etc/profile (where it is applied to all users logging in to the system) is to change the umask settings in a file with the name .profile that is created in the home directory of an individual user. Settings applied in this file are applied for only the user who owns the home directory, so this is a nice method to create an exception for a single user. You could, for example, create a .profile in the home directory of the user root and in there apply the umask setting of 027, whereas the generic umask setting for ordinary users is set to 022 in /etc/profile.

Working with Access Control Lists

Up to now, you've just read about the basic model to apply permissions on a Linux system. When an advanced file system like Ext3 is used, it's possible to add some options to this default model. You'd do this by using the ACL feature. In this section, you'll learn how this technique can be applied to allow for a more flexible security mechanism.

The main reason behind the development of the Linux ACL system was to compensate for the shortcomings of default Linux permissions. Basically, the system had two problems:

- Default Linux permissions do not allow more than one entity to be set as user or group owner of a file.

- In a default Linux permissions scheme, there is no option to set default permissions.

ACLs offer an optional system that can be used to compensate for these shortcomings. In this section you'll learn how to apply this system.

Preparing the File System for ACLs

Before you can use ACLs on a file system, you must add an option to /etc/fstab for all file systems that must support ACLs (all relevant Linux file systems do). The following procedure describes how:

1. Open /etc/fstab with an editor.

2. Select the column in which the mount options are specified. Add the option acl. Repeat this procedure for all file systems in which you want to use ACLs.

3. Remount all partitions in which ACLs have been applied (or restart your server). For example, to remount the root partition so that new settings are applied, use mount -o remount /.

Using ACLs to Grant Permissions to More than One Object

The idea of an ACL is that connected to a file or directory, a list of users and groups is created that has permission on a file or directory. By default, in the inode that is used for the complete administration of files and directories, there simply isn't enough room, and you can't easily change this because of backward compatibility. As a result, you must specify for all devices with which you want to use ACLs that ACLs have to be enabled for that device. Only then can ACLs be set. ACLs can be used on most modern Linux file systems.

■**Note** The /etc/fstab file on Ubuntu server uses UUIDs instead of the device names of your file system. Remember, a UUID is a unique ID that can be assigned to a file system. In the case of an Ext3 file system, for example, this is done with the tune2fs command. For better readability, I've chosen to omit the UUIDs from the examples in this book, and I'll just refer to the device name of the file system.

If ACLs are enabled for a given device, you can use the setfacl command to set them. If this command isn't available, run apt-get install acl first. The use of setfacl is not too hard to understand: for example, setfacl -m u:linda,rwx somefile can be used to add user linda as a trustee (someone who has rights to a file) on the file somefile. This command does not change file ownership, though; it just adds to the ACL a second user who also has rights to the file. The normal output of the ls -l command does not show all users who have rights by means of an ACL, but the + character appears behind the permissions list on that file. To get an overview of all ACLs currently set to a given file, use the getfacl command. The following procedure gives you an opportunity to try it:

1. Make sure that you are root and then create a file somewhere in the file system. You can use the touch command to create an empty file; for example, use touch somefile to create the file somefile.

2. Now use getfacl somefile to monitor the permissions that are set for this file. You will see an overview, as shown in Listing 5-7, indicating only the default permissions that are granted to user, group, and others.

Listing 5-7. *Before Applying an ACL,* getfacl *Just Displays Normal User, Group, and Others Information*

```
myserver:~# touch somefile
myserver:~# getfacl somefile
# file: somefile
# owner: root
# group: root
user::rw-
group::r--
other::r--
```

3. Now use the command setfacl -m g:account:rw somefile (you must have a group with the name *account* for this to work). The group will now be added as a trustee to the file, which can be seen when you use getfacl on the same command again. Listing 5-8 provides an example of this.

Listing 5-8. *After Adding Another Trustee,* getfacl *Will Show Its Name and the Rights You Have Granted to This Trustee*

```
myserver:~# touch somefile
myserver:~# getfacl somefile
# file: somefile
# owner: root
# group: root
user::rw-
group::r--
group:account:rw-
mask::rw-
other::r--
```

Working with ACL Masks

In the example in Listing 5-8, you can see what happens when a simple ACL is created: not only is a new entity added as the trustee of the object but a mask setting is also added. The mask is the summary of the maximum of permissions an entity can have on the file. This mask is not very important because it is modified automatically when new permissions are set with the ACL. However, the mask can be used to reduce the permissions of all trustees to a common denominator. Because it's set automatically when working with ACLs, I recommend that you just ignore the ACL masks: it makes things very complicated if you try to modify them in a useful way.

Using Default ACLs

A default ACL can be applied on a directory. When using a default ACL, you can specify the permissions that new files and directories will get when they are created in a given directory. Therefore, you can consider default ACLs as a umask setting that is applied on a directory only. If a directory has a default ACL, all files will get the permissions specified in that default ACL. Also, subdirectories will get the permissions from the default ACL, and these permissions will be set as their own permissions as well. If a default ACL exists for a directory, the umask setting is not used for that directory.

To set a default ACL, the setfacl command must be used with the -d option. Otherwise, it can be used with parameters as seen earlier. The following example will apply a default ACL to somedir:

```
setfacl -d -m group:account:rwx somedir
```

Because this command uses the -d option, a default ACL is set for all entities that currently are listed as trustees of the directory. You can see in Listing 5-9 that the command getfacl is used to display the permissions currently applied to that directory.

Listing 5-9. *Displaying the Default ACL for a Directory*

```
myserver:~# getfacl somefile
# file: somedir
# owner: root
# group: root
user::rwx
group::r-x
other::r-x
default:user::rwx
default:group::r-x
default:group:account:rw-
default:mask::rwx
default:other::r-x
```

The nice thing about working with default ACLs is that the rights that are granted in a default ACL are automatically added for all new files and directories created in that directory. However, you should be aware that when you apply a default ACL to a directory, files and directories that currently exist within that directory are not touched by this default ACL. If you want to change permission settings in ACLs for existing files and directories, use the setfacl command with the option -R (recursive).

ACL Limitations

You should also be aware of the limitations of working with ACLs, such as the fact that ACLs are not cumulative (which is also the case for the normal Linux permissions). Let's imagine the not-so-realistic situation in which user stacey is the owner of a file and has only read permission. She is also a member of the group sales, which is a trustee of the same file and has read-write permission. So, when the permissions for this user are calculated, she will not have both read and write permissions. When determining the effective permission, the operating system will check if she is the owner of the file. She is, and so the operating system will look no further and the permissions for the owner are applied. The permissions for the group are ignored.

The problem of nonaccumulation becomes even more complex if a process belongs to more than one group. When determining group rights, the group from which the process will get its rights is selected randomly.

Another problem when working with ACLs is that many applications still don't support them. For example, most backup applications cannot handle ACLs, and your database probably doesn't either. However, changes are coming, and some applications have begun supporting ACLs. One of these is the Samba file server, which uses ACLs extensively to emulate the working of Windows rights (check Chapter 10 for complete coverage of this server). Also, some of the basic Linux utilities such as cp, mv, and ls currently support ACLs. However, you should always check that the utility you want to use supports ACLs before you start using it.

Applying File Attributes

When working with permissions, there's always a combination between a user or group object and the permissions that these user or group objects have on a file or directory. An alternate but seldom-used method of securing files on a Linux system is to work with attributes, which do their work regardless of the user who accesses the file. Of course, the difference is that the owner of a file can set file attributes, whereas other users (except for the almighty root) cannot.

For file attributes, an option must be provided in /etc/fstab before they can be used. This is the user_xattr option that can be seen in the fstab example in Listing 5-7. Here's a list of the useful attributes that can be applied:

- A: This attribute ensures that the file access time of the file is not modified. Normally, every time a file is opened, the file access time must be written to the file's metadata, which slows system performance. So, on files that are accessed on a regular basis, the A attribute can be used to disable this feature.

■**Tip** You don't like the access time being modified at all? In this case, use the noatime option in /etc/fstab to specify that this feature be disabled for all files on a volume.

- a: This attribute allows a file to be modified but not removed.

- c: If you are using a file system that supports volume-level compression, this file attribute makes sure that the file is compressed the first time the compression engine is activated. This attribute is currently ignored by Ext2/Ext3 file systems.

- D: This attribute makes sure that changes to files are written to disk immediately and not to cache first. This is a useful attribute on important database files to make sure that they don't get lost between file cache and hard disk. Using this option decreases the risk of losing data because of a power failure, for instance.

- d: This attribute ensures that the file is not backed up in backups when the dump utility is used.

- I: This attribute enables indexing for the directory in which it is enabled. You'll thus enjoy faster file access for primitive file systems such as Ext3 that don't use a B-tree database for fast access to files. Users cannot set this attribute using chattr; it will be managed by file system–specific utilities.

■**Note** A B-tree is a tree data structure that keeps data sorted, even if changes occur. A file system can operate very quickly using a B-tree.

- j: This attribute ensures that on an Ext3 file system the file is first written to the journal; only after that it is written to the data blocks on hard disk.

- s: This attribute overwrites the blocks in which the file was stored with zeros after the file has been deleted. This makes sure that recovery of the file is not possible after it has been deleted. This attribute is not currently supported by Ext2/Ext3 file systems.

- u: This attribute saves undelete information. A utility can then be developed that works with that information to salvage deleted files. This attribute is not currently supported by Ext2/Ext3 file systems.

■**Note** Although you can use quite a few attributes, you should be aware that most of them are rather experimental and are useful only if an application is used that can work with the given attribute. For example, it doesn't make sense to apply the u attribute if no application has been developed that can use this attribute to recover deleted files.

Use the chattr command if you want to apply attributes. For example, use chattr +s somefile to apply the attribute s to somefile. Need to remove the attribute again? Use chattr -s somefile. For an overview of all attributes that can be used, use the lsattr command.

Apply Quota to Allow a Maximum Amount of Files

User quota is a completely different way to apply restrictions to control how users can create files and directories. By using quota, the amount of space that a user can occupy is limited. Configuring user quota is a simple five-step procedure:

1. Install the quota software.

2. Prepare the file system in which you want to use quota.

3. Initialize the quota system.

4. Apply quota to users and groups.

5. Start the quota service.

Before starting to apply quota, you should first realize how it must be applied. Quotas are always user- or group-related and apply to a complete volume or partition. That is, if you have one disk in your server with one partition on it that holds your complete root file system, and you apply a quota of 100 MB for user zeina, this user can create no more than 100 MB of files anywhere on the file system.

When working with quotas, you need to apply a hard limit, a soft limit, and a grace period. The *soft limit* is a limit that cannot be surpassed on a permanent basis. (The user can create more data than the quota allows on a temporary basis.) The *grace period* is the length of time that the user can temporarily exceed the soft limit. The *hard limit* is an absolute limit; after it's reached (or when the grace period elapses, whichever is sooner), the user can't create new files.

Working with soft and hard limits is confusing at first glance, but it has some advantages: if a user has more data than the soft limit allows, she still can create new files and isn't stopped in her work immediately. She will, however, get a warning to create some space before the hard limit is reached.

Installing the Quota Software

To work with quotas, it makes sense that the quota software must be installed. You'll do this with the apt-get install quota command, and you'll notice soon enough whether you need to run it. If you try to use one of the quota management utilities (such as edquota) when the quota software has not been installed yet, you'll see a message that it has to be installed first.

Preparing the File System for Quota

Before you can use the quota software to limit the amount of disk space that a user can use on a given file system, you must add an option to /etc/fstab for all file systems that must support quota. Here's the procedure:

1. Open /etc/fstab with an editor.

2. Select the column with options. Add the option usrquota if you want to apply quota to users and grpquota for groups. Repeat this procedure for all file systems in which you want to use quota.

3. Remount all partitions in which quota has been applied (or restart your server). For example, to remount the root partition so that new settings are applied, use `mount -o remount /`.

Initializing Quota

Now that you've finished the preliminary steps, you need to initialize the quota system. This is necessary because all file systems have to be searched for files that have already been created, and for a reason that's probably obvious: existing files count toward each user's quota, so a report must be created in which the quota system can see which user owns which files. The report generated by this quota initialization is saved in two files: `aquota.user` is created to register user quotas, and `aquota.group` is created for group quotas.

To initialize a file system for the use of quotas, you need to use the `quotacheck` command. This command can be used with some options, and I'll list only the most important ones here:

- `-a`: This option ensures that all file systems are searched when initializing the quota system.

- `-u`: This option ensures that user information is searched. This information will be written to the `aquota.user` file.

- `-g`: This option ensures that group information is searched as well. This information is written to the `aquota.group` file.

- `-m`: Use this option to make sure that no problems will occur on file systems that are currently mounted.

- `-v`: This option ensures that the command will work in verbose mode to show exactly what it is doing.

So, the best way to initialize the quota system is to use the `quotacheck -augmv` command, which (after awhile) creates the files `aquota.user` and `aquota.group` to list all quota information for current users.

Setting Quota for Users and Groups

Now that the quota databases have been created, it's time for the real work because you're ready to apply quota to all users and groups on your system. You'll do this with the `edquota` command, which uses the `nano` editor to create a temporary file. This temporary file is where you'll enter the soft and hard limits you've decided upon for your users and groups. If, for example, you want to apply a soft limit of 100,000 blocks and a hard limit of 110,000 blocks for user florence, follow these steps:

Tip The `edquota` command works only with blocks, not bytes, kilobytes, or anything else. So, to set quota properly, you need to know the block size that's currently used. To find that block size, use the `dumpe2fs | less` command. You'll find the block size in the second screen.

---

1. Issue the command `edquota -u florence`.

2. In the editor screen, six numbers specify the quota for all file systems on your computer. The first of these numbers is the number of blocks that are currently being used by the user you're creating the quota file for. The second and third numbers are important as well: the second number is the soft limit for the number of blocks, and the third number is the hard limit on blocks in kilobytes. The fifth and sixth numbers do the same for inodes, which roughly equal the number of files you can create on your file system. The first and fourth numbers are used to record the number of blocks and inodes that are currently being used for this user.

3. Close the editor and write the changes in the quota files to disk.

In this procedure, you learned that quota can be applied to the number of inodes and blocks. If quotas are used on inodes, they specify the maximum number of files that can be created. Most administrators think it doesn't make sense to work that way, so they set the values for these to 0. A value of 0 indicates that this item currently has no limitation.

After setting the quota, if the soft limit and hard limit are not set to the same value, you need to use the `edquota -t` command to set the grace time. This command opens another temporary file in which you can specify the grace time you want to use, either in hours or in days. The grace time is set per file system, so there's no option to specify different grace time settings for different users.

Once you have set quotas for one user, you may want to apply them to other users. Instead of following the same procedure for all users on your system, you can use the `edquota -p` command. For example, `edquota -p florence alex` copies the quotas currently applied for user florence to user alex.

■**Caution** To set quotas, the user you are setting quotas for must be known to the quota system. This is not done automatically. To make sure that new users are known to the quota system, you must initialize the quota system again after creating the new users. I recommend setting up a `cron` job (see the "Setting the System to Your Hand" section in Chapter 6 to do this automatically at a reasonable interval).

When all the quotas have been set the way you want, you can use the `repquota` command to monitor the current quota settings for your users. For example, the `repquota -aug` command shows current quota settings for all users and groups on all volumes. Now that you've set all the quotas you want to work with, you just have to start the quota service, and you'll do this with the `/etc/init.d/quota start` command.

Understanding Pluggable Authentication Modules

In the normal situation, the local user database in the Linux files `/etc/passwd` and `/etc/shadow` is checked at login to a Linux workstation. In a network environment, however, the login program must fetch the required information from somewhere else (for example, an LDAP directory service such as OpenLDAP). But how does the login program know where it has to search for authentication information? That's where the PAMs come in, and PAMs are what makes the login procedure on your workstation flexible. Using a PAM in conjunction with nsswitch.conf, you can redirect any application that has to do anything related to authentication to any service that handles authentication. A PAM is used, for example, if you want to authenticate with a private key stored on a USB stick, to enable password requirements, to prevent the root user from establishing a telnet session, and in many other situations. The only thing you need is a PAM that supports your authentication method.

The main advantage of a PAM is its modularity. In a PAM infrastructure, anything can be used for authentication, provided there's a PAM module for it. So, if you want to implement some kind of strong authentication, ask your supplier for a PAM module and it will work. PAM modules are stored in the directory /lib/security, and the configuration files specifying how these modules must be used (and by which procedures) are in /etc/pam.d. Listing 5-10 is an example of just such a configuration file, in which the login procedure learns that it first has to contact an LDAP server before trying any local login.

Listing 5-10. *Sample PAM Configuration File*

```
auth        sufficient   /lib/security/pam_ldap.so
account     sufficient   /lib/security/pam_ldap.so
password    sufficient   /lib/security/pam_ldap.so
session     optional     /lib/security/pam_ldap.so
auth        requisite    pam_unix2.so
auth        required     pam_securetty.so
auth        required     pam_nologin.so
#auth       required     pam_homecheck.so
auth        required     pam_env.so
auth        required     pam_mail.so
account     required     pam_unix2.so
password    required     pam_pwcheck.so      nullok
password    required     pam_unix2.so        nullok use_first_pass use_authok
session     required     pam_unix2.so
session     required     pam_limits.so
```

The authentication process features four different instances, and they are reflected in Listing 5-10. Authentication is handled in the first instance; these are the lines that start with the keyword auth. During the authentication phase, the user login name and password are first checked, followed by the validity of the account and other account-related parameters (such as login time restrictions). This happens in the lines that start with account. Then, all settings relating to the password are verified (the lines that start with password). Last, the settings relating to the establishment of a session with resources are defined; this happens in the lines that start with session.

The procedure that will be followed upon completion of these four instances is defined by calling the different PAM modules. This occurs in the last column of the example configuration file in Listing 5-10. For example, the module pam_securetty can be used to verify that the user root is not logging in to a Linux computer via an insecure terminal. The keywords sufficient, optional, required, and requisite are used to qualify the degree of importance that the conditions in a certain module are met. Except for the first four lines (which refer to the connection a PAM has to make to an LDAP server), conditions defined in all modules must be met; they are all *required*. Without going into detail, this means that authentication will fail if one of the conditions implied by the specified module is not met.

When enabling a server for logon to an LDAP server (as in the example in Listing 5-10), four lines are added to the default PAM configuration file in /etc/pam.d/login. They are the first four lines, and they offer an alternative for valid authentication by using the pam_ldap.so module. Passing the conditions imposed by these first four modules is sufficient to authenticate successfully, but it is not required. Sufficient in this context means that if, for example, the instance auth passes all the conditions defined in pam_ldap.so, that's enough for local authentication. The local Linux authentication mechanism will no longer be used because the user can authenticate against the LDAP server in this case. For this to work, you of course need a valid user account that has all the required Linux properties on the LDAP server.

■**Note** Configuring LDAP is beyond the scope of this book, but have a look at www.padl.com, for example, for more information about this subject.

A nice thing about this example PAM configuration file is that it first sees whether the LDAP server can be used to authenticate to the network. The default Linux login mechanism is used only if this procedure doesn't work. The workings of this default mechanism are defined from the fifth line on in the example configuration file.

By default, many services on Ubuntu Server are PAM-enabled. (You can see this from a simple ls command in the directory /etc/pam.d, which will show you that there is a PAM file for login, su, sudo, and many other programs. I won't cover all of them here, but will explain a bit about some when the time is relevant.) The true flexibility of PAM is in its modules, which you can find in /lib/security. Each of these modules has a specific function. The next section provides a short description of some of the more interesting modules. But, before we dive into that, you'll quickly learn how to set a secure default policy.

Creating a Default Security Policy

In a PAM environment, every service should have its own configuration for PAM. However, the world isn't perfect, and a given service may not have a PAM configuration. In this case, I recommend creating /etc/pam.d/other as a PAM configuration file. This file is processed by all PAM applications that don't have their own configuration file. If you really want to know whether your system is secure, give it the contents detailed in Listing 5-11.

Listing 5-11. *Configuring PAM for Security in* /etc/pam.d/other

```
auth        required        pam_warn.so
auth        required        pam_deny.so
account     required        pam_warn.so
account     required        pam_deny.so
password    required        pam_warn.so
password    required        pam_deny.so
session     required        pam_warn.so
session     required        pam_deny.so
```

All four phases in the authentication process call two modules: pam_warn and pam_deny. The pam_warn module generates a warning and writes that to your log environment (/var/log/messages by default). Next, for all these instances, the module pam_deny is called. This simple module will just deny everything. The results? All modules will handle authentication properly, as defined in their own configuration file, but when that file is absent, this generic configuration will make sure that all access is denied.

■**Tip** Want to know if a program is PAM-enabled? Use ldd programname. For example, use ldd /usr/bin/passwd to find the library files used by this command. If the modules libpam_misc and libpam are listed, the module is PAM-enabled. And so it should have its own configuration file for handling user authentication.

Discovering PAM Modules

The usefulness of a system like PAM is entirely determined by its modules. Some of these modules are still experimental, and others are pretty mature and can be used to configure a Linux system. I'll discuss some of the most important modules in the following sections.

pam_deny

As seen in Listing 5-11, the pam_deny module can be used to deny all access. It's very useful if used as a default policy to deny access to the system.

pam_env

The module pam_env is used to create a default environment for users when logging in. In this default environment, several system variables are set to determine what the environment a user is working in looks like. For example, there is a definition of a PATH variable in which some directories are included that must be in the search path of the user. To create these variables, pam_env uses a configuration file in /etc/security/pam_env.conf. In this file, several variables are defined, each with its own value to define essential items like the PATH environment variable.

pam_limits

Some situations require an environment in which limits are set to the system resources that a user can access. Think, for example, of an environment in which a user can use no more than a given number of files at the same time. To configure these limitations, you would modify the /etc/security/limits.conf file. To make sure that the limitations that you set in /etc/security/limits.conf are applied, use the pam_limits module.

In /etc/security/limits.conf, limits can be set for individual users as well as groups. The limits can be applied to different items, some of which are listed here:

- fsize: Maximum file size

- nofile: Maximum number of open files

- cpu: Maximum CPU time in minutes

- nproc: Maximum number of processes

- maxlogins: Maximum number of times this user can log in simultaneously

The following code presents two examples of how these limitations can be applied. In the first line, the user ftp is limited to start a maximum of one process simultaneously. Next, everyone who is a member of the group student is allowed to log in four times simultaneously.

```
ftp                     hard      nproc         1
@student        -                 maxlogins   4
```

When applying these limitations, you should remind yourself of the difference between hard and soft limits: a hard limit is absolute, and a user cannot exceed it. A soft limit can be exceeded, but only within the settings that the administrator has applied for these soft limits. If you want to set the hard limit to the same as the soft limit, use a – character, as seen in the previous code example for the group student.

pam_mail

This useful module looks at the user's mail directory and indicates whether there is any new mail. It is typically applied when a user logs in to the system with the following line in the relevant PAM configuration file:

```
login    session     optional     pam_mail.conf
```

pam_mkhomedir

If a user authenticates to a machine for the first time and doesn't have a home directory yet, pam_mkhomedir can be applied to create this home directory automatically. This module will also make sure that the files in /etc/skel are copied to the new home directory. This module is especially useful in a network environment in which users authenticate through NIS or LDAP and do not always work on the same machine. However, it's recommended in such situations to centralize user home directories on an NFS server so that no matter where a user logs in to a server, a home directory will always be present. Chapter 8 contains more information about configuring an NFS server. The disadvantage of pam_mkhomedir is that if the module is not applied correctly, a user may end up with home directories on many different machines in your network.

pam_nologin

If an administrator needs to conduct system maintenance like installing new hardware, and the server must be brought down for a few moments, the pam_nologin module may prove useful. This module makes sure that no users can log in when the file /etc/nologin exists. So before you perform any maintenance, make sure to create this file. The user root will always be allowed to log in to the system, regardless of whether this file exists or not.

pam_permit

Pam_permit is by far the most insecure PAM service available. It does only one thing: it grants access—*always*—no matter who tries to log in. All security mechanisms will be completely bypassed in this case, and even users who don't have a valid user account can use the services that are configured to use pam_permit. The only sensible use of pam_permit is to test the PAM awareness of a certain module or to disable account management completely and create a system that is wide open to everyone.

pam_rootok

This module lets user root access services without entering a password. It's used, for example, by the su utility to make sure the user root can su to any account, without having to enter a password for that user account.

pam_securetty

In the old days when telnet connections were still very common, it was important for the user root never to use a telnet session for login because telnet sends passwords in clear text over the network. For this purpose, the securetty mechanism was created: a file /etc/securetty can be created to provide a list of all TTYs from which root can log in. By default, these include only local TTYs 1 through 6. On Ubuntu Server, this module is still used by default, which means that you can limit the TTYs in which root can log in by manipulating this file.

pam_tally

This very useful module can be used to keep track of attempts to access the system. It also allows the administrator to deny access if too many attempts fail. The PAM module pam_tally works with an application that uses the same name pam_tally that can be used to set the maximum amount of failed logins that are allowed. All attempts are logged by default in the /var/log/faillog file. If this module is called from a configuration file, be sure to at least use the options deny=n and lock_time. The first determines the maximum number of login attempts a user can make, and the second determines how long an account will be locked after that number of login attempts has been reached. The value given to lock_time is expressed in seconds by default.

pam_time

Based upon the configuration file /etc/security/time.conf, the pam_time module is used to limit the times between which users can log in to the system. You can use this module to limit the access for certain users to specific times of the day. Also, access can be further limited to services and specific TTYs that the user logs in from. The configuration file time.conf uses lines with the following form:

```
services;ttys;users;times
```

The next line is an example of a configuration line from `time.conf` that denies access to all users except root (the ! character in front of the times is used to deny access). This might be a perfect solution to prevent users from breaking into a system that they shouldn't be trying to log in to anyway.

```
login ; tty* ; !root ; !Al0000-2400
```

pam_unix

This is probably the most important of all modules: it is used to redirect authentication requests through the /etc/passwd and /etc/shadow files. The module can be used with several arguments, such as `nullok` and `try_first_pass`. The `nullok` argument allows a user with an empty password to connect to a service, and the `try_first_pass` argument will always try the password a user has already used (if a password is asked for again). Notice that many PAM configuration files include a line to call the common configuration file `common-auth`. The `pam_unix` file is called from here.

pam_warn

The `pam_warn` module is particularly useful with log errors: its primary purpose is to enable logging information about proposed authentication or password modification. For example, it can be used in conjunction with the `pam_deny` module to log information about users trying to connect to your system.

Configuring Administrator Tasks with sudo

Once upon a time, if the system administrator wanted to perform his administration tasks, he would do that as root. However, this has some security risks, the most important of which is that you might make a mistake and thus remove everything from your server by accident. Therefore, on Ubuntu Server, the root account is disabled by default. It doesn't even have a password, so you can't log in as root after a default installation. To perform tasks for which root privileges are required, use the `sudo` mechanism instead.

The idea of `sudo` is that specific administrator tasks can be defined for specific users. If one such user wants to execute one of the `sudo` commands that she has been granted access to, she has to run it with `sudo`. For example, where normally the user root would type `shutdown -h` to shut a machine down, a random user with `sudo` privileges would type `sudo shutdown -h now`. Next, the user enters his password and the machine shuts down.

Because `sudo` is the basic mechanism on Ubuntu to perform tasks that normally are reserved for root only, after a normal installation every administration tasks is performed that way. As discussed in Chapter 2, if you first run as an ordinary user the `sudo passwd root` command, you can then set a password for the user root and do your work as root anyway. This technique can be quite handy for administration of a server for which root privileges are required all the time. After all, you have to work in the way that you like best.

To create a `sudo` configuration, you need to use the editor `visudo`. This editor is used to open a temporary file with the name /etc/sudoers. In this file, you can define all `sudo` tasks that must be available on your server. You should never open the /etc/sudoers file for editing directly because that involves the risk of completely locking yourself out if you make an error.

■**Tip** On Ubuntu Server, `visudo` uses the text editor nano by default. If you are a Linux veteran who is used to Vi, you probably won't like this. Want to use Vi instead of nano? Use the command `export VISUAL=vi`. Like what you see? Put it as the last line in `/etc/profile`. From now on, every time that you use either `visudo` or `edquota`, Vi is started instead of nano. In this book, I'm using the Vi alternative because it automatically saves all files in the locations where they have to be saved.

As you can see in Listing 5-12, the default configuration in `/etc/sudoers` is rather simple.

Listing 5-12. *Default Configuration in* `/etc/sudoers`

```
root@RNA:/etc# cat sudoers
# /etc/sudoers
#
# This file MUST be edited with the 'visudo' command as root.
#
# See the man page for details on how to write a sudoers file.
# Host alias specification
# User alias specification

# Cmnd alias specification

# Defaults

Defaults        !lecture,tty_tickets,!fqdn

# User privilege specification
root    ALL=(ALL) ALL

# Members of the admin group may gain root privileges
%admin ALL=(ALL) ALL
```

It's really just two lines of configuration. The first line is `root ALL=(ALL) ALL`, which specifies that user root has the right to run all commands from all machines. Next, you can see that the same is true for all users who belong to the user group `admin`. Typically, this is only the user you have created during the installation of Ubuntu Server. If, for example, you would like to specify that user linda is allowed to run the command `/sbin/shutdown` no matter which host she is connecting from, add the following line:

```
linda   ALL=/sbin/shutdown
```

This line consists of three parts. In the first part, the user name is entered. (Instead of the name of a specific user, you can refer to groups as well, but, if you do that, make sure to put a % sign before the group name.) The second part—ALL in this example—refers to the name of the host where the user is logged on. Here, that host name has no limitations, but you can specify the name of a specific machine to minimize the risk of abuse by outsiders. Next, the command that this user is allowed to use (`/sbin/shutdown`, no options) is specified. This means that the user is allowed to run all options that can be used with this command. If you want to allow the user just one option, you need to include that option in the command line. If that's the case, all options that do not match the pattern you have specified in sudoers are specifically denied.

Now that the sudo configuration is in place, the specified user can run his commands. To do this, the complete command should be referred to because the directories that typically house the root commands (/sbin, /usr/sbin) are not in the search path for normal users. So, user linda should use the following command to shut down the machine:

```
sudo /sbin/shutdown -h now
```

Summary

In this chapter, you learned how to configure local security on your server by using user accounts, groups, and permissions. I introduced some advanced file-system security options: ACLs and user-extended attributes. Next, you read about some important internal mechanisms: PAM and sudo. Your server ought to be relatively secure by now, so let's proceed to Chapter 6, in which you'll learn how to let the system do exactly what you want it to do. I'll cover topics like process management, the boot procedure, and kernel management.

CHAPTER 6

■■■

Setting the System to Your Hand
Management of Processes, Boot Procedure, Kernel, and Hardware

After reading the first five chapters of this book, you should have your server up, running, and secure. Up to now, however, you haven't really changed the way processes on your server are running. So in this chapter, you will learn how to customize and optimize your server.

We'll have a look at some important aspects of your server that can be tuned and modified to increase its efficiency. First, I'll talk about process monitoring and management. Then, I'll talk about cron and how you can use it to automate process execution. After that, you'll learn about the system boot procedure, followed by kernel and hardware management.

Process Monitoring and Management

Everything you do on a Linux server is handled as a process by that server, so it's very important that you know how to manage these processes. In this section, you'll learn how to start and stop processes, which processes can be used, and how to run and manage processes in both the foreground and background. You will also learn how to use cron and schedule processes for future execution.

Different Kinds of Processes

It depends on the way you look at them, but you could say that Linux basically has two different kinds of processes: automatic and interactive. The automatic processes include services that are started automatically when you boot your server—they are known as *daemons*. The upstart process that is responsible for an important part of your server's boot procedure takes care that these processes are started properly. Daemons are service processes that run in the background; in other words, they do not write their output directly to the standard output. The interactive processes are started by users from a shell. Any command started by a user and producing output on the standard output is an interactive process.

To start an interactive process, a user needs to type the corresponding command. The process then runs as a child process from the shell in which the user entered the command. The process will do its work and will terminate when it's finished. While terminating, it will write its exit status to its parent (which is the shell if the process was an interactive process). Only after a child process has told its parent that it has terminated can it be closed properly. In case the parent is no longer present (which is generally considered an error condition), the child process will become a so-called zombie process, and it won't be possible to perform any management on the process except for trying to restart the parent process. In general, zombie processes are the result of bad programming. You should try to upgrade (or maybe rewrite) your software if you see too many of them.

The concepts of parent and child processes are universal on your system. The init process is started by upstart (which I'll cover later) as the first process; from there, all other processes are started. You can get an overview of the hierarchical process structure by using the pstree command, which provides a result such as that shown in Listing 6-1.

Listing 6-1. *The* pstree *Command Shows Relations Between Parent and Child Processes*

```
init ----apache2----5*[apache2]
       |--atd
       |--cron
       |--dd
       |--dhclient3
       |--events/0
       |--5*[getty]
       |--khelper
       |--klogd
```

Although interactive processes are important to users working on your machine, daemon processes are more important on a server because those daemon processes usually provide the services that are needed on a server. Daemon processes typically run in the background and normally don't send any output to the terminal. To see what they're doing, you must check the log files to which the daemon processes write. Generally speaking, it's a good idea to start with /var/log/messages if you're looking for daemon output. From a perspective of process management, it doesn't really matter if you're working with daemon or interactive processes; both can be handled the same way using the same commands.

Foreground and Background

When working with interactive processes, it can be useful to know that processes can run in the foreground and in the background. A foreground process takes up the current terminal, which gives optimal control of the process; the background process runs without an interface and has to be interrupted with a special command before it can be stopped or parameters can be passed to it. It might be useful for processes that take some time to complete. Before talking about the way you can start and manage processes that run in the background, let's talk about some process details so that you can understand what's happening.

A process always works with three standard file handlers that determine where the process should send its output and accept its input. They are the standard input (STDIN), the standard output (STDOUT), and the standard error (STDERR). Normally, when a process is running in the foreground, the STDIN is the keyboard, the STDOUT is the terminal the process is working on, and the STDERR is also the terminal that the process is working on. As you learned in Chapter 2, you can change them all by using redirection (for example, `grep -i blah * 2> /dev/null` would redirect the error output of the `grep` command to the null device).

It can be a little confusing that the three file descriptors don't change when you decide to run a process in the background. When it starts, the STDIN, STDOUT, and STDERR for a process are set; once they are set, they stay like that no matter what you do to the process. Therefore, you can run a long command like `find / -name "*" -exec grep -ls something {} \;` as a background job, but you'll still see its output and errors on your screen if you haven't redirected STDERR as well. If you don't want to see errors, you should use redirection to send STDOUT and STDERR somewhere else: by putting `> /somewhere` after the command, you are redirecting the standard output to a file called `/somewhere`; and by using `2> /dev/null`, you can arrange for all errors to be redirected to the null device.

■Tip Want to know what's really happening? In the `/proc` file system, you can see how STDIN, STDOUT, and STDERR are defined. Check the directory with the process ID (PID) of the process as its name (see the section "Managing Processes" later in this chapter for more details on process IDs). In this directory, activate the subdirectory `fd` (short for "file descriptors"). You'll see a list of all files the process currently has open—these are the so-called file descriptors. Number 0 is STDIN, 1 is STDOUT, and 2 is STDERR. Use the command `ls -l` to check what they are linked to, and you will know how STDIN, STDOUT, and STDERR are set for this process. If the subdirectory `fd` is empty, you're probably dealing with a daemon process that has no file descriptors.

Now that you know what to expect when working with processes in the background, it's time to learn how you can tell a process that it should be a background process. Basically, you can do this in one of two ways:

- Put an & after the name of the command when starting it. This makes it a background job immediately. For example, use `nmap 192.168.1.10 > ~/nmap.out &` to run the nmap command as a background process. What's the advantage of this? While waiting for the command to produce its output, you can do something else.

- Interrupt the process with the Ctrl+Z key sequence and then use the `bg` command to restart it in the background.

Once the command is running as a background job, you can still control it. Use the `jobs` command for an overview of all current background processes. You'll see a list of all interactive processes that have been started as a background job from the same shell environment. In front of each of these processes, you can see their current job number, and this job number can be used to manage the process with the `fg` command. For example, if `jobs` gives you a result such as

```
RNA:~# jobs
[1]-  Running        cat /dev/sda > /dev/null &
[2]+  Running        find / -name "*" -exec grep -ls help \; > /dev/null &
```

and you want to be able to terminate the cat command with Ctrl+C, use fg 1 to bring the cat command to the foreground again.

Managing Processes

As a Linux administrator, process management is a major task. If, for example, your server is reacting very slowly, you can probably find a process that's causing the problem. If this is the case, you need to know how to terminate that process, or maybe how you can reset its priority so that it can still do its work while not stopping other processes. The following sections describe what you need to know to perform daily process management tasks.

Tuning Process Activity

If something isn't going well on your server, you want to know about it. So, before you can conduct any process management, you need to tune process activity. Linux has an excellent tool that allows you to see exactly what's happening on your server: the top utility. From this utility you can see everything you need to know. It is very easy to start top: use the top command. When the utility starts, you'll see something like Figure 6-1.

```
top - 11:45:07 up 2 min,  2 users,  load average: 0.28, 0.20, 0.08
Tasks:  53 total,   1 running,  52 sleeping,   0 stopped,   0 zombie
Cpu(s):  2.7%us,  8.4%sy,  0.0%ni, 83.9%id,  3.2%wa,  0.2%hi,  1.7%si,  0.0%st
Mem:    515956k total,   125960k used,   389996k free,     4568k buffers
Swap:   409616k total,        0k used,   409616k free,    83404k cached

  PID USER      PR  NI  VIRT  RES  SHR S %CPU %MEM    TIME+  COMMAND
    1 root      15   0  2908 1844  524 S  0.0  0.4   0:01.04 init
    2 root      RT   0     0    0    0 S  0.0  0.0   0:00.00 migration/0
    3 root      34  19     0    0    0 S  0.0  0.0   0:00.00 ksoftirqd/0
    4 root      RT   0     0    0    0 S  0.0  0.0   0:00.00 watchdog/0
    5 root      10  -5     0    0    0 S  0.0  0.0   0:00.02 events/0
    6 root      10  -5     0    0    0 S  0.0  0.0   0:00.00 khelper
    7 root      10  -5     0    0    0 S  0.0  0.0   0:00.00 kthread
   30 root      17  -5     0    0    0 S  0.0  0.0   0:00.00 kblockd/0
   31 root      20  -5     0    0    0 S  0.0  0.0   0:00.00 kacpid
   32 root      20  -5     0    0    0 S  0.0  0.0   0:00.00 kacpi_notify
   90 root      10  -5     0    0    0 S  0.0  0.0   0:00.01 kseriod
  115 root      21   0     0    0    0 S  0.0  0.0   0:00.00 pdflush
  116 root      15   0     0    0    0 S  0.0  0.0   0:00.02 pdflush
  117 root      16  -5     0    0    0 S  0.0  0.0   0:00.00 kswapd0
  118 root      16  -5     0    0    0 S  0.0  0.0   0:00.00 aio/0
 1798 root      10  -5     0    0    0 S  0.0  0.0   0:00.00 ksuspend_usbd
 1800 root      10  -5     0    0    0 S  0.0  0.0   0:00.00 khubd
```

Figure 6-1. *The* top *utility gives you everything you need to know about the current state of your server.*

Using top to Monitor System Activity

The top window consists of two major parts. The first (upper) part provides a generic overview of the current state of your system. These are the first five lines in Figure 6-1. In the second (lower) part of the output, you can see a list of processes, with information about the activity of these processes.

The first line of the top output starts with the current system time. This time is followed by the "up" time; in Figure 6-1, you can see that the system has been up for only a few minutes. Next, you see the number of users currently logged in to your server. The end of the first line contains some very useful information: the load average. This line shows three different numbers. The first is the load average for the last minute, the second is the load average for the last 5 minutes, and the third is the load average for the last 15 minutes.

The load average is displayed by a number that indicates the current activity of the process queue. The value here is the number of processes that are waiting to be handled by the CPU on your system. On a system with one CPU, a load average of 1.00 indicates that the system is completely busy handling the processes in the queue, but there are no processes waiting in the queue. If the value increases past 1.00, the processes are lining up, and users may experience delays while communicating with your server. It's hard to say what a critical value exactly is. On many systems, a value anywhere between 1 and 4 indicates that the system is just busy, but if you want your server to run as smoothly as possible, make sure that this value exceeds 1.00 only rarely.

If an intensive task (such as a virus scanner) becomes active, the load average can easily rise to a value of 4. It may even happen that the load average reaches an extreme number like 254. In this case, it's very likely that processes will wait in the queue for so long that they will die spontaneously. What exactly indicates a healthy system can be determined only by doing some proper baselining of your server. In general, 1.00 is the ideal number for a one-CPU system. If your server has hyperthreading, dual-core, or two CPUs, the value would be 2.00. And, on a 32-CPU system with hyperthreading enabled on all CPUs, the value would be 64. So the bottom line is that each (virtual) CPU counts as 1 toward the overall value.

The second line of the top output shows you how many tasks currently are active on your server and also shows you the status of these tasks. A task can have four different statuses:

- *Running*: In the last polling interval, the process has been active. You will normally see that this number is rather low.

- *Sleeping*: The process has been active, but it was waiting for input. This is a typical status for an inactive daemon process.

- *Stopped*: The process is stopping. Occasionally, you'll see a process with the stopped status, but that status should disappear very soon.

- *Zombie*: The process has stopped, but it hasn't been able to send its exit status back to the parent process. This is a typical example of bad programming. Zombie processes will sometimes disappear after a while and will always disappear when you have rebooted your system.

The third row of top provides information about current CPU activity. This activity is separated into different statistics:

- us: CPU activity in user space. Typically, these are commands that have been started by normal users.

- sy: CPU activity in system space. Typically, these are kernel routines that are doing their work. Although the kernel is the operating system, kernel routines are still often conducting work on behalf of user processes or daemons.

- id: CPU inactivity, also known as the *idle loop*. A high value here just indicates that your system is doing nothing.

- wa: For "waiting," this is the percentage of time that the CPU has been waiting for new input. This should normally be a very low value; if not, it's time to make sure that your hard disk can still match up with the other system activity. If your CPU utilization is high, this should be the first parameter to check because a high workload on the CPU might be caused by a slow I/O channel.

- hi: For "hardware interrupt," this is the time the CPU has spent communicating with hardware. It will be rather high if, for example, you're reading large amounts of data from an optical drive.

- si: For "software interrupt," this is the time your CPU has spent communicating with software programs. It should be rather low on all occasions.

- st: This parameter indicates the time that is stolen by the virtualization hypervisor (see Chapter 13 for more details about virtualization and the hypervisor) from a virtual machine. On a server that doesn't use any virtualization, this parameter should be set to 0 at all times. If there is a virtual machine that is very active on your server, this parameter will increase from time to time because it measures activity in the host operating system; the host operating system has to share CPU cycles with the virtual machine.

The fourth and fifth lines of the top output display the memory statistics. These lines show you information about the current use of physical RAM (memory) and swap space. (Similar information can also be displayed using the free utility.) An important thing that you should see here is that not much swap space is in use. Swapping is bad because the disk space used to compensate for the lack of physical memory is approximately 1,000 times slower than real RAM.

If all memory is in use, you should take a look at the balance between buffers and cache. *Cache* is memory that is used to store files recently read from the server's hard drive. When files are stored in the cache, the request can be handled very quickly the next time a user requests the same file, thus improving the general speed of the server. Cache is good, and having a lot of it isn't bad at all.

A *buffer* is a region of memory reserved for data that still has to be written to the server's hard drive. After the data has been written to the buffers, the process that owns the data gets a signal that the data has been written. This means that the process can go on doing what it was doing and has to wait no longer. Once the disk controller has time to flush the buffers, it will flush them. Although using buffers is helpful, there is a disadvantage: everything that was stored in the server's buffers will be lost in case of a power outage if it hasn't yet been written to disk. And that's where the journal becomes useful: when the server reboots, the journal is read to recover the damaged files as fast as possible (see Chapter 4 for more information about journaling).

The bottom line of monitoring the cache and buffers parameter is that it is occupied memory that can be freed as soon as it is needed for something else. If a process has a memory request, the server can clear these memory areas immediately to give the memory that becomes available to the process in need.

The lower part of the `top` window provides details about the process that's most active in terms of CPU usage. It will be the first process listed, and the line also displays some usage statistics:

- *PID*: Every process has a unique process ID. Many tools such as `kill` need this PID for process management.

- *User*: This is the name of the user ID the process is using. Many processes run as root, so you will see the user name root rather often.

■Note For well-programmed processes, it's generally not a problem that they're running as root. It's a different story, though, for logging in as the user root.

- *PRI*: This is the priority indication for the process. This number is an indication of when the process will get some CPU cycles again. A lower value indicates a higher priority so that the process will have its share of CPU cycles sooner. The value RT indicates that it is a real-time process and is therefore given top priority by the scheduler.

- *NI*: The nice value of the process. See "Setting Process Priority" later in this chapter for more details on nicing processes.

- *VIRT*: The total amount of memory that is claimed by the process.

- *RES*: The resident memory size is the amount of memory that is actually mapped to physical memory. In other words, it represents the amount of process memory that is not swapped.

- *SHR*: The amount of shared memory is what the process shares with other processes. You'll see this quite often because processes often share libraries with other processes.

- *S*: This is the status of the process; they're the same status indications as the ones in the second line of the `top` screen.

- *%CPU*: This is the amount of CPU activity that the process has caused in the last polling cycle (which is typically every five seconds).

- *%MEM*: This is the percentage of memory that the process used in the last polling cycle.

- *TIME+*: This indicates the total amount of CPU time that the process has used since it was first started. You can display this same value by using the `time` command, followed by the command that you want to measure the CPU time for.

- *Command*: This is the command that started the process.

As you have seen, the `top` command really provides a lot of information about current system activity. Based upon this information, you can tune your system so that it works in the most optimal way.

Other Tools to Monitor System Activity

Although top is not the only tool that you can use for process monitoring, it's the most important. Its major benefit is that it shows you almost all you need to know about your system's current activity, but you should be aware that top itself takes up system resources as well, thus skewing the parameters that it shows. Some other good performance-monitoring tools are available as well:

- ps: This tool gives a list of processes.

- uptime: This tool shows how long the server is up and gives details about the load average as well. Basically, it displays the same output as the first line of output of the top command.

- free: Use this tool to show information about memory usage. Use the -m option to display the result in megabytes.

Terminating Processes

In your work as an administrator, you'll need to terminate misbehaving processes on a regular basis. When terminating a process, you'll send it a predefined signal. In general, the three important ones are SIGHUP, SIGKILL, and SIGTERM.

If you send the SIGHUP signal to a process, it doesn't really terminate the process, but just forces it to reread its configuration files. This is very useful to make sure that changes you made to configuration files are applied properly. Next is SIGKILL, which is sent to a process when someone uses the infamous kill -9 <PID> command to terminate a process. In this command, the -9 is a numerical representation for the SIGKILL signal. (Check the signal(7) man page for more details about signals and their numerical representations.) The SIGKILL signal doesn't terminate a process nicely: it just cuts it off, and the results can be severe because the process doesn't have an opportunity to save open files. Therefore, SIGKILL will definitely damage any open files and possibly even lead to system instability. So use it only as a last resort.

SIGTERM is the third signal that a process will always listen to. When a process receives this signal, it shuts down gracefully. It closes all open files and also tells its parent that it's gone. Using SIGTERM is the best way to terminate processes you don't need anymore.

Commands for Process Termination

You can use different commands to terminate a process. The following list provides a short description of the most important ones:

- kill: This is one of the most commonly used commands to terminate processes. It works with the PID of the process you need to kill. If a special signal needs to be sent to a process, the signal is commonly referred to with its numeric argument (for example, kill -9 1498), but you can use kill --sigkill <pid> instead. If no signal is referred to, the default SIGTERM signal (15) is sent to the process.

- killall: The major disadvantage of kill is that it works with one or more PIDs and thus isn't the best solution to kill more than one process at once. If you need to kill more than one process, you'd better use killall, which works with the name of the process. For example, killall httpd kills all instances of the Apache web server that are currently active on your server. By default, killall sends SIGTERM to the processes you want to kill. If you need it to do something else, add the name or number of the signal you want to send to the process. For example, use killall -SIGKILL httpd to kill all instances of the Apache web server.

■Tip The killall command works with processes that have exactly the name you've specified. It doesn't work for processes that have that name somewhere in the command line that was started to invoke them. Thus, killall won't kill these processes. To kill these processes anyway, you'll need to issue a somewhat more complex command. The following command kills all processes that have the text "evolution" somewhere in the command line: kill `ps aux | grep evolution | grep -v grep | awk '{ print $2 }'`. The technique used in this line is referred to as command substitution, which means that the result of a command is used as input for another command. In this example, the command ps aux | grep evolution | grep -v grep | awk '{ print $2 }' results in a list of PIDs of all processes that have the text "evolution" somewhere in the command line. This list is next used by the kill command to terminate all these processes. You do want to be very sure about what you type before you run this command because a typo will kill processes that you maybe don't want to.

- top: Killing a process from top is easy. From the top interface, press the k key. You'll first be asked for the PID of the process you want to kill. Enter it, and then you'll be asked what signal to send to the process. Specify the numeric value of the signal and press Enter. This terminates the process.

- pkill: The pkill command is useful if you want to kill a process based on any information about the process. This command is related to the pgrep command, which allows you to find process details easily. For example, you can use pkill to kill all processes owned by a certain user: pkill -U 501 kills all processes owned by the user with UID 501. Because it knows many ways to refer to processes that you want to terminate, pkill is a very convenient command.

Using ps to Get Details About Processes

Before killing a process, you most likely want some more information about it. Of course, you can use top to do this, but the utility has the disadvantage that it shows only the most active processes in its standard output. You can run it in batch mode, though, to get a complete list of all processes. Use top -b to obtain this result. If you need to manage a process that isn't among the most active processes, the ps utility is very useful. By using the right parameters, this command will show all processes that are currently active on your server and, combined with grep, it offers a flexible way to find exactly what you were looking for.

If you don't use any options with ps, it will just show you the processes that are interactive and that you own. Normally, this will be a rather short list. As a system administrator, you probably want to see a complete list of all processes. Now there is something funny with the ps command: you can use it in the BSD-style UNIX syntax, but also with the System V-style syntax.

■**Note** In the history of UNIX, two different flavors of UNIX developed: the BSD style and the System V style. Both flavors had different ways of doing things. In some Linux commands, Linux tries to make both users happy by implementing both flavors in one command. Therefore, the ps command has two different styles you can use.

You probably don't care what kind of syntax you're using, and you just want to see a list of active processes. This can be done by using the ps -ef command. Alternatively, ps -aux does this as well; check Listing 6-2 for an example of the output of this command. Both commands provide a complete list of all processes that are running on your system, and it's just a matter of taste as to which you prefer. Although ps has some options to do sorting, instead of remembering what these options do, you can use grep to do some filtering. For example, ps -ef | grep httpd shows detailed information, but only about the output line where the httpd string occurs.

Listing 6-2. *The* ps -aux *Command Displays a Complete List of All Processes on the Server*

```
root@ubuntu:~# ps aux
USER      PID %CPU %MEM   VSZ   RSS TTY      STAT START   TIME COMMAND
root        1  0.0  0.3  2908  1844 ?        Ss   11:43   0:01 /sbin/init
root        2  0.0  0.0     0     0 ?        S    11:43   0:00 [migration/0]
root        3  0.0  0.0     0     0 ?        SN   11:43   0:00 [ksoftirqd/0]
root        4  0.0  0.0     0     0 ?        S    11:43   0:00 [watchdog/0]
root        5  0.0  0.0     0     0 ?        S<   11:43   0:00 [events/0]
root        6  0.0  0.0     0     0 ?        S<   11:43   0:00 [khelper]
root        7  0.0  0.0     0     0 ?        S<   11:43   0:00 [kthread]
root       30  0.0  0.0     0     0 ?        S<   11:43   0:00 [kblockd/0]
root       31  0.0  0.0     0     0 ?        S<   11:43   0:00 [kacpid]
root       32  0.0  0.0     0     0 ?        S<   11:43   0:00 [kacpi_notify]
root       90  0.0  0.0     0     0 ?        S<   11:43   0:00 [kseriod]
root      115  0.0  0.0     0     0 ?        S    11:43   0:00 [pdflush]
root      116  0.0  0.0     0     0 ?        S    11:43   0:00 [pdflush]
...
root     4202  0.0  0.1  5084   968 ?        Ss   11:44   0:00 /usr/sbin/sshd
root     4213  0.0  0.4  7864  2472 ?        Ss   11:44   0:00 sshd: root@pts/
root     4215  0.0  0.3  4048  1780 pts/0    Ss   11:44   0:00 -bash
root     4237  0.0  0.1  2564   996 pts/0    R+   12:02   0:00 ps aux
```

Setting Process Priority

Killing a process may improve the performance of your server, but what if you still need that process? In this case, resetting its priority (*renicing*) may be an option. To understand what the commands `nice` and `renice` are doing, we first need to have a look at how the process scheduler works.

Every system uses a process queue. All processes sit in this queue to wait for some CPU cycles. So, if three processes are named A, B, and C, they will each get an equal number of CPU cycles. If a process still needs more cycles after the process has been handled, it reenters the queue. Because it was the last process that was handled, it rejoins the process queue at the end.

This all sounds pretty fair to all processes, but it just doesn't work in some cases. Imagine that process A is the company database that causes 90 percent of all the workload on your server, and processes B and C are less important. In this case, you'd want to give process A a higher priority, and give a slightly lower priority to the other two processes. This is exactly what the `nice` and `renice` commands do. Both commands work with a numeric argument from –20 up to 19. If a process has the `nice` value –20 (which means that it is not nice at all to other processes), it gets the most favorable scheduling (highest priority), and if it gets 19, it gets the least favorable scheduling.

Giving a `nice` value of –20 to a very important process may look like a good solution. But you should never do this. A very busy process that gets a `nice` value of –20 will exclude all other processes. Because, for example, kernel processes such as writing to disk also need to enter the process queue, you could give your database the highest priority, but then the database wouldn't be able to write its data to disk. So that wouldn't work. Let's just say that –20 is a `nice` value you should never use. If you want to `renice` a process, do it carefully, such as by increasing or decreasing the `nice` value of a process in increments of 5.

Several methods are available to `renice` processes:

- `nice`: The `nice` command can be used to start a process with a given `nice` value. For example, `nice 10 find / -name "*" -exec grep -ld help {} \;` starts the `find` command with a lower priority. The disadvantage of this command is that you have to know beforehand that you are going to want to adjust the `nice` value of a process.

- `renice`: The `renice` command is used to change the priority of a running command. This command normally works with the PID of the process you want to `renice`. For example, `renice -10 1234` increases the priority of process 1234.

- `top`: A very convenient way to `renice` a process is to use the `top` interface. From this interface, press the n key. You'll then be asked to enter the PID of the process you want to `renice`. After entering this PID, enter the new `nice` value you want this process to have.

Executing Processes Automatically

On a server system, it's often important that processes are executed at a regular predefined time, and Linux offers the `cron` facility to do this. It works with two parts: a daemon called `crond` and some configuration files that the administrator can use to specify when the processes should be started. Both parts ensure that the command is executed at regular times. Apart from cron, the at command can be used to run a command just once.

Configuring cron

The cron service is activated by default. It checks its configuration files every minute to see if something needs to be done. The cron process looks for configuration data in different places:

- The generic file /etc/crontab can contain lines that tell cron when to execute a given command.

- In the directory /etc/cron.d, an administrator can put a file that defines what should happen, and when. When installing software packages, you'll see that some files are automatically created in here as well.

- Every user can have its own cron configuration file, telling the system when to execute certain tasks. A user can enter the command crontab -e to create a personal crontab configuration file.

- The directories /etc/cron.hourly, cron.daily, cron.weekly, and cron.monthly are used to activate jobs once per hour, per day, per week, or per month, respectively. These directories contain files that are activated every hour, day, week, or month.

Working with the cron time activation mechanisms makes it very easy for an administrator to start jobs on a regular basis. The scripts in these directories are just regular shell scripts that make sure the job gets done. So all you have to do is include a shell script that activates the job you want to start. These scripts can be very simple: just a line that starts the service is enough.

Note Some daemons need to be restarted to make sure that changes are activated, but this isn't true for cron, which rereads its configuration every minute to see whether any new jobs have been scheduled.

---

cron User Jobs

You can set up your system to allow individual users to start their cron jobs. Such a configuration starts with the files /etc/cron.allow and /etc/cron.deny. A user who is listed in /etc/cron.allow or who isn't listed in /etc/cron.deny is capable of adding cron jobs. If /etc/cron.allow exists, only this file is evaluated and settings in /etc/cron.deny are ignored. If both files don't exist, only root can create cron jobs. The cron configuration files for individual users are stored in the directory /var/spool/cron/crontabs. The crontab command can be used to edit these files. Next we'll look at some examples of the crontab command in action.

■**Note** By default, the `crontab` command uses the `nano` editor to do its work. The problem with `nano`, however, is that it doesn't write its configuration files to the right location by default. To fix this, as root add the following line to the end of /etc/profile: `export VISUAL=vim`. After logging in again, `vim` will be used as the default editor for `crontab` and some other editor-related commands as well. The advantage? The right file will be created at the right location automatically.

- `crontab -e`: This creates or edits `cron` jobs for the user who executes the command. Again, `nano` is used as the editor to modify these files.

- `crontab -l`: This command displays a list of all jobs that are scheduled for the current user.

- `crontab -r`: This command deletes all jobs for the current user.

In the `cron` files, you use lines to define what should happen, and each line specifies one command. The lines consist of six fields each: the first five specify when the command should be activated, and the last field specifies what command should be activated. The following code is an example of such a line:

```
*/5 8-18 * * 1-6 fetchmail mailserver
```

The easiest part to understand in this line is the actual command: `fetchmail mailserver`. This command makes sure that incoming mail is fetched from `mailserver`. Then, in the first five fields, you can see an indication of the times that it should happen. These fields have the following meanings:

- *Minutes*: This field specifies the minute when the command should be executed. It has a range from 0 to 59. Always specify something for this field; if you don't, the command will run every minute. In the example, the construct */5 is used to specify that the command should run every 5 minutes.

- *Hours*: This field specifies the hour that the command should run. Possible values are between 0 and 23. In the example, you can see that the command will run every hour between 8 and 18.

- *Day of the Month*: Use this field to execute a command only on given days of the month. This field is often not specified.

- *Month*: Use this field to specify in which month of the year the command should run.

- *Day of Week*: This field specifies on which day of the week the command should run. The range is 0 to 7, and both of the values 0 and 7 should be used to specify that the command should run on Sunday.

■**Note** You normally will not use it, but, if you ever want to work with the /etc/crontab file, be aware that, between the time setting and the command you want to execute, the name of the user whose account should be used to execute the command is entered. For example, 0 17 * * * root /sbin/shutdown -h now would make sure the system shuts down automatically every day at 5 p.m. by using the permissions of the user root.

Executing Once with at

The cron mechanism is used to execute commands automatically on a regular basis. If you want to execute a command just once, at is the solution you need. The at mechanism comprises different parts:

- The service atd: Make sure it is started if you want to schedule commands to run once.

- The files /etc/at.allow and /etc/at.deny: Used to specify which users can and cannot schedule commands with at.

- The at command: Used to schedule a command.

- The atq command: Used to display an overview of all commands that currently have been scheduled.

- The atrm command: Used to delete jobs from the at execution queue.

Scheduling a job with the at command is not hard; just use the at command followed by the time when you want to run the command, for example at 17:00. This command opens the interactive at prompt, where you'll enter the commands you want to schedule for execution at the specific time. When you've finished entering the names of commands, use the Ctrl+D key sequence to close the interactive at prompt, and the commands will be scheduled.

The at command has different options to specify when exactly a command should be executed. Some of the most useful options are listed here:

- HH:MM: In its most elementary form, time is indicated in an *HH:MM* format; for example an entry of 17:00 will execute the command the next time it is 17:00 hours.

- am/pm: If you don't like the *HH:MM* notation, use am/pm instead; for example, at 5 pm.

- DDMMYY HH:MM: To run a command at a specific time on a specific day, you can use a full day specification as well.

Other options are available. For example, you can use words to tell at when to run a command. For example, at teatime tomorrow would run the command at 4 p.m. the next day. Check the at man page for more details.

Tuning the Boot Procedure

It's important that you know what happens during the boot procedure of your computer for two reasons. First, you need to know how it works to be able to perform troubleshooting.

Second, you need to be aware of what happens if you want to make sure that a service is activated automatically. In the Linux boot procedure, the following phases can be distinguished:

- The boot loader GRUB is executed.

- The upstart process is started.

- The initial boot phase is executed.

- The runlevel is activated.

In the next subsections, you'll learn in detail how these phrases work and how you can modify the boot procedure.

Managing the GRUB Boot Loader

The BIOS of every computer has a setting for the device that should be used for booting by default. Often, the server will try to initiate the boot procedure from its hard drive. It reads the very first sector of 512 bytes (the master boot record, or MBR), in which it finds the GRUB primary boot loader in the first 446 bytes. After that are the 64 bytes in which the partition table is stored; and to finish, in the last 2 bytes are where a magic code is written. Upon installing your server, the installation program writes the GRUB boot code onto the hard drive. This code makes sure that your server is started automatically. However, you can also interrupt the automatic startup by pressing the Esc key. Figure 6-2 shows the menu that you'll see in this case.

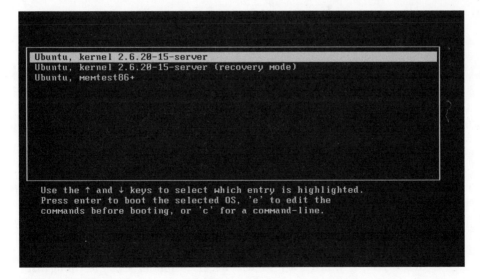

Figure 6-2. *The GRUB boot menu allows you to interrupt the boot procedure.*

The GRUB Configuration File

GRUB has a text configuration file—/boot/grub/menu.lst—that defines all options from the boot menu. Here, you can specify the different boot options on your server. Listing 6-3 shows the data that is normally in the GRUB configuration file just after installation of Ubuntu Server. For better readability, I removed all the comment sections from this file.

Listing 6-3. *Default GRUB* menu.lst *File*

```
default        0
timeout        3
hiddenmenu


title          Ubuntu 8.04, kernel 2.6.24-16-server
root           (hd0,0)
kernel         /boot/vmlinuz-2.6.24-16-server\
 root=UUID=1aa61aba-4b23-4e9d-9718-289f1c84a3a ro quiet splash
initrd         /boot/initrd.img-2.6.24-16-server
quiet


title          Ubuntu 8.04, kernel 2.6.24-16-server (recovery mode)
root           (hd0,0)
kernel         /boot/vmlinuz-2.6.24-16-server\
 root=UUID=1aa61aba-4b23-4e9d-9718-e289f1c84a3a ro single
initrd          /boot/initrd.img-2.6.24-16-server

title           Ubuntu, memtest86+
root            (hd0,0)
kernel         /boot/memtest86+.bin
```

This file consists of several parts. The first is the general section, which defines some options that determine how the menu is used. Next are three sections, each devoted to one of the three different boot menu options.

The first parts of the GRUB boot menu are the generic options. The example file shown in Listing 6-3 has three of them. The option default 0 specifies that the first section in menu.lst should be executed as the default section. Next, timeout 3 is used to give the user 3 seconds to interrupt the startup procedure. If the user doesn't do anything during these 3 seconds, the server will continue with the boot process. The last generic boot option is hiddenmenu. As you can guess, this option causes the boot menu to be hidden by default. If the user presses the Esc key at this moment, the menu in Figure 6-2 will be displayed.

In the second part, the first item in the boot menu is specified. This item has the title Ubuntu, kernel 2.6.20-15 server, which is defined with the title option. Next, everything that is needed to start the server is defined. First is the name of the root device that should be read. This line is needed for GRUB to know where it can find the kernel that it should load. In this example, this is the device root (hd0,0), which corresponds to /dev/sda1 or /dev/hda1. However, because the device names are not known at this stage in the boot procedure, it's not possible to refer to these device names, so that's why (hd0,0) is used. Check the file /boot/grub/device.map to see how these device mappings are currently defined.

After specifying the root device, the kernel itself is referred to in the line that starts with `kernel /boot/vmlinuz`. This line also specifies all the options that are required to load the kernel properly. Some of the more common options are as follows:

- `root`: This option refers to the device where the root file system is found. It's possible to refer to common device names such as `/dev/sda1` here. To add increased flexibility, however, file system UUIDs are used. In case your root is on a logical volume, you'll see the logical volume device name here. Check Chapter 4 for more details, or use the `dumpe2fs` command to see parameters that are set for your Ext2/Ext3 file systems.

- `ro`: Use this option to make sure that the root device is mounted read-only at this stage. This is necessary so that you'll be able to perform a file system check later during the system boot.

- `quiet`: This option suppresses most messages that are generated while booting. If you want to see exactly what happens, remove this option from `menu.lst`.

- `splash`: Use this option to show a splash screen. In general, this is a graphical screen that is shown to the user during the boot process. You don't want this option on a server; you should disable it so that you can see what happens when the server comes up.

- `vga`: Use this option to specify the VGA mode as a hexadecimal argument when booting. This line determines the number of columns and lines used when starting your system. As an alternative to a value such as `0x314`, you can use the option `ask`. In that case, you can enter the mode you want to use when booting.

- `ide`: You can use this option to specify the mode that should be used for starting the IDE device. Use `ide=nodma` if you suspect that your server might have problems initializing IDE in DMA mode.

- `acpi`: The advanced configuration and power interface (ACPI) option allows you to specify what to do with this sometimes problematic technique. By default, ACPI is on. Use `acpi=off` if you suspect that it's causing some problems.

- `noresume`: If your system was suspended, this option will just ignore that fact and start a new system. While starting this new system, the suspended system is terminated. Because normally you wouldn't suspend a server, you probably don't need this option, either.

- `nosmp`: Use this option if symmetric multiprocessing (SMP) is causing you any trouble. But be aware that you'll be using only one CPU if this option is used.

- `noapic`: The advanced programmable interrupt controller (APIC) allows you to use interrupts with many more outputs and options than when using normal interrupts. However, this option can cause problems; so use `noapic` if you think that your system can't properly handle APICs.

- `maxcpus`: This option tells your kernel how many CPUs to work with. Use `maxcpus=0` to force all off except the primary processor.

- edd: This option specifies whether enhanced disk drive (EDD) support should be used. If you suspect that it's causing problems, switch it off here.

- single: This option is used only in recovery mode. It starts single-user mode, in which a minimal amount of services is started so that the administrator can perform troubleshooting.

The following line specifies what to load as the initial RAM drive (initrd). The use of an initrd is very important on modern Linux systems because it's used to load the kernel modules that are needed to boot the system.

The other menu items that are defined in this boot menu work in more or less the same way: each starts with a specification of the root device and then a referral to the kernel that should be loaded.

One of the nice features of GRUB is that it reads its configuration dynamically, which means that if you made any modifications to the options used in menu.lst, you don't have to recompile or reinstall GRUB. This is a huge advantage as compared with LILO, the boot loader from the early days of Linux, in which you had to run the lilo command after all changes or modifications to the configuration. Any changes that you make to menu.lst will show immediately the next time you restart your server.

Installing GRUB

Installing GRUB is not something that you'll do very frequently because it's installed by default. However, if your GRUB ever causes a problem when booting your server, you may need to reinstall it. Before you do this, however, you'll have to boot your server from the installation CD-ROM. From the boot menu on the CD-ROM, select the option to rescue a broken system. After answering some generic questions about your server, a menu will offer different options (see Figure 6-3). From this menu, you can choose to reinstall the GRUB boot loader to reinstall GRUB directly. Or you may choose to select a shell in either your root device or your installer's environment. When choosing this latter option, you can use the command grub-install /dev/sda to reinstall GRUB.

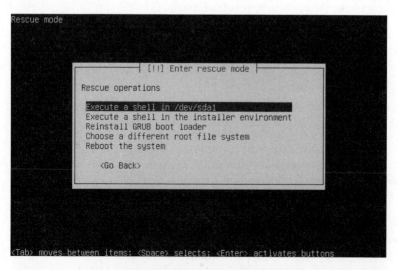

Figure 6-3. *It's relatively easy to reinstall GRUB from the rescue environment.*

Working with the GRUB Boot Menu

When GRUB runs, it displays a boot menu. (Remember to press the Esc key when booting your server in silent mode.) From the boot menu, you will normally have a choice between the three different sections that are defined in `/boot/grub/menu.lst`. Normally you will select the first option to boot the server. If you want to use your server for XEN virtualization, select the XEN option from the boot menu. (This option is available only if you selected the XEN software when installing your server. See Chapter 13 for more on XEN.) The failsafe option is the one you need if you run into trouble, and finally, you can select the Memory Check option if you suspect that you have problems with your server's RAM.

■ **Note** The failsafe option is more than just a single-user mode. A minimal number of services are loaded in single-user mode, but the kernel is loaded in the normal way. Selecting the failsafe option from the boot menu starts the single-user mode, but the kernel is also started with minimal options to increase chances that you can boot successfully.

If the default startup option from the GRUB menu is not good enough, select the item that you want to start and press the e key. You'll next see a window like the one in Figure 6-4.

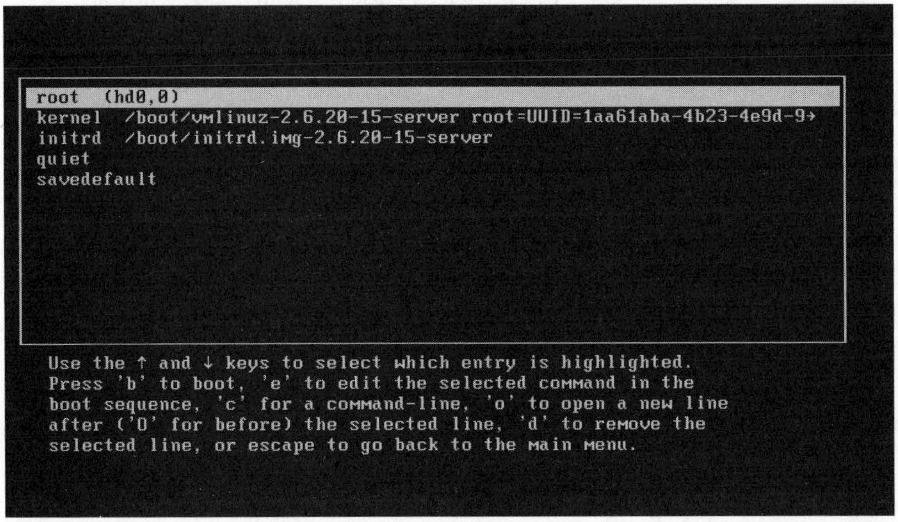
root (hd0,0)
kernel /boot/vmlinuz-2.6.20-15-server root=UUID=1aa61aba-4b23-4e9d-9→
initrd /boot/initrd.img-2.6.20-15-server
quiet
savedefault
Use the ↑ and ↓ keys to select which entry is highlighted.
Press 'b' to boot, 'e' to edit the selected command in the
boot sequence, 'c' for a command-line, 'o' to open a new line
after ('O' for before) the selected line, 'd' to remove the
selected line, or escape to go back to the main menu.

Figure 6-4. *After pressing the e key, you can choose from more details when booting your server.*

You'll now see the selected boot item in more detail. Every line in the selected item can be edited from this interface. From this interface, you can perform the following tasks:

- Press b to boot: Use this option if you want to boot your computer with the selected settings.

- Select a line and press the e key to edit the selected line. This option is very convenient if you know that you have made an error in a certain line and you want to fix it.

- Press c to open the GRUB command line. This not-so-intuitive interface allows you to type GRUB-specific commands to tell your server what you want to do. If GRUB still is capable of showing you some boot options, you probably won't use this option much.

- Press o or O to open a new line. On this line, you can add new options that you want to pass to GRUB while starting your machine. For example, if you want to start your server in troubleshooting mode instead of its normal startup mode, type **single** to start single-user mode.

- Press d to remove a line from the menu.

- Press Esc to return to the main menu. From there, you can press Enter to continue booting.

Upstart

After GRUB, the kernel is loaded. In the old days, the kernel loaded the init process that read its configuration file /etc/inittab. Since Ubuntu 7.04, however, a new program is used instead. The Upstart program is responsible for the remainder of the boot procedure. To start your computer, it still uses a boot method that looks a lot like the one that was used in the old days.

The most important part of Upstart is found in the /etc/event.d directory. It's here that Upstart looks for a definition of all the jobs it has to start, and there's a file for every job. Next, you'll find a description of all the available jobs:

- control-alt-delete: This job defines what should happen when a user presses the Ctrl+Alt+Del key sequence. The default behavior is that the system will reboot. If you don't like that, open the /etc/event.d/control-alt-delete file and replace this shutdown command with something else.

- logd: This job makes sure that the log process /sbin/logd is started. This process ensures that all log messages generated by daemons on your server can be logged.

- rc0-rc6: A Linux computer uses the concept of *runlevels*, which are used to define what services have to be started when booting your server. The scripts with the names rc0 up to rc6 define what should happen in the corresponding runlevels. Typically, Ubuntu Server is started in runlevel 2. This master script makes sure that all services normally required in that runlevel are launched. Later in this chapter you'll learn how to define what happens in a given runlevel.

- rc-default: This script determines the default runlevel, which is normally runlevel 2 on Ubuntu Server. If you want to use something else for the default runlevel, you should create a file with the name /etc/inittab that contains the following line: id:N:initdefault:. In this line, N refers to the number of the runlevel that you want to activate.

- rcS: This script is used to ensure compatibility with System V startup scripts. Ubuntu Server still uses these old scripts to start services, and you can read in more detail how to configure them in the section "Runlevels" later in this chapter.

- rcS-sulogin: Normally, single-user mode is used for troubleshooting, and no administrator password is asked for. Of course, this is a serious security issue, and some measures have to be taken. The rcS-sulogin service makes sure that the root password has to be provided every time the single-user mode is entered.

- sulogin: In this script, the administrator can specify the message that a user should see when entering single-user mode.

- tty1-tty6: On Ubuntu Server, virtual terminals are used. To activate a virtual terminal, the key sequences Ctrl+Alt+F1 up to Ctrl+Alt+F6 have to be used. The services files in /etc/event.d specify what needs to be done when activating one of these virtual terminals. If you want to have more than six virtual terminals, copy one of these files to (for example) a file with the name tty8 (never use tty7 because it is by default used for the graphical environment). Next, change the last line of this file to reflect the name of the TTY it is related to. See Listing 6-4 for an example.

Listing 6-4. *The TTY Files Specify What Should Happen on a Virtual Console*

```
root@ubuntu:~# cat /etc/event.d/tty1
# tty1 - getty
#
# This service maintains a getty on tty1 from the point the system is
# started until it is shut down again.

start on runlevel 2
start on runlevel 3
start on runlevel 4
start on runlevel 5

stop on runlevel 0
stop on runlevel 1
stop on runlevel 6

respawn
exec /sbin/getty 38400 tty1
```

As you have seen, the Upstart service activates services as specified in the different files in /etc/event.d. This is pretty much the same as what happened on older versions of Ubuntu Server that still used the init process. One of the most important tasks of Upstart is that it's also responsible for starting all the services that are needed on your server. To do this, it uses the concept of runlevels.

Runlevels

The default runlevel on Ubuntu Server is runlevel 2, in which all the services that have to be started are referred to. Before entering runlevel 2, Ubuntu Server passes through runlevel S. In this runlevel, all the essential services that are always required on your server are started. The configuration of both works in more or less the same way.

To understand the working of a runlevel, you need to understand two components: the service scripts and the scripts that execute these service scripts. All the service scripts are found in the /etc/init.d directory, and they are used to start fundamental services such as the mounting of file systems as well as network services like your Apache server. To specify which of these scripts have to be executed when starting your server, two runlevel-related directories are used. The first of these directories is /etc/rcS.d, and on a system that follows a default installation, the second of them is /etc/rc2.d. In the /etc/rcS.d directory, services are started that are always needed, whereas in the /etc/rc2.d directory, services are started that are specific to a given runlevel.

To make sure that a service starts automatically during system initialization, a symbolic link is created in the /etc/rcS.d directory. The name of this link starts with an S, followed by a two-digit number, followed by the name of the script in /etc/init.d that the link refers to. All these links are processed when booting your server, and they are processed in alphabetical order. So S01blah is processed before S99blah.

The same thing happens for the runlevel directories, except that when working with runlevels, there is an option to change the current runlevel. When changing a runlevel, some scripts may have to be started as well. To do this, more symbolic links are created. The name of these links starts with K, followed by a two-digit number. Listing 6-5 shows an example of the default runlevel 2.

Listing 6-5. *To Determine What Is Started and What Is Stopped in a Runlevel, Some Symbolic Links Are Processed*

```
root@ubuntu:/etc/rc2.d# ls -l
total 4
-rw-r--r-- 1 root root 556 2007-04-10 17:46 README
lrwxrwxrwx 1 root root  18 2007-07-29 07:34 S10sysklogd -> ../init.d/sysklogd
lrwxrwxrwx 1 root root  15 2007-07-29 07:34 S11klogd -> ../init.d/klogd
lrwxrwxrwx 1 root root  15 2007-07-29 07:36 S15bind9 -> ../init.d/bind9
lrwxrwxrwx 1 root root  23 2007-07-29 07:36\
 S17mysql-ndb-mgm -> ../init.d/mysql-ndb-mgm
lrwxrwxrwx 1 root root  19 2007-07-29 07:36 S18mysql-ndb -> ../init.d/mysql-ndb
lrwxrwxrwx 1 root root  15 2007-07-29 07:36 S19mysql -> ../init.d/mysql
lrwxrwxrwx 1 root root  17 2007-07-29 07:32 S20makedev -> ../init.d/makedev
lrwxrwxrwx 1 root root  15 2007-07-29 07:36 S20rsync -> ../init.d/rsync
lrwxrwxrwx 1 root root  13 2007-07-29 11:44 S20ssh -> ../init.d/ssh
lrwxrwxrwx 1 root root  13 2007-07-29 07:36 S89atd -> ../init.d/atd
lrwxrwxrwx 1 root root  14 2007-07-29 07:36 S89cron -> ../init.d/cron
lrwxrwxrwx 1 root root  17 2007-07-29 07:36 S91apache2 -> ../init.d/apache2
lrwxrwxrwx 1 root root  18 2007-07-29 07:33 S99rc.local -> ../init.d/rc.local
lrwxrwxrwx 1 root root  19 2007-07-29 07:33 S99rmnologin -> ../init.d/rmnologin
```

If you want to make sure that a given service is started automatically, it follows that you first need to make sure that it has a service script in /etc/init.d. If it does, you next need to make a symbolic link for this service. If it is a service that has to be started when your server is booting, you just need a start link in /etc/rcS.d. If it is a service that you want to be included in your server's runlevels, you need to create a start link as well as a stop link in the directory of the default runlevel, which would be /etc/rc2.d in most cases. So let's see how this works for the imaginary service blahd.

1. To include blahd in system startup, make sure that it has a start script in /etc/init.d. If blahd was developed to be used on either Debian or Ubuntu Linux, it will have such a script. Let's say that the name of this script is /etc/init.d/blah. If you can write a decent Bash shell script, open the example script /etc/init.d/skeleton and change it to start the blah service instead of the default foo service.

2. If blahd is a nonessential service, you should include it in the default runlevel. Therefore, you're going to create two symbolic links in /etc/rc2.d, and to put the service in the right place, you should first analyze its dependencies. If it depends on some other service to be started first, give it a relatively high number after the S, such as S50. If it doesn't depend on anything, you can give it a relatively low number. The inverse is true for the kill scripts that make sure that the service is stopped once you quit the runlevel: scripts that depend on many other services but don't have dependencies themselves get a low number; scripts that don't depend on other services get a high number.

3. Now create the links. To create the start link, first use cd /etc/rc2.d and then ln -s ../init.d/blah S10blahd. Next, to create the kill link, use ln -s ../init.d/blah K90blahd. When restarting your server, the service will now be executed automatically.

■**Tip** When determining the proper load number for a script, on Ubuntu Server you can always assume that all device drivers are initialized, local file systems have been mounted, and networking is available after the S40 scripts have been processed. So in case of doubt, use S41 or higher.

Making Service Management Easier

When reading the information about starting services in the preceding section, maybe you began to suspect that it's not really easy. And you know what? You're right. Even with the modern Upstart system, Ubuntu Server is still compatible with the old way of starting services (System V); you can use one of the many tools available for System V service management to make service configuration easier. One of these tools is sysv-rc-conf. Use apt-get install sysv-rc-conf to install it. Once installed, you can start it with the command sysv-rc-conf, and what follows is an interface similar to that shown in Figure 6-5. From this interface, you'll see all the services available on your server. To make sure that a given service is started, move the arrow key to the right location in the runlevel columns for the runlevel in which you want the service started; then press the spacebar to select it. All required symbolic links will be automatically created for you.

```
 SysV Runlevel Config    -: stop service   =/+: start service   h: help   q: quit

 service         1       2       3       4       5       0       6       S
 -------------------------------------------------------------------------------
 alsa-utils    [ ]     [█]     [ ]     [ ]     [ ]     [ ]     [ ]     [ ]
 apache2       [ ]     [X]     [X]     [X]     [X]     [ ]     [ ]     [ ]
 atd           [ ]     [X]     [X]     [X]     [X]     [ ]     [ ]     [ ]
 bind9         [ ]     [X]     [X]     [X]     [X]     [ ]     [ ]     [ ]
 bootclean     [ ]     [ ]     [ ]     [ ]     [ ]     [ ]     [ ]     [ ]
 bootlogd      [ ]     [ ]     [ ]     [ ]     [ ]     [ ]     [ ]     [ ]
 console-s$    [ ]     [ ]     [ ]     [ ]     [ ]     [ ]     [ ]     [X]
 cron          [ ]     [X]     [X]     [X]     [X]     [ ]     [ ]     [ ]
 dns-clean     [ ]     [ ]     [ ]     [ ]     [ ]     [ ]     [ ]     [X]
 halt          [ ]     [ ]     [ ]     [ ]     [ ]     [X]     [ ]     [ ]
 hdparm        [ ]     [ ]     [ ]     [ ]     [ ]     [ ]     [ ]     [ ]
 keyboard-$    [ ]     [ ]     [ ]     [ ]     [ ]     [ ]     [ ]     [X]
 killprocs     [X]     [ ]     [ ]     [ ]     [ ]     [ ]     [ ]     [ ]



 Use the arrow keys or mouse to move around.      ^n: next pg      ^p: prev pg
                        space: toggle service on / off
```

Figure 6-5. *The* sysv-rc-conf *tool makes service management a lot easier.*

■**Tip** Don't worry about service management too much. You will find that after installing a package with apt-get, most service management tasks are accomplished automatically. So you just have to see whether the required link is really created as well. Everything usually works just fine.

Managing Hardware

One of the hardest challenges when working with Linux is making your hardware do what you want it to do. Many times, the real cause for not being able to get your hardware to work is the lack of the right drivers. Many hardware vendors still think that Windows is the only operating system on Earth, so they don't offer any Linux drivers for their devices. This means that it's up to the open source community to do the work. Often this goes very well, especially if the specifications of the hardware are clear. However, in some cases, hardware vendors think that their product is unique and therefore are unwilling to share their code specifications with the rest of the world, which makes it sometimes nearly (sometimes completely) impossible to produce the right drivers.

In this subsection you'll learn what you can do to get your hardware working. To begin with, you'll have a look at the kernel and its capability to add load modules to get your hardware working. Related to the kernel, I'll also talk about the initial RAM drive (initrd) and how you can configure it to load additional modules while booting. Next, I'll talk about udev and the way it has changed hardware management on modern Linux distributions. At the end of this chapter, you'll learn how the lspci and lsusb commands can be useful for finding out what kind of hardware you are using. You'll also learn how the sysfs file system can help you manage hardware.

Kernel Management

The kernel is the heart of the operating system; it is the software layer that sits directly on top of the hardware and makes it possible to do something useful with that hardware. With Ubuntu Server, you are working with a default kernel in which certain functionality is enabled and other functionality is not. I'll now explain how the kernel is organized and what you can do to tune it to your needs.

Working with Modules

On all modern Linux distributions, kernels are modular—which means that the core of the operating system is in the kernel file itself, but lots of drivers that aren't needed by default are dynamically loaded as modules. The idea of this modularity is an increased efficiency—if a driver is needed, its module is loaded; if it isn't needed, the module isn't loaded either. It's really as simple as that.

As an administrator, you'll find that module management is an important task. With Ubuntu Server, modules are installed in the directory /lib/modules/`uname -r`. As you can see, command substitution is used in this directory name: the command uname -r gives the correct version of the current kernel; by using this command in the directory path, you can be sure always to refer to the right path in which kernel modules can be found. Under this directory, you can find a directory structure in which all modules are stored in an organized way, according to the type of module. You can recognize the kernel modules in this directory structure by their file name: all kernel modules have the extension .ko.

You should be aware how modules are loaded. The good thing is that on a default installation, most of your hardware is detected automatically, and the required modules are loaded automatically as well. So in most cases there is no need to do anything. Sometimes, however, some tuning of the load process of modules is required. In the next subsection you can read how.

Loading Modules

You can load modules in one of three methods: manually, from initrd, or by udev. Let's see how this process works.

Tuning initramfs

As soon as your system boots, it immediately needs some modules, such as the modules necessary to access the root device on your server. These modules are loaded by the initial RAM file system (initrd), which is loaded from GRUB. Normally, this initial RAM drive is created automatically, and you don't have to worry about it. However, you may need to tune your own initrd in some situations; in this case, the mkinitramfs command can be used.

■**Note** The correct way to refer to `initrd` is to call it the initial RAM file system (`initramfs`). In the old days, the `initramfs` was referred to as the `initrd`. It basically is the same thing, and you can use either term to refer to it.

To create your own `initramfs`, the first thing you should tune is the `/etc/initramfs-tools/initramfs.conf` file. This file is used to specify generic options that should be used on your `initramfs`, such as a time-out parameter that specifies how long you'll have to interrupt the boot procedure. Normally, it's not necessary to change anything in this file. Also, there is the `/etc/ initramfs-tools/modules` file, in which you refer to the modules that you want to be loaded automatically. Next, in the `/etc/initramfs-tools/scripts` directory you can create scripts that allow the `mkinitramfs` command to find the proper modules. Done all that? Then it's time to run the `mkinitramfs` command to create your own `initramfs`.

When using `mkinitramfs`, the command needs the option `-o` to specify the name of the output file it needs to create; for example, `mkinitramfs -o newinitrd`. Once created, it is a good idea to copy `newinitrd` to the `/boot` directory; everything your kernel needs to boot the system must be in this directory. Next, tune `/boot/grub/menu.lst` to make sure the new `initramfs` is included in one of the GRUB sections (be aware that in the `menu.lst` file it is referred to as `initrd` when doing so):

1. Open `/boot/grub/menu.lst` with your favorite editor.

2. Copy the default section that is used to boot your system in the file. This will result in this section occurring twice in the `menu.lst` file.

3. Change the title of the default boot section to something else ("test with new initrd" would be a decent name while you are still testing) and make sure the `initrd` line refers to the new `initrd` that you just created. This would result in something like the following lines:

```
title      Test with new initrd
root       (hd0,0)
kernel     /boot/vmlinuz-2.6.24-16-server root=/dev/sda1 ro quiet splash
initrd     /boot/newinitrd
```

4. Reboot your server, and while rebooting, select the new GRUB menu item to test if the new `initrd` is working properly. If it does, change `/boot/grub/menu.lst` to make the test section permanent.

Loading Modules on Boot

Normally, the kernel ensures that all modules you need when booting your server are loaded when the hardware that requires them is detected. In some situations, though, this doesn't work out. If not, you can make sure that the module is loaded anyway by including it in the `/etc/modules` configuration file. The structure of this file is not complicated; just specify the names of all the modules that you want to load, one per line, and they will be loaded when you reboot your server. The following listing shows an example of the contents of this file:

```
root@RNA:/etc# cat modules
# /etc/modules: kernel modules to load at boot time.
#
# This file contains the names of kernel modules that should be loaded
# at boot time, one per line. Lines beginning with "#" are ignored.

loop
lp
sbp2
fuse
```

Need to add a new module? Make sure that it is listed in this file and it will be loaded when your server restarts.

Loading Modules Manually

Modules can be managed manually as well, which can be useful when testing new hardware devices. Here are the commands:

- lsmod: This command displays a list of all currently loaded modules. In this list, you'll also see the current status of the module. The output of lsmod is given in four columns (as can be seen in Listing 6-6). The first column provides the name of the module. The second column shows its size. In the third column, a 0 indicates that the module currently is not used. Everything greater than 0 indicates that the module is in use. The last column shows the name of other modules that require this module to be loaded.

Listing 6-6. *Output of* lsmod

```
root@ubuntu:/etc/init.d# lsmod
Module                  Size  Used by
ipv6                  273344  20
lp                     12324  0
af_packet              23688  2
snd_ens1371            27552  0
gameport               16520  1 snd_ens1371
snd_ac97_codec         97952  1 snd_ens1371
ac97_bus                3200  1 snd_ac97_codec
snd_pcm_oss            44416  0
snd_mixer_oss          17408  1 snd_pcm_oss
snd_pcm                79876  3 snd_ens1371,snd_ac97_codec,snd_pcm_oss
snd_seq_dummy           4740  0
snd_seq_oss            32896  0
snd_seq_midi            9600  0
snd_rawmidi            25472  2 snd_ens1371,snd_seq_midi
snd_seq_midi_event      8448  2 snd_seq_oss,snd_seq_midi
snd_seq                52464  6\
 snd_seq_dummy,snd_seq_oss,snd_seq_midi,snd_seq_midi_event
snd_timer              23684  2 snd_pcm,snd_seq
```

```
...
capability                    5896  0
commoncap               8192  1 capability
```

- modprobe: If you want to load a module by hand, the modprobe command is the way to
  do it. The importance of this command is that it will do a dependency check. Some
  modules need another module to be present before they can do their job, and modprobe
  makes sure that these dependencies are fulfilled. To load the dependent modules, it
  looks in the configuration file modules.dep, which is created automatically by the depmod
  command (see later in this section). Loading a module with modprobe isn't hard; if, for
  example, you want to load the module vfat by hand, just use the modprobe vfat command. In the early days, modprobe had an alternative: the insmod command. But insmod
  has the disadvantage that it doesn't check for dependencies, so you probably shouldn't
  use it anymore.

- rmmod: An unused module still consumes system resources. It usually won't be much
  more than 50 KB of system memory, but some heavy modules (such as the XFS module
  that offers support for the XFS file system) can consume up to 500 KB. On a system that
  is short on memory, this is a waste, and you can use rmmod followed by the name of the
  module you want to remove (for example, rmmod ext3). This command will remove the
  module from memory and free up all the system resources it was using. A more modern
  alternative for rmmod is the modprobe -r command. The major difference is that modprobe
  -r takes dependencies into consideration as well.

- modinfo: Have you ever had the feeling that a module was using up precious system
  resources without knowing exactly what it was doing? Then modinfo is your friend. This
  command will show some information that is compiled in the module itself. As an
  example, you can see how it works on the pcnet32 network board driver in Listing 6-7.
  Especially for network boards, the modinfo command can be very useful because it
  shows you all the parameters the network board is started with (for instance, its duplex
  settings), which can be handy for troubleshooting.

Listing 6-7. *The* modinfo *Command Shows What a Module Is Used For*

```
myserver # modinfo pcnet32
root@ubuntu:/etc/init.d# modinfo pcnet32
filename:       /lib/modules/2.6.20-15-server/kernel/drivers/net/pcnet32.ko
license:        GPL
description:    Driver for PCnet32 and PCnetPCI based etherboards
author:         Thomas Bogendoerfer
srcversion:     8C4DDF304B5E88C9AD31856
alias:              pci:v00001023d00002000sv*sd*bc02sc00i*
alias:              pci:v00001022d00002000sv*sd*bc*sc*i*
alias:              pci:v00001022d00002001sv*sd*bc*sc*i*
depends:        mii
vermagic:       2.6.20-15-server SMP mod_unload 686
parm:           debug:pcnet32 debug level (int)
parm:           max_interrupt_work:pcnet32 maximum events\
  handled per interrupt (int)
```

```
parm:            rx_copybreak:pcnet32 copy breakpoint for\
 copy-only-tiny-frames (int)
parm:            tx_start_pt:pcnet32 transmit start point (0-3) (int)
parm:            pcnet32vlb:pcnet32 Vesa local bus (VLB) support (0/1) (int)
parm:            options:pcnet32 initial option setting(s) (0-15) (array of int)
parm:            full_duplex:pcnet32 full duplex setting(s) (1) (array of int)
parm:            homepna:pcnet32 mode for 79C978 boards (1\
 for HomePNA, 0 for Ethernet, default Ethernet (array of int)
root@ubuntu:/etc/init.d#
```

- depmod: The depmod command is used to generate the modules dependency file in /lib/modules/`uname -r`. The name of this file is modules.dep, and it simply contains a list of all dependencies that exist for modules on your system. As can be seen in Listing 6-7, modules normally know what dependencies they have (indicated by the depends field). The depmod command just analyzes this data and makes sure that the dependency file is up to date. There's normally no need to run this command manually because it's started automatically when your system boots. If, however, you've installed new kernel modules and you want to make sure the dependency file is up to date, run depmod manually.

The Role of the sysfs File System

When trying to understand what happens with your hardware, you need to take the sysfs file system into consideration. This file system is created dynamically by the kernel, and it is mounted in the /sys directory. In this file system you can find configuration information that relates to the way your system loads modules. Consider the /sys/devices/pci0000:00 directory shown in Listing 6-8. You'll find a subdirectory for each device that was found on the PCI bus. In the names of these subdirectories, the PCI ID is used.

Listing 6-8. *The* /sysfs *Keeps Information About Drivers that Are Used*

```
root@mel:/sys/devices/pci0000:00# ls
0000:00:00.0  0000:00:1a.1  0000:00:1c.2  0000:00:1d.2  0000:00:1f.3
0000:00:01.0  0000:00:1a.7  0000:00:1c.3  0000:00:1d.7  0000:00:1f.5
0000:00:03.0  0000:00:1b.0  0000:00:1c.4  0000:00:1e.0  power
0000:00:19.0  0000:00:1c.0  0000:00:1d.0  0000:00:1f.0  uevent
0000:00:1a.0  0000:00:1c.1  0000:00:1d.1  0000:00:1f.2
```

It's not hard to find out which device is using which PCI ID. To do this, you can use the lspci command. An example of usage of this command is shown in Listing 6-9.

Listing 6-9. *To Find Out What Device Is On What PCI ID, Use* lspci

```
root@mel:/sys/devices/pci0000:00# lspci

00:00.0 Host bridge: Intel Corporation 82P965/G965 Memory Controller Hub (rev 02)
00:01.0 PCI bridge: Intel Corporation 82P965/G965 PCI Express Root Port (rev 02)
00:03.0 Communication controller: Intel Corporation\
 82P965/G965 HECI Controller (rev 02)
00:19.0 Ethernet controller: Intel Corporation 82566DC\
```

```
Gigabit Network Connection (rev 02)
00:1a.0 USB Controller: Intel Corporation 82801H (ICH8 Family)\
 USB UHCI Controller #4 (rev 02)
00:1a.1 USB Controller: Intel Corporation 82801H (ICH8 Family)\
 USB UHCI Controller #5 (rev 02)
00:1a.7 USB Controller: Intel Corporation 82801H (ICH8 Family)\
 USB2 EHCI Controller #2 (rev 02)
00:1b.0 Audio device: Intel Corporation 82801H (ICH8 Family)\
 HD Audio Controller (rev 02)
00:1c.0 PCI bridge: Intel Corporation 82801H (ICH8 Family)\
 PCI Express Port 1 (rev 02)
00:1c.1 PCI bridge: Intel Corporation 82801H (ICH8 Family)\
 PCI Express Port 2 (rev 02)
00:1c.2 PCI bridge: Intel Corporation 82801H (ICH8 Family)\
 PCI Express Port 3 (rev 02)
00:1c.3 PCI bridge: Intel Corporation 82801H (ICH8 Family)\
 PCI Express Port 4 (rev 02)
00:1c.4 PCI bridge: Intel Corporation 82801H (ICH8 Family)\
 PCI Express Port 5 (rev 02)
00:1d.0 USB Controller: Intel Corporation 82801H (ICH8 Family)\
 USB UHCI Controller #1 (rev 02)
00:1d.1 USB Controller: Intel Corporation 82801H (ICH8 Family)\
 USB UHCI Controller #2 (rev 02)
00:1d.2 USB Controller: Intel Corporation 82801H (ICH8 Family)\
 USB UHCI Controller #3 (rev 02)
00:1d.7 USB Controller: Intel Corporation 82801H (ICH8 Family)\
 USB2 EHCI Controller #1 (rev 02)
00:1e.0 PCI bridge: Intel Corporation 82801 PCI Bridge (rev f2)
00:1f.0 ISA bridge: Intel Corporation 82801HB/HR (ICH8/R)\
 LPC Interface Controller (rev 02)
00:1f.2 IDE interface: Intel Corporation 82801H (ICH8 Family)\
 4 port SATA IDE Controller (rev 02)
00:1f.3 SMBus: Intel Corporation 82801H (ICH8 Family) SMBus Controller (rev 02)
00:1f.5 IDE interface: Intel Corporation 82801H (ICH8 Family)\
 2 port SATA IDE Controller (rev 02)
01:00.0 VGA compatible controller: nVidia Corporation GeForce 8600 GTS (rev a1)
03:00.0 IDE interface: Marvell Technology Group Ltd. 88SE6101\
 single-port PATA133 interface (rev b1)
07:02.0 Ethernet controller: Realtek Semiconductor Co., Ltd.\
 RTL-8169 Gigabit Ethernet (rev 10)
07:03.0 FireWire (IEEE 1394): Texas Instruments TSB43AB22/A\
 IEEE-1394a-2000 Controller (PHY/Link)
```

Suppose that you want to know more about the network card that uses the Intel chip set. At the top of the lspci output, you can find its PCI ID, which is 00:19.0. The complete configuration relating to this PCI ID is located in the sysfs file system inside the /sys/devices/ pci0000:00/0000:00:19.0 directory. You can now change to this directory to get an overview of the configuration that is stored for this device. You'll find a set of configuration files that will tell you exactly what the device is all about. For instance, you can find the driver file, which is a symbolic link and in this example refers to /sys/bus/pci/drivers/e1000 (see Listing 6-10). So this network board is using the e1000 driver! If you are having problems with the network board, this information might help you. For instance, you now know what driver to update to try solving its current problems.

Listing 6-10. *From the* sys *File System, You Get Information About the Drivers Your Hardware Uses*

```
root@mel:/sys/devices/pci0000:00/0000:00:19.0# ls -l
total 0
-rw-r--r-- 1 root root    4096 2008-05-19 04:06 broken_parity_status
-r--r--r-- 1 root root    4096 2008-05-19 04:03 class
-rw-r--r-- 1 root root     256 2008-05-19 04:03 config
-r--r--r-- 1 root root    4096 2008-05-19 04:03 device
lrwxrwxrwx 1 root root       0 2008-05-19 02:24 driver\
 -> ../../../bus/pci/drivers/e1000
-rw------- 1 root root    4096 2008-05-19 04:06 enable
-r--r--r-- 1 root root    4096 2008-05-19 04:03 irq
-r--r--r-- 1 root root    4096 2008-05-19 04:06 local_cpus
-r--r--r-- 1 root root    4096 2008-05-19 04:06 modalias
-rw-r--r-- 1 root root    4096 2008-05-19 04:06 msi_bus
drwxr-xr-x 3 root root       0 2008-05-19 02:24 net
drwxr-xr-x 2 root root       0 2008-05-19 04:06 power
-r--r--r-- 1 root root    4096 2008-05-19 04:03 resource
-rw------- 1 root root  131072 2008-05-19 04:06 resource0
-rw------- 1 root root    4096 2008-05-19 04:06 resource1
-rw------- 1 root root      32 2008-05-19 04:06 resource2
lrwxrwxrwx 1 root root       0 2008-05-19 02:24 subsystem -> ../../../bus/pci
-r--r--r-- 1 root root    4096 2008-05-19 04:06 subsystem_device
-r--r--r-- 1 root root    4096 2008-05-19 04:06 subsystem_vendor
-rw-r--r-- 1 root root    4096 2008-05-19 02:24 uevent
-r--r--r-- 1 root root    4096 2008-05-19 04:03 vendor
```

Installing Your Own Custom Kernel

In the early days of Linux, it was often necessary to recompile your own kernel. Today this process is almost never necessary. Here's why:

- In the old days, drivers were included in the kernel. To add a driver, you had to recompile the kernel. Today's drivers are modular; you just have to load them. In some situations, however, you need to recompile the driver, not the kernel itself.

- In early Linux versions, to tune the Linux kernel, you had to recompile it. Now you can write parameters to tune the kernel directly to the /proc file system. For instance, to tell your server that it has to do packet forwarding between its network boards, you have to write the value 1 to the /proc/sys/net/ipv4/ip_forward file. You can do that by using the echo "1" > /proc/sys/net/ipv4/ip_forward command.

- Some Linux servers are supported by external parties, which don't like you to change the kernel (you could even lose support when doing it).

The kernels that are used on Ubuntu Linux (no matter what version of the operating system you're using) are pretty close to the official Linux kernels as found on `ftp.kernel.org`. Ubuntu distinguishes between the Linux kernel (the so-called vanilla kernel) and the kernel that Ubuntu uses, which is installed automatically for the hardware platform that you are using. When using special software, such as XEN (see Chapter 13), an additional kernel may be installed as well. To use them, the GRUB boot menu will be automatically modified as necessary.

You can create your own binary kernel from the kernel sources. This is referred to as compiling the kernel, and it's a four-step procedure:

1. Install the kernel sources for your platform.

2. Configure the kernel using a command such as `make menuconfig`.

3. Build the kernel and all its modules.

4. Install the new kernel.

Installing the Kernel Source Files

In some situations—if you want to build a custom kernel, for example—the kernel sources may have to be present. This is mainly the case if you need to be able to add new functionality to the kernel, such as to compile a module for a certain piece of hardware for which you have only the source code and no compiled version. To install the kernel sources, use the following procedure:

1. Use the command `apt-cache search linux-source` to see a list of all kernel sources that are suitable for your server. See Listing 6-11 for an example.

2. Now, as root, use the `apt-get install` command to install the sources that you want to use; for instance, use `apt-get install linux-source-2.6.20`. If this command causes an error message, run `apt-get update` before you start.

3. After downloading the kernel sources, an archive file is placed in `/usr/src/`. Now you need to extract this file by using `tar -jxvf linux-source-2.6.20.tar.bz2`. This command will create a subdirectory and put the new kernel sources in it.

4. To make sure that you don't run into problems later, you now need to create a symbolic link to the directory that was just created in `/usr/src`. The name of this link is `linux`: `ln -sf linux-source-2.6.20 linux`. The kernel sources are now ready and waiting for you to do anything you want.

Listing 6-11. *Before Installing Kernel Sources, Use* apt-cache search *to Find Out What Sources Are to Be Used on Your Server*

```
root@ubuntu:/# apt-cache search linux-source
xen-source-2.6.16 - Linux kernel source for version 2.6.17 with Ubuntu patches
linux-source - Linux kernel source with Ubuntu patches
linux-source-2.6.20 - Linux kernel source for version 2.6.20 with Ubuntu patches
```

Configuring the Kernel

You should compile your own kernel if some modifications to the default kernel are required or if some new functionality has to be included in your default kernel. This latter scenario is the more realistic because the default kernel on Ubuntu Server is flexible enough to meet most situations. Because of its modularity, it will do the right things in almost any circumstances. But, in general, you would want to recompile a kernel for four reasons:

- You need access to a new type of hardware that isn't yet supported by the kernel. This option is pretty rare now that most hardware is supported by loading kernel modules dynamically.

- You need some specific feature that isn't available in the default binary kernel yet.

- You really need to strip the kernel to its essential components, removing everything that isn't absolutely necessary.

- You are running Ubuntu Server on old hardware that the default binary kernel doesn't support.

To tune a kernel, you need to create a new configuration for it, and you can choose among several methods of tuning what you do and don't need in your kernel:

- Run make config if you want to create the .config file that is needed to compile a new kernel completely by hand. The one drawback is that if you realize that you've made a mistake in the previous line after entering the next line, there's no going back.

- Use make oldconfig after installing patches to your kernel. This command makes sure that only the settings for new items are prompted for.

- Use make menuconfig if you want to set all kernel options from a menu interface.

- Use make xconfig to tune kernel options from an X-windows interface.

If you are configuring kernel settings with make menuconfig, you're working from a menu interface in which kernel functionality is divided into different sections. Each of these sections handles different categories of kernel options. For example, the File Systems section handles everything related to the available file systems, and Networking is the place to activate some obscure networking protocol.

After opening the selection of your choice, you'll get access to the individual parameters. For many of these parameters, you won't necessarily see immediately what it's used for. If so, use the Tab key to navigate to the Help button while the parameter is selected and then press Enter. You'll be provided with a description of the selected option that in most cases will be very informative as to whether this is a reasonable option to use. Most options have three possibilities. First, it can be selected with an * character, which means that the selected functionality is hard-coded in the kernel. Second, it can be selected with an M (not available for all options), which means that the selected component will be available as a kernel module. Third, you can choose not to select it at all.

Build the New Kernel

After specifying what you need and what you don't in the new kernel, you must build the new kernel. This involves running the gcc compiler to write all the changed kernel source files to one new kernel program file. To do this, you'll use the make-kpkg kernel-image command. This reads all the changes that you made to your kernel and writes the new kernel to a Debian package with the name kernel-image-<version>.deb, which is then placed in /usr/src.

Install the New Kernel

After creating the Debian package with make-kpkg kernel-image, you have to install it. Use the command dpkg -i kernel-image-<version>.deb, which not only installs the new kernel but also updates your GRUB configuration. Next, reboot your server, and the new kernel will be used.

Hardware Management with udev

When earlier kernel modules were loaded by specifying them in /etc/modules.conf and later /etc/modprobe.conf, on a recent Ubuntu Server the udev system is the most common way of loading kernel modules; in fact, udev is the central service to handle hardware initialization on your server. It's implemented as the daemon udevd, which is started at a very early stage in the boot process.

When the kernel detects a device by some event that occurs on one of the hardware busses, it tells udev about the device. After receiving a signal from the kernel that a device has been added or removed, udev initializes this device. Then it creates the proper device files in the /dev directory. This all is a major improvement in the way devices are handled on a Linux system. In older versions of Linux, a device file existed for all devices that could possibly exist. Now, a device file is created only for devices that are really present. This is the task of udev. After initializing the device, udev informs all applications about the new device through the hardware abstraction layer (HAL).

One problem with udev is that it loads at a stage when some devices have already been initialized. Think, for example, about the hard disk your system is working from. To initialize these devices properly, udev parses the sysfs file system, which is created in the directory /sys when the kernel is starting. This file system contains configuration parameters and other information about devices that have already been initialized.

As an administrator, it is useful to know that udev can be monitored using the udevmonitor tool. Listing 6-12 shows what happens in the udevmonitor when a USB stick is plugged in the system.

Listing 6-12. *In* udevmonitor *You Can See Exactly What Happens When a Device Is Connected to Your System*

```
SFO:/ # udevmonitor
udevmonitor prints the received event from the kernel [UEVENT]
and the event which udev sends out after rule processing [UDEV
]

UEVENT[1158665885.090105] add@/devices/pci0000:00/0000:00:1d.7
/usb4/4-6
UEVENT[1158665885.090506] add@/devices/pci0000:00/0000:00:1d.7
/usb4/4-6/4-6:1.0
UEVENT[1158665885.193049] add@/class/usb_device/usbdev4.5
UDEV   [1158665885.216195] add@/devices/pci0000:00/0000:00:1d.7         /usb4/4-6
UDEV   [1158665885.276188] add@/devices/pci0000:00/0000:00:1d.7         /usb4/4-6/4-➡
6:1.0
UDEV   [1158665885.414101] add@/class/usb_device/usbdev4.5
UEVENT[1158665885.500944] add@/devices/pci0000:00/0000:00:1d.7         /usb4/4-6/4-6.1
UEVENT[1158665885.500968] add@/devices/pci0000:00/0000:00:1d.7         /usb4/4-6/4-➡
6.1/4-6.1:1.0
UEVENT[1158665885.500978] add@/class/usb_device/usbdev4.6
UDEV   [1158665885.604908] add@/devices/pci0000:00/0000:00:1d.7         /usb4/4-6/4-6.1
UEVENT[1158665885.651928] add@/module/scsi_mod
UDEV   [1158665885.652919] add@/module/scsi_mod
UEVENT[1158665885.671182] add@/module/usb_storage
UDEV   [1158665885.672085] add@/module/usb_storage
UEVENT[1158665885.672652] add@/bus/usb/drivers/usb-storage
UDEV   [1158665885.673200] add@/bus/usb/drivers/usb-storage
UEVENT[1158665885.673655] add@/class/scsi_host/host0
UDEV   [1158665885.678711] add@/devices/pci0000:00/0000:00:1d.7\
              /usb4/4-➡
6/4-6.1/4-6.1:1.0
UDEV   [1158665885.854067] add@/class/usb_device/usbdev4.6
UDEV   [1158665885.984639] add@/class/scsi_host/host0
UEVENT[1158665890.682084] add@/devices/pci0000:00/0000:00:1d.7/usb4/4-     6/4-➡
6.1/4-6.1:1.0/host0/target0:0:0/0:0:0:0
UEVENT[1158665890.682108] add@/class/scsi_device/0:0:0:0
UDEV   [1158665890.858630] add@/devices/pci0000:00/0000:00:1d.7/usb4/4-6/4   -6.1/4-➡
6.1:1.0/host0/target0:0:0/0:0:0:0
UEVENT[1158665890.863245] add@/module/sd_mod
UEVENT[1158665890.863971] add@/bus/scsi/drivers/sd
UDEV   [1158665890.864828] add@/module/sd_mod
UDEV   [1158665890.865941] add@/bus/scsi/drivers/sd
UEVENT[1158665890.875674] add@/block/sda
UEVENT[1158665890.875949] add@/block/sda/sda1
```

```
UEVENT[1158665890.880180] add@/module/sg
UDEV   [1158665890.880180] add@/class/scsi_device/0:0:0:0
UEVENT[1158665890.880207] add@/class/scsi_generic/sg0
UDEV   [1158665890.906347] add@/module/sg
UDEV   [1158665890.986931] add@/class/scsi_generic/sg0
UDEV   [1158665891.084224] add@/block/sda
UDEV   [1158665891.187120] add@/block/sda/sda1
UEVENT[1158665891.413225] add@/module/fat
UDEV   [1158665891.413937] add@/module/fat
UEVENT[1158665891.427428] add@/module/vfat
UDEV   [1158665891.436849] add@/module/vfat
UEVENT[1158665891.449836] add@/module/nls_cp437
UDEV   [1158665891.451155] add@/module/nls_cp437
UEVENT[1158665891.467257] add@/module/nls_iso8859_1
UDEV   [1158665891.467795] add@/module/nls_iso8859_1
UEVENT[1158665891.489400] mount@/block/sda/sda1
UDEV   [1158665891.491809] mount@/block/sda/sda1
```

The interesting part of this rather lengthy listing is that you can see exactly how udev interacts with the /sys file system that contains information about devices. First, the kernel detects the new device. At that moment, almost nothing is known about the nature of the device; udev sees only the PCI ID for the device (you can reveal these IDs with the lspci command as well). Based on this PCI information, udev can communicate with the device and it finds out what kernel modules need to be loaded to communicate with the device. You can see this in the lines where the scsi_mod and usb_storage modules are added. Based on that information, udev finds out that an sda and sda1 are present on the device. After finding that out, it can read the file system signature and load the proper modules for that as well; in this case, these are the fat and vfat modules. Once the proper file system drivers are loaded, some support modules can be used to read the files that are on the stick. Finally, the file system on the device is mounted automatically. As you can see, working with udev makes "automagic" loading of modules a lot less magical than it was.

When working with udev, you can do some tweaking. For instance, imagine a server that has two network boards. One of those network boards would be known as eth0, whereas the other one would be available as eth1. You can use the configuration files that you'll find in the /etc/udev/rules.d directory if you want to change the device names that are associated with the network cards. In this directory, you can find files that define rules for all hardware devices that support working with rules on your server. For instance, there is the file with the name 70-persistent-net.rules. You can see the contents of this file in Listing 6-13.

Listing 6-13. *The* 70-persistent-net.rules *File Determines How Your Network Boards Are Initialized*

```
root@mel:/etc/udev/rules.d# cat 70-persistent-net.rules
# This file was automatically generated by the /lib/udev/write_net_rules
# program run by the persistent-net-generator.rules rules file.
#
# You can modify it, as long as you keep each rule on a single line.
```

```
# PCI device 0x8086:0x104b (e1000)
SUBSYSTEM=="net", ACTION=="add", DRIVERS=="?*",\
 ATTR{address}=="00:19:d1:ed:82:07", ATTR{type}=="1",\
 KERNEL=="eth*", NAME="eth0"


# PCI device 0x10ec:0x8169 (r8169)
SUBSYSTEM=="net", ACTION=="add", DRIVERS=="?*",\
 ATTR{address}=="00:0c:f6:3f:5d:bb", ATTR{type}=="1",\
 KERNEL=="eth*", NAME="eth1"
```

As you can see, this file matches the MAC addresses of your network boards with their device names. Imagine that this configuration is wrong, and you want to make sure that MAC address 00:0c:f6:3f:5d:bb is available as eth0 in the future. Just change the eth name of the device, and udev will do the rest for you. Likewise, configuration scripts are available for almost all other devices. Some of them tend to be pretty complex, though, and you shouldn't touch them if you don't have a deep understanding of shell scripting.

Working with udev has one other major advantage as well: it ensures that your storage devices can be referred to by unique names. *Unique names* are names that relate to the devices, and they don't ever change—no matter how and where the device is loaded. Normally a storage device gets its device name (/dev/sda and so on) based on the order that it is plugged into the system: the first storage device gets /dev/sda, the second storage device gets /dev/sdb, and so on. When activating a device, udev generates more than just the device name /dev/sda, and so on. For storage devices, some links are created in the directory /dev/disk. These links are in the following subdirectories and all contain a way to refer to the disk device:

- /dev/disk/by-id: This subdirectory contains information about the device based on the vendor ID and the name of the device. Because this name never changes during the life of a device, you can use these device names as an alternative to the /dev/sda devices that may change in an uncontrolled way. The only disadvantage is that the /dev/disk/by-id names are rather long.

- /dev/disk/by-path: This subdirectory contains links with a name that is based on the bus position of the device.

- /dev/disk/by-uuid: In this subdirectory, you can find links with a name that is based on the serial number (the UUID) of the device.

Because the information in /dev/disk won't change for a device the next time it is plugged in, you can create udev rules that work with that information and make sure that the same device name is always generated. The udev rules for storage devices are in /etc/udev/rules.d/60-persistent-storage.rules, in which you can create a persistent link that makes sure that a device is always initialized with the same device name. This solution can be used for disk devices and other devices as well. Just have a look at the files in /etc/udev/rules.d to see how the different device types are handled.

Summary

In this chapter, you learned how to manage and customize your server. In the first part of this chapter, you learned how to manage processes with utilities such as `top`, `ps`, and `kill`. After that, you learned how to schedule processes to run in the future. Next, you read about the boot procedure, which may help you when troubleshooting or optimizing your server's boot procedure. In the last part of this chapter, you read about the kernel and hardware management. In Chapter 7, you'll learn how to create shell scripts on Ubuntu Server.

CHAPTER 7

■ ■ ■

Running It Any Way You Like
An Introduction to Bash Shell Scripting

Knowing your way around commands on Linux is one thing. But if you really want to understand what is happening on Ubuntu Server, you must at least be able to read shell scripts. On Ubuntu Server, many things are automated with shell scripts. For example, the entire startup procedure consists of ingenious shell scripts that are tied together. As an administrator, it's very useful to know how to do some shell scripting yourself.

For these reasons, this chapter will give you an introduction to Bash shell scripting. After a short introduction, you'll learn about the most important components that you'll see in most shell scripts, such as iterations, functions, and some basic calculations. Notice that this chapter is meant to give a basic overview of the way that a shell script is organized and should help you write a simple shell script. It's not meant to be a complete tutorial that discusses all elements that can be used in a script.

Before You Even Start

If you know how to handle your Linux commands properly, you can perform magic. But imagine the magic when combining multiple Linux commands in a shell script. Shell scripting is a fine art, and you aren't going to learn it by just studying this chapter: you need to do it yourself, again and again. Expect to spend a few frustrating hours trying it without success. You should know that that is only part of the fun because you'll get better bit by bit. It takes practice, though. I hope you'll find the examples in this chapter inspiring enough to start elaborating on them, improving on them, and converting them to your own purposes.

To Script or Not to Script?

Before you start writing shell scripts, you should ask whether a shell script is really the best solution. In many cases, other approaches are available and maybe even preferable. Instead of using the Bash shell as your scripting language, you can use Perl or write a complete program in C. Each of these solutions has advantages and disadvantages.

That said, Bash offers some important advantages as a scripting language:

- Bash scripts are relatively easy to understand and to write.

- You don't have to compile a Bash script before you can start using it. The only thing you need on the computer where you will run your shell script is the shell for which the script is written. The Bash shell is omnipresent, so it's no problem performing tasks with your script on other Linux computers as well.

- A shell script is platform independent. You can run the same script on a Solaris machine, a Power PC, or an Intel machine. It just doesn't matter.

- Although Bash is almost always present, you can get even greater portability by using the Bourne shell (/bin/sh) instead of Bash. Bourne shell scripts run on any flavor of Linux and even different brands of UNIX, without the need to install anything else on your server.

The most important disadvantage of using Bash to create your script, however, is that it is relatively slow. It's slow because the shell always has to interpret the commands that it finds in the script before it can do its job. For contrast, a C program is compiled code, optimized to do its work on the hardware of your computer directly and therefore is much faster. Of course, it's also much more difficult to create such a program.

What Shell?

Many shells are available for Linux. When writing a shell script, you should be aware of that and choose the best shell for your script. A script written for one shell will not necessarily run on another. Bash is the best choice to write shell scripts on Linux. Bash is compatible with the UNIX Bourne shell /bin/sh, which has been used on UNIX since the 1970s. The good thing about that compatibility is that a script that was written to run on /bin/sh will work on Bash as well. However, the opposite is not necessarily true because many new features have been added to Bash that don't exist in the traditional UNIX Bourne shell.

On Ubuntu, dash is used as the default shell. You can see this in most system scripts that call #!/bin/sh, which is a link to /bin/dash, on the first line of the script. However, because I have had problems with dash and scripting on several occasions, I recommend using Bash for scripting. You can ensure that Bash is used by including #!/bin/bash on the first line of each script you create.

You'll likely occasionally encounter Linux shells other than Bash or dash. The most important of these includes the Korn shell (/bin/ksh), which is the default shell on Sun Microsystems' Solaris. An open source derivative of that shell is available as the Public Domain Korn Shell /bin/pdksh. Another popular shell is the C shell, which on Linux exists as /bin/tcsh. The C shell is especially popular among C programmers because it has a scripting language that closely resembles the C programming language. You'll sometimes encounter C shell users in a Linux environment. The Korn shell, however, is not used often in Linux environments because almost all its important features are also offered by Bash.

Both the Korn shell and the C shell are incompatible with Bash, and this incompatibility could prevent you from running a C shell script in a Bash environment. However, there is a solution, and that's to include the so-called shebang in your shell script. This is an indicator of the program that must be used when executing the script. The shebang consists of the pound sign (#), followed by an exclamation mark, followed by the name of the required command interpreter. If the program that is referred to by the shebang is present on your system, the script will run, no matter what shell environment you're currently in as a user. Listing 7-1 shows a script that starts with a shebang.

Listing 7-1. *Shell Scripts Should Always Start with the Shebang*

```
#!/bin/bash
#
# myscript [filename]
#
# Use this script to....
```

Basic Elements of a Shell Script

Some elements should occur in all shell scripts. First, as you've just read, every shell script should start with the shebang. After this, it's a good idea to add some comment lines to explain what the script is for. A comment line starts with a pound sign, which ensures that the line is not interpreted by the shell. Of course, how you create your scripts is entirely up to you, but starting every script with some comment that explains how to use the script will make your scripts much easier to use. It's really a matter of perspective: you know exactly what you're doing at the moment you're writing the script, but months or years later you might have forgotten what your shell script is all about.

The first line in a good comment shows the exact syntax to be used for launching it. After the syntax line, it's normally a good idea to explain in two or three lines what exactly your script is doing. Such an explanation makes it much easier for others to use your script the right way. If the script starts growing, you might even add comments at other places in the script. It's not a bad idea to start every new chunk of code with a short comment, just to explain what it's doing. One day you'll be glad that you took the few extra seconds to add a comment or two.

Apart from the comments, your script naturally includes some commands. All legal commands can be used, and you can invoke Bash internal commands as well as work with external commands. An internal command is loaded into memory with Bash and therefore can execute very fast. An external command is a command that is somewhere on disk, and this is its main disadvantage: it needs to be loaded first and that takes time. Listing 7-2 is a shell script that although rather simple, still includes all the basic elements.

Listing 7-2. *Example of a Simple Shell Script That Contains All Basic Elements*

```
#!/bin/bash
#
# This is just a friendly script. It echoes "Hello World" to the person
# who runs it.
#
# Usage: hello
#
echo 'Hello World!'
exit 0
```

In the example script, you can see some things happening. After the comment, the echo command is used to greet the user who runs the script. Notice that the text to be echoed to the screen is placed between single quotes. These are also called "strong quotes," and they make sure that the shell does not actually interpret anything that appears between them. In this example, it's a good idea to use them because the exclamation mark has a special meaning for the shell.

Also note that after the successful termination of the script, the exit 0 command is used. This command generates the so-called exit status of the script; it tells the parent shell whether the script executed successfully. Normally, the exit status 0 is used to indicate that everything went well. If some problems were encountered executing the script, an exit status value of 1 can be used. Any other exit status can be used at the discretion of the programmer. Using more than just 0 and 1 as values for exit status can make troubleshooting much easier. Using an exit status is important in more complex shell scripts because you can decide that something else needs to happen based on the success or failure of your script.

■Tip Did you know that you can request the exit status of the last command executed by the shell? Typing **echo $?** displays the exit status of that command as a numerical value.

Making It Executable

Now that you created your shell script, it's time to do something with it. You can execute it with several different options:

- Activate it as an argument of your shell.

- "Source" the script.

- Make it executable and run it.

If you just need to check that the script works, the easiest way to test it is as a shell argument. To do this, you have to start a new shell that starts the script for you. If the name of your script is hello, you can start the script with the bash hello command.

This method starts a subshell and executes the script from there. If a variable is set in this subshell, it's available within that subshell only, not in the parent shell. If you want to set a variable from a shell script and make sure that that variable is available in the parent shell as well, use the source command to run the shell script. You'll learn more about variables later in "Changing Variables."

■Tip Want a variable that's set in a script to be available in all subshells? Use the export command when defining the variable. However, there's no way to define a variable in a subshell that will also be set in the parent shell.

The second way to execute a script is with the source command. This command is referred to by entering a dot, followed by a space and the name of the script. For example, the script with the name hello can be started with . hello.

The important difference with the source command is that no subshell is started, and the script runs directly from the current shell. The result is that all variables that are defined when running the script are also available after running the script. This can be both useful and confusing. The source method is often used to include another script in a generic script. In this other script, for example, some system variables are set. Listing 7-3 shows how this works in the script that starts networking: /etc/init.d/networking. As you can see in about the approximate middle of the listing, the . /lib/lsb/init-functions command is included to set some generic functions that should be used in this script.

Listing 7-3. *The Sourcing Method Is Used to Include Scripts Containing Variables in Many Startup Scripts*

```
#!/bin/sh -e
### BEGIN INIT INFO
# Provides:          networking
# Required-Start:    mountkernfs ifupdown $local_fs
# Required-Stop:     ifupdown $local_fs
# Default-Start:     S
# Default-Stop:      0 6
### END INIT INFO


PATH="/usr/local/sbin:/usr/local/bin:/sbin:/bin:/usr/sbin:/usr/bin"


[ -x /sbin/ifup ] || exit 0


. /lib/lsb/init-functions



case "$1" in
start)
        log_action_begin_msg "Configuring network interfaces"
        type usplash_write >/dev/null 2>/dev/null && usplash_write "TIMEOUT 120"
 || true
        if [ "$VERBOSE" != no ]; then
            if ifup -a; then
networking
```

The last and possibly the most frequently used method to run a script is to make it an executable first. Do this by adding the execute permission to your script, as in the following command:

```
chmod +x hello
```

Next, you can simply run the script:

```
./hello
```

Notice that in this example the script is executed as `./hello`, not just `hello` (assuming that the script is in the current directory). This is because you need to indicate that the script must run from the current directory. As a default security feature, no Linux shell looks for executable code in the current directory. Excluding the current directory from the search path ensures that a user or an administrator who runs a command always runs the proper command from the search path, not some rogue command that was installed in the current directory. Without the `./`, Bash would search for `hello` in its current PATH setting and would probably not find it.

■**Note** The shell PATH variable is used to specify a list of directories that should always be searched for executable files. You can see its contents by using the `echo $PATH` command.

One last remark before diving into real scripting: always be careful about what you name your script and try to avoid names that already exist. For example, you might be tempted to use `test` as the name of a test script. This would, however, conflict with the `test` command that's installed on all Linux systems by default. Want to see whether the name of your script is already used by some other command? Use the `which` command to search all directories set in the PATH variable for a binary with the name you've entered. Listing 7-4 shows the result of this command issued for the `test` command.

Listing 7-4. *Using* which *to Check Whether a Command with a Given Name Already Exists*

```
root@RNA:/# which test
/usr/bin/test
```

Making a Script Interactive

It's cool if your script can execute a list of commands, but it'll be much better if you can make it interactive. This way, the script can ask a user for input, and the user decides how the script should be run. To make a script interactive, use the `read` command followed by the name of a variable. This variable is used as a label to the input of the user, but the great thing is that you can use it later in the script to check exactly what the user entered. Listing 7-5 is an example of an interactive script. You'll also learn a new method to display script output on the screen.

Listing 7-5. *Making Your Script Interactive*

```
#!/bin/bash
#
# Send a message to the world
#
# Usage: ./hello

cat << EOF
Tell us, what message do you want to tell the world today? Don't hesitate, anything
```

```
is allowed, just tell me what friendly message you want to enter.
EOF

read MESSAGE
echo "$MESSAGE"
```

In the script of Listing 7-5, the first new item that you see is the so-called here document, which is an alternative way to echo text to the user's screen. It's particularly useful if you want to display some lines of text on the user's screen. The advantage of using this construction is that you open it by using cat << followed by anything. In this example, I used EOF (end of file), but if you want to use "mydoggie" instead, that's fine as well. Just make sure that the opening statement for the here document is on a line of its own. Next, enter all the text you want to enter and close the here document by referring to the text that you entered to open the here document on a single line. In the example from Listing 7-5, this means that you just put EOF on a line by itself.

After the here document, the read command asks the user for some input. The input is placed in the temporary variable MESSAGE, which is echoed in the last line of the script. Also notice that no $ character is required to define the variable, but one is necessary to display the contents of the variable. Otherwise, echo would have no way of knowing that you are referring to a variable. One more remark about the use and definition of variables: I like to write them all uppercase. Why? It makes a script more readable. Listing 7-6 shows what exactly this script will do when you run it.

Listing 7-6. *Running the Interactive Script*

```
SFO:~/bin # ./hello
Tell us, what message do you want to pass to the world today? Don't hesitate,
anything is allowed, just tell me what friendly message you want to enter
Good morning folks
Good morning folks
```

Working with Arguments

Although making a script interactive is a good way to get user input, it does have a disadvantage: it requires a user who provides input to your script. This is not ideal because many scripts are created to run automatically. Instead, such scripts can be started with specific parameters that are specified as arguments when the script is launched. For example, you would run the hello script from the previous section, just as ./hello hi to let it output the text hi. In this example, hi is the argument used by this script.

To work with arguments that are provided when activating the script, you need names for them. The first argument is named $1, the second argument is $2, and so forth, up to $9 ($10 would be interpreted as $1, followed by a 0). So you're basically limited to the use of only nine arguments. If you need more than nine, use $@ as explained next in the "Referring to Arguments" section. The name of the script itself is referred to by using $0. Listing 7-7 is a simple example of a script that can work with arguments.

Listing 7-7. *Working with Arguments*

```
#!/bin/bash
#
# Script that allows you to greet someone
# Usage: ./hello [name]

echo "Hello $1, how are you today"
```

Let's imagine that you activate this script by entering ./hello linda on the command line. This means that when calling the script, $1 is filled with the value linda. When called in the actual code line, the script will therefore echo "Hello linda, how are you today" on the screen of the user. When working with arguments, you must be aware that every single word you enter is interpreted as a separate argument. You can see this if you execute the example script by entering ./hello mister president. As the result, only the text "Hello mister, how are you today" is displayed. This is because your script has no definition for $2.

Do you want to make sure that cases like this are handled correctly? Use the construction $* to denote an unknown number of arguments. So, to handle any number of arguments, without knowing beforehand how many arguments are going to be used, edit the script in Listing 7-7, as shown in Listing 7-8.

Listing 7-8. *Handling an Unknown Number of Arguments*

```
#!/bin/bash
#
# Script that allows you to greet one or more persons
# Usage: ./hello [name1] [name2] ... [namen]
echo "Hello $*, how are you today"
```

Referring to Arguments

In Listing 7-8, you saw that $* is used to refer to a number of arguments that is unknown at the time of running the script. And you can refer to other arguments that you might be using in other ways:

- $*: Refers to all arguments, treating them as one string

- $@: Refers to all arguments, treating each argument as a string on its own

- $#: Shows how many arguments were used when first running the script

Sounds complicated, doesn't it? Let's have a look at an example to show how it works. In Listing 7-9, I'm using the for i in ... do ... done construction to show the difference between $* and $@. I'll explain in more detail later how the for i in construction works, but all you have to know for now is that it looks at its arguments and performs an action for every element that it sees.

Listing 7-9. *Showing the Difference Between* $*$ *and* $@

```
#!/bin/bash
# Script that shows the difference between $* and $@
# Usage: ./showdifference [arguments]

echo "\$* shows $*"
echo "\$# shows $#"
echo "\$@ shows $@"
echo "The name of the script itself is $0"

echo showing the interpretation of \$*
for i in "$*"
do
     echo $i
done

echo showing the interpretation of \$@
for i in "$@"
do
     echo $i
done
```

Listing 7-10 shows what this script does when activated.

Listing 7-10. *Showing the Working of the Script from Listing 7-9*

```
root@RNA:~/scripts# ./showdifference a b c d e f
$* Shows a b c d e f
$# shows 6
$@ shows a b c d e f
The name of the script is ./showdifference
showing the interpretation of $*
a b c d e f
showing the interpretation of $@
a
b
c
d
e
f
root@RNA:~/scripts#
```

Now let's try to understand all this. In the first part of the script (the lines that start with echo), we show the result of using the different items when running this script. You may notice that the lines start with a / before the $. This / makes sure that the $ is not interpreted the first time. The second time the same $ is referred to, I'm not using the / because we actually want to see a real result.

Next, in the for i in ... loops a temporary variable with the name i is defined. You can understand the use of this variable as "for each element in ... ," whereby every element in turn is temporarily put in the variable i. Now, for every element encountered in $* in the first loop, the command echo $i is executed. The result of this is that the name of the element (which is an argument in this script) is echoed to the screen.

The difference between $* and $@ becomes clear from this example. Where just one element is seen in the first loop, every argument is treated as an element on its own in the loop that uses $@. So, to make sure that from a range of arguments every argument is treated as an argument on its own, use $@.

Working with Variables

Variables play an important role in creating a good working shell script. In the previous section, you learned how variables are used to store the arguments that are entered when activating a script. And you can define variables in other ways as well. This section explores more of the possibilities when working with variables.

Command Substitution

One way of handling variables automatically is to use command substitution, which is a technique that puts the result of a command in a variable that can be used in a script (or on the command line). This technique is especially useful if you need to work with information that changes often or automatically, such as the version of the kernel that you're using. To use command substitution, put the command you want to use between backquotes; for example echo `whoami` would put the result of the whoami command in the echo command. An alternative way of writing this is echo $(whoami). Notice that there's really no difference between these two.

An example could be a script that refers to the directory in which kernel modules are installed. The name of this directory changes with every kernel update that is installed, so it's not really a good idea to use hard references to this directory in your scripts. Command substitution is an ideal solution.

The name of the current kernel version can be displayed with the uname -r command. So, instead of referring to the directory /lib/modules/2.6.20 (or whatever the name of the module directory for the currently loaded kernel is), you can refer to /lib/modules/`uname -r` instead. The example script in Listing 7-11 shows how command substitution is used.

Listing 7-11. *Example of Command Substitution*

```
#!/bin/bash
#
# Copy a kernel module to the appropriate directory
# Usage: ./modcop

echo Enter the full path name of the file that you want to copy
read FILE
cp $FILE /lib/modules/`uname -r`
```

In this example, the script first asks the user to input the complete name of the file that should be copied. Next, it will copy the file to the directory where the current kernel stores its kernel modules.

Changing Variables

Sometimes the name of a variable needs to be changed. To do this, you need to define a new variable that's based on the value of an old variable. This may be useful, for example, to change the argument that a user has entered when starting the script. When changing a variable, you should be aware that you can redefine all variables except arguments that were entered when starting the script ($1, $2, and so on). So, if you need to do something to the value that is assigned to an argument, put the current value of the argument in a new variable and change it. The example in Listing 7-12 shows how to put the result of an existing variable in a new variable.

Listing 7-12. *Assigning the Value of Existing Variables to New Variables*

```
#!/bin/bash
#
# Greet the user in a friendly way
# Usage: ./hello <firstname> <surname>

NAME="$1 $2"
echo hello $NAME
```

If, for example, a user named Linda Thomson starts the script by using the ./hello Linda Thomson command, the script will output "hello Linda Thomson" to the screen. Put in this way, it is not extremely useful to put the current values of $1 and $2 in a new variable called NAME. If, however, you want to change the value currently assigned to a variable, it can be very useful to assign the value of old variables to a temporary new variable. The next section makes this clear.

Substitution Operators

Within a script, it may be important to check whether a variable really has a value assigned to it before the script continues. To do this, Bash offers *substitution operators*. By using substitution operators, you can assign a default value if a variable doesn't have a value currently assigned, and much more. Table 7-1 provides an overview of the substitution operators with a short explanation of their use.

Table 7-1. *Substitution Operators*

Operator	Use
${parameter:-value}	Show value if parameter is not defined.
${parameter=value}	Assign value to parameter if parameter does not exist at all. This operator does nothing if parameter exists, but doesn't have a value.
${parameter:=value}	Assign value if parameter currently has no value, or if parameter doesn't exist at all.

Continued

Table 7-1. *Continued*

Operator	Use
${parameter:?value}	Show a message that is defined as value if parameter doesn't exist or is empty. Using this construction will force the shell script to be aborted immediately.
${parameter:+value}	If parameter does have a value, the value is displayed. If it doesn't have a value, nothing happens.

Substitution operators can be hard to understand. To make it easier to see how they work, Listing 7-13 provides some examples. In all these examples, something happens to the $BLAH variable. You'll see that the result of the given command is different depending on the substitution operator that's used. To make it easier to discuss what happens, I added line numbers to the listing. Notice that when trying this yourself, you should omit the line numbers.

Listing 7-13. *Using Substitution Operators*

```
1. sander@linux %> echo $BLAH
2.
3. sander@linux %> echo ${BLAH:-variable is empty}
4 variable is empty
5. sander@linux %> echo $BLAH
6.
7. sander@linux %> echo ${BLAH=value}
8. value
9. sander@linux %> echo $BLAH
10. value
11. sander@linux %> BLAH=
12. sander@linux %> echo ${BLAH=value}
13.
14. sander@linux %> echo ${BLAH:=value}
15. value
16. sander@linux %> echo $BLAH
17. value
18. sander@linux %> echo ${BLAH:+sometext}
19. sometext
```

The example of Listing 7-13 starts with the echo $BLAH command, which reads the variable BLAH and shows its current value. Because BLAH doesn't have a value yet, nothing is shown in line 2. Next, a message is defined in line 3 that should be displayed if BLAH is empty. As you can see, the message is displayed in line 4. However, this doesn't assign a value to BLAH, which you see in lines 5 and 6 where the current value of BLAH is asked again. In line 7, BLAH finally gets a value, which is displayed in line 8. The shell remembers the new value of BLAH, which you can see in lines 9 and 10 where the value of BLAH is referred to and displayed. In line 11, BLAH is redefined but it gets a null value. The variable still exists; it just has no value here. This is demonstrated when echo ${BLAH=value} is used in line 12; because BLAH has a null value at that moment, no new value is assigned. Next, the construction echo ${BLAH:=value} is used to assign a new value to BLAH. The fact that BLAH really gets a value from this is shown in lines 16 and 17. Finally, the construction in line 18 is used to display sometext if BLAH currently does have a value. Notice that this doesn't change anything to the value that is assigned to BLAH at that moment; sometext just indicates that it has a value and that's all.

Pattern-Matching Operators

You've just seen how substitution operators can be used to do something if a variable does not have a value. You can consider them a rather primitive way of handling errors in your script. A pattern-matching operator can be used to search for a pattern in a variable and modify the variable if that pattern is found. This can be very useful because it allows you to define a variable exactly the way you want. For example, think of the situation in which a user enters a complete pathname of a file, but only the name of the file itself (without the path) is needed in your script.

The pattern-matching operator is the way to change this. Pattern-matching operators allow you to remove part of a variable automatically. Listing 7-14 is an example of a script that works with pattern-matching operators.

Listing 7-14. *Working with Pattern-Matching Operators*

```
#!/bin/bash
#
# script that extracts the file name from a file name that includes the complete path
# usage: stripit <complete file name>

filename=${1##*/}
echo "The name of the file is $filename"
```

When executed, the script shows the following result:

```
sander@linux %> ./stripit /bin/bash
the name of the file is bash
```

Pattern-matching operators always try to locate a given string. In this case, the string is */. In other words, the pattern-matching operator searches for a /, preceded by another character. In this pattern-matching operator, ## is used to search for the longest match of the provided string, starting from the beginning of the string. So, the pattern-matching operator searches for the last / that occurs in the string and removes it and everything that precedes the / as well. You might ask how the script comes to remove everything in front of the /. It's because the pattern-matching operator refers to */ and not to /. You can confirm this by running the script with /bin/bash/ as an argument. In this case, the pattern that's searched for is in the last position of the string, and the pattern-matching operator removes everything.

This example explains the use of the pattern-matching operator that looks for the longest match. By using a single #, you can let the pattern-matching operator look for the shortest match, again starting from the beginning of the string. If, for example, the script in Listing 7-14 used filename=${1#*/}, the pattern-matching operator would look for the first / in the complete file name and remove that and everything before it.

You should realize that in these examples the * is important. The pattern-matching operator ${1#*/} removes the first / found and anything in front of it. The pattern-matching operator ${1#/} removes the first / in $1 only if the value of $1 starts with a /. However, if there's anything before the /, the operator will not know what to do.

These examples showed how a pattern-matching operator is used to start searching from the beginning of a string. You can start searching from the end of the string as well. To do so, a % is used instead of a #. This % refers to the shortest match of the pattern, and %% refers to its longest match. The script in Listing 7-15 shows how this works.

Listing 7-15. *Using Pattern-Matching Operators to Start Searching at the End of a String*

```
#!/bin/bash
#
# script that isolates the directory name from a complete file name
# usage: stripdir <complete file name>

dirname=${1%%/*}
echo "The directory name is $dirname"
```

While executing, you'll see that this script has a problem:

```
sander@linux %> ./stripdir /bin/bash
The directory name is
```

As you can see, the script does its work somewhat too enthusiastically and removes everything. Fortunately, this problem can be solved by first using a pattern-matching operator that removes the / from the start of the complete file name (but only if that / is provided) and then removing everything following the first / in the complete file name. The example in Listing 7-16 shows how this is done.

Listing 7-16. *Fixing the Example from Listing 7-15*

```
#!/bin/bash
#
# script that isolates the directory name from a complete file name
# usage: stripdir <complete file name>

dirname=${1#/}
dirname=${1%%/*}
echo "The directory name is $dirname"
```

As you can see, the problem is solved by using ${1#/}. This construction starts searching from the beginning of the file name to a /. Because no * is used here, it looks for a / only at the very first position of the file name and does nothing if the string starts with anything else. If it finds a /, it removes it. So, if a user enters usr/bin/passwd instead of /usr/bin/passwd, the ${1#/} construction does nothing at all. In the line after that, the variable dirname is defined again to do its work on the result of its first definition in the preceding line. This line does the real work and looks for the pattern /*, starting at the end of the file name. This makes sure that everything after the first / in the file name is removed and that only the name of the top-level directory is echoed. Of course, you can easily edit this script to display the complete path of the file: just use dirname=${dirname%/*} instead.

So, to make sure that you are comfortable with pattern-matching operators, the script in Listing 7-17 gives another example. This time, though, the example does not work with a file name, but with a random text string.

Listing 7-17. *Another Example with Pattern Matching*

```
#!/bin/bash
#
# script that extracts the file name from a file name that includes the complete path
# usage: stripit <complete file name>

BLAH=babarabaraba
echo BLAH is $BLAH
echo 'The result of ##ba is '${BLAH##*ba}
echo 'The result of #ba is '${BLAH#*ba}
echo 'The result of %%ba is '${BLAH%ba*}
echo 'The result of %ba is '${BLAH%%ba*}
```

When running it, the script gives the result shown in Listing 7-18.

Listing 7-18. *The Result of the Script in Listing 7-17*

```
root@RNA:~/scripts# ./pmex
BLAH is babarabaraba
The result of ##ba is
The result of #ba is barabaraba
The result of %%ba is babarabara
The result of %ba is
root@RNA:~/scripts#
```

Performing Calculations in Scripts

Bash offers some options that allow you to perform calculations from scripts. Of course, you're not likely to use them as a replacement for your spreadsheet program, but performing simple calculations from Bash can be useful. For example, you can use calculation options to execute a command a number of times or to make sure that a counter is incremented when a command executes successfully. The script in Listing 7-19 provides an example of how counters can be used.

Listing 7-19. *Using a Counter in a Script*

```
#!/bin/bash
counter=1
while true
do
      counter=$((counter + 1))
      echo counter is set to $counter
done
```

As you can see, this script uses a construction with while (which is covered in more detail in the "Using while" section). The construction is used to execute a command as long as a given condition is met. In this example, the condition is simple: you must be able to execute the true command successfully. This won't be a problem: the name of the command is true because it always executes successfully. That is, true always gives an exit status of 0, which tells the shell that it has executed with success, just like the false command always gives the exit status of 1.

What has to happen if the condition is met is specified between the do and done. First, the line counter=$((counter + 1)) takes the current value of the variable counter (which is set in the beginning of the script) and increments that by 1. Next, the value of the variable counter is displayed with the line echo counter is set to $counter. Once that's happened, the condition is checked again and the command is executed again as well. The result of this script will be that you see a list of numbers on your screen that's updated very quickly. Does it go too fast? Just add a line with the command sleep 1 in the loop. Now the calculation of the new value of counter is performed only once per second.

Although the previous example explains how a simple calculation can be performed from a script, it isn't very useful. Listing 7-20 provides a more useful one. I once had to test the durability of USB sticks for a computer magazine. As you have probably heard, some people think that the life of flash storage is limited. After a given number of writes, according to some people, the stick dies. Such a claim called for a test, which can be performed through the following shell script with the name killstick:

Listing 7-20. *Script to Test USB Sticks*

```
#!/bin/bash
#
# Script to test USB sticks
#
# usage: killstick <mountpoint of the stick>
#
counter=0
while cp /1MBfile $1
do
    sync
    rm -rf $1/1MBfile
    sync
    counter=$((counter + 1))
    echo Counter is now set to $counter
done
echo Your stick is now non-functional
```

The script again starts with a little explanation of how it works. To run this script, you first need to mount the stick on a certain mount point, and this mount point needs to be declared by specifying it as an argument to the script. Next, a while loop is started. The command that needs to execute successfully is cp /1MBfile $1. You can use this script on a stick of any size, but before starting it, make sure that all the available disk space on the stick is used—with the exception of 1 MB. Next, create a file with a size of 1 MB (or just a little smaller). This way you'll make sure that the controller of the stick isn't playing any tricks on you, and the write always occurs at the same spot.

As long as the file copy is successful, the commands in the do loop are executed. First, the file is synchronized to the stick using the sync command to make sure that it isn't just kept somewhere in memory. Next, it's immediately removed again, and this removal is synchronized to the physical storage media. Finally, the calculation is used again to increment the counter variable by 1. This continues as long as the file can be copied successfully. When copying fails, the while loop is terminated and the echo Your stick is now non-functional command is displayed, thus allowing you to know exactly how often the file could be copied to the stick.

> **■Note** Would you like to know how many writes it takes to kill a stick completely? As it turns out, flash memory has improved enormously over the last few years, and you can expect the memory chip to support at least 100,000 writes. In many cases, however, more than 1,000,000 writes can be performed without any problem.

So far, we've dealt with only one method to do script calculations, but you have other options as well. First, you can use the external expr command to perform any kind of calculation. For example, the following line produces the result of 1 + 2:

```
sum=`expr 1 + 2`; echo $sum
```

As you can see, a variable with the name sum is defined, and this variable gets the result of the command expr 1 + 2 by using command substitution. A semicolon is then used to indicate that what follows is a new command. After the semicolon, the command echo $sum shows the result of the calculation.

The expr command can work with addition, and other types of calculation are supported as well. Table 7-2 summarizes the options.

Table 7-2. expr *Operators*

Operator	Meaning
+	Addition (1 + 1 = 2)
-	Subtraction (10 – 2 = 8)
/	Division (10 / 2 = 5)
*	Multiplication (3 * 3 = 9)
%	Modulus—calculates the remainder after division; this works because expr can handle integers only (11 % 3 = 2)

When working with these options, you'll see that they all work fine with the exception of the multiplication operator *. Using this operator results in a syntax error:

```
linux: ~> expr 2 * 2
expr: syntax error
```

This seems curious, but can be easily explained. The * has a special meaning for the shell, as in ls -l *. When the shell parses the command line, it interprets the * (you don't want it to do that here). To indicate that the shell shouldn't touch it, you have to escape it. Therefore, change the command as follows:

```
expr 2 \* 2
```

Alternatively, you could have escaped the * with single quotes by using the following command:

```
expr 2 '*' 2
```

Another way to perform some calculations is to use the internal command let. Just the fact that let is internal makes it a better solution than the external command expr: it can be loaded from memory directly and doesn't have to come all the way from your computer's hard drive. Using let, you can make your calculation and apply the result directly to a variable, as in the following example:

```
let x="1 + 2"
```

The result of the calculation in this example is stored in the variable x. The disadvantage of working this way is that let has no option to display the result directly as can be done when using expr. For use in a script, however, it offers excellent capabilities. Listing 7-21 shows a script in which let is used to perform calculations.

Listing 7-21. *Performing Calculations with* let

```
#!/bin/bash
#
# usage: calc $1 $2 $3
# $1 is the first number
# $2 is the operator
# $3 is the second number
let x="$1 $2 $3"
echo $x
```

If you think that we've now covered all methods to perform calculations in a shell script, you're wrong. Listing 7-22 shows another method that you can use.

Listing 7-22. *Another Way to Calculate in a Bash Shell Script*

```
#!/bin/bash
#
# usage: calc $1 $2 $3
# $1 is the first number
# $2 is the operator
# $3 is the second number
x=$(($1 $2 $3))
echo $x
```

You saw this construction when you read about the script that increases the value of the variable counter. Note that the double pair of parentheses can be replaced by one pair of square brackets instead, assuming that the preceding $ is present.

Using Flow Control

Up until now, you haven't read much about the way in which the execution of commands can be made conditional. The technique for enabling this in shell scripts is known as flow control. Bash offers many options to use flow control in scripts:

- if: Use if to execute commands only if certain conditions were met. To customize the working of if some more, you can use else to indicate what should happen if the condition isn't met.

- case: Use case to work with options. This allows the user to further specify the working of the command when he runs it.

- for: This construction is used to run a command for a given number of items. For example, you can use for to do something for every file in a specified directory.

- while: Use while as long as the specified condition is met. For example, this construction can be very useful to check whether a certain host is reachable or to monitor the activity of a process.

- until: This is the opposite of while. Use until to run a command until a certain condition has been met.

The following subsections cover flow control in more detail. Before going into these details, however, you can first read about the test command. This command is used to perform many checks to see, for example, whether a file exists or whether a variable has a value. Table 7-3 shows some of the more common test options. For a complete overview, consult its man page.

Table 7-3. *Common Options for the* test *Command*

Option	Use
test -e $1	Checks if $1 is a file, without looking at what particular kind of file it is.
test -f $1	Checks if $1 is a regular file and not (for example) a device file, a directory, or an executable file.
test -d $1	Checks if $1 is a directory.
test -x $1	Checks if $1 is an executable file. Note that you can test for other permissions as well. For example, -g would check to see if the SGID permission (see Chapter 5) is set.
test $1 -nt $2	Controls if $1 is newer than $2.
test $1 -ot $2	Controls if $1 is older than $2.
test $1 -ef $2	Checks if $1 and $2 both refer to the same inode. This is the case if one is a hard link to the other (see Chapter 4 for more on inodes).
test $1 -eq $2	Sees if the integers $1 and $2 are equal.

Continued

Table 7-3. *Continued*

Option	Use
test $1 -ne $2	Checks if the integers $1 and $2 are not equal.
test $1 -gt $2	Gives true if integer $1 is greater than integer $2.
test S1 -lt $2	Gives true if integer $1 is less than integer $2.
test $1 -ge $2	Sees if integer $1 is greater than or equal to integer $2.
test $1 -le $2	Checks if integer $1 is less than or equal to integer $2.
test -z $1	Checks if $1 is empty. This is a very useful construction to find out if a variable has been defined.
test $1	Gives the exit status 0 if $1 is defined.
test $1=$2	Checks if the strings $1 and $2 are the same. This is most useful to compare the value of two variables.
test $1 != $2	Sees if the strings $1 and $2 are not equal to each other. You can use ! with all other tests to check for the negation of the statement.

You can use the test command in two ways. First, you can write the complete command, as in test -f $1. This command, however, can be rewritten as [-f $1]. Most of the time you'll see the latter option only because people who write shell scripts like to work as efficiently as possible.

Using if...then...else

Possibly the classic example of flow control consists of constructions that use if...then... else. Especially if used in conjunction with the test command, this construction offers various interesting possibilities. You can use it to find out whether a file exists, if a variable currently has a value, and much more. Listing 7-23 provides an example of a construction with if...then...else that can be used in a shell script.

Listing 7-23. *Using* if *to Perform a Basic Check*

```
#!/bin/bash
if [ -z $1 ]
then
    echo You have to provide an argument with this command
    exit 1
fi

echo the argument is $1
```

The simple check from the Listing 7-23 example is used to see if the user who started your script provided an argument. If he or she didn't, the code in the if loop becomes active, in which case it displays the message that the user needs to provide an argument and then terminates the script. If an argument has been provided, the commands within the loop aren't executed, and the script will run the line echo the argument is $1, and in this case echo the argument to the user's screen.

Also notice how the syntax of the if construction is organized. First, you have to open it with if. Then, separated on a new line (or with a semicolon), then is used. Finally, the if loop is closed with an fi statement. Make sure that all those ingredients are used all the time or your loop won't work.

■**Note** You can use a semicolon as a separator between two commands. So ls; who would first execute the command ls and then the command who.

The example in Listing 7-23 is rather simple, and it's also possible to make if loops more complex and have them test for more than one condition. To do this, use else or elif. By using else within the loop, you can make sure that something happens if the condition is met, but it allows you to check another condition if the condition is not met. You can even use else in conjunction with if (elif) to open a new loop if the first condition isn't met. Listing 7-24 is an example of the latter construction.

Listing 7-24. *Nesting* if *Loops*

```
if [ -f $1 ]
then
     echo "$1 is a file"
elif [ -d $1 ]
     echo "$1 is a directory"
else
     echo "I don't know what \$1 is"
fi
```

In this example, the argument that was entered when running the script is checked. If it is a file (if [-f $1]), the script tells the user that. If it isn't a file, the part under elif is executed, which basically opens a second loop. In this second loop, the first test performed is to see if $1 is perhaps a directory. Notice that this second part of the loop becomes active only if $1 is not a file. If $1 isn't a directory either, the part after else is run, and the script reports that it has no idea what $1 is. Notice that for this entire construction, only one fi is needed to close the loop.

You should know that if .. then ... else constructions are used in two different ways. You can write out the complete construction as in the previous examples, or you can use constructions that use && and ||. These so-called separators are used to separate two commands and establish a conditional relationship between them. If && is used, the second command is executed only if the first command is executed successfully (in other words, if the first command is true). If || is used, the second command is executed only if the first command isn't true. So, with one line of code, you can find out if $1 is a file and echo a message if it is:

```
[ -f $1 ] && echo $1 is a file
```

Note that this can be rewritten differently as well:

```
[ ! -f $1 ] || echo $1 is a file
```

■**Note** This example only works as a part of a complete shell script. Listing 7-25 shows how the example from Listing 7-24 is rewritten if you want to use this syntax.

In case you don't quite follow what is happening in the second example: it performs a test to see if $1 is not a file. (The ! is used to test if something is not the case.) Only if the test fails (which is the case if $1 is indeed a file), it executes the part after the || and echoes that $1 is a file. Let's have a look (see Listing 7-25) at how you can rewrite the script from Listing 7-24 with the && and || tests.

Listing 7-25. *The Example from Listing 7-24 Rewritten with* && *and* ||

```
([ -z $1 ] && echo please provide an argument; exit 1) || (([ -f $1 ] && echo $1 is\
 a file) || ([ -d $1 ] && echo $1 is a directory || echo I have no idea what $1 is))
```

■**Note** You'll notice in Listing 7-25 that I used a \ at the end of the line. This slash makes sure that the carriage return sign at the end of the line is not interpreted and is used only to make sure that you don't type two separated lines. I've used the \ for typographical reasons only. In a real script, you'd just put all code on one line (which wouldn't fit on these pages without breaking it, as I've had to do). I'll use this convention in some later scripts as well.

If you understand what the example script from Listing 7-24 does, it is not really hard to understand the script in Listing 7-25 because it does the same thing. However, you should be aware of a few things. First, I added a [-z $1] test to give an error if $1 is not defined. Next, the example in Listing 7-25 is all on one line. This makes the script more compact, but it also makes it a little harder to understand what is going on. I used brackets to increase the readability a little bit and also to keep the different parts of the script together. The parts between brackets are the main tests, and within these main tests some smaller tests are used as well.

Let's have a look at some other examples with if ... then ... else. Consider the following line, for example:

```
rsync -vaze ssh --delete /srv/ftp 10.0.0.20:/srv/ftp || echo "rsync failed" | mail
admin@mydomain.com
```

Here, the rsync command tries to synchronize the content of the directory /srv/ftp with the content of the same directory on some other machine. If this succeeds, no further evaluation of this line is attempted. If something happens, however, the part after the || becomes active and makes sure that user admin@mydomain.com gets a message.

Another more complex example could be the following script that checks whether available disk space has dropped below a certain threshold. The complex part lies in the sequence of pipes used in the command substitution:

```
if [ `df -m /var | tail -n1 | awk '{print $4} '` -lt 120 ]
then
     logger running out of disk space
fi
```

The important part of this piece of code is in the first line, where the result of a command is used in the `if` loop by using backquoting, and that result is compared with the value 120. If the result is less than 120, the following section becomes active. If the result is greater than 120, nothing happens. As for the command itself, it uses the `df` command to check available disk space on the volume where /var is mounted, filters out the last line of that result, and from that last line filters out the fourth column only, which in turn is compared with the value 120. And if the condition is true, the `logger` command writes a message to the system log file. This example isn't really well organized; the following rewrite does exactly the same, but makes it somewhat more readable:

```
[ `df -m /var | tail -n1 | awk '{print $4}'` -lt $1 ] && logger running out of
disk space
```

This shows why it's fun to write shell scripts: you can almost always make them better.

Case

Let's start with an example this time (see Listing 7-26). Create the script, run it, and then try to explain what it's done.

Listing 7-26. *Example Script with Case*

```
#!/bin/bash
# Your personal soccer expert
# usage: soccer

cat << EOF
Enter the name of the country you think will be world soccer champion in 2010.
EOF

read COUNTRY
# translate $COUNTRY into all uppercase
COUNTRY=`echo $COUNTRY | tr a-z A-Z`

# perform the test
case $COUNTRY in
     NEDERLAND | HOLLAND | NETHERLANDS)
     echo "Yes, you are a soccer expert "
     ;;
     DEUTSCHLAND | GERMANY | MANNSCHAFT)
     echo "No, they are the worst team on earth"
     ;;
     ENGLAND)
     echo "hahahahahahaha, you must be joking"
```

```
    ;;
    *)
    echo "Huh? Do they play soccer?"
    ;;
esac
```

In case you didn't guess, this script can be used to analyze the next World Cup championship (of course you can modify it for any major sports event you like). It will first ask the person who runs the script to enter the name of the country that he or she thinks will be the next champion. This country is put in the $COUNTRY variable. Notice the use of uppercase for this variable; it's a nice way to identify variables easily if your script becomes rather big. Because the case statement that's used in this script is case sensitive, the user input in the first part is translated into all uppercase using the tr command. Using command substitution with this command, the current value of $COUNTRY is read, translated to all uppercase, and assigned again to the $COUNTRY variable using command substitution. Also notice that I made it easier to distinguish the different parts of this script by adding some additional comments.

The body of this script consists of the case command, which is used to evaluate the input the user has entered. The generic construction used to evaluate the input is as follows:

```
alternative1 | alternative2)
command
;;
```

So the first line evaluates everything that the user can enter. Notice that more than one alternative is used on most lines, which makes it easier to handle typos and other situations where the user hasn't typed exactly what you were expecting him to type. Then on separate lines come all the commands that you want the script to execute. In the example, just one command is executed, but you can enter 100 lines to execute commands if you like. Finally, the test is closed by using ;;. Don't forget to close all items with the double semicolons; otherwise, the script won't understand you. The ;; can be on a line by itself, but you can also put it directly after the last command line in the script.

When using case, you should make it a habit to handle "all other options." Hopefully, your user will enter something that you expect. But what if he doesn't? In that case, you probably do want the user to see something. This is handled by the *) at the end of the script. So, in this case, for everything the user enters that isn't specifically mentioned as an option in the script, the script will echo "Huh? Do they play soccer?" to the user.

Using while

You can use while to run a command as long as a condition is met. Listing 7-27 shows how while is used to monitor activity of an important process.

Listing 7-27. *Monitoring Process Activity with* while

```
#!/bin/bash
#
# usage: monitor <processname>
```

```
while ps aux | grep $1
do
      sleep 1
done

logger $1 is no longer present
```

The body of this script consists of the command ps aux | grep $1. This command monitors for the availability of the process whose name was entered as an argument when starting the script. As long as the process is detected, the condition is met, and the commands in the loop are executed. In this case, the script waits one second and then repeats its action. When the process is no longer detected, the logger command writes a message to syslog.

As you can see from this example, while offers an excellent method to check whether something (such as a process or an IP address) still exists. If you combine it with the sleep command, you can start your script with while as a kind of daemon and perform a check repeatedly. For example, the script in Listing 7-28 would write a message to syslog if due to an error the IP address suddenly gets lost.

Listing 7-28. *Checking if the IP Address Is Still There*

```
#!/bin/bash
#
# script that monitors an IP address
# usage: ipmon <ip-address>

while ip a s | grep $1/ > /dev/null
do
      sleep 5
done

logger HELP, the IP address $1 is gone.
```

Using until

Although while does its work as long as a certain condition is met, until is used for the opposite: it runs until the condition is met. This can be seen in Listing 7-29, in which the script monitors whether the user, whose name is entered as the argument, is logged in.

Listing 7-29. *Monitoring User Login*

```
#!/bin/bash
#
# script that alerts when a user logs in
# usage: ishere <username>

until who | grep $1 >> /dev/null
do
      echo $1 is not logged in yet
```

```
        sleep 5
done

echo $1 has just logged in
```

In this example, the who | grep $1 command is executed repeatedly. In this command, the result of the who command that lists users currently logged in to the system is grepped for the occurrence of $1. As long as that command is not true (which is the case if the user is not logged in), the commands in the loop will be executed. As soon as the user logs in, the loop is broken and a message is displayed to say that the user has just logged in. Notice the use of redirection to the null device in the test, ensuring that the result of the who command is not echoed on the screen.

Using for

Sometimes it's necessary to execute a series of commands, whether for a limited or an unlimited number of times. In such cases, for loops offer an excellent solution. Listing 7-30 shows how you can use for to create a counter.

Listing 7-30. *Using* for *to Create a Counter*

```
#!/bin/bash
#
# counter that counts from 1 to 9
for (( counter=1; counter<10; counter++ )); do
      echo "The counter is now set to $counter"
done
exit 0
```

The code used in this script isn't difficult to understand: the conditional loop determines that as long as the counter has a value between 1 and 10, the variable counter must be automatically incremented by 1. To do this, the construction counter++ is used. As long as this incrementing of the variable counter continues, the commands between do and done are executed. When the specified number is reached, the loop is left, and the script will terminate and indicate with exit 0 to the system that it has done its work successfully.

Loops with for can be pretty versatile. For example, you can use it to do something on every line in a text file. The example in Listing 7-31 illustrates how this works.

Listing 7-31. *Displaying Lines from a Text File*

```
#!/bin/bash
for i in `cat /etc/passwd`
do
      echo $i
done
```

In this example, for is used to display all lines in /etc/passwd one by one. Of course, just echoing the lines is a rather trivial example, but it's enough to show how for works. If you're using for in this way, you should notice that it cannot handle spaces in the lines. A space would be interpreted as a field separator, so a new line would begin after the space.

One more example with `for`: in this example, `for` is used to ping a range of IP addresses. This is a script that one of my customers likes to run to see whether a range of machines is up and running. Because the IP addresses are always in the same range, starting with 192.168.1, there's no harm in including these first three bits in the IP address itself. Of course, you're free to work with complete IP addresses instead.

Listing 7-32. *Testing a Range of IP Addresses*

```
#!/bin/bash
for i in $@
do
      ping -c 1 192.168.1.$i
done
```

Notice the use of $@ in this script. This operator allows you to refer to all arguments that were specified when starting the script, no matter how many there are.

Using a Stream Editor

In scripting, some fixed Bash functionality can be used, such as if...then...else, for, read, and others that you've read about in this chapter. To make a script really powerful, external utilities can be used as well. One of these is the stream editor sed. In this section, I'll introduce you to some sed basics.

The stream editor sed can be compared with grep. Although grep is merely used to find patterns in files, the purpose of sed is to do something to these patterns as well. To accomplish this, a sed command consists of different parts. In the first part, you indicate what exactly you want the command to do. Then you specify what it has to search for. Next, a pattern can be specified to indicate the replacement text, and finally you can specify how a replacement has to take place. You can see an example of this in the following line:

```
sed "s/english/french/g" languages.txt
```

In this example, the action that has to be performed is a substitution (s). The text that has to be located is english, and its replacement text is french. Finally, the letter g indicates that the command has to be executed until matches are found. Also notice that the command that sed has to execute is always between quotes; this is to prevent the shell from interpreting the text string.

If you want to modify the file with sed, you can use the -i (edit in place) option. For instance, sed -i "s/English/French/g" languages.txt would replace the word English in languages.txt with French everywhere it is found.

If you want to work safely with sed and avoid accidental erasure of the original file contents, it is better not to write the result of the replacement directly to the original file. So omit the option -i, which will write any modifications that it makes in the original text to STDOUT. If you want these modifications to be saved somewhere, you need to write it to a new file. The most common way to do this is by redirection to a temporary file. If required, the temporary file can be used later to overwrite the original file. To accomplish this, the preceding example would be modified in the following way:

```
sed "s/english/french/g" languages.txt > languages2.txt
```

Next, you can copy the new output file over the old file.

■**Caution** Never redirect the output to the file that you are analyzing, as in `sed "s/English/French/g"` `languages.txt > languages.txt`. It will completely erase the content of the file!

Another useful task that can be accomplished with `sed` is to remove text from a file. In that case, just add empty replacement text, as seen in the following example:

```
sed "s/something//g" list.txt
```

Of course you then have to make sure that the result is then written to some temporary file.

Also very useful is the option to remove any lines that match a certain pattern from a file. For example, the following command would remove user sander from the `/etc/passwd` file:

```
sed "/sander/d" /etc/passwd
```

Notice that no substitution is used in this example; instead, the d (delete) command removes the line. You can even make it somewhat more complicated by removing an empty line. In this case, you need to use a regular expression. The next example shows how:

```
sed "/^$/d" /myfile
```

The special construction used here is a regular expression that searches for the beginning of the line, indicated by a ^, which is followed immediately by the end of the line, which is indicated by a $. Because there's nothing between the two of them, this construction helps you to find empty lines.

Working with Functions

The function is an element that can be very useful in longer shell scripts. A *function* is a subroutine in a script that is labeled with a name. Using functions makes it easier to refer to certain command sequences that have to be used more than once in a script. For instance, you could create a generic error message if something went wrong. You can define functions in two ways. You can use something like this:

```
function functionname
{
     command1
     command2
     commandn
}
```

Or you could do it this way:

```
functionname ()
{
    command1
    command2
    commandn
}
```

To increase the readability of a script, it's a good idea to use functions if certain code sequences are needed more than once. Listing 7-33 is an example of a script in which a function is used to display an error message. This script is a replacement for the file command, with the difference that the script displays a more elegant error message.

Listing 7-33. *Displaying Error Codes Using Functions*

```
#!/bin/bash
# This script shows the file type
#
# usage: filetype $1
function noarg
{
    echo "You have made an error"
    echo "When running this script, you need to specify the name of the file"
    echo "that you want to check"
    exit 1
}

if [ -z $1 ]; then
    noarg
else
    file $1
fi
exit 0
```

In Listing 7-33, the function has the name noarg. In it, some text is specified that has to be echoed to the screen when the function is called. The function basically defines an error message, so it makes sure that the script terminates with an exit status of 1. As you can see, the function is called just once in this script, when a user forgets to enter the required argument.

A Complex Scripting Example

Let's discuss one more script—one that provides a rather complex example in which process activity is monitored (see Listing 7-34). To do this, the script will periodically check the most active process, and if this script's activity rises above a threshold, it will send an e-mail to the user root.

Listing 7-34. *Complex Scripting Example*

```
#!/bin/bash
# Script that monitors the top-active process. The script sends an email to the user
# root if utilization of the top active process goes beyond 80%. Of course, this
# script can be tuned to do anything else in such a case.
#
# Start the script, and it will run forever.

while true
do
        # Check if we have a process causing high CPU load every 60 seconds
        sleep 10
        BLAH=`ps -eo pcpu,pid -o comm= | sort -k1 -n -r | head -1`
        USAGE=`echo $BLAH | awk '{ print $1 }'`
        USAGE=${USAGE%.*}
        PID=`echo $BLAH | awk '{print $2 }'`
        PNAME=`echo $BLAH | awk '{print $3 }'`

        # Only if we have a high CPU load on one process, run a check within 7 sec.
        # In this check, we should monitor if the process is still that active
        # If that's the case, root gets a message
        if [ $USAGE -gt 70 ]
        then
                USAGE1=$USAGE
                PID1=$PID
                PNAME1=$PNAME
                sleep 7
                # FIX MIJ
        BLAH2=`ps -eo pcpi,pid -o comm= | sort -k1 -n -r | head -1`
                USAGE2=`echo $BLAH2 | awk '{ print $1 } '`
                USAGE2=${USAGE2%.*}
                PID2=`echo $BLAH2 | awk '{print $2 }'`
                PNAME2=`echo $BLAH2 | awk '{print $3 }'`

                # Now we have variables with the old process information and
                # with the new information

                [ $USAGE2 -gt 70 ] && [ $PID1 = $PID2 ] && mail -s "CPU load of\
$PNAME is above 70%" root < .
        fi
done
```

Again, you can see that this script comprises several parts. The first thing that happens is that a variable with the name BLAH is defined. In this variable, three values are stored for the most active process: the first value indicates CPU usage, the second value indicates the PID of that process, and the third value refers to the name of the process. These three values are stored in the variables USAGE, PID, and PNAME. Notice that the script performs a pattern-matching operation on the variable USAGE. This is to make the value of this variable a whole number, such as 81 instead of a fractional number like 81.9. (This is necessary because Bash cannot perform calculations on fractional numbers.) Also notice the use of the awk command, which plays an essential role in the script, and that's to strip the value of the different fields that are stored in the variables BLAH and BLAH2.

In the second part, the script looks to see whether the CPU utilization of the most active process is higher than 70 percent. If it is, a second check is made to get the usage, name, and PID of that process at that time. These values are stored in the variables USAGE2, PID2, and PNAME2.

In the third part, the script determines whether the script that has a CPU utilization greater than 70 percent in the first run is the same as the script with the highest CPU utilization in the second run. If so, a message is sent to the user root.

Summary

In this chapter, you learned about some basic ingredients of shell scripts. This chapter is in no way a complete overview of everything that can be used in a shell script; it's just meant to familiarize you with the basic ingredients of a script, so that you can analyze scripts that are used on your server or write simple scripts yourself to simplify tasks that you have to perform repeatedly. In Chapter 8, you'll learn how to set up networking on Ubuntu Server.

■ ■ ■

Making a Connection

Configuring the Network Interface Card and SSH

What is a server without a network connection? Of no use whatsoever. We've already explored the possibilities of the Linux operating system itself, and now we need to talk about the network. In this chapter, you'll learn how to configure the network card. Also, I'll talk about setting up remote connections using SSH. And you'll learn some basic steps to troubleshoot a network connection.

Configuring the Network Card

When installing your server, the installer automatically configures your server's network board to get its IP configuration from a DHCP server. As you read in Chapter 1, you can configure it to use a static IP address instead. Also, after installing a server, it's possible to change the IP address assignment of your server's network card. Let's see how this works.

When your server boots, it starts the networking script from /etc/init.d. The script reads the configuration that is stored in the /etc/network directory, paying particular attention to the /etc/network/interfaces file. This configuration file stores the entire configuration of the network board. Listing 8-1 shows an example configuration for a server that has two Ethernet network cards.

Listing 8-1. *Example Configuration for a Network Board*

```
root@ZNA:~# cat /etc/network/interfaces
# This file describes the network interfaces available on your system
# and how to activate them. For more information, see interfaces(5).

# The loopback network interface
auto lo
iface lo inet loopback
```

```
# The primary network interface
auto eth0
iface eth0 inet static
        address 192.168.1.33
        netmask 255.255.255.0
        network 192.168.1.0
        broadcast 192.168.1.255
        gateway 192.168.1.254
        # dns-* options are implemented by the resolvconf package, if installed
        dns-nameservers 193.79.237.39
        dns-search lan

#The second network board
auto eth1
iface eth1 inet static
      address 10.0.0.10
      netmask 255.255.255.0
      network 10.0.0.0
      broadcast 10.0.0.255
```

As you can see from the configuration file, the server has activated three network devices. The first is lo, which is the loopback interface. It's required for many services to function, even if your server has no network connection at all. Typically, it uses the IP address 127.0.0.1.

In most cases, an Ethernet network board is used to connect with the rest of the world. This network board is represented by the name eth0 if it's the first, and names such as eth1 and so on for the next cards. The definition of each of the network cards starts with auto eth*n*, in which *n* is the number of the network interface. This line is used to start the network board automatically when your server boots. Although you can omit this line, you need to use the ifup or ifconfig commands (as described in a bit) to start the network board by hand. In most situations, you don't want to do that, so make sure that the line that starts with auto is used at all times.

Following the auto line, there is a definition of the interface itself. In this example, a server is configured with two static IP addresses (which is what you typically want for a server). If you need DHCP on an interface, make sure that the iface line reads iface eth*n* inet dynamic. Following is the rest of the configuration for the network board. You'll need address, netmask, network, and broadcast in all cases. The other options are optional.

To show the current network configuration of your server, the ifconfig command is the easiest command to use. For more versatile management of your network board, you should use the ip command, which is discussed later in this chapter. Listing 8-2 is an example of the output of ifconfig. Especially notice the address given by the inet addr parameter, which is the IP address your server uses to connect to the rest of the world.

Listing 8-2. *The* ifconfig *Command Shows the Current Network Configuration*

```
root@RNA:/etc/network# ifconfig
eth0      Link encap:Ethernet  HWaddr 00:0C:29:03:C4:1C
          inet addr:192.168.1.70  Bcast:192.168.1.255  Mask:255.255.255.0
          inet6 addr: fe80::20c:29ff:fe03:c41c/64 Scope:Link
```

```
         UP BROADCAST RUNNING MULTICAST  MTU:1500  Metric:1
         RX packets:2627 errors:0 dropped:0 overruns:0 frame:0
         TX packets:335 errors:0 dropped:0 overruns:0 carrier:0
         collisions:0 txqueuelen:1000
         RX bytes:282945 (276.3 KiB)  TX bytes:35050 (34.2 KiB)
         Interrupt:16 Base address:0x2000

lo       Link encap:Local Loopback
         inet addr:127.0.0.1  Mask:255.0.0.0
         inet6 addr: ::1/128 Scope:Host
         UP LOOPBACK RUNNING  MTU:16436  Metric:1
         RX packets:14 errors:0 dropped:0 overruns:0 frame:0
         TX packets:14 errors:0 dropped:0 overruns:0 carrier:0
         collisions:0 txqueuelen:0
         RX bytes:700 (700.0 b)  TX bytes:700 (700.0 b)
```

Now that you know where the server stores its network configuration, you can also change it directly in this file. This is useful if you want to change the IP address of your network card quickly, for example. Next, you can restart the network card with the ifdown and ifup commands, after which the new configuration is activated. Or you can use /etc/init.d/networking restart if you want to reread the configuration for all your network interfaces.

Using ifup, ifdown, and Related Tools

The ifup and ifdown commands make managing a network board easy, and these tools are simple: call the tool followed by the name of the network board that you want to manage. For example, ifup eth0 starts network card eth0 and ifdown eth0 stops it again.

Another useful tool to manage the network card is ifplugstatus, which shows the state of a network interface. As seen in Listing 8-3, this utility shows if a link is detected on a network interface. (If the ifplugstatus utility hasn't been installed yet, use apt-get install ifplugd.)

Listing 8-3. *The* ifplugstatus *Tool Shows the Current Connection State of a Network Boar*

```
root@RNA:/# ifplugstatus
lo: link beat detected
eth0: link beat detected
```

Using ifconfig

The ifconfig command is used to manage a network interface card. The command has been around for years, so it's not the most flexible command, but it'll still do the job. And the biggest advantage is that it's a relatively easy command to use. If you just use the ifconfig command without any parameters, you'll see information about the current configuration of the network cards in your server. You saw an example of this in Listing 8-2.

Displaying Information with `ifconfig`

The `ifconfig` command provides different kinds of information about a network card. It starts with the name of the protocol used on the network card. The protocol is indicated by (for example) `Link encap: Ethernet`, which states that it is an Ethernet network board. Almost all modern LAN interfaces will show you Ethernet as the link encapsulation type. Then, if applicable, the MAC address is given as the `HWaddr` (hardware address). This address is followed by first the IPv4-related address information and then the IPv6 address information if IPv6 hasn't been disabled. Then several statistics about the network board are given. Pay special attention to the `RX packets` (received packets) and `TX packets` (transmitted packets) because you can see from these statistics what the network board is doing and whether any errors have occurred. You typically shouldn't see any errors at all.

Apart from the information about the physical network cards that are present in your server, you'll also always see information about the loopback device (`lo`), which is the network interface that's used for internal purposes on your server. You need this loopback device because some services depend on it; for example, the graphical environment that's used on Linux is written on top of the IP stack offered by the loopback interface.

Configuring a Network Card with `ifconfig`

Although the server is provided with an IP address upon installation, it's important for you to be able to manage IP address configuration on the fly, using the `ifconfig` command. Fortunately, it's relatively easy to configure a network board in this way: just add the name of the network board you want to configure, followed by the IP address you want to use on that network board (for example, `ifconfig eth0 192.168.1.125`). This command will configure `eth0` with a default class C subnet mask of 255.255.255.0, which indicates that the first three bytes of the IP address are a part of the network address and that the last byte is the unique host identifier within that network.

■**Tip** Not sure which `eth` device number is used? You can manage this via the `udev` mechanism. In the `/etc/udev/rules.d/70-persistent-net.rules` file, a mapping is made between the MAC address and interface number of your network cards; see the section about `udev` in Chapter 6 for more details. So if you want your `eth1` device to be presented as `eth20`, this is the place where you can change the device number.

If you need something other than a default subnet mask, add an extra parameter. An example of this is the `ifconfig eth0 172.16.18.18 netmask 255.255.255.0 broadcast 172.16.18.255` command, which configures the `eth0` device with the given IP address and a 24-bit subnet mask. Note that this example uses a nondefault subnet mask. If this happens, you have to specify the broadcast address that's used to address all nodes in the same network as well; the `ifconfig` command just isn't smart enough to realize that you're using a nondefault IP address and to calculate the right broadcast address accordingly.

Bringing Interfaces Up and Down with `ifconfig`

Apart from adding an IP address to a network board, you can use the `ifconfig` command to bring a specific network board up or down. For example, `ifconfig eth0 down` shuts down the interface, and `ifconfig eth0 up` brings it up again with its default settings as specified in the `/etc/network/interfaces` configuration file. This is useful if you want to test a new configuration, but you're not sure whether it will really work properly.

Instead of using `ifconfig` to manipulate your network card, you can also use `ifup` and `ifdown`. These commands allow you to bring a network card up or down easily, and without changing the configuration of a given network board. For example, to bring a network board down, use `ifdown eth0`; to bring it up again, use `ifup eth0`. In both cases, the default configuration for the network board as specified in `/etc/network/interfaces` is applied.

Using Virtual IP Addresses with `ifconfig`

Another rather useful way of using `ifconfig` is to add virtual IP addresses, which are just secondary IP addresses that are added to a network card. A network board with virtual IP addresses can listen to two different IP addresses, which is useful if you are configuring services on your server that all need their own IP addresses. Think of different virtual Apache web servers, for example.

You can use the virtual IP address within the same address range or on a different one. To add a virtual IP address, add `:n` where n is a number after the name of the network interface. For example, `ifconfig eth0:0 10.0.0.10` adds the address 10.0.0.10 as a virtual IP address to eth0. The number after the colon must be unique, so you can add a second virtual IP address with `ifconfig eth0:1 10.0.0.20`, and so on. When you use the `ifconfig` tool to display the current configuration of your server, you'll see all virtual IP addresses that are configured, as shown in Listing 8-4.

Listing 8-4. *The* `ifconfig` *Tool Shows Virtual IP Addresses*

```
root@ZNA:~# ifconfig eth0:0 10.0.0.10
root@ZNA:~# ifconfig eth0:1 10.0.0.20
root@ZNA:~# ifconfig
eth0      Link encap:Ethernet  HWaddr 00:0C:29:A0:A5:80
          inet addr:192.168.1.33  Bcast:192.168.1.255  Mask:255.255.255.0
          inet6 addr: fe80::20c:29ff:fea0:a580/64 Scope:Link
          UP BROADCAST RUNNING MULTICAST  MTU:1500  Metric:1
          RX packets:3035 errors:0 dropped:0 overruns:0 frame:0
          TX packets:199 errors:0 dropped:0 overruns:0 carrier:0
          collisions:0 txqueuelen:1000
          RX bytes:240695 (235.0 KiB)  TX bytes:19035 (18.5 KiB)
          Interrupt:18 Base address:0x1400

eth0:0    Link encap:Ethernet  HWaddr 00:0C:29:A0:A5:80
          inet addr:10.0.0.10  Bcast:10.255.255.255  Mask:255.0.0.0
          UP BROADCAST RUNNING MULTICAST  MTU:1500  Metric:1
          Interrupt:18 Base address:0x1400
```

```
eth0:1    Link encap:Ethernet  HWaddr 00:0C:29:A0:A5:80
          inet addr:10.0.0.20  Bcast:10.255.255.255  Mask:255.0.0.0
          UP BROADCAST RUNNING MULTICAST  MTU:1500  Metric:1
          Interrupt:18 Base address:0x1400

lo        Link encap:Local Loopback
          inet addr:127.0.0.1  Mask:255.0.0.0
          inet6 addr: ::1/128 Scope:Host
          UP LOOPBACK RUNNING  MTU:16436  Metric:1
          RX packets:0 errors:0 dropped:0 overruns:0 frame:0
          TX packets:0 errors:0 dropped:0 overruns:0 carrier:0
          collisions:0 txqueuelen:0
          RX bytes:0 (0.0 b)  TX bytes:0 (0.0 b)
```

Using the ip Tool

Although the ifconfig tool can still be used to display information about the configuration of a network card, it's not the only tool available. A more flexible (but also more difficult) tool is ip. The ip tool has many options that allow you to manage virtually all aspects of the network connection. For example, you can use it to configure an IP address, but it manages routing as well, which is something that ifconfig can't do.

■**Note** The ip tool offers more than ifconfig. Its syntax is also more difficult, so many people stick to using ifconfig instead. To be honest, it doesn't really matter because they can both be used for the same purposes in almost all cases. If you really want to be sure not to run into trouble, you should use ip, however.

The first option you use after the ip command determines exactly what you want to do with the tool. This first option is a reference to the so-called object, and each object has different possibilities. The following objects are available:

- link: Used to manage or display properties of a network device

- addr: Used to manage or display IPv4 or IPv6 network addresses on a device

- route: Used to manage or display entries in the routing table

- rule: Used to manage or display rules in the routing policy database

- neigh: Used to manage or display entries in the ARP cache

- tunnel: Used to manage or display IP tunnels

- maddr: Used to manage or display multicast addresses for interfaces

- mroute: Used to manage or display multicast routing cache entries

- monitor: Used to monitor what happens on a given device

Each of these objects has options of its own. The easiest way to learn about these options is to use the ip command, followed by the object, and then followed by the keyword help. For example, ip address help provides information on how to use the ip address command, as shown in Listing 8-5.

Listing 8-5. *The* ip address help *Command Gives Help on Configuring IP Addresses with the* ip *Tool*

```
root@ZNA:~# ip address help
Usage: ip addr {add|del} IFADDR dev STRING
       ip addr {show|flush} [ dev STRING ] [ scope SCOPE-ID ]
                            [ to PREFIX ] [ FLAG-LIST ] [ label PATTERN ]
IFADDR := PREFIX | ADDR peer PREFIX
          [ broadcast ADDR ] [ anycast ADDR ]
          [ label STRING ] [ scope SCOPE-ID ]
SCOPE-ID := [ host | link | global | NUMBER ]
FLAG-LIST := [ FLAG-LIST ] FLAG
FLAG   := [ permanent | dynamic | secondary | primary |
            tentative | deprecated ]
```

It can be quite a challenge to find out how the help for the ip tool works, so I'll give you some help with this help feature. To understand what you need to do, you must first analyze the Usage: lines. In this output, you see two of them: a usage line that starts with ip addr {add|del} and another that starts with ip addr {show|flush}. Let's have a look at the first one.

The complete usage line is ip addr {add|del} IFADDR dev STRING. You can add or delete an IP address that is referred to by IFADDR from a device (dev) that is referred to by STRING. Now a string is just a string, and that can be anything, but that's not the case for the IFADDR part. Therefore, you can find an explanation of that part in the next section of the help output: IFADDR := PREFIX | ADDR peer PREFIX [broadcast ADDR] [anycast ADDR] [label STRING] [scope SCOPE-ID]. In this line, the help explains that you have to use a PREFIX or an ADDR statement, which might be followed by several options such as the broadcast address, the anycast address, a label, or a SCOPE-ID. Now that you understand how help works, let's have a look at some examples.

Displaying IP Address Setup Information with the ip Tool

A common use of the ip tool is to display information about the use of IP addresses for a given interface. The command to use is ip address show. Note that if it is clear exactly what you want and there can be no confusion between options, you can specify the options used with the ip command in short form, such as ip a s, which accomplishes the same thing as ip address show. This command displays the information shown in Listing 8-6.

Listing 8-6. *Showing* ip *Address Configuration with* ip address show

```
root@ZNA:~# ip address show
1: lo: <LOOPBACK,UP,10000> mtu 16436 qdisc noqueue
    link/loopback 00:00:00:00:00:00 brd 00:00:00:00:00:00
    inet 127.0.0.1/8 scope host lo
    inet6 ::1/128 scope host
```

```
        valid_lft forever preferred_lft forever
2: eth0: <BROADCAST,MULTICAST,UP,10000> mtu 1500 qdisc pfifo_fast qlen 1000
    link/ether 00:0c:29:a0:a5:80 brd ff:ff:ff:ff:ff:ff
    inet 192.168.1.33/24 brd 192.168.1.255 scope global eth0
    inet 10.0.0.10/8 brd 10.255.255.255 scope global eth0:0
    inet 10.0.0.20/8 brd 10.255.255.255 scope global secondary eth0:1
    inet6 fe80::20c:29ff:fea0:a580/64 scope link
        valid_lft forever preferred_lft forever
```

If you look hard enough, you can see that the result of ip address show is almost the same as the result of ifconfig. It's just presented differently.

Monitoring Device Attributes

Another simple use of the ip tool is to show device attributes, which you can do with the ip link show command. This command shows usage statistics for the device you specified, but no address information. Listing 8-7 provides an example of its output.

Listing 8-7. *Use the* ip link show *Command for an Overview of Link Attributes*

```
root@ZNA:~# ip link show
1: lo: <LOOPBACK,UP,10000> mtu 16436 qdisc noqueue
    link/loopback 00:00:00:00:00:00 brd 00:00:00:00:00:00
2: eth0: <BROADCAST,MULTICAST,UP,10000> mtu 1500 qdisc pfifo_fast qlen 1000
    link/ether 00:0c:29:a0:a5:80 brd ff:ff:ff:ff:ff:ff
```

The information displayed by ip link show is related to the activity on the network board. Of particular interest are the device attributes returned for each of the devices (they're displayed in brackets right after the name of the device). For example, in most cases you can see the attributes BROADCAST,MULTICAST,UP for a normal network interface card. The BROADCAST attribute indicates that the device is capable of sending broadcasts to other nodes in the network, the MULTICAST attribute indicates that the device can also send multicast packets, and UP indicates that the device is working. The command also shows all IP protocol attributes, such as the maximum transmission unit (mtu) that is used on the interface.

Setting the IP Address

Just as with the ifconfig tool, you can use the ip tool to assign an IP address to a device. To do this, you could use a command like ip address add 10.0.0.10/16 brd + dev eth0. This command sets the IP address to 10.0.0.10 for eth0. With this IP address, a 16-bit subnet mask is used, which is indicated by the /16 directly behind the IP address. The broadcast address is calculated automatically, which is indicated with the brd + construction. Once you have set the IP address with the ip tool, you can use the following command to check whether it's set correctly: ip address show dev eth0.

As with the ifconfig command, you can add more than one IP address to a network interface when using the ip tool as well. And it isn't hard: just use ip address add 10.0.0.20/16 brd + dev eth0 and 10.0.0.20 with its specified properties is added as a second IP address to eth0. You should, however, note the difference between the secondary IP addresses that are added with ifconfig and the IP addresses that are added with the ip tool. An address added with `ip` won't show up when you use `ifconfig`. So, when using secondary IP addresses, make sure that you use the right tool to check their properties.

Managing IPv6

Currently, IPv4 is the default protocol on most servers. However, because it has some serious shortcomings, a new version of the IP protocol began development a few years ago. Because this draft for IP version 5 just didn't make it, the new generation of Internet protocol is referred to as *IPv6*, and it's this version that's installed by default on Ubuntu Server, so you can use it as an alternative to IPv4. In this section, you'll learn about the properties of IPv6 and how to configure it on your server. This section isn't meant as an in-depth coverage of IPv6 and all its properties. Instead, it aims to help you configure IPv6 on a server and see whether it's useful in your environment.

IPv6 Addressing

Before you start the actual implementation of IPv6, you should know about its peculiarities, of which the first and most important is the address length. Although IPv4 has to work with 32-bit addresses that are grouped in 4 groups of 8 bits (such as 192.168.1.13) and that theoretically allow for approximately 4,000,000,000 unique addresses, IPv6 offers a 128-bit address space, which yields more than enough IP addresses to assign one to every square meter of the Earth's surface, including the oceans. Opposite to the decimal-written IPv4 addresses, the IPv6 addresses are written in hexadecimal and split into 16-bit groups. An example of such an address is `2bad:babe:5655:8812:0BFC:1234:0:1234`. Not really something you would care to memorize.

If an IPv6 address has more than one group of 16 bits with the value of 0, you can abbreviate this using the double colon (`::`). For example, the IPv6 address `2bad:0:0:0:0:1234:5678:90ab` can also be written as `2bad::1234:5678:90ab`, and `0:0:0:0:0:0:0:1` is just `::1`. This clever shortcut makes working with IPv6 addresses much easier. Another nice feature of IPv6 is that you can share an IP address among different NICs so that several network cards listen to the same IP address. This easy-to-implement method is for load balancing.

Because more than enough bits are available in an IPv6 address, there's a default division between the network part of the address and the node part of the address. This is an important advantage of IPv4, in which you must use a subnet mask to specify which part of the address refers to the network and which part refers to the node on that network. So with IPv6 you don't need to struggle with subnet masks any more.

The last 64 bits of an IPv6 address are normally used as the node ID. This node ID is a so-called IEEE EIA-64 ID, which on Ethernet consists of the 48-bit MAC address with `FFFE` added between the vendor identifier and the node identifier. If a network interface doesn't have a MAC address, the node ID is randomly generated.

Because the IPv6 address includes the MAC address, something important follows: the node in an IPv6 network can determine its own IPv6 address. All that a node must do is listen on the network to check for the address that's in use. Next, it can add its own MAC address, transform that to an IEEE EIA-64 ID, and it'll be able to communicate with the rest of the network automatically. So there goes the need for the DHCP server that was required for automatic address configuration in IPv4 as well.

If you really need it, an IPv6 address can work with a subnet mask. By default, this subnet mask for all addresses is /64 (64 bits), which specifies that the first half of the IPv6 address refers to the network, but you can use something other than this default subnet mask as well. However, the last 64 bits of an address are always reserved for the node address, so you can't use them in the subnet mask.

Address Types

In IPv6, you can use different types of addresses:

- *Link local addresses*: These IP addresses are used if no specific information about the network configuration could be found. They're intended for local use only, and they always start with FE80 in the first two bytes. They aren't routable, but they are necessary for neighbor discovery (see the next section, "The Neighbor Discovery Protocol"). Link local addresses are always created automatically if IPv6 is enabled.

- *Site local addresses*: These are similar to addresses that are defined in the private address ranges for IPv4. They cannot be addressed from nodes outside this network. Site local addresses always start with FEC0 and have a default 48-bit subnet mask. The last 16 bits can be used for internal subnetting. Site local addresses are not created automatically.

- *Aggregatable global unicast addresses*: These are the "normal" worldwide unique addresses that are used on IPv6 networks. They are assigned by an administrator and always start with a 2 or 3 (binary 001).

- *Multicast addresses*: These addresses are used to address groups of nodes. They always start with FF.

- *Anycast addresses*: This is the IPv6 alternative for a broadcast address. When using anycast, the IPv6 node gets an answer from any node that matches the anycast criteria.

- In IPv6, broadcast addresses are not used.

On a single Linux host that uses IPv6 (which by default is the case on Ubuntu Server), you'll always find more than one IPv6 address:

- A loopback address (::1) is used on the loopback interface.

- A link local address is generated automatically for every interface.

- If the administrator has configured it, every interface has a unicast address. This can be a site local address, an aggregatable global unicast address, or both.

Neighbor Discovery Protocol

One of the design goals of IPv6 was to make network configuration easier. For this purpose, the neighbor discovery protocol was defined in RFC 2461 (see www.ietf.org/rfc-rfc2461.txt). The purpose of this protocol is to provide an automatic IP address assignment: neighbor discovery makes sure that a node can automatically find routers, addresses, prefixes, and other required configuration information, just by looking at what happens on the network.

In the neighbor discovery protocol, a router advertises all relevant information such as the best next hop. Individual nodes check their neighbors and keep information about the neighbors in the neighbor cache, so that they always have current and reliable information about the rest of the network. In the neighbor cache, a node keeps information such as addresses of neighbors, a list of prefixes (IPv6 addresses) that are in use by the neighbors, and a list of routers that can be used as default routers. So, the neighbor discovery protocol really makes IPv6 a plug-and-play protocol.

Assigning IPv6 Addresses in Ubuntu Server

On Ubuntu Server, you can use `ip` as well as `ifconfig` to configure an IPv6 address. All required kernel modules are loaded by default, so, with regard to that, no extra work needs to be done. Let's look at the following examples of how to configure IPv6 on your server:

- `ifconfig eth0 inet6 add 2000:10:20:30:20c:29ff:fec7:82f6/64`: This command configures `eth0` with an IPv6 address that is an aggregatable global unicast address (a worldwide unique address). Note that the second part of the address assigned here is the IEEE EIA-64 ID of the network interface card that the address is added to. You need to configure only one address per LAN in this way, and all other nodes will get the aggregatable global unicast address assigned automatically by means of the neighbor discovery protocol. To make this a functional IPv6 address, you should also make sure that the EIA-64 ID of your network card matches your MAC address. To get to an EIA-ID from the MAC address, you should insert `ff:fe` in the middle of the MAC address and put a 2 in front of it. For instance, the MAC address `00:19:d1:ed:82:07` would get the EIA-ID of `219:d1ff:feed:8207`.

- `ip address add 2000:10:20:30:20c:29ff:fec7:82f6/64 dev eth0`: This is exactly the same as the command used in the previous example, with the exception that the `ip` tool is used instead of `ifconfig`.

- `ip address add fec0:10:20:30:29ff:fec7:82f6 dev eth0`: This command adds a site address to interface `eth0`. Note that this also has to be performed for just one node per LAN. Instead of using the `ip` tool, you can do the same with `ifconfig eth0 inet6 add fec0:10:20:30:29ff:fec7:82f6 dev eth0`.

- `route -A inet6`: This command shows information about current IPv6 routes.

- `route -A inet6 add 2000::/3 gw 3ffe:ffff:0:f101::1`: This adds a route in which all addresses that start with binary 001 (decimal notes as 2) will be sent to the specified default gateway.

Once your IPv6 interface is set up, you'll probably want to test its operation as well. You can find some tools in the Linux `iputils` package such as the `ping6` utility that you can use to ping other hosts to check for their availability. Note that when using `ping6`, you always need to specify the interface you want to send the ping packets from: for example, `ping6 -I eth0 fe80::2e0:18ff:fe90:9205`.

Also in the same `iputils` package are the `traceroute6` tool that can be used to trace the route to a given destination and the `tracepath6` tool, which does more or less the same thing but without the need to use superuser privileges. You can read more about these tools in the "Troubleshooting Network Connections" section of this chapter.

Managing Routes

You've read about how a network interface is provided with an IP address. But to be completely functional on the network, you have to specify some routes as well. These routes allow you to communicate with computers on other networks; conversely, they allow computers on other networks to communicate with your server.

As a minimal requirement, you need a default route. This route specifies where to send packets that don't have a destination on the local network. The router used for the default route is always on the same network as your server; just consider it to be the door that helps you get out of the local network. Your server typically gets the information about the default router that it should use from the /etc/network/interfaces file. To set the default route, two tools can be used: the ip tool and the route utility. The ifconfig utility was never meant to create or maintain routes, so you can't use it for this purpose.

Setting the Default Route with route

The old command to set the default route is route. If no options are used, it will display a list of all routes that are currently defined on this host. Listing 8-8 provides an example. When using the route command without options, it will always try to resolve the name for a given IP address, which takes some time. If you don't want any name resolution to be performed, use the option -n, which makes the command a lot faster.

Listing 8-8. *Use the* route *Command to Get an Overview of All Routes That Are Currently Configured*

```
root@ZNA:~# route
Kernel IP routing table
Destination     Gateway         Genmask         Flags   Metric  Ref     Use Iface
localnet        *               255.255.255.0   U       0       0       0 eth0
10.0.0.0        *               255.0.0.0       U       0       0       0 eth0
default         192.168.1.254   0.0.0.0         UG      0       0       0 eth0
```

Several columns are displayed in the output of the route command, as you can see in Listing 8-8. The first column provides the destination, which is the network or host that a route is defined for. Next is the gateway, which is the router that needs to be contacted to reach the specified destination. An asterisk (*) in the gateway column indicates that the local-host is the gateway for that destination. For external routers used as the destination, you'll see the IP address (or name) of that router. Next is the genmask, which is the subnet mask used on the specified destination. Then come the flags, metric, ref, and use columns, all of which reveal more detailed information about this route. Finally, the iface column reveals what network interface is used to route packets.

To specify a route, you need to provide a minimum of two pieces of information: what network you want to add an entry for and what router is used as a gateway. All the other information is added automatically. For example, if you want to specify that the router with IP address 192.168.1.254 should be used as the default gateway, use the route add default gw 192.168.1.254 command.

If you need to change the default gateway, you should be aware that you first have to remove the old route. Use the route del command to do this. For example, to remove the current setting for the default gateway, use route del default gw.

Using the `ip` Tool to Specify the Default Gateway

If you know what information has to be entered when defining a route, it's easy to do it with either the `ifconfig` or the `ip` tool. The only differences are minor changes in the syntax that's used. To set the default gateway to 192.168.1.254 using the `ip` tool, use the `ip route add default via 192.168.1.254` command. This command makes sure that all packets sent to nonlocal destinations are sent through 192.168.1.254. Likewise, you can delete the default route with `ip route del default`.

Storing Routing Information

When you enter information, such as the default gateway, from the command line, it will be lost the next time you reboot your server. To make sure that the information remains after a reboot, store it in the `/etc/network/interfaces` file. This file is read every time the network is activated. The entry used in this file to store the default route isn't complex:

```
gateway 192.168.1.254
```

If you have just one network card in your server, include it in the entry for your network card. If you want to specify a default route per network card (for example, one for your private internal network and one for the public external network), you can specify a default route setting for each of the network cards.

Configuring the DNS Resolver

If you want to manually configure a network connection as the last part, you need to specify what DNS name server to use. This is the so-called *DNS resolver*. With Linux, you do this by modifying the `/etc/resolv.conf` file. Typically, this file will contain the IP address of at least two DNS name servers and a search domain. The name server specifications indicate what DNS name server should be contacted to translate DNS names to IP addresses, and vice versa. Specify at least two name servers, so that if the first one cannot be reached, the second one can do the job. The search domain specifies what domain name should be appended if an incomplete host name is used. On Ubuntu Server, this is typically set to `lan`. Listing 8-9 is an example of the content of the `/etc/resolv.conf` file.

Listing 8-9. *Example of the* `/etc/resolv.conf` *File*

```
nameserver 192.168.1.10
nameserver 193.79.237.39
search lan
```

In this example, you see that name server 192.168.1.10 is used as the default name server, and all DNS requests will be sent to it. If this server cannot be reached, only then will the second server in the list (193.79.237.39) be contacted. Make sure to always specify the addresses of two name servers. You can specify a third name server if you like, but it probably will never be used (just because of the slim chance that the first and second names are both unavailable). You'll see that the third line of the Listing 8-9 example specifies the search domain. For example, if a user uses the command `ping ftp`, which includes an incomplete host name, the name of the domain specified with the search option in `resolv.conf` is added automatically to it (this works only if there really is a host with the name `ftp` in your local network).

The Role of the `nsswitch.conf` File

Most people take it for granted that DNS resolves host names to IP addresses, but this isn't necessarily so. Every Linux box has the `/etc/nsswitch.conf` file that determines what exactly should happen when translating a host name to an IP address and vice versa. This file specifies many things, but only the following lines are important for resolving host names:

```
hosts:        files dns
networks:     files
```

These two lines specify that when resolving host names and network names, the files should be searched first, and the DNS subsystem should be used only if the files have no information about the given host. Thus, an administrator can make sure that frequently accessed host names are resolved locally, with the DNS server being contacted only when the files don't have information about a particular host. The most important file used for resolving names to IP addresses is the `/etc/hosts` file.

Using the `/etc/hosts` File

One of the oldest ways to resolve host names to IP addresses (and vice versa) is to use the `/etc/hosts` file. It's rather primitive because the file has to be maintained on every single host where you need it, and no synchronization is established between hosts. But it's also a very efficient way to supply information that needs to be available locally.

Note To resolve the problem of decentralized management, the Network Information Service (NIS, formerly known as Yellow Pages) was invented by Sun. It's rarely used now because most companies keep their hosts-related information in DNS files.

Using the `/etc/hosts` file makes resolving names faster and reduces Internet traffic, and you can use it to add any host names that need to be available only locally. Listing 8-10 shows the contents of this file as it is created after a default installation of Ubuntu Server.

Listing 8-10. *Example of the* `/etc/hosts` *File*

```
root@ZNA:~# cat /etc/hosts
127.0.0.1          localhost
192.168.1.33    ZNA.lan ZNA

# The following lines are desirable for IPv6 capable hosts
::1     ip6-localhost ip6-loopback
fe00::0 ip6-localnet
ff00::0 ip6-mcastprefix
ff02::1 ip6-allnodes
ff02::2 ip6-allrouters
ff02::3 ip6-allhosts
root@ZNA:~#
```

As you can see, the contents of this file are rather simple. First, you specify the IP address of the host, which can be an IPv4 or an IPv6 address. Next, the fully qualified host name of the host is specified. This is the name of the host itself, followed by its DNS suffix. Last, the short host name is used. Alternatively, you can just provide the IP address followed by the name of the host you want to add, as in the following line:

```
192.168.1.180   RNA
```

On a modern Linux server, it's not necessary to set up /etc/hosts except for local name resolving. Network name resolution is typically managed by DNS. So you'll always need your own host name and IP address in this file. This is configured automatically when installing Ubuntu Server.

Configuring Network Card Properties with the ethtool Command

Up to now, we've talked about stuff related to IP addresses. But the network card itself has settings that you may need to modify, and you'll use the ethtool command to do this. With it, you can change network board properties such as link speed and duplex mode. Don't overestimate this tool, however. Some Ethernet cards are not supported, and the only way to change settings on them might be through the network card's BIOS settings. Let's start by displaying some information: use ethtool -i eth0 to see an overview of driver properties that are currently used, as shown in Listing 8-11.

Listing 8-11. *The* ethtool -i *Command Provides an Overview of Driver Properties*

```
root@ZNA:~# ethtool -i eth0
driver: pcnet32
version: 1.33
firmware-version:
bus-info: 0000:00:11.0
```

To change duplex settings and link speed on your network board, you'll use the -s option, followed by one of these arguments:

- speed: This option changes the speed. Valid options are 10, 100, and 1000 (all of them expressing megabits per second).

- duplex: This option changes the duplex settings. Set it to half or full.

- port: This option specifies what port to use. This option is used for network interfaces with different ports available (which is not very common). Valid choices are tp, aui, bnc, mii, and fibre.

- autoneg: This option indicates whether you want to use auto negotiation to discover the settings that are used on the network. Valid choices are on and off.

So, for example, if you want to change the settings of your network card to full duplex and a link speed of 1000 Mbps, use ethtool -s eth0 speed 1000 duplex full. Now there is a problem when using ethtool like this because you need to enter these settings again the next time you start your server. If you don't want to do that all the time, you can create a simple script that contains all the settings. The following procedure describes how to do this:

1. Use Vi to create a script: `vim /etc/init.d/ethtool`.

2. Append the following lines (change them to reflect the settings that you need to use):

```
#!/bin/bash
ETHTOOL="/usr/sbin/ethtool"
DEV="eth0"
SPEED="1000 duplex full"
case "$1" in
start)
echo -n "Setting eth0 speed…";
$ETHTOOL -s $DEV speed $SPEED;
echo " done.";;
stop)
;;
esac
exit 0
```

3. Make this script executable using the command `chmod +x /etc/init.d/ethtool`.

4. Run the `update-rc.d` command to update your runlevels. This process ensures that this script will be executed in all appropriate runlevels. Run it as follows: `update-rc.d ethtool defaults`.

■**Note** The `update-rc.d` command is available to add startup scripts to the System-V–style boot procedure. You can use it on any script, as long as the script fits these minimal requirements: the script should use a case construction; within the case, there should be a `start)` and a `stop)` section. If your script complies with these requirements, you can add it to your runlevels.

Besides the brief summary you get about your network board when you use the `-i` option with `ethtool`, there are also some other useful options. For instance, you can get some very detailed statistics about your network board when using `ethtool -S`, as you can see in Listing 8-12.

■**Note** The drivers of some network boards don't support `ethtool`. Therefore, in some cases this command shows nothing at all. If that happens, your network card doesn't support `ethtool`, and there's nothing you can do about it.

Listing 8-12. *The* ethtool –S *Tool Gives Very Detailed Statistics About Network Cards*

```
root@mel:~# ethtool -S eth0
NIC statistics:
     rx_packets: 1691
     tx_packets: 319
     rx_bytes: 183662
     tx_bytes: 37876
     rx_broadcast: 1441
     tx_broadcast: 72
     rx_multicast: 0
     tx_multicast: 6
     rx_errors: 0
     tx_errors: 0
     tx_dropped: 0
     multicast: 0
     collisions: 0
     rx_length_errors: 0
     rx_over_errors: 0
     rx_crc_errors: 0
     rx_frame_errors: 0
     rx_no_buffer_count: 0
     rx_missed_errors: 0
     tx_aborted_errors: 0
     tx_carrier_errors: 0
     tx_fifo_errors: 0
     tx_heartbeat_errors: 0
     tx_window_errors: 0
     tx_abort_late_coll: 0
     tx_deferred_ok: 0
     tx_single_coll_ok: 0
     tx_multi_coll_ok: 0
     tx_timeout_count: 0
     tx_restart_queue: 0
     rx_long_length_errors: 0
     rx_short_length_errors: 0
     rx_align_errors: 0
     tx_tcp_seg_good: 0
     tx_tcp_seg_failed: 0
     rx_flow_control_xon: 0
     rx_flow_control_xoff: 0
     tx_flow_control_xon: 0
     tx_flow_control_xoff: 0
     rx_long_byte_count: 183662
     rx_csum_offload_good: 1504
     rx_csum_offload_errors: 0
```

```
rx_header_split: 0
alloc_rx_buff_failed: 0
tx_smbus: 0
rx_smbus: 0
dropped_smbus: 0
```

Note Some people seem to think that `ethtool` is the most important tool for proper functioning of your network. In fact, it isn't. In the early days of switched Ethernet, auto negotiate settings didn't work that well. Nowadays, auto negotiate works fine at almost all times. Therefore, you will find that in most situations you can do perfectly without `ethtool`.

Troubleshooting Network Connections

Once you have finished the setup tasks I just described, you should have a working network connection. But even if it's working fine right now, you might at some point need to perform some tuning and troubleshooting, and that's exactly what this section is about. Here, you'll learn how to test that everything is working the way it should and how to monitor what is happening on the network itself, as well as on the network interface. The tools I'm talking about in this section are the top-notch troubleshooting tools.

Testing Connectivity

After configuring a network card, you want to make sure it's working correctly. For this, the `ping` command is your friend, and more so because it's easy to use: enter the command followed by the name or address of the host you want to test connectivity to, such as `ping www.ubuntu.com`. This forces `ping` to start continuous output, which you can interrupt by using the Ctrl+C key sequence. You can also send a limited number of packets; for example, the `ping -c 3 192.168.1.254` command sends just three packets to the specified host. If you use `ping` in a clever way, you can test a lot of things with it. I recommend using it in the following order:

1. Ping the localhost. If you pass this test, you've verified that the IP stack on your local machine is working properly.

2. Ping a machine on the local network by using its IP address: if this works, you've verified that IP is properly bound to the network board of your server and that it can make a connection to other nodes on the network. If it fails, you need to check the information you've entered with the `ifconfig` or `ip` commands; you may have made an error entering the subnet mask for your network interface.

3. Ping a machine on the Internet using its IP address. A good bet is 137.65.1.1, which is a name server that hasn't failed me in the last 15 years. Of course, you can use any other host as long as you know its IP address. If the ping is successful, you've verified that the routers between the localhost and the destination are all working. If it fails, there's an error somewhere in the routing chain. Check `route -n` or `ip route show` on your local-host to see if the default route is defined.

4. Ping a machine on the Internet using its DNS name. If this succeeds, everything is working. If this step fails (but test 3 was successful), make sure you've entered the name of the DNS server that should be used in /etc/resolv.conf. If this is okay, check to see if your DNS server is working.

In many cases, you'll use the ping command without options. But some options can be useful, as seen in Table 8-1.

Table 8-1. *Useful* ping *Options*

Option	Description
-c count	Specifies the number of packets to be sent. The ping command terminates automatically after reaching this number.
-l device	Specifies the name of the network device that should be used. Useful on a computer with several network devices.
-i seconds	Specifies the number of seconds to wait between individual ping packets. The default setting is one second.
-f	Sends packets as fast as possible, but only after a reply comes in.
-l	Sends packets without waiting for a reply. If used with the -f option, this may cause a denial-of-service attack on the target host and the host may stop functioning properly or even crash. Apart from the unknown harm that this may do to the target server, you may find yourself blacklisted or even charged with a criminal offense. Because this is such a very dangerous option, only the user root is allowed to use it.
-t ttl	Sets the time to live (TTL) for packets that are sent. This indicates the maximum number of routers that each packet may pass through on its way to a destination. The TTL is decremented by one by each router it passes until the TTL becomes 0, which means that the packet won't be routed any more.
-b	Sends packets to the broadcast address of the network. This prompts a reply from every host that's up and allowed to answer to ping packets.

■**Note** To protect against a denial-of-service attack, many hosts are configured not to answer a ping request. Therefore, when testing connectivity, make sure that you use a host that's allowed to answer.

The ping command is not just used to test that a connection can be established; you can also use it to check the roundtrip delay between your computer and a given host. The elapsed time is an important indication of the quality of the network connection. To check the roundtrip delay, have a look at the time parameter that's listed in the result of the ping command. Listing 8-13 provides an example in which ping is used to send four packets to www.ubuntu.com.

Listing 8-13. *Testing Connectivity to* www.ubuntu.com

```
root@ZNA:~# ping -c 4 www.ubuntu.com
PING www.ubuntu.com (82.211.81.158) 56(84) bytes of data.
64 bytes from arctowski.ubuntu.com (82.211.81.158): icmp_seq=1 ttl=51 time=22.0 ms
```

```
64 bytes from arctowski.ubuntu.com (82.211.81.158): icmp_seq=2 ttl=51 time=10.7 ms
64 bytes from arctowski.ubuntu.com (82.211.81.158): icmp_seq=3 ttl=51 time=18.6 ms
64 bytes from arctowski.ubuntu.com (82.211.81.158): icmp_seq=4 ttl=51 time=20.8 ms

--- www.ubuntu.com ping statistics ---
4 packets transmitted, 4 received, 0% packet loss, time 3015ms
rtt min/avg/max/mdev = 10.741/18.092/22.057/4.417 ms
```

Testing Routability

If you can ping your default router, but you can't ping a given host on the Internet, it's probably obvious that something is wrong with one of the routers between your network and the destination host. You can use the `traceroute` command to find out exactly where things are going wrong (use `apt-get install traceroute` to install `traceroute` first). The `traceroute` command uses the TTL value of the UDP datagrams it sends out.

■**Note** A datagram is a packet sent over the OSI model network layer.

The idea is that, when the TTL value reaches 0, the packet is discarded by the router and a message is sent back to the sender. When starting, `traceroute` uses a TTL value of 0, which causes the packet to be discarded by the very first router. This is how `traceroute` identifies the first router. Next, it sends the packet to the target destination again, but with a TTL of 1, which, as you can see, causes the packet to be discarded by the second router. Things continue in this manner until the packet reaches its final destination.

To use `traceroute`, you normally put the host name as the argument, such as `traceroute www.ubuntu.com`. It's possible as well to use the IP address of a host, which will produce a result as seen in Listing 8-14.

Listing 8-14. *Testing a Network's Route with* traceroute

```
root@ZNA:~# traceroute www.ubuntu.com
traceroute to www.ubuntu.com (82.211.81.158), 30 hops max, 40 byte packets
 1  192.168.1.254 (192.168.1.254)  72.668 ms  10.361 ms  176.306 ms
 2  195.190.249.90 (195.190.249.90)  3.353 ms  9.199 ms  10.351 ms
 3  42.ge-4-0-0.xr1.3d12.xs4all.net (194.109.5.49)  6.386 ms  7.237 ms  16.421 ms
 4  0.so-6-0-0.xr1.tc2.xs4all.net (194.109.5.10)  11.407 ms  11.447 ms  9.599 ms
 5  217.149.46.21 (217.149.46.21)  31.989 ms  29.321 ms  22.756 ms
 6  sl-bb21-ams-8-0.sprintlink.net (217.149.32.41)  13.415 ms  13.244 ms  12.569 ms
 7  213.206.131.46 (213.206.131.46)  11.147 ms  12.282 ms  11.222 ms
 8  ae-0-56.mp2.Amsterdam1.Level3.net (4.68.120.162)  7.862 ms ae-0-54.mp2.Amster\
dam1.Level3.net (4.68.120.98)  11.796 ms ae-0-52.mp2.Amsterdam1.Level3.net\
 (4.68.120.34)  11.000 ms
 9  as-0-0.bbr2.London2.Level3.net (4.68.128.110)  21.047 ms ae-1-0.bbr1.London2.\
```

```
Level3.net (212.187.128.46)  35.125 ms as-0-0.bbr2.London2.Level3.net\
(4.68.128.110)  17.183 ms
10  ae-15-53.car1.London2.Level3.net (4.68.117.79)  18.917 ms  17.388 ms ae-25-52.\
car1.London2.Level3.net (4.68.117.47)  18.992 ms
11  tge9-3-146.core-r-1.lon2.\
mnet.net.uk (212.187.196.82)  14.699 ms  17.381 ms  15.293 ms
12  85.133.32.134 (85.133.32.134)  27.130 ms  33.310 ms  37.576 ms
13  82.211.81.76 (82.211.81.76)  16.784 ms  20.140 ms  17.556 ms
14  * * *
15  * * *
16  * * *
17  * * *
```

With the `traceroute` command, you'll see every router that's passed. For each router, the name of the router is displayed, followed by its IP address and then the roundtrip times of the three packets that were sent to that router. You'll often see that a router replies with only a string of three asterisks (* * *), which indicates that the router forwards packets normally but is configured not to reply to ping packets for security reasons.

Testing Availability of Services

When the `ping` and `traceroute` commands show that everything is working, you're the proud owner of a working network interface. Next you can test the availability of two kinds of services: those on your computer itself and those on external computers. Because so many tools are available to test service availability, I won't try to cover them all, but I do want to discuss two of the most popular. First is the `netstat` tool, which you can use to test for the availability of services on the host where you run the command. And second is `nmap`, which is used to test availability on other hosts.

■**Caution** Some administrators consider any use of `nmap` on their hosts or their network as an attack against their security, so they don't allow it. I once used it in a hotel room in the United States to see if my server in Amsterdam was still offering all its services, and the hotel network shut me off immediately. In these circumstances, it can be a real pain to get your connection back, so be careful.

Using `netstat` to Check Your Server

If you want to know what services are available on your server and what these services are doing, the `netstat` command is an excellent choice. However, because many of its options require you to be root, I recommend that you use `netstat` as root only. To see the most useful information offered by `netstat`, use the `-platune` options, which make sure that you see information about programs connected to ports (`-p`) and what ports are actually listening (`-l`). Other options show you everything there is to show (`-a`), do that for TCP (`-t`) as well as UDP (`-u`), without translating IP addresses to DNS names (`-n`), and with extended information (`-e`).

If you think that netstat -platune offers too much information, use netstat -tulp instead. The results are slightly less verbose, which makes it easier to get the data you really need. Listing 8-15 shows the first screen of output generated by netstat -platune.

Listing 8-15. *The* netstat -platune *Command Provides an Exhaustive Overview of Everything Happening on Your Computer*

```
root@ZNA:~# netstat -platune
Active Internet connections (servers and established)
Proto Recv-Q Send-Q Local Address      Foreign Address     State   User\
       Inode       PID/Program name
tcp      0      0 127.0.0.1:3306         0.0.0.0:*                   LISTEN    103\
       12937       3839/mysqld
tcp      0      0 0.0.0.0:80          0.0.0.0:*        LISTEN    0\
       13209       3965/apache2
tcp      0      0 10.0.0.20:53        0.0.0.0:*        LISTEN    104\
       13737       3737/named
tcp      0      0 10.0.0.30:53        0.0.0.0:*        LISTEN    104\
       13735       3737/named
tcp      0      0 10.0.0.10:53        0.0.0.0:*        LISTEN    104\
       13733       3737/named
tcp      0      0 192.168.1.33:53     0.0.0.0:*        LISTEN    104\
       12821       3737/named
tcp      0      0 127.0.0.1:53        0.0.0.0:*        LISTEN    104\
       12819       3737/named
tcp      0      0 127.0.0.1:953       0.0.0.0:*        LISTEN    104\
       12824       3737/named
tcp6     0      0 :::53                  :::*        LISTEN\
     104       12816       3737/named
tcp6     0      0 :::22                  :::*        LISTEN\
       0       13585       4150/sshd
tcp6     0      0 ::1:953                :::*        LISTEN\
     104       12825       3737/named
tcp6     0      0 ::ffff:192.168.1.33:22  ::ffff:192.168.1.6:4197 ESTABLISHED0\
       13761       4229/1
tcp6     0    164 ::ffff:192.168.1.33:22  ::ffff:192.168.1.7:9688 ESTABLISHED0\
       13609       4158/0
udp      0      0 0.0.0.0:1024        0.0.0.0:*            104\
       12822       3737/named
udp      0      0 10.0.0.20:53        0.0.0.0:*            104\
       13736       3737/named
udp      0      0 10.0.0.30:53        0.0.0.0:*            104\
       13734       3737/named
udp      0      0 10.0.0.10:53        0.0.0.0:*            104\
       13732       3737/named
udp      0      0 192.168.1.33:53     0.0.0.0:*            104\
       12820       3737/named
udp      0      0 127.0.0.1:53        0.0.0.0:*            104\
```

```
         12818      3737/named
udp6     0       0 :::1025               :::*          104\
         12823      3737/named
udp6     0       0 :::53                 :::*          104\
         12815      3737/named
```

As you can see, the `netstat` command yields a lot of information when used with the `-platune` options. Table 8-2 explains the information displayed in Listing 8-15.

Table 8-2. *Information Offered by* `netstat -platune`

Item	Explanation
Proto	The protocol that's used; can be TCP or UDP.
Recv-Q	The number of packets waiting in the receive queue for this port at the moment that `netstat` was used.
Send-Q	The number of packets waiting to be sent from this port at the moment that `netstat` was used.
Local address	The local socket address (the local IP address followed by the port number that's used).
Foreign address	The address of the foreign host (if any) that currently has an open connection to this host.
State	The current state of the protocol connected to the mentioned port.
User	The numeric user ID of the user with whose permissions the process was started.
Inode	The inode(s) of files that currently are opened by the process.
PID/program name	The PID and name of the program that has currently claimed the mentioned port.

As you can see, `netstat` provides a complete overview of what's happening on your server. It's especially useful if you get error messages like "port already in use." In combination with the grep utility, it's easy to learn what port program is currently holding a port open and, if required, to terminate that program. For example, to find out what program is currently occupying port 80, use `netstat -platune | grep 80`. This returns a line like this:

```
root@ZNA:~# netstat -platune | grep 80
tcp      0       0 0.0.0.0:80       0.0.0.0:*        LISTEN      0\
         13209      3965/apache2
```

From this line, you can see that an Apache web server with a PID of 3965 is currently listening on port 80. Want to remove it? Use `kill 3965` and it's gone.

Using nmap to Check Service Availability on Remote Servers

The `netstat` command is a useful tool, but it works only on the host where you run it. Sometimes, when you cannot connect to a given service on a given host, you'd like to know if the service is available at all. You can do this with the `nmap` command. (Use `apt-get install nmap` to install it.) Like most powerful network tools, `nmap` also works best if you are root.

The nmap command is an expert tool that helps you find out exactly what's happening at another host. If you use it properly, the owner of that host will never even know that you were there. However, you should be aware that running a so-called *port scan* to monitor open ports on a given host is considered an intrusion by many administrators, so be careful about what you're doing with it because you might run into trouble if you use nmap on a host that isn't yours and you haven't notified its owner.

If you really want to keep things simple, just use nmap without arguments. For example, nmap 192.168.1.69 performs a basic scan on host 192.168.1.69 to find what common ports are open on it. This gives good results for day-to-day use; see Listing 8-16 for an example.

Listing 8-16. *The* nmap *Command Shows You What Services Are Offered by a Host*

```
root@ZNA:~# nmap 192.168.1.69

Starting Nmap 4.20 ( http://insecure.org ) at 2007-08-01 11:08 EDT
Interesting ports on 192.168.1.69:
Not shown: 1693 closed ports
PORT     STATE SERVICE
22/tcp    open  ssh
111/tcp   open  rpcbind
139/tcp   open  netbios-ssn
445/tcp   open  microsoft-ds
MAC Address: 00:18:8B:AC:C9:54 (Dell)

Nmap finished: 1 IP address (1 host up) scanned in 0.626 seconds
```

A very common reason why the test shown in Listing 8-16 could fail is that nmap normally tries to ping its targets first. On many hosts, ping commands are administratively prohibited, dropped, or ignored. And these hosts won't reveal anything when you issue nmap on them. To make sure that they're working even when you cannot ping, use the -P0 option to disable ping. Another useful option is -O, which tries to guess the operating system that is on the target host. And if you want to make sure that both TCP and UDP ports are scanned, you should include -sT and -sU as well. So the command becomes somewhat longer: nmap -sT -sU -P0 -O 192.168.1.69 would scan the target host with all those options. You'll notice that because nmap has to do a lot more work with these options, it takes considerably longer for the command to complete. Listing 8-17 shows the result of this scan.

Listing 8-17. *You Have Lots of Options to Specify How* nmap *Should Do Its Work*

```
root@ZNA:~# nmap -sT -sU -P0 -O 192.168.1.69

Starting Nmap 4.20 ( http://insecure.org ) at 2007-08-01 11:11 EDT
Interesting ports on 192.168.1.69:
Not shown: 3176 closed ports
PORT       STATE      SERVICE
22/tcp     open       ssh
111/tcp    open       rpcbind
139/tcp    open       netbios-ssn
```

```
445/tcp      open           microsoft-ds
68/udp       open|filtered  dhcpc
111/udp      open|filtered  rpcbind
631/udp      open|filtered  unknown
5353/udp     open|filtered  zeroconf
32768/udp    open|filtered  omad
MAC Address: 00:18:8B:AC:C9:54 (Dell)
Device type: general purpose
Running: Linux 2.6.X
OS details: Linux 2.6.14 - 2.6.17
Uptime: 0.176 days (since Wed Aug 1 07:23:05 2007)
Network Distance: 1 hop

OS detection performed. Please report any incorrect results at➥
http://insecure.org/ nmap/submit/ .
Nmap finished: 1 IP address (1 host up) scanned in 1482.860 seconds
```

In the last command, you'll most likely get a better result, but there's still a problem: the scan is rather noisy, and so the target host might log messages to tell its owner that you're using nmap on it. There's nothing wrong with that in most cases, but if you really want to put nmap through a thorough security test, you should use some stealth options such as -sF (FIN-scan), -sX (X-mas tree scan), or -sN (NULL-scan). All of these options use specific properties of the IP protocol to perform a stealth scan so that the target host never knows you were there. The disadvantage of these scan options is that they don't always work! On many modern operating systems, you'll find that the operating system ignores them, so you'll end up waiting a long time without a result.

Monitoring the Network Interface

Two useful tools are available to monitor what's happening on your servers' network cards. IPTraf offers a menu-driven interface from which you can monitor protocol activity, and the iftop utility shows how much bandwidth is used by a given connection.

Monitoring Protocol Activity with IPTraf

IPTraf is another useful tool to see what's happening on the network. It's not installed by default, however, so make sure that it's installed before you try to launch it from the command line with the iptraf command. (If it's not installed yet, use apt-get install iptraf.) After launching it as root, you'll see the menu interface (see Figure 8-1). You have several options in this interface:

- *IP traffic monitor*: This option tells IPTraf to monitor what's happening on the network interfaces in your server. You can select one particular network interface, but it's possible to check all the interfaces as well. When a connection is established, you'll see the connection happening in real time, indicating with what other node the connection is established and how many packets are flowing across that connection.

Figure 8-1. *The IPTraf tool offers different menu options to see what's happening on your server.*

- *General interface statistics*: This option provides generic information on what's happening on a network board. You'll see information such as the number of packets sent and received by the network interface, which is a good statistical overview of what's happening on a network board.

- *Detailed interface statistics*: As you would guess, this option provides more detail, such as the number of sent packets of a specific protocol type (see Figure 8-2).

```
IPTraf
 Statistics for eth0

                 Total      Total    Incoming   Incoming   Outgoing   Outgoing
                Packets     Bytes     Packets     Bytes     Packets     Bytes
    Total:          50      13738         28       2014         22      11724
    IP:             50      12930         28       1514         22      11416
    TCP:            41      12228         19        812         22      11416
    UDP:             9        702          9        702          0          0
    ICMP:            0          0          0          0          0          0
    Other IP:        0          0          0          0          0          0
    Non-IP:          0          0          0          0          0          0


    Total rates:_____       Broadcast packets:           9
                                           Broadcast bytes:           828

    Incoming rates:

                                           IP checksum errors:          0
    Outgoing rates:


 X-exit
```

Figure 8-2. *If you choose to view the detailed interface statistics, you'll see how many packets of a given protocol type are sent on an interface.*

- *Statistical breakdown*: This option lets you divide the incoming information into different columns, sorted by the protocols in use.

- *LAN station monitor*: This option provides an overview of the most active stations on the LAN. However, be aware that only those packets coming in on the host where you are running IPTraf are seen, unless you're connected directly to the monitoring port of a switch.

Apart from these options that you can use to specify how IPTraf should do its work, you also have a filter option and a configure option. The filter option is used to specify what kind of packets you want to see, and the configure option is used to configure IPTraf itself. For example, there's an option that allows you to specify what colors are used in the IPTraf interface.

Monitoring Bandwidth Usage with the `iftop` Utility

The `iftop` utility is simple but efficient. It shows you who has an open connection to a network card on your server and how much bandwidth they're consuming. It displays a summary total of transmitted and received packets for the selected network card, but a progress bar also provides a visual indication of the actual bandwidth usage of the given connection. As root, run `iftop` from the command line (if it's not installed yet, use `apt-get install iftop` to install it), and it will display the results window shown in Figure 8-3. On servers with more than one network card, don't forget to specify on which network card you want to run `iftop`. You can do that with the option `-i`; for instance, `iftop -i eth1` would show you usage statistics for `eth1`.

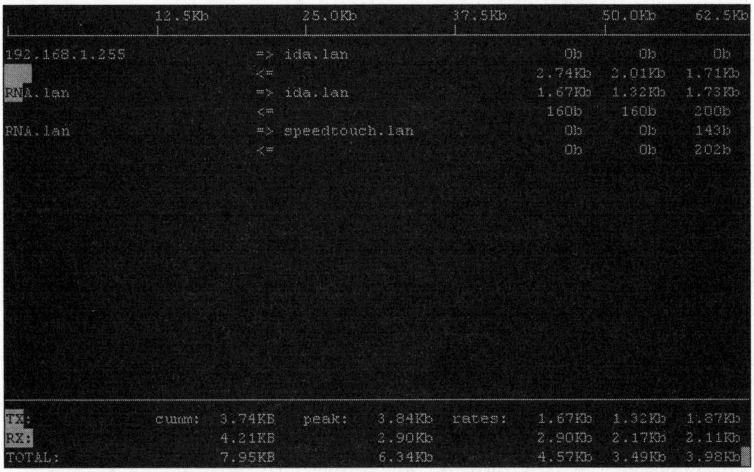

Figure 8-3. *The `iftop` utility displays actual bandwidth usage on your server.*

Monitoring Network Traffic

So, you've seen the tools that will help you monitor the local network cards of your server, but there are also some excellent tools to see what's happening on the network. The mother of all of these tools is tcpdump, which just dumps IP packets on the console you run it from. This tool is for the hardcore system administrator because it provides lots of information that normally scrolls by much too fast to see what's happening. Listing 8-18 shows the results of the tcpdump command.

Listing 8-18. *When Using* tcpdump, *You'll See Packet Headers Flying by on Your Server's Console*

```
root@RNA:/ # tcpdump
16:00:21.044803 IP ida.lan.9603 > RNA.lan.ssh: . ack 2705288 win 64503
16:00:21.044856 IP RNA.lan.ssh > ida.lan.9603: P 2705420:2705632(212) ack 12377 win\
 13936
16:00:21.044945 IP RNA.lan.ssh > ida.lan.9603: P 2705632:2705844(212) ack 12377 win\
 13936
16:00:21.045023 IP ida.lan.9603 > RNA.lan.ssh: . ack 2705632 win\
 64159
16:00:21.045076 IP RNA.lan.ssh > ida.lan.9603: P 2705844:2705976(132) ack 12377 win\
 13936
16:00:21.045166 IP RNA.lan.ssh > ida.lan.9603: P 2705976:2706188(212) ack 12377 win\
 13936
16:00:21.045220 IP RNA.lan.ssh > ida.lan.9603: P 2706188:2706320(132) ack 12377 win\
 13936
16:00:21.045267 IP ida.lan.9603 > RNA.lan.ssh: . ack 2705976 win 65535
16:00:21.045336 IP RNA.lan.ssh > ida.lan.9603: P 2706320:2706452(132) ack 12377 win\
 13936
...
23826 packets captured
24116 packets received by filter
288 packets dropped by kernel
```

Wireshark is built on top of tcpdump and can be used to view network packets from a graphical interface. This allows you to see what protocols are used, who is sending the packets, and even what is inside them. Before starting with these tools, however, you should know one thing: you can monitor only what you can see. If you're on a shared network in which every node sees every packet coming by, it's easy to monitor everything sent by all hosts on the network. But this isn't the case on modern switched networks.

If your computer is connected to a switch, you can see only those packets that are addressed to the host from where you run the monitoring software. To see the packets sent by others, you need a specialized tool, like the ARP poisoning tool Ettercap. (This is a very dangerous tool that can severely disturb network communications, and I won't be covering it in this book.) Another way of seeing all packets that are sent on the network is to connect the computer on which you're capturing packets to your switch's management port. This allows you to see all the packets sent on the network.

Using tcpdump

Because tcpdump is a very straightforward tool, it does exactly what its name promises: it dumps TCP packets on the console of your machine so you can see all packets received by the network board of your server. By default, it shows the first 96 bytes of every packet, but, if you need more details, you can start it with the -v option, or even the -vv option, so that it will be more verbose.

On a very busy server, tcpdump isn't very useful. The information passes by way too fast to see what's happening, so it makes sense to pipe its output to a file and grep that file for the information that you really need. Although tcpdump is an excellent tool for capturing packets, it isn't the best solution if you want to do something with the captured packets afterward. That would be Wireshark.

Analyzing Packets with Wireshark

Wireshark provides a graphical interface that you can use to capture and analyze packets, so it doesn't work directly on a server that's running without X. Also, you wouldn't want to install a complete GUI environment on your server just to run Wireshark. Instead of using it from your server directly, I recommend running it from a graphical workstation that is connected on the same network. It would show you the same information, anyway.

To start Wireshark, as root install it using apt-get install wireshark. Then run the wireshark command from the run command box, which you can open from the graphical console with Ctrl+F2. To start a Wireshark capture session, select Capture ➤ Interfaces. From the pop-up window, select the interface that you want to use to perform your packet capture (see Figure 8-4). Click Start to start the packet capture.

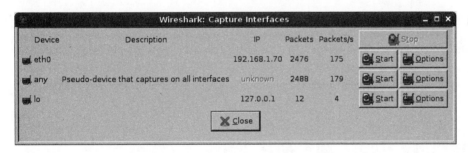

Figure 8-4. *Before starting a Wireshark packet capture, select the interface you want to perform the packet capture on and then click Start.*

Wireshark now starts filling its buffers. You won't see any packet contents while this is happening. To see the content of the packet buffer, you need to click the Stop button. As a result, you'll see the window shown in Figure 8-5. From this window you can sort packets and see packet details. To sort packets, click one of the columns. By default, they're sorted on the number they came in with, but if you click the Source column, you can sort the packets by their source address; and if you click the Protocol column, you can sort the packets by the protocol that was used. Any of the columns in the results window can be clicked to filter the information.

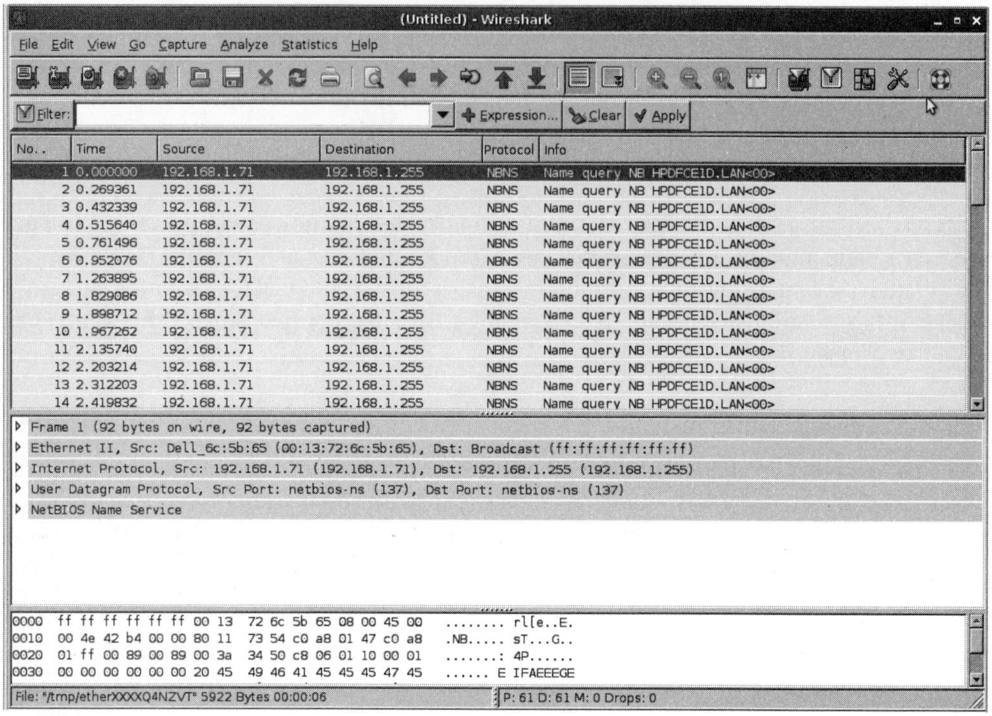

Figure 8-5. *You can browse the contents of packets from this results window.*

Click one of the packets to display more detail. For every packet that's captured, you can analyze all its layers. The top part of the Wireshark capture results window displays just the list of packets, but after selecting a packet in the lower part, you'll see the packet's different headers. If you really need to see details of any of these parts, click the part you want to zoom in on to display its contents. You might even see passwords being sent in plain text over the network.

Connecting Remotely with SSH

The essence of SSH is its security, and public and private keys naturally play an important role in it. On first making contact, the client and the server exchange public and private keys. In this communication, the server creates a key based on its private key—the so-called *host key*—and uses it as its proof of identity. When connecting, the server sends its public key to the client. If this is the first time the client has connected to this host, the host replies with the message shown in Listing 8-19.

Listing 8-19. *Establishing an SSH Session with an Unknown Host*

```
root@ZNA:~# ssh 192.168.1.70
The authenticity of host '192.168.1.70 (192.168.1.70)' can't be established.
RSA key fingerprint is fd:07:f6:ce:5d:df:6f:a2:84:38:c7:89:f1:3a:a6:34.
Are you sure you want to continue connecting (yes/no)? yes
```

```
Warning: Permanently added '192.168.1.70' (RSA) to the list of known hosts.
Password:
Last login: Tue Jul 31 15:34:15 2007 from ida.lan
root@RNA:~#
```

If the client trusts that this is really the intended host, it should answer yes to the request, in which case the host is then added to the .ssh/known_hosts file in the home directory of the user who initiated the SSH session. The next time the client connects to the host, this file is checked to see if the host is already known. The check is based on the public key fingerprint of the host, which is a unique checksum related to the public key of the host. The connection is established only if this check matches the name and public key of the server that the client is connecting to. If these two pieces of data don't match, it's very likely that the host the client is trying to connect to isn't the intended host, and the connection is refused.

Once the identity of the server you want to connect to is established, a secured channel is set up between the client and server. These secured channels are established by a session key, which is an encryption key that's the same on both the server and the client and encrypts all data sent between the two machines. The client and the server negotiate this session key based on their public keys. One of the things determined in this negotiation is the protocol that should be used. For example, session keys can use different encryption protocols such as 3DES, Blowfish, or IDEA.

After establishing the secured channel, the user on the client is asked for credentials; if nothing is configured, a prompt asks the user to enter his user name and password. Alternatively, the user can authenticate with his public/private key pair, thus proving that he really is the user that he says he is, but some more things have to be configured before that can happen.

All this might sound pretty complicated, but the nice thing is that the user doesn't notice any of it. The user just has to enter a user name and a password. If, however, you want to move beyond simple password-based authentication, it's necessary to understand what's happening.

Working with Public/Private Key Pairs

The security of SSH relies on the use of public/private key pairs. By default, the client tries to authenticate using RSA or DSA key pairs. To make this work, the server must have the client's public key, which is something that you have to configure by hand, as you'll see later. When the client has a public/private key pair, it generates an encrypted string with its private key. If the server can decrypt this string using the client's public key, the client's identity is authenticated.

When using public/private key pairs, you can configure different things. First, the user needs to determine what cryptographic algorithm she wants to use. For this purpose, she can choose between RSA and DSA (DSA is considered stronger). Next, she has to decide if she wants to protect her private key with a passphrase.

Using a passphrase is important because the private key really is used as the identity of the user. Should anyone steal this private key, it would be possible to forge the identity of the key's owner, so it's a very good idea to secure private keys with a passphrase.

Working with Secure Shell

Basically, Secure Shell is a suite of tools that consists of three main programs and a daemon: sshd. Before being able to use it, of course, you have to install it using `apt-get install openssh-server` (you might have installed it already using the SSH installation pattern when you installed your server). The tools are `ssh`, `scp`, and `sftp`. The first, `ssh`, is used to establish a secured remote session. Let's say that it's like telnet but cryptographically secured. The second, `scp`, is a very useful command that's used to copy files to and from another server where the SSH process is running. The third, `sftp`, is a secure FTP client interface. Using it establishes a secured FTP session to a server that's running the `sshd`.

Two of the best things of all these tools are that they can be used without any preparation or setup, and you can set them up to work entirely according to your needs. They are at once easy-to-use and very specialized tools.

Using the `ssh` Command

The simplest way to work with SSH is to just enter the `ssh` command, followed by the name of the host you want to connect to. For example, to connect to the host `AMS.sandervanvugt.com`, use `ssh AMS.sandervanvugt.com`.

Depending on whether you've connected to that host before, it may check the host credentials or just ask for your password. The `ssh` command doesn't ask for a user name because it assumes that you want to connect to the other host with the same identity that you're logged in with locally. If you'd rather log in with another user account, you can indicate this intention in one of two ways. You can specify the user name and follow it with an at sign (@) when establishing the connection to the remote host, and you can also use the `-l` option followed by the name of the user account you want to use to connect to the other host. So `ssh linda@AMS.sandervanvugt.com` and `ssh -l linda AMS.sandervanvugt.com` accomplish the same thing. After establishing a session, use the `exit` command (or Ctrl+D) to close the session and return to your own machine.

Now, it seems a lot of trouble to log in to a remote host if you just need to enter one or two commands. If you face this situation often, it's good to know that you can just specify the name of the command at the end of the `ssh` command: `ssh -l linda@AMS.sandervanvugt.com ls -l` provides a long listing of files that user linda has in her home directory at the other host. Of course, this isn't the most realistic example of how to use "one command only" sessions to a host, but you probably can see its value when working from shell scripts.

Using `scp` to Copy Files Securely

The `scp` command is another part of the SSH suite that you'll definitely like. It's used to copy files securely. If you know how the `cp` command works, you'll know how to handle `scp`. The only difference is that it requires a complete network pathname, including the names of the host and the file you want to copy. Also, if you don't want to use the name of the user you are currently logged in as, a user name should be included as well. Consider the following example:

```
scp /some/file linda@AMS.sandervanvugt.com:/some/file
```

This easy command copies `/some/file` to `AMS.sandervanvugt.com` and places it in the directory `/some/file` on that host. Of course, it's possible to do the opposite as well: `scp` root@SFO.sandervanvugt.com:/some/file /some/file copies /some/file from a remote host with the name SFO.sandervanvugt.com to the localhost. You'll like the -r option as well because it allows you to copy a complete subdirectory structure.

Using sftp for Secured FTP Sessions

As an alternative to copying files with scp, you can use the sftp command. This command is used to connect to servers running the sshd program and to establish a secured FTP session with it. From the sftp command, you have an interface that really looks a lot like the normal FTP client interface. All the standard FTP commands work here as well, except that it's secure in this case. For example, you can use the ls and cd commands to browse to a directory and see what files are available and use the get command from there to copy a file to the current local directory.

Configuring SSH

In an SSH environment, a node can be client and server simultaneously. So, as you can imagine, there's a configuration file for both of these aspects. The client is configured in /etc/ssh/ssh_config, and the server uses /etc/ssh/sshd_config. Setting options for the server isn't hard to understand: just put them in the configuration file for the /etc/ssh/sshd_config daemon. For the client settings, however, the situation is more complicated because there are several ways of overwriting the default client settings:

- The generic /etc/ssh/ssh_config file is applied to all users initiating an SSH session. An individual user can overwrite them if he creates a .ssh_config file in the .ssh directory of his home directory.

- An option in /etc/ssh/ssh_config has to be supported by the sshd_config file on the server you are connecting to. For example, if you're allowing password-based authentication from the client side, but the server doesn't allow it, it won't work.

- Options in both files can be overwritten with command-line options.

Table 8-3 is an overview of some of the most useful options that you can use to configure the client in ssh_config.

Table 8-3. *Useful options in* ssh_config

Option	Description
Host	This option restricts the following declarations (up to the next Host keyword) to a specific host. Therefore, this option is applied on a host that a user is connecting to. The host name is taken as specified on the command line. Use this parameter to add some extra security to specific hosts. You can also use wildcards such as * and ? to refer to more than one host name.
CheckHostIP	If this option is set to yes (the default value), SSH will check the host IP address in the known_hosts file. Use this as a protection against DNS or IP address spoofing.

Continued

Table 8-3. *Continued*

Option	Description
Ciphers	This option, which takes multiple arguments, is used to specify the order in which the different encryption algorithms should be tried to use in an SSHv2 session (version 2 is the default SSH version nowadays).
Compression	The yes/no values for this option specify whether to use compression. The default is no.
ForwardX11	This very useful option specifies if X11 connections will be forwarded. If set to yes, graphical screens from an SSH session can be forwarded through a secure tunnel. The result is that the DISPLAY environment variable that determines where to draw graphical screens is set correctly. If you don't want to enable X forwarding by default, use the -X option on the command line when establishing an SSH session.
LocalForward	This option specifies that a TCP/IP port on the local machine is forwarded over SSH to the specified port on a remote machine. (See "Generic TCP Port Forwarding" later in this chapter for more details.)
LogLevel	Use this option to specify the level of verbosity for log messages. The default value is INFO. If this doesn't go deep enough, VERBOSE, DEBUG, DEBUG1, DEBUG2, and DEBUG3 provide progressively more information.
PasswordAuthentication	Use this option to specify whether or not you want to use password authentication. By default, password authentication is used. In a secure environment in which keys are used for authentication, you can safely set this option to "no" to disable password authentication completely.
Protocol	This option specifies the protocol version that SSH should use. The default value is set to 2,1 (which indicates that version 2 should be used first and, if that doesn't work, version 1 is tried). It's a good idea to disable version 1 completely because it has some known security issues.
PubkeyAuthentication	Use this option to specify whether you want to use public key–based authentication. This option should always be set to the default value (yes) because public key–based authentication is the safest way of authenticating.

The counterpart of ssh_config on the client computer is the sshd_config file on the server. Many options that you can use in the ssh_config file are also available in the sshd_config file. However, some options are specific to the server side of SSH. Table 8-4 gives an overview of some of these options.

Table 8-4. *Important Options in* `sshd_config`

Option	Description
AllowTcpForwarding	Use this option to specify whether you want to allow clients to do TCP port forwarding. This is a very useful feature, and you'll probably want to leave it at its default value (yes).
Port	Use this option to specify the port that the server is listening on. By default, sshd is listening on port 22. If the SSH process is connected directly to the Internet, this will cause many people to try a brute-force attack on your server. Consider running the SSH process on some other port for increased security.
PermitRootLogin	Use this option to specify whether you want to allow root logins. To add additional security to your server, consider setting this option to the no value. If set to no, the root user has to establish a connection as a normal user and from there use su to become root or use sudo to perform certain tasks with root permissions.
PermitEmptyPasswords	Use this option to specify if you want to allow users to log in with an empty password. From a security perspective, this isn't a very good idea, so the default no value is suitable in most cases. If, however, you want to run SSH from a script and establish a connection without entering a password, it can be useful to change the value of this parameter to yes.
ChallengeResponseAuthentication	This option specifies whether users are allowed to log in using passwords. If you want to add additional security to your server by forcing users to log in with public/private key pairs only, give this parameter the value no.
X11Forwarding	Use this option to specify if you want to allow clients to use X11 forwarding. On Ubuntu Server, the default value for this parameter is yes.

Using Key-Based Authentication

Now that you know all about the basics of SSH, let's look at some of the more advanced options. One of the most important is key-based authentication, which SSH uses via public/private key–based authentication. Before diving into the configuration of key-based authentication, let's first have a look on how these keys are used.

A Short Introduction to Cryptography

In general, you can use two methods for encryption: symmetric and asymmetric. Symmetric encryption is faster but less secure, and asymmetric encryption is slower but more secure. In a symmetric key environment, both parties use the same key to encrypt and decrypt messages. With asymmetric keys, a public and a private key are used, and this is the important technique that's used for SSH.

If asymmetric keys are used, every user needs his own public/private key pair and every server needs a pair of them as well. Of these keys, the private key must be protected at all times; if the private key is compromised, the identity of the owner of the private key is compromised as well. In short, stealing a user's private key is like stealing their identity. Therefore, a private key is normally stored in a very secure place where no one other than its owner can access it; typically this is in ~/.ssh. The public key, on the other hand, is available to everyone.

Public/private keys are generally used for three purposes: encryption, authentication, and non-repudiation.

To send an encrypted message, the sender encrypts the message with the public key of the receiver who can decrypt it with the matching private key. This scenario requires that before you send an encrypted message, you have the public key of the person you want to send the message to.

The other options are to use public/private keys for authentication or to prove that a message has not changed since it was created. This method is known as nonrepudiation. In the example of authentication, the private key is used to generate an encrypted token, the salt. If this salt can be decrypted with the public key of the person who wants to authenticate, that proves that the server really is dealing with the right person, and access can be granted. However, this technique requires the public key to be copied to the server before any authentication can occur, which is also the case when keys are used to prove that a message hasn't been tampered with.

Using Public/Private Key–Based Authentication in an SSH Environment

When SSH key-based authentication is used, you must make sure that for all users who need to use this technology, the public key is available on the servers they want to log in to. When logging in, the user creates an authentication request that's signed with the user's private key. This authentication request is matched to the public key of the same user on the server where that user wants to be authenticated. If it matches, the user is allowed access; if it doesn't, user access is denied.

Public/private key–based authentication is enabled by default on Ubuntu Server, so it's only when no keys are present that the server prompts users for a password. The following steps provide a summary of what happens when a user tries to establish an SSH session with a server:

1. If public key authentication is enabled (the default), SSH checks the .ssh directory in the user's home directory to see if a private key is present.

2. If a private key is found, SSH creates a packet with some data in it (the salt), encrypts that packet with the private key, and sends it to the server. The public key is also sent with this packet.

3. The server now checks whether a file with the name authorized_keys exists in the home directory of the user. If it doesn't, the user can't be authenticated with his keys. If the file does exist, and the public key is an allowed key (and also is identical to the key that was previously stored on the server), the server uses this key to check the signature.

4. If the signature is verified, the user is granted access. If the signature can't be verified, the server prompts the user for a password instead.

All this sounds pretty complicated, but it really isn't. Everything happens transparently if it has been set up right. Also, there's hardly any noticeable delay when establishing a connection. It normally takes no more than a second.

Setting Up SSH for Key-Based Authentication

The best way to explain how to set up SSH for key-based authentication is by working through an example. In the following procedure, key-based authentication is enabled for the user root.

1. On the desktop where root is working, use the `ssh-keygen -t dsa -b 1024` command. This generates a public/private key pair of 1,024 bits. Listing 8-20 shows what happens.

Listing 8-20. *Generating a Public/Private Key Pair with* `ssh-keygen`

```
workstation # ssh-keygen -t dsa -b 1024
Generating public/private dsa key pair.
Enter file in which to save the key (/root/.ssh/id_dsa) :
Enter passphrase (empty for no passphrase):
Enter same passphrase again:
Your identification has been saved in /root/.ssh/id_dsa.
Your public key has been saved in /root/.ssh/id_dsa.pub.
The key fingerprint is:
59:63:b5:a0:c5:2c:b5:b8:2f:99:80:5b:43:77:3c:dd root@workstation
```

I'll explain what happens. The user in this example uses the `ssh-keygen` command to generate a public and a private key. The encryption algorithm used to generate this key is DSA, which is considered more secure than its alternative, RSA. The option `-b 1024` specifies that 1024-bit encryption should be used for the key. The longer this number, the more secure it is. Notice, however, that a many-bits encryption algorithm also requires more system resources to use it. After generating the keys, the command prompts you to save it somewhere. By default, a directory with the name `.ssh` is created in your home directory and, within this directory, a file with the name `id_dsa`. This file contains the private key.

Next, you're prompted to enter a passphrase, which is an important extra layer of protection that can be added to the key. Because anyone who has access to your private key (which isn't that easy) can forge your identity, your private key should always be protected with a passphrase. After entering the same passphrase twice, the private key is saved, and the related public key is generated and saved in the `/root/.ssh/id_dsa.pub` file. Also, a key fingerprint is generated. This fingerprint is a summary of your key, a checksum that's calculated on the key to alert you if the key has been changed. Make sure that your passphrase is not too easy to guess; a weak passphrase makes a strong key useless.

2. After creating the public/private key pair, you must transfer the public key to the server. The ultimate goal is to place the contents of the `id_dsa.pub` file in the `/root/.shh/authorized_keys` file on the server. But you can't simply copy the file to the `authorized_keys` destination file because other keys may already be stored there. Therefore, first use `scp` to copy the file to a temporary location. The command `scp /root/.ssh/id_dsa.pub root@server:/root/from_workstation_key.pub` would do the job.

3. Now that the public key is on the server, you have to put it in the `authorized_keys` file. Before doing this, though, make sure that the `.ssh` directory exists on the server in the home directory of the user root, and that it has user and group root as its owner and permission mode 700. Then, on the server with `/root` as your current directory, use `cat from_workstation_key.pub >> .ssh/authorized_keys`. This command appends the content of the public key file to the `authorized_keys` file, thus not overwriting any file that may have been there already.

4. Hopefully, no errors have occurred, and you've been successful. Go back to your workstation and start an SSH session to the server in which you just copied your public key to the `authorized_keys` file. You'll notice that you are no longer prompted for a password, but for a passphrase instead. This proves that everything worked. Do notice, however, that you need to repeat this procedure for every key-secured server with which you want to be able to establish a session.

Working with keys as described in these steps is an excellent way to make SSH authentication more secure. But there's a drawback: if you need to establish an SSH session automatically from a shell script or `cron` job, it's not very handy if you're first prompted for a key. Therefore, some method is needed to execute such jobs automatically. One solution is to create a special user account with limited permissions and without a passphrase on its private key. Another solution is to run `ssh-agent`, which caches the keys before they are used (you'll learn how to do this in the next section).

Caching Keys with `ssh-agent`

You can use `ssh-agent` to save yourself from constantly having to enter private keys. With this program, you can cache keys for a given shell environment. After starting `ssh-agent` from a shell prompt, you need to add the passphrase for the private key that belongs to it. This is something that you'll do for a specific shell, so after you close that specific shell or load another shell, you'll need to add the passphrase to that shell again.

After adding a passphrase to `ssh-agent`, the passphrase is stored in RAM, and only the user who added the key to RAM can read it from there. Also, `ssh-agent` listens only to the `ssh` and `scp` commands that you've started locally, so there's no way you can access a key that is kept by `ssh-agent` over the network. So you can be sure that using `ssh-agent` is pretty secure. Apart from being secure, it's pretty easy as well. Enabling `ssh-agent` and adding a passphrase to it is a simple two-step procedure:

1. From the shell prompt, use ssh-agent followed by the name of the shell you want to use it from. For example, use ssh-agent /bin/bash to activate ssh-agent for the Bash shell.

2. Now type ssh-add. You'll be prompted for the passphrase of your current private key, and you'll then see the message identity added, followed by the private key whose passphrase is added to ssh-agent.

■**Tip** Secure Shell is a great way of accessing other hosts. But did you know that you can also use it to mount a file system on a remote computer? All modern versions of SSH support this feature: just use sshfs for access to all the files and directories on the remote server, just like a local user on that server. If you know how to mount a directory with the mount command, working with sshfs is easy. For example, the command sshfs linda@AMS:/data /mnt allows access to the /data directory on the remote server and connects that directory to /mnt on the local server. Secure Shell is not installed by default, so use apt-get install sshfs to install it on your server.

Tunneling Traffic with SSH

Apart from establishing remote login sessions, copying files, and executing commands on remote hosts, you can also use SSH for TCP port forwarding. When used like this, SSH is a simple VPN solution with the capability of tunneling to almost any unsecured protocol over a secured connection. In this section, I'll first talk about X forwarding and then you'll see how to forward almost any protocol using SSH.

X Forwarding

Wouldn't it be useful if you could start an application on a server, where all the workload is performed by the server while you control the application from your client? Well, you can with SSH X forwarding. To use X forwarding, you first must establish an SSH session to the server you want to connect to. Next, from this SSH session, you start the graphical application, which will draw its screen on your workstation while doing all the work on the server itself.

Sounds good? Establishing such an environment has only two requirements:

- Make sure that the X11Forwarding option is set to yes in /etc/ssh/sshd_config on the server.

- Connect to the server with the ssh -X command from your client. Alternatively, you can set the X11Forwarding option in the client configuration file /etc/ssh/ssh_config, which allows you to forward graphical sessions by default. This poses a minor security problem, however, so this setting is not enabled by default on Ubuntu Server.

Now that you have established the SSH session with your server, start your favorite graphical program. The program itself will be executed at the remote host, and you'll see the screen locally.

> **Note** X-forwarding sessions with SSH are really cool, but there is a limitation: you need an X server on the client from which you are establishing the SSH session. This X server is used as the driver for your graphical hardware, and the application that you want to run on your client needs it to display its screens. This won't be a problem on Linux, UNIX, or Macintosh machines because an X server is present by default. It's a problem on Windows, however. The most common SSH client for Windows is PuTTY, which, although very useful, doesn't contain an X server. A good X server for Windows is Xming, which is a free X server that you can download from the Internet.

Generic TCP Port Forwarding

X is the only service for which port forwarding is hard-coded in the SSH software. For everything else, you need to do it by hand using the -L (local forwarding) or the -R (remote port forwarding) options. Let's have a look at the example in Figure 8-6.

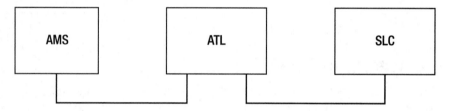

Figure 8-6. *Example network*

This network has three nodes: AMS is the node in which the administrator is working; ATL is the node in the middle; and AMS has a direct connection to ATL, but not to SLC which is behind a firewall. ATL does have a direct connection to SLC and is not obstructed by any firewall.

The following command illustrates a simple case of port forwarding:

```
linda@AMS:~> ssh -L 4444:ATL:110 linda@ATL
```

In this example, user linda forwards connections to port 4444 on her localhost to port 110 on the host ATL as user linda on that host. This is how you would establish a secure session to the insecure POP service on that host, for example. The localhost first establishes a connection to the SSH server running on ATL. This SSH server connects to port 110 at ATL, whereas ssh binds to port 4444 on the localhost. Now an encrypted session is established between local port 4444 and server port 110: everything sent to port 4444 on the localhost really goes to port 110 at the server. If, for example, you configured your POP mail client to get its mail from local port 4444, it would really get it from port 110 at ATL.

Notice that a nonprivileged port is used in this example. Only user root can connect to a privileged port with a port number lower than 1024. No matter what port you are connecting to, you should always check in the /etc/services services configuration file, in which port numbers are matched to names of services, what the port is normally used for (if anything), and use netstat -platune | grep <your-intended-port> to make sure that the port is not already in use.

A little variation on local port forwarding, as just seen, is remote port forwarding. If you want to try it, forward all connections on a remote port at a remote server to a local port on your machine. To do this, use the -R option as in the following example:

```
linda@AMS:~> ssh -R 4444:AMS:110 linda@ATL
```

In this example, user linda connects to host ATL (see the last part of the command). On this remote host, port 4444 is addressed by using the construction -R 4444. This remote port is redirected to port 110 on the localhost. As a result, anything going to port 4444 on ATL is redirected to port 110 on AMS. This example would be useful if ATL were the client and AMS were the server running a POP mail server that user linda wants to connect to.

Another very useful instance is when the host you want to forward to cannot be reached directly, perhaps because it is behind a firewall. In this case, you can establish a tunnel to another host that is reachable with SSH. Imagine that in Figure 8-6, the host SLC is running a POP mail server that our user linda wants to connect to. This user would use the following command:

```
linda@AMS:~> ssh -L 4444:SLC:110 linda@ATL
```

In this example, linda forwards connections to port 4444 on her localhost to server ATL that is running SSH. This server, in turn, forwards the connection to port 110 on server SLC. Note that, in this scenario, the only requirement is that ATL has the SSH service activated; no sshd is needed on SLC for this to work. Also note that there is no need for host AMS to get in direct contact with SLC because that's what ATL is used for.

In these examples, you learned how to use the ssh command to accomplish port forwarding, but this isn't the only way of doing it. If a port-forwarding connection needs to be available all the time, you can put it in the ssh configuration file at the client computer. Put it in .ssh/config in your home directory if you want it to work for your user account only, or put it in /etc/ssh/ssh_config if you want it to apply for all users on your machine. The parameter that should be used as an alternative to ssh -L 4444:ATL:110 would be LocalForward 4444 ATL:110.

Summary

In this chapter you learned how to set up a network connection. First, we explored how an IP address is assigned to a network interface card. We covered IPv4 addresses as well as IPv6 addresses. Following that, you read how to troubleshoot a network connection using basic commands such as ping and traceroute, or advanced tools such as nmap and Wireshark. In the last part of this section, you learned how to create a remote session with SSH. In the next chapter, you'll find out how to set up networking services such as NTP, DHCP, and DNS on your server.

■■■

## CHAPTER 9

Configuring Network Infrastructure Services Using DNS, DHCP, and NTP

Linux servers are often used to configure services that help make networking happen. These services include DNS for name resolution, DHCP for IP address configuration, and NTP for time services. In this chapter, you'll read how to configure them. You'll also read how to enable some common Linux services using `xinetd`.

Configuring DNS

As you would expect, IP (Internet protocol) is used for all communications on the Internet. This protocol specifies unique IP addresses that computers use to talk to one another. To contact a computer, you just need to know its IP address. One of the most important reasons why the domain name system (DNS) was developed is because computers work better with numbers than humans do, and humans tend to prefer names. So, DNS translates IP addresses to DNS names (and back from DNS names to IP addresses). In this chapter, you'll learn how to configure DNS on Ubuntu Server.

Methods of Name Resolution

Before going into detail about configuring DNS servers, you first need to learn exactly what DNS is and how it works. In this section, you'll read about the differences between DNS and other methods of resolving names. You'll also find out how the DNS hierarchy is structured and what roles the different types of DNS servers play in this hierarchy.

DNS is not the only solution that you can use for name resolving. Let's have a quick look at two of the alternative methods: the `/etc/hosts` file and Sun's Network Information System (NIS).

Managing Host Name Information with the `/etc/hosts` File

Before centralized systems such as NIS and DNS were introduced, every host kept its own file that mapped IP addresses to names. In the days when the Internet was called (D)ARPANet and was still a very small network, this was a feasible solution, although the administrator had to make sure that these files were updated properly. Such a mechanism still exists, but in the form of the /etc/hosts file. In this file, you can keep a list of commonly used names and their IP addresses. Ubuntu Server creates this file by default to make sure that the localhost can be resolved. Listing 9-1 shows an example of the file. Note that you can still use this file as an addition to DNS. Depending on the settings in /etc/nsswitch.conf, its contents will be checked first before any DNS lookup.

Listing 9-1. *Displaying the Contents of* /etc/hosts

```
root@RNA:~# cat /etc/hosts
127.0.0.1      localhost
127.0.1.1      RNA.lan RNA

# The following lines are desirable for IPv6 capable hosts
::1     ip6-localhost ip6-loopback
fe00::0 ip6-localnet
ff00::0 ip6-mcastprefix
ff02::1 ip6-allnodes
ff02::2 ip6-allrouters
ff02::3 ip6-allhosts
```

Using NIS to Manage Name Resolution

A more convenient method that you can use to keep mappings between host names and IP addresses is Sun's NIS, also known as the Yellow Pages. This system uses a database for important configuration files on a server, such as the /etc/hosts file, the /etc/passwd file, and /etc/shadow. As an administrator, you can determine for yourself what files to manage with NIS. These files are converted to NIS maps, which are the indexed files that comprise the NIS database. In NIS, one server is configured as the master server, which maintains the NIS database. All nodes are configured as NIS clients and send their name resolution requests to the NIS master. To provide redundancy, NIS can also use slave servers, which offer a read-only copy of the NIS master database. However, the master server is the single point of administration.

Although NIS was a good solution to manage relevant information within a network, it never became very popular as an Internet-level name service mainly because NIS does not provide a hierarchical solution, only flat databases. All these flat databases are managed by local administrators, and there's no relation among the databases that are used in different NIS domains.

The large amount of information on the Internet today makes it impossible to get quick results from a structure like NIS. For this reason, most organizations that still use NIS are phasing it out and configuring DNS to resolve host names to IP addresses and LDAP to manage user information (therefore, NIS is not covered in this book).

Managing Search Order with the /etc/nsswitch.conf File

Although DNS is the main system used for name resolution, it's not the only one. You can set it up in parallel with a NIS system and the /etc/hosts file. If you do this, the order in which the

different systems are searched is important. The search order is determined by the
/etc/nsswitch.conf file; see Listing 9-2 for an example.

Listing 9-2. *Contents of the* /etc/nsswitch.conf *File*

```
root@RNA:~# cat /etc/nsswitch.conf
# /etc/nsswitch.conf
#
# Example configuration of GNU Name Service Switch functionality.
# If you have the 'glibc-doc-reference' and 'info' packages installed, try:
# 'info libc "Name Service Switch"' for information about this file.

passwd:         compat
group:          compat
shadow:         compat

hosts:          files dns
networks:       files

protocols:      db files
services:       db files
ethers:         db files
rpc:            db files

netgroup:       nis
```

For all the important information on your server, the nsswitch.conf file contains an indication of where it should be searched. In the case of hosts and network information, the
example file is pretty clear: it first checks local configuration files and only after that does it
check the DNS hierarchy. This means that you can use /etc/hosts to override information as
defined in DNS.

Structure of the DNS Hierarchy

The most important advantage offered by DNS is that it's organized in a hierarchical manner.
This makes the system very scalable because it can be extended by simply adding another
branch to the tree-like hierarchy.

On top of the hierarchy are the root servers, which have one purpose only: to provide
information about the top-level domains (TLDs). Some fixed domain names are used for top-
level domains, including .com, .org, and .info. TLDs exist for all countries as well, such as
.nl, .uk, .fr, and so on. Within these TLDs, persons and organizations can create their own
domains, which can contain subdomains as well. For example, an organization could create a
domain called example.com and, within the structure of example.com, it could create some subdomains as well, such as east.example.com and west.example.com.

The number of subdomains is virtually unlimited, although it becomes hard to work
with more than four or five levels of domains. No one wants to type www.servers.east.nl.
sandervanvugt.com all the time, do they? Figure 9-1 provides an example of the partial DNS
hierarchy.

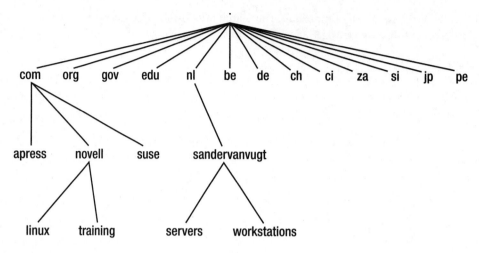

Figure 9-1. *Example of a part of the DNS hierarchy*

Master and Slave Servers

Within the DNS hierarchy, different servers are responsible for the data in specific domains (and sometimes subdomains as well). These are the so-called name servers and the part of the hierarchy that they are responsible for is the zone. A zone can include more than just one domain; for example, if one name server is responsible for everything in sandervanvugt.nl, including the subdomain's servers and workstations, the complete zone is sandervanvugt.nl. If, however, there's a subdomain called sales.sandervanvugt.com that has its own name server, the subdomain would be a zone by itself that is not part of sandervanvugt.com. Speaking in a very generic way, a zone is just a branch of the DNS hierarchy.

All zones should have at least two name servers. The first is the master name server, which is ultimately responsible for the data in a zone. For fault tolerance and to make the information more accessible, it's a good idea to use one or more slave servers as well. These slave servers will periodically get an update of all the data on the master server by means of a zone transfer; this is the process the master server uses to update the database on the slave server.

Note that DNS uses a single-master model: updates are performed on the master server and nowhere else, and the databases on the slave servers are read-only. You should also know that the name servers do not need to be in the zone that they are responsible for. For example, the name server of a given domain will often be hosted by the Internet provider that (of course) has its own domain. You can maintain your own DNS server, and it's useful to do so if your organization is larger than average, but you don't have to. You can also just purchase a domain and have your Internet server do the name server maintenance work.

Connecting the Name Servers in the Hierarchy

Because DNS uses a hierarchy, the servers in DNS need to know about each other, and this is a two-way process by its very nature. First, all servers in subordinate zones need to know where to find the root servers of the DNS hierarchy. Equally, the servers of the upper-level zones need to know how to find the servers of lower-level zones. You can very well create your own DNS domain called mynicednsdomain.com and run your DNS server in it, but it doesn't make sense if the DNS server that's responsible for the .com domain doesn't know about it. This is because a client trying to find your server will first ask the name server of the domain above your zone if it knows where to find authoritative information for your domain.

This is why DNS domain names need to be registered. Only then can the manager of the domain above yours configure your name server as the responsible name server for your domain. This is the delegation of authority.

It also helps to understand what happens when a user tries to resolve a DNS name that it doesn't know about already. The next procedure describes what happens:

1. To resolve DNS names, you need to configure the DNS resolver on the user's workstation or on the server that needs to be part of the DNS hierarchy. The DNS resolver is the part of the workstation where the user has configured how to find a DNS server. On a Linux system, this happens in the /etc/resolv.conf file.

2. Based on the information in the DNS resolver, the client contacts its preferred name server and asks that server to resolve the DNS name, no matter what server it is and where on Earth the server is running. So, if the client tries to resolve the name www.sandervanvugt.nl, it first asks its preferred name server. The advantage is that the client's name server can consult its cache to find out whether it has recently resolved that name for the client. If it knows the IP address of the requested server, the DNS name server returns that information to the client immediately.

3. If the name server of the client doesn't know the IP address of the requested server, it sees whether a forwarder is configured. (A *forwarder* is just a server that a name server contacts if it can't resolve a name by itself.)

4. If no forwarder is configured, the DNS name server contacts a name server of the root domain and asks that name server how to contact the name server of the top-level domain it needs. In the example in which you want to reach the host www.sandervanvugt.nl, this is the name server for the .nl domain.

5. Once the name server of the client finds the name server address of the top-level domain, it contacts it and asks for the IP address of the authoritative name server for the domain it's looking for. In our example, this would be the name server for sandervanvugt.nl.

6. Once the name server of the client finds out how to reach the authoritative name server for the domain the client asks for, it contacts that name server and asks to resolve its name. In return, the name server of the client receives the IP address it needs.

7. Ultimately, the IP address of the desired server is returned to the client, and contact can be established.

Resource Records

To answer all name resolution requests, your DNS server needs to maintain a database in which it maintains the *resource records*, which contain different types of data to find specific information for a domain. Table 9-1 presents some of the most important types of data that can be maintained in that database. Later in this chapter you'll learn how to add these resource records to the DNS database. Listing 9-3 shows an example of the DNS database in which different resource record types are used. You'll find an explanation of the resource record types in Table 9-1.

Listing 9-3. *Contents of the* example.com *Zone File*

```
RNA:/ # cat /etc/bind/db.example.com
$TTL 2D
@                IN SOA          SFO.example.com.     root.SFO.example.com. (
                                 2006080700           ; serial
                                 3H                   ; refresh
                                 1H                   ; retry
                                 1W                   ; expiry
                                 1D )                 ; minimum


example.com.     IN MX           10 mail.example.com.
example.com.     IN NS           lax.example.com.
sfo              IN A            201.100.100.10
lax              IN A            201.100.100.40
web              IN CNAME        sfo.example.com.
```

Table 9-1. *Using the Important Resource Records*

Resource Record	Use
MX	This resource record finds the mail servers for your domain. In the first column, you'll find the name of the domain they are used for, and the fourth column reveals the primary mail server. The number 10 indicates the priority of this mail server. If more than one mail server is present in the domain, the mail server with the lowest priority number is used first. Following the priority number is the DNS name of the mail server.
NS	This resource record provides a list of name servers for this domain. Typically, you must have this resource record for all master and slave name servers of the domain. The first column reveals the name of the domain, and the fourth column provides the name of the server itself. Notice the dot at the end of the server name, which indicates it as an absolute name (a name that refers to the root of the DNS hierarchy directly).
A	The A resource record is used to define the relation between a host name and an IP address. The first column mentions the name of the host as it occurs in this domain, and the fourth column provides the IP address of this host.
CNAME	The CNAME ("common name") resource record is used to define an alias, which is just a nickname that is used for a host. A CNAME should always refer to the real name of the host. Aliases can be useful if one server hosts many DNS names. In that case, use an A resource record for "myserver" and create CNAMEs that refer to the A resource record for all services provided by your server. This way, if you have to change the IP address of your server, you'll change it only once.

Introducing Forward and Reverse DNS

Before I start talking about the actual configuration of DNS, you need to know about reverse DNS. Translating names into IP addresses is one task of the DNS server, and its other task is translating IP addresses to names. This translation from address to name is called *reverse DNS*, and it's necessary if you want to find the real name that is used by a given IP address. This feature is useful if you want names in your log files instead of IP addresses, but, if you want all IP addresses translated to names, you should realize that this comes at a cost in performance. For this reason, many services and commands allow you to specify whether to use reversed name resolution. To make name resolution for your domain possible, you should always configure it when setting up a DNS hierarchy.

To create a reverse DNS structure, you need to configure a zone in the `in-addr.arpa` domain, under which a structure is created that contains the inverse IP addresses for your network. If, for example, you're using the class C network 201.10.19.0/24, you should create a DNS domain with the name `19.10.201.in-addr.arpa`. Within this zone, you next have to create a pointer (PTR) resource record for all of the hosts that you want to include in the DNS hierarchy.

When working with reverse DNS, you should be aware of one important limitation: it doesn't know how to handle non-default subnet masks. In other words, it works only if you have the complete network, and it doesn't work if you've registered a couple of IP addresses only with your IP. If you have only one (or very few) IP addresses out of a complete range, you should ask your IP to set up reverse DNS for you.

Configuring DNS

When setting up DNS, you have to configure a series of configuration files, and in this section you'll learn how these relate to each other. At this point, make sure that the DNS server is installed by using `apt-get install bind9` as root.

/etc/bind/named.conf

The `/etc/bind/named.conf` file is the master configuration file for your DNS server. Listing 9-4 provides an example. The `named.conf` file is a master configuration file that contains all you need to get a working DNS set up. To set up your own additional zones, you have to use the `/etc/bind/named.conf.local` file.

Listing 9-4. *Default* /etc/bind/named.conf *File*

```
root@RNA:~# cat /etc/bind/named.conf
// This is the primary configuration file for the BIND DNS server named.
//
// Please read /usr/share/doc/bind9/README.Debian.gz for information on the
// structure of BIND configuration files in Debian, *BEFORE* you customize
// this configuration file.
//
// If you are just adding zones, please do that in /etc/bind/named.conf.local
```

```
include "/etc/bind/named.conf.options";

// prime the server with knowledge of the root servers
zone "." {
        type hint;
        file "/etc/bind/db.root";
};

// be authoritative for the localhost forward and reverse zones, and for
// broadcast zones as per RFC 1912

zone "localhost" {
        type master;
        file "/etc/bind/db.local";
};

zone "127.in-addr.arpa" {
        type master;
        file "/etc/bind/db.127";
};

zone "0.in-addr.arpa" {
        type master;
        file "/etc/bind/db.0";
};

zone "255.in-addr.arpa" {
        type master;
        file "/etc/bind/db.255";
};



include "/etc/bind/named.conf.local";
```

Several other files are called from the main configuration file (/etc/bind/named.conf). Before starting to configure your own DNS server, let's look at how these files relate to each other:

- /etc/bind/named.conf.local: This file contains the DNS zones that you set up on your server.

- /etc/bind/named.conf.options: In this file you'd put generic options that define the working of your DNS server.

- *The db files*: These are database files that store the information for specific zones. Every zone has its own db file, so there should be many of these db files on a completely configured DNS server. For example, the following code lines that come from /etc/bind/named.conf refer to the database for the localhost zone:

```
zone "localhost" {
        type master;
        file "/etc/bind/db.local";
};
```

When setting up your own DNS server, it can be quite hard to configure the right files in the right way. So let's do a setup for the example.com zone.

■**Tip** If you want to set up a working DNS environment, you should have your own DNS domain, which you can get from your IP. If you don't have your own DNS domain, you can use the example.com domain. This domain is not used for real on the Internet and can therefore be used by anyone who wants to set up a local-only DNS test environment.

---

1. Don't touch the /etc/bind/named.conf file. It contains default settings, and you never need to modify it on Ubuntu Server.

2. Open the /etc/bind/named.conf.local file with an editor and use the following code:

```
zone "example.com" in {
        allow-transfer { any; };
        file "/etc/bind/db.example.com";
        type master;
};
```

3. In this example configuration, the zone "example.com" statement is used as a defini- tion of the zone that you want to use. After the definition of the zone itself and between brackets, specify the options for that zone. In this example, they are as follows:

   - allow-transfer { any; };: This option specifies what name servers are allowed to synchronize their databases with the information in this database.

   - file "/etc/bind/db.example.com";: This line indicates what file contains the spe- cific configuration for this zone.

   - type master;: This option indicates the definition of the master name server for this zone.

4. You've now defined the file in which the DNS server can find the specific configuration for example.com. Next, you need to set up reversed name resolution as well. If example.com is using the IP network 201.100.100.0, you should open /etc/bind/ named.conf.local once more and enter the following code:

```
zone "100.100.201.in-addr.arpa" {
        type master;
        file "/etc/bind/db.100.100.201";
};
```

5. Now that you've set up the basic structure for DNS, you need to create the database files in /etc/bind that contain the actual configuration of the DNS zones. I'll explain how to do this and all your available options in the next few sections.

Using named.conf Options

Before you create the database files that you refer to in the named.conf file and its related files, let's have a look at some of the options that you can use in the /etc/bind/named.conf file and its related /etc/bind/named.conf.local and /etc/bind/named.conf.options files.

Ubuntu Server uses the /etc/bind/named.conf.options file to include options in the DNS configuration. This file is included with the line include "/etc/bind/named.conf.options"; in /etc/bind/named.conf. Listing 9-5 shows the file as it is by default.

Listing 9-5. *The* /etc/bind/named.conf.options *File Contains Generic Options for Your* bind *Name Server*

```
root@RNA:~# cat /etc/bind/named.conf.options
options {
        directory "/var/cache/bind";

        // If there is a firewall between you and name servers you want
        // to talk to, you might need to uncomment the query-source
        // directive below.  Previous versions of BIND always asked
        // questions using port 53, but BIND 8.1 and later use an unprivileged
        // port by default.

        // query-source address * port 53;

        // If your ISP provided one or more IP addresses for stable
        // name servers, you probably want to use them as forwarders.
        // Uncomment the following block, and insert the addresses replacing
        // the all-0's placeholder.

        // forwarders {
        //      0.0.0.0;
        // };

        auth-nxdomain no;    # conform to RFC1035
        listen-on-v6 { any; };

        // By default, name servers should only perform recursive domain
        // lookups for their direct clients.  If recursion is left open
        // to the entire Internet, your name server could be used to
        // perform distributed denial-of-service attacks against other
        // innocent computers.  For more information on DDoS recursion:
        // http://cve.mitre.org/cgi-bin/cvename.cgi?name=CVE-2006-0987
```

```
    allow-recursion { localnets; };

    // If you have DNS clients on other subnets outside of your
    // server's "localnets", you can explicitly add their networks
    // without opening up your server to the Internet at large:
    // allow-recursion { localnets; 192.168.0.0/24; };

    // If your name server is only listening on 127.0.0.1, consider:
    // allow-recursion { 127.0.0.1; };
};
```

As you see in the example file in Listing 9-5, you have quite a few options. In the example file, many options are disabled by default ,and others are just not available. Let's have a look at some of the more common options:

- `options { .... };`: Use this statement to indicate the start and the end of the section that contains the options. All generic options need to be in this section, so notice the structure used by this statement. It starts with a bracket, it ends with a bracket, and all specific options are defined between the brackets. When putting this in manually, do not forget the semicolon after the last bracket.

- `directory "/var/cache/bind";`: You can use this parameter to define the location in which all DNS configuration files are stored. If an incomplete file name is used anywhere in one of the DNS configuration files, the DNS name server looks for it in this directory. If, however, an absolute file name (a file with a complete directory reference) is used, it just follows the absolute file name. Also note the semicolon at the end of the line; this is an important syntax feature.

- `notify no;`: This option indicates that slave servers should not be notified of changes, which leaves it completely to the slave server to make sure that it is up to date. If you want an alert to be sent to a slave server when a change occurs, change this setting to `notify yes;`.

- `forwarders;`: By default, if your DNS server gets a request to resolve a name for which it is not responsible, it starts querying a root server of the DNS hierarchy to find the required information. You can change this behavior by using a forwarder, which is another DNS name server that typically has a large cache that it uses to resolve names very quickly. You could, for example, use your IP's DNS name server as a DNS forwarder.

Zone Definition in `/etc/bind/named.conf.local`

Among the most important DNS server options is the definition of zones. As you can see in the example in Listing 9-4, the first zone that is defined is the zone ".". This refers to the root of the DNS domain. The definition is required to hook up your DNS server to the rest of the DNS hierarchy. To do this, the zone definition in `/etc/bind/named.conf` indicates that a list of name servers for the root domain can be found in the `db.root` file. Listing 9-6 is a portion of the contents of that file.

Listing 9-6. *The* db.root *File Makes Sure That Your DNS Server Can Contact Other Servers in the DNS Hierarchy*

```
root@RNA:~# cat /etc/bind/db.root

; <<>> DiG 9.2.3 <<>> ns . @a.root-servers.net.
;; global options:  printcmd
;; Got answer:
;; ->>HEADER<<- opcode: QUERY, status: NOERROR, id: 18944
;; flags: qr aa rd; QUERY: 1, ANSWER: 13, AUTHORITY: 0, ADDITIONAL: 13

;; QUESTION SECTION:
;.                               IN      NS

;; ANSWER SECTION:
.                       518400  IN      NS      A.ROOT-SERVERS.NET.
.                       518400  IN      NS      B.ROOT-SERVERS.NET.
...
.                       518400  IN      NS      L.ROOT-SERVERS.NET.
.                       518400  IN      NS      M.ROOT-SERVERS.NET.

;; ADDITIONAL SECTION:
A.ROOT-SERVERS.NET.     3600000 IN      A       198.41.0.4
B.ROOT-SERVERS.NET.     3600000 IN      A       192.228.79.201
...
L.ROOT-SERVERS.NET.     3600000 IN      A       198.32.64.12
M.ROOT-SERVERS.NET.     3600000 IN      A       202.12.27.33

;; Query time: 81 msec
;; SERVER: 198.41.0.4#53(a.root-servers.net.)
;; WHEN: Sun Feb  1 11:27:14 2004
;; MSG SIZE  rcvd: 436
```

The db Files

The zone files of your DNS server are stored in the /etc/bind directory, and the name of these files typically starts with "db" (although nothing says that you have to name them this way). The named.conf file specifies where to look for these database files. The next part you need to understand is how this file is structured to define your DNS zone. In Listing 9-7 you can see the example that I introduced in Listing 9-3.

Listing 9-7. *Contents of the* example.com *Zone File*

```
RNA:/ # cat /etc/bind/db.example.com
$TTL 2D
@               IN SOA          SFO.example.com.        root.SFO.example.com. (
                                2006080700              ; serial
                                3H                      ; refresh
```

```
                         1H                      ; retry
                         1W                      ; expiry
                         1D )                     ; minimum

example.com.    IN MX            10 mail.example.com.
example.com.    IN NS            lax.example.com.
sfo             IN A             201.100.100.10
lax             IN A             201.100.100.40
web             IN CNAME         sfo.example.com.
```

As you can see, the zone file starts with generic settings. First, the TTL 2D parameter speci-fies a validity of two days if your slave server cannot synchronize with the master. Next to be defined are the SOA settings for your server, which are the settings for the authoritative name server of this domain. Notice the mail address for the administrator of your DNS server: root.SFO.example.com. After that, you see the following synchronization settings:

- serial: This number should be changed every time you change the database on the master server. By changing it, a slave server that wants to synchronize with the master server can see that an update has occurred and start the zone transfer. Notice that the serial number typically consists of the current year, current month, and current day, fol-lowed by two digits that indicate the event number. For example, after the third change on December 12, 2007, the serial number would be 07121202.

- refresh: This indicates the interval used on a slave server between updates from the zone information at the master server.

- retry: If the update fails the first time the slave server tries to synchronize, this interval specifies how long it should wait before trying again.

- expiry: If a slave server fails to contact the master server for a longer period, this setting indicates how long before the information at the slave server expires. After expiration, the slave server no longer answers DNS queries.

- minimum: This is the length of time that a negative response is cached on this server.

Following the generic information, you can see the definition of the resource records. In the previous example, only the four most common resource records are used. (A more com-plete overview was provided in "Resource Records" earlier in this chapter.)

Configuring Reversed Lookup

Until this moment, we've looked at just normal name resolution in which a name is resolved into an IP address. As I've mentioned, on a DNS server, you need reversed name resolution as well. To configure reversed lookup, you first need to set up the /etc/bind/named.conf.local file with the information about the zone you want to configure it for. As discussed earlier, this part of the configuration should look like the following lines:

```
zone "100.100.201.in-addr.arpa" {
        type master;
        file "/etc/bind/db.100.100.201";
};
```

Next, you need to set up the zone file for reverse lookup as well. Listing 9-8 shows a typical reverse lookup file. As instructed in the named.conf.local file, this definition comes from the /etc/bind/db.100.100.201 file.

Listing 9-8. *Example of a Reverse Lookup DNS Zone File*

```
$TTL 2D
@    N SOA    SFO.example.com.   root.SFO.example.com. (
                2006080700      ; serial
                3H              ; refresh
                1H              ; retry
                1W              ; expiry
                1D )            ; minimum


"                   IN NS            lax.example.com.
10                  IN PTR           sfo.example.com.
40                  IN PTR           lax.example.com.
```

You can see that Listing 9-8 uses one resource records type that's specific for a reverse DNS zone: the PTR record. As shown in Table 9-1, this record is used to connect a partial IP address (10 and 40 in Listing 9-8) to a complete DNS name.

Testing Your Name Server

After setting up the DNS name server, it's time to (re)start and test it. First, use the /etc/init.d/bind9 restart command (or start it if it wasn't started yet). Next, use ps aux | grep named to check whether the named process is really running. Then make sure that your local named process on your server is used for name resolving. Next, use the ping command to any host name to check if you can contact a server by its name. If this succeeds, your DNS server is working properly. If it fails, make sure that all your configuration files are set up properly.

If the ping command fails, you can use the host command for detailed testing of your DNS server. The general syntax of this command is host computer nameserver. For example, use host myhost 193.79.237.39 to query the specific name server 193.79.237.39 about the records it has for host myhost. Next, the host command reveals the IP address that's related to that host (according to the name server). The opposite is possible as well; for example, the command host 82.211.81.158 provides the name of the host you've queried. You can use the host command without referring to a specific DNS server, in which case the DNS servers as mentioned in /etc/resolv.conf are used. Listing 9-9 shows three examples of the host command in action.

Listing 9-9. *Using the host Command to Test a DNS Server*

```
root@RNA:~# host www.ubuntu.com 193.79.237.39
Using domain server:
Name: 193.79.237.39
Address: 193.79.237.39#53
Aliases:
```

```
www.ubuntu.com has address 82.211.81.158
root@RNA:~# host 82.211.81.158
158.81.211.82.in-addr.arpa domain name pointer arctowski.ubuntu.com.
root@RNA:~# host www.ubuntu.com
www.ubuntu.com has address 82.211.81.158
```

Configuring DHCP

Your network probably has a lot of computers that need an IP address and other IP-related information in their configuration. You can, of course, enter all this information by hand on each individual workstation, but it's much easier to automate this process with a dynamic host configuration protocol (DHCP) server. Let's see how to set this up on Ubuntu Server.

Understanding the DHCP Protocol

DHCP is a broadcast-based protocol. A client that's configured to obtain an IP address via DHCP sends a broadcast on startup to try to find one or more DHCP servers in the network. The client uses the DHCPDISCOVER packet to do this. If a DHCP server sees the DHCPDISCOVER packet coming by, it answers with a DHCPOFFER packet, in which it offers an IP address and related information.

If the client receives a DHCPOFFER from more than one DHCP server, it chooses only one. It's very difficult to determine beforehand what IP configuration information the client will work with, which is one of the reasons why you should take care that no more than one DHCP server is available per broadcast domain to offer a configuration to the DHCP clients.

To indicate that the client wants to use the IP address and related information offered by a DHCP server, it returns a DHCPREQUEST, thus asking to work with that information. The DHCP server then indicates that it's okay by returning a DHCPACK (acknowledgment) to the client. From this moment on, the client can use the IP address.

A lease time is associated with each offering from a DHCP server, and this lease time determines how long the client can use an IP address and associated information. Before the lease ends, the client has to send another DHCPREQUEST to renew its lease. In most cases, the server answers such a request by extending the lease period and sending the client a DHCPACK. If it's not possible to extend the lease for some reason, the client receives a DHCPNACK (negative acknowledgment). This indicates that the client cannot continue its use of the IP address and associated information. If this happens, the client has to start the process all over again, beginning with the DHCPDISCOVER packet.

When the client machine is shut down, it informs the server that it no longer needs the IP address by sending a DHCPRELEASE over the network. That IP address then becomes available for use by other clients.

One of the things that you should note in all this is that DHCP is a broadcast-based protocol, which means that if the DHCP server is on a different subnet than the DHCP client, the client cannot reach it directly. If this is the case, a DHCP relay agent is needed that forwards DHCP requests to a DHCP server. You'll learn how to configure all this in the "The DHCP Relay Agent" section.

Creating the DHCP Server Configuration

To operate a DHCP server on your network, you need to configure two components: the DHCP service itself and the /etc/dhcp3/dhcpd.conf configuration file. You'll learn how to operate these components in the next subsections.

The DHCP Process

The first part of the DHCP server is the DHCP process itself. Its name is dhcpd3 and it resides in the /usr/sbin directory after you've installed it using the apt-get install dhcp3-common dhcp3-server command as root. Of course, it has some startup scripts in /etc/init.d as well. You can use /etc/init.d/dhcp4-server start to start it; and the options stop, restart, and force-reload work as well.

The /etc/dhcp/dhcpd.conf Configuration File

The main configuration file for the DHCP server is /etc/dhcp3/dhcpd.conf. Everything is configured in this file except startup parameters for the DHCP server. Listing 9-10 is an example configuration file that contains some of the most important options from the example file that's copied to your server after installation of the DHCP server.

Listing 9-10. *The DHCP Server's Main Configuration File is* /etc/dhcp3/dhcpd.conf

```
root@RNA:~# cat /etc/dhcp3/dhcpd.conf
#
# Sample configuration file for ISC dhcpd for Debian
#
# $Id: dhcpd.conf,v 1.4.2.2 2002/07/10 03:50:33 peloy Exp $
#

# option definitions common to all supported networks...
option domain-name "fugue.com";
option domain-name-servers toccata.fugue.com;

option subnet-mask 255.255.255.224;
default-lease-time 600;
max-lease-time 7200;

#subnet 204.254.239.0 netmask 255.255.255.224 {
#   range 204.254.239.10 204.254.239.20;
#   option broadcast-address 204.254.239.31;
#   option routers prelude.fugue.com;
#}

# The other subnet that shares this physical network
#subnet 204.254.239.32 netmask 255.255.255.224 {
#   range dynamic-bootp 204.254.239.10 204.254.239.20;
#   option broadcast-address 204.254.239.31;
```

```
#  option routers snarg.fugue.com;
#}

#subnet 192.5.5.0 netmask 255.255.255.224 {
#  range 192.5.5.26 192.5.5.30;
#  option name-servers bb.home.vix.com, gw.home.vix.com;
#  option domain-name "vix.com";
#  option routers 192.5.5.1;
#  option subnet-mask 255.255.255.224;
#  option broadcast-address 192.5.5.31;
#  default-lease-time 600;
#  max-lease-time 7200;
#}

# Hosts which require special configuration options can be listed in
# host statements.   If no address is specified, the address will be
# allocated dynamically (if possible), but the host-specific information
# will still come from the host declaration.

#host passacaglia {
#  hardware ethernet 0:0:c0:5d:bd:95;
#  filename "vmunix.passacaglia";
#  server-name "toccata.fugue.com";
#}

# Fixed IP addresses can also be specified for hosts.   These addresses
# should not also be listed as being available for dynamic assignment.
# Hosts for which fixed IP addresses have been specified can boot using
# BOOTP or DHCP.   Hosts for which no fixed address is specified can only
# be booted with DHCP, unless there is an address range on the subnet
# to which a BOOTP client is connected which has the dynamic-bootp flag
# set.
#host fantasia {
#  hardware ethernet 08:00:07:26:c0:a5;
#  fixed-address fantasia.fugue.com;
#}

# If a DHCP or BOOTP client is mobile and might be connected to a variety
# of networks, more than one fixed address for that host can be specified.
# Hosts can have fixed addresses on some networks, but receive dynamically
# allocated addresses on other subnets; in order to support this, a host
# declaration for that client must be given which does not have a fixed
# address.   If a client should get different parameters depending on
# what subnet it boots on, host declarations for each such network should
# be given.   Finally, if a domain name is given for a host's fixed address
# and that domain name evaluates to more than one address, the address
# corresponding to the network to which the client is attached, if any,
```

```
# will be assigned.
#host confusia {
#   hardware ethernet 02:03:04:05:06:07;
#   fixed-address confusia-1.fugue.com, confusia-2.fugue.com;
#   filename "vmunix.confusia";
#   server-name "toccata.fugue.com";
#}

#host confusia {
#   hardware ethernet 02:03:04:05:06:07;
#   fixed-address confusia-3.fugue.com;
#   filename "vmunix.confusia";
#   server-name "snarg.fugue.com";
#}

#host confusia {
#   hardware ethernet 02:03:04:05:06:07;
#   filename "vmunix.confusia";
#   server-name "bb.home.vix.com";
#}
```

The configuration file also starts with some generic options that aren't included in a particular section of the configuration file and therefore apply to all sections that are defined. The first of these is option domain-name "fudge.com";. This line sets the default domain name, and you should usually change it. Then the names of DNS servers are referred to with option domain-name-servers toccata.fudge.com;. Notice that there's no need to use an IP address here; assuming that the DNS resolver is set up as it should be, you can use names here.

When editing the DHCP configuration file by hand, make sure that each line is terminated with a semicolon, or else your DHCP server will complain and refuse to start. Next, the following three lines specify a non-default subnet mask and define the leases:

```
option subnet-mask 255.255.255.224;
default-lease-time 600;
max-lease-time 7200;
```

By default, a lease is specified in minutes, so the default lease time expires after 10 hours, and the maximum lease time is 120 hours. Following the generic options, some example subnets are specified. Let's have a look at one of them:

```
#subnet 192.5.5.0 netmask 255.255.255.224 {
#   range 192.5.5.26 192.5.5.30;
#   option name-servers bb.home.vix.com, gw.home.vix.com;
#   option domain-name "vix.com";
#   option routers 192.5.5.1;
#   option subnet-mask 255.255.255.224;
#   option broadcast-address 192.5.5.31;
#   default-lease-time 600;
#   max-lease-time 7200;
#}
```

A range of five IP addresses is defined in this subnet, which is on the network with IP address 192.5.5.0. Then the specific options for this subnet are defined. Some options were already defined in the global part of the configuration file; if that's the case for your options, the subnet-specific option just overwrites the global option. One option in this example needs some explanation, though: broadcast-address is needed here because a non-default address class is used on the subnet. Every time that non-default address classes are used, you must specify the broadcast address for that network as well.

Next are two host definitions that contain settings for specific hosts:

```
host passacaglia {
  hardware ethernet 0:0:c0:5d:bd:95;
  filename "vmunix.passacaglia";
  server-name "toccata.fugue.com";
}

host fantasia {
  hardware ethernet 08:00:07:26:c0:a5;
  fixed-address fantasia.fugue.com;
}
```

To make sure that the setting is applied to the right host, the MAC address is referred to for every host definition. This happens with the definition of the hardware ethernet address. Then three other options are used. The option filename is used to refer to a boot file that is to be loaded by a client. This file can be offered by a Trivial FTP (TFTP) server, which is just a very simple FTP server that you can configure to hand out files in a convenient way to nodes on the network.

Just enable the TFTP server as a part of your xinetd configuration (see "Starting Services with xinetd" later in this chapter) and then put the file with the name mentioned here in the /tftpboot directory (which you'll have to create manually), and the host will be capable of downloading this file. The filename option is useful for diskless workstations because it allows them to download a boot image.

If a client is booting from a boot image file that has been delivered by a server, it can be useful for the client to know what server it's dealing with. To specify this, the server-name option is used in the host definition for passacaglia. It should contain the name of your DHCP server. The last new option that you see here is fixed-address, which is used to pass a fixed IP address to the client. If DNS is set up correctly, a resolvable DNS name can be used as well.

Advanced DHCP Configuration Options

Based on the information so far, you can set up a DHCP server that doesn't use any complicated options, but some advanced configuration options may be interesting as well. You'll read about three of them in this section. First, "Integrating DHCP and DNS" discusses how to set up dynamic DNS (DDNS), so that the DHCP server tells the DNS server when it has handed out a new configuration. Then the DHCP relay agent describes how you can let one DHCP server serve all subnets in your network.

Integrating DHCP and DNS

If you want clients to be accessible by their names, you need to tell the DNS server whenever the DHCP server has handed out a new IP address to the client. To make this work, you need to configure the configuration files for both DNS and DHCP. The first thing you need to do is create a cryptographic key that can be used to authorize the update. You can generate this key with the dnssec-keygen command (which is installed automatically when installing a DNS server), as in the following example:

```
dnssec-keygen -a HMAC-MD5 -b 128 -n HOST ddns
```

This command generates two keys in the current directory. To make sure that they are secure, it's a good idea to create a dedicated directory for these files, such as in /var/lib/named/keys. You should also make sure that the private key file is accessible by only root. A part of the key name is a random number. The names could be the following, for example:

```
Kddns.+157+03212.key
Kddns.+157+03212.private
```

These two files contain the key that has to be used in clear text:

```
RNA:~ # cat Kddns.+157+03212.key
ddns. IN KEY 512 3 157 WVf7JaWqrfoIe4AtT9GGug==
```

Now first edit the DNS named.conf.local configuration file to include this key. The example in Listing 9-11 shows how to use the key for the zone example.com and its associated reverse DNS zone.

Listing 9-11. *Securing* named.conf.local *with a Key for Dynamic DNS Updates*

```
key ddns {
    algorithm HMAC-MD5;
    secret WVf7JaWqrfoIe4AtT9GGug==;
};

zone "example.com" in {
    type master;
    file "example.zone";
    allow-update { key ddns ;};
};

zone "1.168.192.in-addr.arpa" in {
    type master;
    file "1.168.192.zone";
    allow-update { key ddns ;};
};
```

As you can see in this example, a new section is created for the key, specifying its algorithm as well as the key that's used. (Make sure that the named.conf.local file is readable for root only if you include a key in it!) Next, the allow-update (key ddns ;}; statement is used for all zones that need this key for dynamic DNS updates. Note that ddns is just the name of the key, and you can choose any name you like here.

Next, make sure that the appropriate DDNS code is added in the dhcpd.conf file. The example in Listing 9-12 works with the example DNS configuration just shown, but feel free to customize it to your own configuration.

Listing 9-12. *Including DDNS code in the* dhcpd.conf *File*

```
ddns-update-style interim;
ddns-updates on;

key ddns {
    algorithm HMAC-MD5;
    secret WVf7JaWqrfoIe4AtT9GGug==;
}

zone 100.100.201.in-addr.arpa. {
    key ddns;
}

zone example.com. {
    key ddns;
}
```

You should take note of a few things in this example. First, when referring to a DNS zone, make sure that you put a dot after the name of the zone because it doesn't work without one. So example.com. is good, and example.com isn't. The ddns-update-style parameter is then used to specify how the updates need to take place. You have two options—interim and ad-hoc—but ad-hoc is deprecated, so you should use only interim here. Then the parameter ddns-updates on is used to activate DDNS. Last, as in the named.conf configuration file, the key must be specified in this configuration file as well. Of course, it must be the same as the key that's specified in the named.conf file. Now start the DHCP server and the DNS server, and DDNS is working.

■**Note** If the client gets its host name from the DHCP server, you have some more work to do. It's important that the client always gets the same host name, and you can ensure this by including the option host-name in the definition of the specific host in the dhcpd.conf configuration file. In this same definition of the client, you must specify the MAC address for each client equally by using the hardware parameter. An example of this follows:

```
host somehost.example.com {
    hardware ethernet 00:0C:29:E8:35:5A;
    ddns-hostname "somehost";
    ddns-domainname "example.com";
    option host-name "somehost";
```

The DHCP Relay Agent

A DHCP broadcast is received only by clients on the local network because they cannot cross routers. But it's impractical to install a DHCP server on every single network. As an alternative, you can of course install the DHCP server on a server that's configured with more than one network board (a multihomed server), so it can serve all the networks it's connected to. An alternative is to use a DHCP relay agent, which is a service that forwards packets to the DHCP server. You can run it on any server on the network or on a router. Almost every hardware router has embedded functionality that lets it act as a DHCP relay agent.

If you want to install a relay agent on a Linux server, you need the dhcp-relay package; use apt-get install dhcp3-relay to install it. While installing this package, you are prompted to enter the configuration you want to use. The following procedure summarizes the steps to take:

1. After entering the command apt-get install dhcp3-relay, a screen pops up and asks you to enter the names or IP addresses that your server should relay DHCP requests to. Enter these names in a space-separated list and press Enter to continue.

2. Next, you need to enter the names of the interfaces that the DHCP relay process should listen on. If you know that DHCP relay requests will come in through eth1 only, for example, make sure to enter eth1 here and click OK to continue.

3. Enter a list of additional options that you want to pass to the DHCP relay daemon (although it normally won't be necessary to use any of these options). After selecting OK, your settings will be written to the /etc/default/dhcp3-relay configuration file, and the dhcprelay3 process is started.

■Tip Need to change any of the options used while installing the dhcp3-relay package? Open the /etc/default/dhcp3-relay file, modify any of the parameters you see there, and restart the service using the /etc/init.d/dhcp3-relay restart command.

After its installation, you can configure the relay agent from the /etc/default/dhcp3-relay file in which you'll find the INTERFACES parameter. Use it to specify on which network cards the relay agents should listen for DHCP broadcasts. You can configure it to listen on eth0 and eth1 by adding INTERFACES="eth0 eth1" to the dhcp-relay file.

Next, you need to specify the IP address of the DHCP server. To do this, add it as a parameter to the DHCP_SERVERS parameter. After configuring these options, use /etc/init.d/dhcrelay start to start the relay agent.

Configuring NTP

For many networked applications, knowing the correct time is essential for proper operation. On the Internet, the network time protocol (NTP) is the de facto standard for time synchronization. In this section, you'll learn how to configure your server as an NTP time server as well as an NTP client. I'll cover the following subjects:

- Working with NTP

- Configuring a stand-alone NTP time server

- Configuring your server to fetch its time from a time reference source

- Tuning NTP operations

How NTP Works

The basic idea of NTP is that all servers on the Internet can synchronize time with one another. In this way, a global time can be established so that only minimal differences exist in the time setting on different servers. To reach this goal, all servers communicate the same time, no matter what time zone they are in. This time is known as coordinated universal time (UTC): a server receives its time in UTC and then calculates its local time from that by using its time zone setting.

To specify what time your server is using, you have to edit the /etc/default/rcS configuration file, where you'll find the UTC= setting. To use UTC on your server, make sure its value is set to yes; if you don't want to use UTC, set it to UTC=no.

The local time zone setting is maintained in the /etc/localtime binary file, which is created upon installation and contains information about your local time zone. To change it afterward, you need to make a link of the configuration file that contains information on your local time zone. You can find these files in /usr/share/zoneinfo. Next, link the appropriate file to the /etc/localtime file, for example: sudo ln -sf /usr/share/zoneinfo/MET /etc/localtime. This will change your local time zone setting to the MET time zone.

Synchronizing time with other servers in an NTP hierarchy uses the concept of *stratum*. Every server in the NTP hierarchy has a stratum setting between 1 and 15, but with a stratum of 16 being used to signify that a clock is not currently synchronized at all. The highest stratum level that a clock can use is 1. Typically, this is a server that's connected directly to an atomic clock with a very high accuracy. The stratum level that is assigned to a server that's directly connected to an external clock depends on the type of clock that's used. In general, though, the more reliable the clock is, the higher the stratum level will be.

A server can get its time in two different ways: by synchronizing with another NTP time server or by using a reference clock. If a server synchronizes with an NTP time server, the stratum used on that server will be determined by the server it's synchronizing with: if a server synchronizes with a stratum 3 time server, it automatically becomes a stratum 4 time server.

If, on the other hand, a reference clock is used, a server does not get its time from a server on the Internet, but instead determines its own time. Again, the default stratum used is determined by the type and brand of reference clock that's used. If it's a very reliable clock, such as one synchronized via GPS, the default stratum setting will be high. If a less-reliable clock (such as the local clock in a computer) is used, the default stratum will be lower.

If a server gets its time from the Internet, it makes sense to use Internet time and use a very trustworthy time server. If no Internet connection is available, use an internal clock and set the stratum accordingly (which means lower). If you're using your computer's internal clock, for example, it makes sense to use a low stratum level, such as 5.

Configuring a Stand-Alone NTP Time Server

Just two elements are needed to make your own NTP time server: the configuration file and the daemon process. First, make sure that all required software is installed by running apt-get install ntp-server as root. The name of the daemon process is ntpd, and you can start it by using the /etc/init.d/ntpd startup script. After making all proper settings to its configuration file /etc/ntp.conf, you can start the daemon process manually by using /etc/init.d/ntp start.

The content of the /etc/ntp.conf NTP configuration file really doesn't have to be very complex. Basically, you just need three lines to create an NTP time server, as seen in Listing 9-13.

Listing 9-13. *Example* ntp.conf *Configuration*

```
server 127.127.1.0
fudge 127.127.1.0      stratum 10
server ntp.yourprovider.somewhere
```

The first line in Listing 9-13 specifies what NTP should use if the connection with the NTP time server is lost for a longer period: this line makes sure that the local clock in your server will not drift too much by making a reference to a local clock. Every type of local clock has its own IP address from the range of loopback IP addresses. The format of this address is 127.127.<t>.<i>; the third byte refers to the type of local clock that is used, and the fourth byte refers to the instance of the clock your server is connected to. The default address to use to refer to the local computer clock is 127.127.1.0. Notice that all clocks that can be used as an external reference clock connected locally to your server have their own IP address. The documentation of your clock tells you what address to use.

■**Tip** Even if your server is connected to an NTP server that's directly on the Internet, it makes sense to use at least one local external reference clock on your network as well. This way you can ensure that time synchronization continues if the Internet connection fails for a longer period.

The second line defines what should happen when the server falls back to the local external reference clock mentioned on the first line. This line starts with the keyword fudge to indicate an abnormal situation. Here, the local clock should be used, and the server sets its stratum level to 10. By using this stratum, the server indicates that it's not very trustworthy, but ensures that it can be used as a time source if necessary.

The last line in Listing 9-13 shows what should happen under normal circumstances. This line normally refers to an IP address or a server name on the network of the Internet provider. This line will always be used if nothing strange is happening.

Pulling or Pushing the Time

An NTP time server can perform its work in two different ways: by pushing (broadcasting) time across the network, or by allowing other servers to pull the time from it. In the default setting, the NTP server that gets its time from somewhere else regularly asks this server what time is used. When both nodes have their times synchronized, this setting will be incremented to a default value of 1,024 seconds. As an administrator, you can specify how often time needs to be synchronized by using the `minpoll` and `maxpoll` arguments on the line in `/etc/ntp.conf` where the NTP time server is referred to, as shown in Listing 9-14.

Listing 9-14. *Configuring the Synchronization Interval*

```
server 127.127.1.0
fudge 127.127.1.0 stratum 10
server ntp.provider.somewhere minpoll 4 maxpoll 15
```

The `minpoll` setting determines how often a client should try to synchronize its time if time is not properly synchronized, and the `maxpoll` value indicates how often synchronization should occur if time is properly synchronized. The values for the `minpoll` and `maxpoll` parameters are kind of weird logarithmically: they refer to the power of 2 that should be used. Therefore, `minpoll` 4 is actually 2^4 (which equals 16 seconds), and the default value of 1,024 seconds can be noted as 2^{10}. Any value that lies between the values of 4 and 17 can be used.

If you are configuring an NTP node as a server, you can use the broadcast mechanism as well. This makes sense if your server is used as the NTP time server for local computers that are on the same network (because broadcast is not forwarded by routers). If you want to do this, make sure that the `broadcast 192.168.0.255` line (use the broadcast address for your network) is included in the `ntp.conf` file on your server and that the `broadcastclient` setting is used on the client computer.

If you want to configure a secure NTP time server, you should think twice before configuring broadcast. Typically, a broadcast client takes its time from any server in the network, as long as it broadcasts NTP packets on the default NTP port 123. Therefore, someone could introduce a bogus NTP time server with a very high stratum configured to change the time on all computers in your network.

Configuring an NTP Client

The first thing to do when configuring a server to act as an NTP client is to make sure that the time is more or less accurate. If the difference is greater than 1,024 seconds, NTP considers the time source to be bogus and refuses to synchronize with it. Therefore, it's recommended to synchronize time on the NTP client manually before continuing. To manually synchronize the time, the `ntpdate` command is very useful: use it to get time only once from another server that offers NTP services. To use it, specify the name or IP address of the server you want to synchronize with as its argument:

```
ntpdate ntp.yourprovider.somewhere
```

By using this command, you'll make a once-only time adjustment on the client computer. After that, you can set up `ntpd` for automatic synchronization on the client computer.

■**Caution** Too often, `ntpdate` is used only for troubleshooting purposes when the administrator finds out that `ntpd` isn't synchronizing properly. In this case, the administrator is likely to see a "socket already in use" error message. This happens because `ntpd` has already claimed port 123 for NTP time synchronization. You can verify this with the `natstat -platune | grep 123` command, which displays the application currently using port 123. Before `ntpdate` can be used successfully in this scenario, the administrator should make sure that `xntpd` is shut down on the client by using `/etc/init.d/ntp stop`.

If the time difference between server and client is not greater than 1,000 seconds, `ntp.conf` can be configured on the NTP client. A typical NTP client configuration is very simple: you just need to specify the server from which you want to get the time, as in the following example:

```
server 192.168.0.10
```

You might also prefer to set a backup option by using the `fudge` option, as displayed in Listing 9-14, but this is optional. Normally, I recommend that you don't set this option on every single server in the network that's using NTP. As an administrator, you might prefer to set this on one server in your network only and let all other NTP clients in your network get the time from that server. So, to make an NTP hierarchy, I recommend letting one or two servers in the network get their time from a reliable time source on the Internet, such as `pool.ntp.org`. Next, to ensure that an NTP time source is still available when the Internet connection goes down, use the `fudge` option on the same servers. Doing so ensures that they will still be the servers with the highest stratum level in your network, and time services will not be interrupted.

Checking NTP Synchronization Status

After you've started the NTP service on all computers in your network, you probably want to know if it's working correctly. The first tool to use is the `ntptrace` command, which provides an overview of the current synchronization status. When using it, you should be aware that it will always take some time to establish NTP synchronization. The delay occurs because an NTP client normally synchronizes only every 16 seconds, and it might fail to establish correct synchronization the first time it tries. It should normally take no longer than drinking a cup of coffee to establish NTP time synchronization.

Another tool to tune the working of NTP is the `ntpq` command, which offers its own interactive interface from which the status of any NTP service can be requested. As when using the FTP client, you can use a couple of commands to do "remote control" on the NTP server. In this interface, you can use the `help` command to see a list of available commands.

As an alternative, you can run `ntpq` with some command-line options. For example, the `ntpq -p` command gives an overview of current synchronization status. Listing 9-15 provides an example of the result, in which several parameters are displayed:

- `remote`: The name of the other server

- `refid`: The IP address of the server you are synchronizing with

- `st`: The stratum used by the other server

- t: The type of clock used on the other server (L stands for local clock; u for an Internet clock)

- when: The number of seconds since the last poll

- poll: The number of seconds used between two polls

- reach: The number of times the other server has been contacted successfully

- delay: Indicates the time between an NTP request and the answer

- offset: The difference in seconds between the time on your local computer and that on the NTP server

- jitter: The error rate in your local clock, expressed in seconds

Listing 9-15. *Use the* ntpq -p *Command to Slow the Current Synchronization Status on Your Server*

```
root@RNA:~# ntpq -p
     remote           refid      st t when poll reach   delay   offset  jitter
==============================================================================
 fiordland.ubunt 192.36.133.17    2 u   10   64    1    2.247  -357489  0.002
```

Customizing Your NTP Server

I have explained the basic NTP time configuration so far, but you can also conduct some fine-tuning. First are the files that are created automatically by the NTP daemon, and then there are some security settings that you can use in ntp.conf to limit what servers are allowed to get time from your server. In this section, you'll read about the NTP drift file, the NTP log file, and NTP security.

NTP Drift File

No matter how secure the local clock on your computer, it will always be slightly off: either too fast or too slow. For example, a clock may have a lag of two seconds every hour: this difference is referred to as the clock's drift factor, and it's calculated by comparing the local clock with the clock on the server that provides NTP time to the local machine. Because NTP is designed also to synchronize time when the connection to the NTP time server is lost, it's important that the NTP process on your local computer knows what this drift factor is. So, to calculate the right setting for the drift factor, it's very important that an accurate time is used on the other server.

Once NTP time synchronization has been established, a drift file is created automatically. On Ubuntu Server, this file is created in /var/lib/ntp/ntp.drift, and the local NTP process uses it to calculate the exact drifting of your local clock, which thus allows it to compensate for it. Because the drift file is created automatically, you don't need to worry about it. However, you can choose where the file is created by using the driftfile parameter in ntp.conf:

```
driftfile /var/lib/ntp/ntp.drift
```

■**Note** Remember that NTP is a daemon. Like most daemons, it reads its configuration file only when it's first started. So, after all modifications, use `/etc/init.d/ntpd restart` to make sure that the modifications are applied to your current configuration.

NTP Log File

The NTP log file is another file that's created automatically for you. Like all other log files, this is a very important file that allows you to see exactly what happens. If time is synchronized properly, it's not the most interesting log file on your system: it just tells you that synchronization has been established and what server is used for synchronization. After installation, Ubuntu Server is not set up to use its own log file, but you can change that using the `logfile` statement in `/etc/ntp.conf`:

```
logfile  /var/log/ntp
```

Applying NTP Security

If your server is connected to the Internet, it might be interesting to notice that restrictions can be used. If no restrictions are applied, the entire world can access your NTP server. If you don't like that idea, add some lines to `ntp.conf`, as shown in Listing 9-16.

Listing 9-16. *Applying Security Restrictions to Your NTP Time Server*

```
restrict default noquery notrust nomodify
restrict 127.0.0.1
restrict 192.168.0.0 mask 255.255.255.0
```

■**Note** Some Linux distributions configure their NTP service so that no one can access it. Having problems getting time from a server? Make sure that no restrictions have been applied.

The restrictions settings prevent inappropriate conduct of clients. In the first line of Listing 9-16, you can see exactly what is considered inappropriate. In this line, first the default settings for accessing the server are allowed. Then three types of packets are disallowed using `noquery`, `notrust`, and `nomodify`. They make sure that no contact whatsoever is allowed for NTP clients. Then an exception to these settings is created for the local NTP service and all computers in the network 192.168.0.0. Add a restrictions line like the one in Listing 9-16 for every IP address or range of IP addresses that has to be allowed to use the NTP server this way.

Starting Services with `xinetd`

There are two methods to start services. First, you can fire up the service when your system boots, in which case the service occupies its port and waits for incoming connections all the time. But if the service is needed only occasionally, starting it at system boot and keeping it available all the time is a waste of system resources. This is exactly when the second method is preferred; the xinetd process (and its predecessor inetd) were developed to listen on behalf of other processes to see whether a connection comes in. If it does, xinetd starts the process, thus making optimal use of system resources. You'll learn how to configure it in this section.

■**Note** On Ubuntu Server, xinetd is not installed by default. Instead, the legacy inetd service is available. Because xinetd offers the same capabilities—but with much more flexibility—I'm covering just xinetd in this section. Make sure that you have it installed by using apt-get install xinetd.

Setting up xinetd by Hand

The xinetd service consists of three different parts:

- The xinetd daemon

- The default configuration file /etc/xinetd.conf

- The configuration files for individual services in the /etc/xinetd.d directory

Managing the xinetd Daemon

The xinetd service is implemented by the daemon process xinetd, which has a script in /etc/init.d that allows you to start and stop this process automatically. Be aware that xinetd is not activated by default, so start it first using /etc/init.d/xinetd start. This command reads all service configuration files and makes sure that all services that have their enabled status set to on are reachable from that moment on.

From time to time, you'll have to restart the xinetd service because it doesn't automatically check its configuration files for changes. So, if you've made any modifications to the services files, be sure to activate them by using the /etc/init.d/xinetd reload or /etc/init.d/xinetd restart command.

Setting Default Behavior

The configuration of xinetd occurs in two locations. First, there's the /etc/xinetd.conf file that contains generic settings, and then there's the /etc/xinetd.d subdirectory that can contain files to configure individual xinetd services. It can contain service-specific settings as well, but that's not the default way to go on Ubuntu Server; every individual service has its own configuration file in /etc/xinetd.d. On Ubuntu Server, xinetd.conf is just used to refer to the individual configuration files in /etc/xinetd.d and to make sure that they are processed.

Tuning the Individual Services

Every service that works with xinetd has its own configuration file in /etc/xinetd.d. In these configuration files, you'll find options that specify how a service must be started. An example of this is in the configuration file shown in Listing 9-17. The most important of the options is disabled = yes, which is on by default. Because it's on by default, the service won't run until you remove the option or change it to disabled = no. Listing 9-17 shows the configuration file for the time service.

Listing 9-17. *Default Configuration File for the* time *Service*

```
root@RNA:~# cat /etc/xinetd.d/time
# default: off
# description: An RFC 868 time server. This protocol provides a
# site-independent, machine-readable date and time. The Time service sends back
# to the originating source the time in seconds since midnight on January first
# 1900.
# This is the tcp version.
service time
{
        disable          = yes
        type             = INTERNAL
        id               = time-stream
        socket_type      = stream
        protocol         = tcp
        user             = root
        wait             = no
}

# This is the udp version.
service time
{
        disable          = yes
        type             = INTERNAL
        id               = time-dgram
        socket_type      = dgram
        protocol         = udp
        user             = root
        wait             = yes
}
```

Of the options used in this configuration file, only two are really important because the rest of them are set automatically. The first option that you have to tune is the disable option. This option has the value yes by default, which means that the service is not active. To activate the service, set it to disable = no. The second option is user, which specifies what user permissions the option should be started with. Many services are started as root by default. If you can, change it to some other user with not so many permissions.

Tuning Access to Services with TCP Wrapper

If a service runs from xinetd, it can be secured with TCP Wrapper. To ensure that you can use it, install TCP wrapper using apt-get install tcpd as root. Stated in a more general way, if a service is using the libwrap.so library module, you can secure it with TCP Wrapper. Because xinetd uses this module, you can secure it this way. Other services that aren't started with xinetd but do use this library can be secured with TCP Wrapper as well. To check whether a service is capable of working with TCP Wrapper, use the ldd command followed by the complete name of the service you want to check. If libwrap.so is listed, TCP Wrapper works for the service. If it isn't, use a generic firewall such as iptables. See Listing 9-18 for an example.

Listing 9-18. *Checking Whether a Service Can Be Secured with TCP Wrapper*

```
root@RNA:~# ldd /usr/sbin/xinetd
        linux-gate.so.1 =>  (0xffffe000)
        libwrap.so.0 => /lib/libwrap.so.0 (0xb7fd0000)
        libnsl.so.1 => /lib/tls/i686/cmov/libnsl.so.1 (0xb7fb9000)
        libm.so.6 => /lib/tls/i686/cmov/libm.so.6 (0xb7f91000)
        libcrypt.so.1 => /lib/tls/i686/cmov/libcrypt.so.1 (0xb7f63000)
        libc.so.6 => /lib/tls/i686/cmov/libc.so.6 (0xb7e22000)
        /lib/ld-linux.so.2 (0xb7fe3000)
```

TCP Wrapper was developed before xinetd existed and when only its predecessor inetd was available. This service didn't include any way of regulating access to services, so inetd could be used to start tcpd, TCP Wrapper, which in turn could be configured to start the necessary service. The task of tcpd was to check whether a host trying to connect to the service was allowed access or not. The nice thing about tcpd is that it sits between (x)inetd and the service a client is connecting to. Therefore, from the outside it's not possible to see whether tcpd is blocking access to a service or whether the service simply isn't there.

Working with the /etc/hosts.allow and /etc/hosts.deny Configuration Files

TCP Wrapper works with two configuration files to determine whether access is allowed or not: /etc/hosts.allow and /etc/hosts.deny. The first has a list of all hosts that can access a service, and the second contains a list of hosts for which access is denied. TCP Wrapper always first reads the /etc/hosts.allow file. If the host that tries to connect is in there, access is allowed. Only if the name of the hosts is not in /etc/hosts.allow does tcpd check /etc/hosts.deny. If the host is in there, access is blocked; if it isn't, access is allowed. Access is also allowed if one of the two configuration files is empty or does not exist.

■**Caution** Test before you trust that TCP Wrapper is really protecting your services. A small error in the configuration can have the result that TCP Wrapper doesn't work.

The generic syntax of the lines that you can include in the /etc/hosts.allow and /etc/hosts.deny files is not hard to understand:

```
daemon:host[:option : option ...]
```

Of these, daemon is the process involved, host is the list of hosts that you want to allow or deny access to, and option is a list of options you want to include. Note that instead of referring to a specific host or daemon, some generic keywords can be used as well. Table 9-2 summarizes these TCP Wrapper keywords.

Table 9-2. *TCP Wrapper Keywords*

Keyword	Description
ALL	Refers to all daemons or all hosts. Note that you can define an exception to ALL by using the keyword EXCEPT.
LOCAL	This option can be used for host names only and refers to all host names that do not have a dot in their name.
UNKNOWN	All host names for which tcpd cannot identify the name.
KNOWN	All host names that could be identified by their name and matching IP address.
PARANOID	All hosts for which the host name does not match the given IP address.

Let's start with the example shown in Listing 9-19.

Listing 9-19. *Simple Example of* /etc/hosts.allow *and* /etc/hosts.deny

```
RNA: ~ # cat /etc/hosts.allow
ALL: LOCAL
RNA: ~ # cat /etc/hosts.deny
famd, netstatd, ps: ALL
```

In this example, incoming hosts are first matched against the /etc/hosts.allow file, in which access to all services is granted for everything coming in from the localhost. Local processes look no further. For connections coming in from remote hosts, now the /etc/hosts. deny file is checked. In this file, you can see that access is denied to the famd, netstatd, and ps services for all hosts. So, in this example, all other services that are controlled by tcpd can also be accessed by all external hosts. As you notice, this example doesn't show anything very secure, but it's possible to create a more secure configuration (see Listing 9-20).

Listing 9-20. *More Complex Example of* /etc/hosts.allow *and* /etc/hosts.deny

```
RNA: ~ # cat /etc/hosts.allow
ALL: SFO.sandervanvugt.com
in.telnetd: 192.168.1.1
ALL EXCEPT in.telnetd: 192.168.
RNA ~ # cat /etc/hosts.deny
ALL: ALL
```

In this example, you should first notice that a policy is set to specifically deny access for all hosts to all services in /etc/hosts.deny. This is good because it creates a mechanism to control access; if the host doesn't have an entry in /etc/hosts.allow, it doesn't get access to the services that are controlled by tcpd.

Three different lines are specified in the /etc/hosts.allow file in Listing 9-20. The first line grants access to all services for the host SFO.sandervanvugt.com. Then 192.168.1.1 gets access to only the telnet service, and in the third line all other hosts whose IP address starts with 192.168 get access to all services except telnet. Note that order matters in this example:

the TCP Wrapper works on a "first match" basis. If line 2 and line 3 of /etc/hosts.allow had been reversed, the host with IP address 192.168.1.1 would also see a match in the ALL EXCEPT in.telnetd line and would look no further.

Why You Shouldn't Use TCP Wrapper

If a service listens to tcpd, you can build an efficient protection for it. However, this protection is far from perfect. The most important problem is that the service is used only for certain kinds of services. The line ALL:ALL in /etc/hosts.deny could give you a false sense of security, making you believe that everything is secure now. A much better way to implement protection for your server is to use the iptables firewall. Check Chapter 5 for more information on its configuration.

Summary

In this chapter, you learned how to set up some of the most common network infrastructure services. You've seen how to configure name resolution using DNS, and you read about the configuration of the DHCP server and the NTP time server. In the last part of this chapter, I covered the configuration of xinetd as a generic way to start services on your Linux server. In the next chapter, you'll learn how to set up Ubuntu Server as a file server, using Samba and NFS.

## CHAPTER 10

Using Ubuntu Server As a File and Print Server

Configuring CUPS, NFS, and Samba

File servers allow users to store important files at a central location in the network from which it's easy to add security and to allow users to share files. In this chapter, you'll learn how to set up Ubuntu Server as a file server.

A file server also typically offers a print service, which provides an easy and convenient way to share printers on the network. You'll also learn how to set up print services as well.

When using any Linux distribution as a file server, you have to choose the type of file server you want to use. Many options are available, but the Network File System (NFS) and Samba are the two most popular. The type of file server you'll use depends on the kind of client that will use it. If in your network most people work from Windows clients, it makes sense to configure a Samba file server because Samba emulates the Windows Server Message Block (SMB) protocol. This means that the Windows user won't see any difference between the Samba server and a Windows server. If, on the other hand, your user is on a Linux workstation and needs an easy-to-configure and very fast protocol to connect to your Samba server, NFS is the way to go. In this chapter, you'll learn how to set up both of these configurations.

Before discussing file servers, however, you'll learn how to set up a CUPS print server.

Setting Up a CUPS Print Server

The Common UNIX Print System (CUPS) server is a service that you'll really want to use a graphical interface for. Although this server uses a set of configuration files that aren't always that easy to configure, it provides a web page that allows you to perform almost all the tasks necessary to manage a print server.

Adding Printers

To configure your server as a print server, you must first add a printer. If your network doesn't have many printers, you can add the printers individually. For a larger number of printers, you can organize them into groups (classes) to make it easier to manage them. Let's go through the steps to add a printer in CUPS:

1. Install CUPS using `apt-get install cupsys`. This command installs all required CUPS components (including the web management interface) and starts the CUPS service.

■**Note** By default, you have administrative access from the server that runs the CUPS process only. If you want to access the administrative interface from another computer in your network, read the next section, "Sharing Printers," for information on how to do that.

---

2. Open a browser and go to `http://yourserver:631`. By default, the CUPS print server listens on port 631. When accessing it from a browser, you see the management interface shown in Figure 10-1.

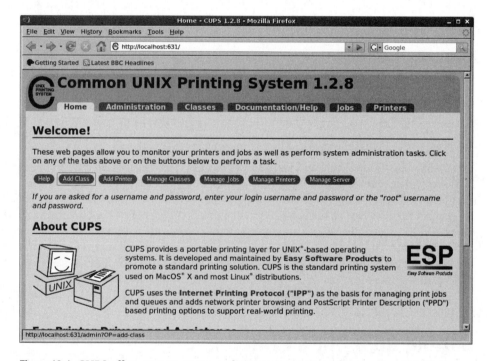

Figure 10-1. *CUPS offers an easy-to-use web management interface on port 631 of your server.*

3. From this interface, click Add Printer. Enter the following information and click Continue when you finish:

   • *Name*: This is the name you want to use to share the printer. You won't be allowed to use spaces in the printer name.

- *Location*: Enter the physical location of your printer.

- *Description*: Provide a description of your printer. Although this field isn't mandatory, the added information does make it easier for a user to connect to the right printer.

4. Next, specify what device the printer is connected to. This is an important option because it relates to the device that your print server has to address when communicating to the printer. This does not have to be a local device, and you can use a remote device over the network. If your printer is attached to your server with USB, you'll see the USB printer listed automatically. If there is a network-enabled printer on the network, you'll probably also see it listed. Apart from the USB interface, the following devices are available by default:

   - *AppSocket/HP JetDirect*: Use this device to communicate to an HP JetDirect or AppSocket-compatible print server.

   - *Internet Printing Protocol (http)*: You can use the Internet printing protocol to address a printer that's shared over the Internet. Use this option to address such a printer over HTTP.

   - *Internet Printing Protocol (ipp)*: Use this option to address an IPP printer using the IPP protocol.

   - *LPD/LPR Host or Printer*: LPD/LPR is the classic way to connect to printers shared by a UNIX or Linux machine. Use this option to address such a printer.

   - *LPT#1*: Choose this option to communicate to a printer that's installed at the parallel printer port LPT1.

   - *SCSI Printer*: This is for printers that are connected to the print server using the SCSI bus.

   - *Serial Port #1/#2*: This is for printers that are connected via a serial interface. (You probably won't need it because serial printers are rarely used.)

5. After selecting the printer port your printer is attached to and clicking OK, you'll see a list of available printer drivers. If your printer is listed here, select it and click Continue. Otherwise, you can specify which printer you want to use by referring to its PostScript Printer Description (PPD) file, which describes how CUPS has to communicate with the printer. You can compare the PPD file to a driver. A limited list of PPD files is installed in /usr/share/ppd/cups-included. If your printer manufacturer supports CUPS, you'll find the PPD file on its web site or on the driver CD. If your printer is not listed there, and your printer manufacturer doesn't give any clue about Linux support for your printer, check the printer page at www.openprinting.org to see what the current support status is for your printer. If it's supported, you'll find a link to the best driver for your printer. Click this link and make sure that the driver is installed in /usr/share/ppd/custom. Next, from the Make/Manufacturer interface, click the Browse button to add this driver (see Figure 10-2). Then click Add Printer to add the printer. When asked for a user name and password, enter the credentials for the user root. Your printer is now added.

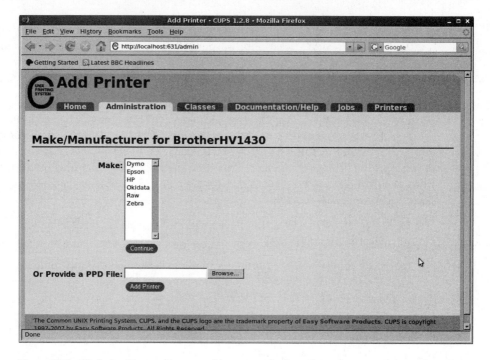

Figure 10-2. *Click the Browse button to browse to the location where you have selected the PPD file for your printer.*

6. Once the printer has been added, you'll see a page with the printer's properties. Make sure that you select the right printer features, such as paper size, resolution, and many other details. After making changes to this page, click the Set Printer Options button to apply the changes. This updates your printer configuration immediately.

Sharing Printers

Once you've added a printer, you'll probably want to share it. By default, only the host localhost has access to your printer. To change this, follow these steps:

1. As root, open the /etc/cups/cupsd.conf file with an editor.

2. Search the line Listen localhost:631 and add a listen line just after it. For example, to add a line that opens the CUPS print server for all nodes at the network 192.168.1.0, add Listen 192.168.1.0/24.

3. From the same configuration file, search the section that starts with `<Location />`. Here you'll find some lines that start with `Allow`. These lines are also required to indicate which remote hosts are allowed to use your CUPS print server. Make sure that you include a line that allows access for all nodes that need it. For example, add `Allow 192.168.1.*` to make sure that all nodes in the specified network can print to your server.

4. If you want to be able to administer your print server from other nodes as well, go to the section that begins with `<Location /admin>` and add an `Allow` line that grants access for the administrator from all required machines as well, such as `Allow 192.168.1.65`.

5. Restart the CUPS print server by issuing the `/etc/init.d/cupsys restart` command as root.

Managing Printers

Once the CUPS printer is installed, you can manage it as well, and the easiest way to do this is from the web interface. Clicking the Printers tab (see Figure 10-3) provides an overview of all available printers, and you'll also see different buttons to manage properties of the printer as well as the jobs handled by that printer. I'll list the most important options offered from this page here:

- *Print Test Page*: Tests your printer.

- *Start Printer*: Activates a printer that has been deactivated by the Stop Printer button. As you can see, only one of these buttons is available at any given moment.

- *Reject Jobs*: Tells the printer to temporarily stop accepting new jobs. This may be a useful option when troubleshooting a printer.

- *Move All Jobs*: Moves all jobs to another printer that's known at this server.

- *Cancel All Jobs*: Stops all jobs that are currently being served.

- *Unpublish Printer*: Removes the printer from the list of available printers.

- *Modify Printer*: Allows you to change the location and description properties of the printer.

- *Set Printer Options*: Changes printer options such as paper size and DPI.

- *Delete Printer*: Removes the printer from the list of available printers.

- *Set As Default*: Makes the printer the default for this machine.

- *Set Allowed Users*: Controls user access to the printer.

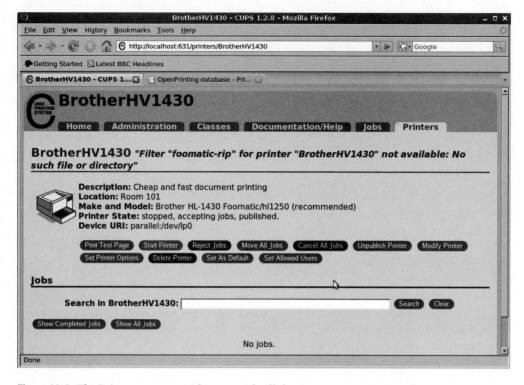

Figure 10-3. *The Printers page provides you with all the management options for your printer.*

Also available from the Printers page is the queue or job list for your printer. You can activate it from Jobs ➤ Show All Jobs, after which you can choose to reprint, hold, cancel, or move individual print jobs.

Accessing CUPS Printers

You have probably set up a CUPS print server because you want to access it as well. In this section, I'll discuss three different ways to access printers:

- Accessing a local CUPS printer from Linux

- Accessing a remote CUPS printer from Windows

- Accessing a remote CUPS printer from Windows using Samba

The first two are covered in the next two sections, but we'll wait until later in this chapter to configure the Samba server to provide access to a CUPS print server (see "Integrating CUPS with Samba").

Accessing a Local CUPS Printer from Linux

Accessing a local CUPS printer from Linux is easy because all CUPS printers appear in your applications automatically. The only minor disadvantage is that after setting up a CUPS printer from the web interface, it doesn't automatically become the default printer. That said, though, it's easy to make your CUPS printer the default printer: from the web management interface that you find at port 631 on your server, select the Printers tab and click Set As Default.

Another useful way of accessing CUPS printers is the command line. You can use the `lpr` command to send a file to a CUPS printer, but you first have to make sure that the command is available on your server (by default it isn't) by typing `apt-get install cupsys-bsd`. Next, as a test, use `lpr -Pnameofyourprinter /etc/hosts` to send the file `/etc/hosts` to the printer that is referred to by using the `-P` option.

Accessing a Remote CUPS Printer from Windows

Because CUPS uses a standard that Windows understands as well, you'll normally have no problem accessing a CUPS printer from Windows. Again, you can access a CUPS printer in two ways: you can add a new printer with the Add Printer wizard and refer to the name of the printer directly, or you can use Samba to access a CUPS printer that's shared by a Samba server. In this section, you'll read how to set it up using the Add Printer wizard in Windows. Although I used Windows XP to set up the CUPS printer, the installation on other Windows versions will be more or less the same.

1. In Windows, select Start ➤ Settings ➤ Printers and Faxes.

2. Click Add a Printer.

3. Specify that you want to create a remote printer and click Next.

4. Select Connect to a printer on the Internet or on a home or office network, and specify the URL of your printer. This URL consists of three parts. First, there is `http://yourserver`. Use the name or the IP address of your server. Next, `/printers` refers to the location on your server where your printers are defined. Next, you should use the printer queue name as it is defined in the CUPS web administration page and as you see it on the Printers page. For example, the complete URL to enter here is something like this: `http://myserver/printers/BrotherHL1430`.

5. After making contact with the printer, Windows displays an interface for you to select the manufacturer and model of your printer. Now complete the wizard to install the CUPS printer on Windows.

Sharing Files with NFS

If you're looking for a service that can offer access to shared files in a fast way, NFS is an excellent choice. NFS is a very convenient way to share files, especially in an environment in which the clients are mainly Linux. It's not uncommon to store the home directories of all users on an NFS server. In this section, I'll cover the following topics:

- Using the NFS server

- Understanding how the NFS server works

- Configuring an NFS server

- Configuring an NFS client

- Monitoring the NFS server

Using the NFS Server

You can use the NFS server to share files with UNIX/Linux servers and clients because every version of UNIX and Linux has native NFS support in the kernel of the operating system. NFS is particularly useful when certain directories must be stored on a central location in the network. You can, for example, use it for access to shared home directories; just make sure that the home directory is stored in a central location on a server and lets users access it when they log in to their workstations. NFS is also very useful for sharing large data directories, such as an installation repository, with other servers using NFS.

One of the most important things to remember about NFS is that its security is rather limited in version 3 of the protocol. Version 4 offers Kerberos to secure the NFS server, but setting up this version is far more difficult. Because most people use NFS for its speed anyway, version 4 hasn't become very successful yet. For trusted file sharing, Samba is a much more convenient solution. Therefore, I'll focus here on version 3 only.

The security that can be applied in NFS version 3 is based on host names or IP addresses. After another host has been granted access to your NFS server, all its users get access to the shared directories as well. It's possible to limit that by granting file permissions to only the user and group owners of a file and by avoiding permissions for others, but that doesn't make for a decent security setting, does it?

To determine the permissions of a user from one machine at another machine, the NFS server checks user IDs. For example, if you have user ID 611 at your client desktop and you access your company's server, you'll automatically get the permission of the user who has UID 611 on the server. To prevent problems with this, you should use NFS in an environment in which user management is centralized with a service such as an NIS or LDAP server. If you just want to use NFS to set up a quick-and-dirty file share (which is the scope of this section), you don't need either one.

Understanding How the NFS Works

A couple of components are involved in offering NFS services. First, there's the NFS server itself, which is provided by the kernel of Ubuntu Server. NFS is one of the services that works with the RPC port mapper, which uses its own port numbers.

Most modern services have their own TCP or UDP port numbers, but this isn't the case with NFS (at least by default). NFS was created a long time ago, when the TCP and UDP port numbers as we know them now weren't very common. Therefore, NFS uses its own kind of port numbers, the remote procedure call (RPC) program numbers. On a modern system, these numbers must be converted to an Internet port number, and this task belongs to the RPC port map program, which is implemented by a process on its own.

When an RPC-based service such as NFS is started, it tells the port mapper what port number it's listening on and what RPC program numbers it serves. When a client wants to communicate to the RPC-based service, it first contacts the port mapper on the server to find out the port number it should use. Once it knows the port number, its requests can be tunneled over the Internet port to the correct RPC port. To find out which RPC program numbers your server is currently listening on, use the `rpcinfo -p` command. Listing 10-1 shows the results of this command. (Make sure to install the kernel NFS server first, using `apt-get install nfs-kernel-server`.)

Listing 10-1. *Displaying RPC Program Numbers with* `rpcinfo -p`

```
SFO:~ # rpcinfo -p
  program  vers  proto  port
   100000    2    tcp    111 portmapper
   100000    2    udp    111 portmapper
   100003    2    udp   2049 nfs
   100003    3    udp   2049 nfs
   100003    4    udp   2049 nfs
   100003    2    tcp   2049 nfs
   100003    3    tcp   2049 nfs
   100003    4    tcp   2049 nfs
   100024    1    udp   1147 status
   100021    1    udp   1147 nlockmgr
   100021    3    udp   1147 nlockmgr
   100021    4    udp   1147 nlockmgr
   100024    1    tcp   2357 status
   100021    1    tcp   2357 nlockmgr
   100021    3    tcp   2357 nlockmgr
   100021    4    tcp   2357 nlockmgr
   100005    1    udp    916 mountd
   100005    1    tcp    917 mountd
   100005    2    udp    916 mountd
   100005    2    tcp    917 mountd
   100005    3    udp    916 mountd
   100005    3    tcp    917 mountd
```

As you can see in this output, NFS is listening to Internet port 2049 for NFS protocol version 2, 3, and 4 calls. Internally it's using RPC port 100003 as well. Before the NFS server is started, you must make sure that the port mapper is started. (This happens automatically when the NFS software is installed.) When the port mapper is started, two service scripts are created. The first is `/etc/init.d/nfs-common`. Some of the common services are started from this script, such as `rpc.lockd`, which takes care of proper NFS file locking. Next, the `nfs-kernel-server` is started. From this service script, the file-sharing services are activated. In total, the NFS server consists of the services in the following list (the names in parentheses are the scripts in `/etc/init.d` that make sure that the service is started):

- `rpc.statd` (`nfs-common`): This helper process is used by `rpc.lockd`. It keeps track of all file locks that are allocated by kernel lock process or `rpc.lockd` and makes sure that they're restored after a crash of the NFS server.

- `rpc.lockd` (`nfs-common`): This process isn't normally needed any more. It was used to make sure that files were locked properly, but now its function is implemented in the Linux kernel. It doesn't harm to start the process anyway, so you'll find the `rpc.lockd` process activated most of the time.

- `rpc.idmapd` (`nfs-common`): The `rpc.idmapd` process is used in NFS version 4 only. It makes sure that user IDs are not matched only at the UID level (a user has the same UID) but also at the user name level. By using this process, the NFS version 4 server can map users with the same name but different UIDs on the machines involved in the NFS setup.

- `rpc.gssd` (`nfs-common`): This service and its helper process `rpc.svcgssd` make sure that a secure connection is established between the NFS client and server before any information is exchanged.

- `rpc.nfsd` (`nfs-kernel-server`): This is the core NFS process because it ensures that NFS services are offered. You need it at all NFS servers. The service is implemented by loading the `nfsd.o` kernel module.

- `rpc.svcgssd` (`nfs-kernel-server`): See `rpc.gssd`.

- `rpc.mountd` (`nfs-kernel-server`): This is the client process that's required to create an NFS mount.

The last part of the NFS server consists of its three configuration files:

- `/etc/default/nfs-common`: This file contains parameters that tune the working of the services started from the `/etc/init.d/nfs-common` script when started.

- `/etc/default/nfs-kernel-server`: This file contains parameters required by the services started from `/etc/init.d/nfs-kernel-server` when started.

- `/etc/exports`: This file specifies the NFS shares.

Configuring an NFS Server

The NFS shares are defined in `/etc/exports`. The generic structure of the lines where this happens is as follows:

```
directory allowed-hosts(options)
```

In this example, `directory` is the name of the directory you want to share (`/share`, for example). Next, `hosts` refers to the hosts that you want to have access to that directory. The following details can be used for the host specification:

- The name of an individual host, either its short name or its fully qualified domain name

- The IP address of an individual host

- A network referred to by its name, such as `*.mydomain.com`

- A network referred to by a combination of IP address and subnetmask, such as `192.168.10.0/255.255.255.0`.

- All networks, referred to by an asterisk

After indicating which hosts are granted access to your server, you need to specify the options with which you want to give access to the NFS share. Table 10-1 lists some of the more popular options.

Table 10-1. *Commonly Used NFS Options*

Option	Meaning
ro	The file system is exported as a read-only file system. No matter what local permissions the user has, writing to the file system is denied at all times, even if the user who makes the connection is root.
rw	The file system is exported as a read-write file system. Users can read and write files to the directory if they have sufficient permissions on the local file system.
root_squash	The user ID of user root is mapped to the user ID 65534, which is mapped to the user nobody by default. This default behavior ensures that a user who is mounting an NFS mount as user root on the workstation does not have root access to the directory on the server. Always use this to secure shares at a server that are frequently accessed by clients.
no_root_squash	With this option, there's no limitation for the root user. He will just have root permissions on the server as well.
all_squash	Use this option if you want to limit the permissions of all users accessing the NFS share. With these options, all users will have the permissions of user nobody on the NFS share. Use this option if you want extra security on your NFS share.
sync	This option ensures that changes to files have been written to the file system before others are granted access to the same file. Although this option doesn't offer the best performance, you should always use it to avoid losing any data.

■Tip After making changes to the /etc/exports file, you must restart the NFS server because NFS is one of the many older UNIX services that reads its configuration only on startup. To restart the NFS server, use /etc/init.d/nfs-kernel-server restart. You don't need to restart the /etc/init.d/nfs-common script after making modifications to /etc/exports.

Tuning the List of Exported File Systems with the exports Command

When the NFS server is activated, it keeps a list of exported file systems in the /var/lib/nfs/xtab file. This file is initialized with the list of all directories exported in the /etc/exports file by invoking the exportfs -a command when the NFS server initializes. With the exportfs command, it's possible to add a file system to this list without editing the /etc/exports file or restarting the NFS server. For example, the following line exports the /srv directory to all servers in the network 192.168.1.0:

```
exportfs 192.168.1.0/255.255.255.0:/srv
```

The exported file system will be created immediately, but it will be available only until the next reboot of your NFS server. If you also want it to be available after a reboot, make sure to include it in the /etc/exports file, too.

Configuring an NFS Client

Now that the NFS server is up and running, you can configure the clients that need to access the NFS server, and you can mount the NFS share either by hand (with the mount command) or automatically from fstab.

Mounting an NFS Share with the mount Command

The fastest way to get access to an NFS shared directory is to issue the mount command from the command line. Just specify the file system type as an NFS file system, indicate what you want to mount and where you want to mount it, and you have immediate access. The following command shows how to get access to the shared directory /opt on server STN via the local directory /mnt:

```
mount -t nfs STN:/opt /mnt
```

Notice the colon after the name of the server; this is a required element to separate the name of the server from the name of the directory that you want to export. Although you can access an NFS shared directory without using any options at all, some options are often used to make it easier to access an NFS mounted share. Table 10-2 summarizes these options.

Table 10-2. *Common NFS Mount Options*

Option	Meaning
soft	Use this option to tell the mount command not to insist indefinitely on mounting the remote share. If the directory could not be mounted after the default time-out value (normally 60 seconds), the mount attempt is aborted. Use this option for all noncritical mounts.
hard	Use this option to tell the mount command that it should continue trying to access the mount indefinitely. But be aware that if the mount is performed at boot time, this option may cause the boot process to hang. Therefore, use this option only on directories that are really needed.
fg	This default option tells the mount command that all mounts must be activated as foreground mounts. The result is that you can do nothing else on that screen as long as the mount could not be completed.
bg	This option performs the mount as a background mount. If the first attempt isn't successful, all other attempts are started in the background.
rsize=n	This option specifies the number of bytes that the client reads from the server at the same time. For compatibility reasons, this size is set to 1,024 bytes by default. NFS version 3 and later can handle much more than this. To increase the performance of your NFS server, set it to a higher value, such as 8,192 bytes.
wsize=n	Use this option to set the maximum number of bytes that can be written simultaneously. Again, the default is 1,024, but NFS 3 and later can handle much more, so specify 8,192 to optimize the write speed for your NFS server.
retry=n	This option specifies the number of minutes a mount attempt can take. The default value is 10,000 (which is 6.94 days). Consider setting it lower to avoid waiting on a mount that can't be established.

Option	Meaning
nosuid	This security option specifies that the SUID and SGID bits cannot be used on the exported file system.
nodev	This option specifies that no devices can be used from the imported file system. This also is a security feature.
noexec	Use this option to avoid starting executable files from the exported file system.

Mount an NFS Share Automatically from `fstab`

Mounting an NFS share with the `mount` command is fine for a mount that you need only occasionally. If you need the mount all the time, you can automate it by using /etc/fstab. If you know how to add entries to /etc/fstab, it isn't difficult to add an entry that mounts an NFS share as well. The only differences with normal mounts are that you have to specify the complete name of the NFS share instead of a device, and that some NFS options must be specified. When mounting from `fstab`, you should always include the `netdev`, `rsize`, `wsize`, and `soft` options for optimal performance. To refer to the server, its name as well as its IP address can be used. Next is an example of such a line:

```
myserver:/myshare        /mylocalmount        nfs
_netdec,rsize=8192,wsize=8192,soft        0 0
```

Monitoring the NFS Server

At the end of this section about NFS, it's time for some information about monitoring the NFS server. You can use two very useful commands: `rpcinfo -p` and `showmount -e`. First, the `rpcinfo -p` command displays a list of all services that are currently registered at the port mapper service on your NFS server. If you can't connect to the NFS server for some reason, this command provides a good check to see whether the server is running properly. Next, the `showmount -e` command displays a list of all file systems that are exported by a remote server. It typically is a utility that you would run from a workstation acting as an NFS client to check a server to see whether the share you intend to connect to is really offered by that server.

Sharing Files with Samba

Sharing files with NFS is useful in a Linux/UNIX environment. If you have many Windows users in your network, they probably won't appreciate your NFS server much because it isn't supported natively by Windows. For those users, we'll have to use the Samba server. Samba is more than just an alternative for NFS; it's an actual replacement for Windows servers. The performance of a Samba server is as good as an average Windows server, and if you need only file-sharing services, Samba provides an excellent alternative. In this section, you'll learn how to configure a Samba server.

Samba Server Possibilities and Impossibilities

In the late 1990s, Microsoft published the specifications of its protocols for file and printer sharing. Based on these specifications, the common Internet file system (CIFS) was defined, and the Samba project team started its free service to provide file and print services to Microsoft clients.

But many things have changed since then. First, Microsoft networking has changed a lot, and Microsoft hasn't published the specifications of its networking protocols since 1998. As a result, the Samba team has had to reverse-engineer these protocols, which means that they had to analyze all new functionality added by Microsoft networking components and then try to build something like it. Sometimes the Samba team succeeded right away, and other times it doesn't work as fast. For example, the Samba developers needed a long time to implement integration with Active Directory in Samba.

The Samba server offers many options that people commonly use in Windows networks, and because it was developed from scratch, Samba is often even faster than the original Microsoft protocols. Also, because it has been ported to many different operating systems, it's used in all environments. Ubuntu Server with a Samba server installed offers an excellent replacement for a Windows server.

■**Note** Let's be realistic. Samba offers excellent file and printer sharing, but lacks Active Directory functionality. If you really need Active Directory, you need Microsoft. But if you need Active Directory functionality, you can probably use Samba as well. Especially when integrated with OpenLDAP, Samba can offer something very similar.

Configuring the Samba Server

The most important role of Samba is as a file server that offers access to shared directories. After installing the Samba server with apt-get install samba, you'll need several elements to configure it:

- A directory to share on the local file system.

- One or more local users who have local Linux permissions on that file system.

- A share that provides network access to the shared directory.

- A user database so Windows users can authenticate with their Windows credentials (which aren't compatible with Linux credentials).

- Services that give access to the shared directory. See whether you have a configuration file with the name /etc/samba/smb.conf; if you don't, run apt-get install samba to install everything you need.

Preparing the Local File System

The first element of a successful Samba file server is a local directory that contains files you want to share. If the main function of your server is to be a file server, you should consider giving this directory its own partition or logical volume to separate it from the other files on your server. I personally like putting Samba shared directories in /srv and creating a logical volume for /srv.

Besides creating the directory, you shouldn't forget about the right permissions. The security for your shared directory is configured partly on the share, but even more so on the local Linux file system. So to make it all work, just create a Linux group, grant permissions to that group, create some users and make them members of the group, and make the group owner of the shared directory. (You can return to Chapter 5 for a refresher on how this all works.) Here are some hints on how to organize the permission part of your Samba:

- Use ACLs if you want to give read access to members of one group but read-write access to members of another group.

- Set the SGID permission on the shared directory to make the group that is owner of the directory the owner of everything created in that directory and its subdirectories.

- Use the sticky bit to prevent users from accidentally deleting each other's files from the shared directory.

It's a good idea to configure access on the local Linux file system before you do anything else on your Samba server. (Many people tend to forget about it otherwise.)

Creating the Share

The second step in the configuration of a Samba server is to configure the share. For this purpose, Samba works with a configuration file with the name /etc/samba/smb.conf. This file configures almost the complete Samba server: general options as well as shares. Listing 10-2 provides an example of a configuration file for the Samba server. I won't discuss it line by line, but you should review it to see how it's organized.

Listing 10-2. *Example of the* smb.conf *Configuration File*

```
[global]
        workgroup = Samba server
        printing = cups
        printcap name = cups
        printcap cache time = 750
        cups options = raw
        map to guest = Bad User
        include = /etc/samba/dhcp.conf
        logon path = \\%L\profiles\.msprofile
        logon home = \\%L\%U\.9xprofile
        logon drive = P:
[homes]
        comment = Home Directories
        valid users = %S, %D%w%S
```

```
        browsable = No
        read only = No
        inherit acls = Yes
[profiles]
        comment = Network Profiles
        path = %H
        read only = No
        store dos attributes = Yes
        create mask = 0600
        directory mask = 0700
[users]
        comment = All users
        path = /home
        read only = No
        inherit acls = Yes
        veto files = /aquota.user/groups/shares/
 [groups]
        comment = All groups
        path = /home/groups
        read only = No
        inherit acls = Yes
[printers]
        comment = All Printers
        path = /var/tmp
        printable = Yes
        create mask = 0600
        browsable = No
[print$]
        comment = Printer Drivers
        path = /var/lib/samba/printers
        write list = @ntadmin root
        force group = ntadmin
        create mask = 0664
        directory mask = 0775
```

The smb.conf configuration file is always divided into different sections. First are the global settings. In the old days you needed the [global] section to define them, but that's no longer the case. In this section, settings are configured that apply to the complete Samba server. Some settings can be configured only here. For example, the definition of the workgroup in workgroup = Samba server is a setting that applies to everything that's offered by your Samba server.

Apart from the global section, some shares are defined as well. Of the shares from the example configuration file, the homes share gives access to the home directories of users, the profiles share allows you to work with Windows profiles, and the printers and print$ shares are created to configure the printing environment. The shares in the example file look at the CUPS printing environment and share it completely with the Samba server. The users and groups shares offer nice examples of how a generic share can be configured.

To add your own share, you need to define a new section in the Samba configuration file. It doesn't matter what name you use for this section, as long as it's unique. Next, specify the parameters that you want to use for the section. Listing 10-3 provides an example in which a share is created for members of the sales group.

Listing 10-3. *Example of a Share with Some Additional Security Features Configured*

```
[sales]
    comment =  Share for the sales department
    path = /srv/samba/sales
    valid users = @ sales
    force user = zeina
    force group = sales
    read only = no
    inherit acls = yes
    veto files = *.mp3
    create mask = 660
```

You'll probably recognize some parameters that are often used on shared directories. Table 10-3 provides an overview of these parameters.

Table 10-3. *Useful Parameters for Shared Folders*

Parameter	Meaning
comment	The text that's used as the value for this parameter is displayed to a user who queries the server for available shares. Use it to explain what the share is used for.
path	This option indicates the path of the local shared Linux directory. In the example, the path is in /srv/samba/. It's a good idea to put all directories shared by the Samba server under one main directory so you can keep a better eye on what exactly is shared on your server. The /srv directory is meant for just that, so use it!
valid users	You read earlier in this chapter that Linux permissions must be configured for the file system on which you keep your shared directory. This doesn't mean that you secure the share only by applying permissions. The valid users parameter is an example of additional security: this parameter can specify a comma-separated list of users who are allowed access to the share. This parameter is empty by default, which allows anyone to connect. It's a good idea to use this parameter followed by the name of a group, as you can see in the example. This allows access only to users who are members of the group you've specified. If you work with group names, make sure to put the @ character before the name of the group to indicate that it is a group. If you want to make sure that some users absolutely don't have access as well, you can use the (rather paranoid) option invalid users to make sure that the specified users are excluded. You could use this option to create an exclusion for a limited number of users who are members of the group that you've granted access.
force user	This parameter can be used to ensure that all files created in this directory get the specified user (zeina in Listing 10-3) as its Linux owner. Don't use this option if you need to see what user created what file in the share.

Continued

Table 10-3. *Continued*

Parameter	Meaning
force group	This option is the equivalent of using the SGID Linux permission on the directory that is shared: it ensures that the specified group becomes the owner of all files that are created in the share. Using either this or the force user option makes sharing files among users in a group really easy.
read only	Without this option, users can't write to the share. By specifying read only = no, you're actually meaning writeable = yes and thus allowing users to write files to the share.
inherit acls	If ACLs are used on the Linux file system, this option makes sure that they are applied to everything created under the directory with the ACL as well. Using this option is a very good idea because you can apply Windows ACLs from the Windows management utilities, and these ACLs integrate perfectly with Linux ACLs. Make sure that you've enabled Linux ACLs for your file system when using this option.
veto files	A veto file is a file that is always denied creation on the share. By using veto files, you can ensure that certain files just cannot be created. As in the example, you should use patterns to indicate exactly what files you don't want to be created. Alternatively, you can specify the names of the files you don't want to exist as well.
create mask	This useful parameter specifies the default permission mode for files that are created in this directory.
directory mask	Use this parameter to set default permissions for new directories.

Configuring User Access

The next important step in the configuration of the Samba server is to specify how user accounts should be handled. Basically, the issue here is that the user connecting to a Samba share is normally a Windows user. Being a Windows user, he comes in with Windows credentials, such as a password that is encrypted with the Windows NTLM password hash. Unfortunately, this method of password encryption isn't compatible with the Linux method, so something must be done to allow Windows users to log in with their Windows password. Basically, this means that some additional authentication service needs to be configured. The following list provides an overview of the available options:

- Configure an additional file in which the names of the Windows users are stored.

- Don't use user authentication at all; work with share-level security.

- Centralize management of Windows user credentials on one server in the network.

- Hook the Samba server up with a Windows domain to handle user authentication.

- Make the Samba server a Windows NT–style domain controller.

- Set up an LDAP directory service and put the local Linux users as well as the Samba users in that.

I don't discuss all of these options here because that would require a book on its own. Instead, I'll discuss in this section the easy method of creating a separate user database. Later in this section, you'll also read how to configure your Samba server as a Windows NT–style domain controller.

To set up a local Samba user database, you'll use the `smbpasswd` command to create a local database containing Samba user names and passwords. You need to create an entry in this file for every user who needs access to the Samba server. Before doing this, however, you must make sure that the user already exists in the local Linux user database. If he doesn't, `smbpasswd` gives an error indicating that it's impossible to create the user. After verifying that the user you want to create as a Samba user already exists as a local user, use `smbpasswd -a username` to create the Samba user as well. After creating the user with `smbpasswd`, he'll be able to connect to Samba shares.

Starting the Services

Three different main services are involved with the Samba software:

- `smbd`: This is the process that allows for the actual file sharing.

- `nmbd`: This service provides NetBIOS naming services, allowing Windows clients to work with their own naming mechanism. For example, this service allows you to browse the network neighborhood and find all Samba services as well.

- `winbind`: This service allows you to bind your Linux environment to a Windows environment that uses Active Directory. With it, you can log in to Active Directory as a Linux user.

To make your Samba server fully operational, you have to make sure that these three services are started when your machine is booted. After installation, a script with the name `/etc/init.d/samba` is created. From this script, `nmbd` and `smbd` are started automatically when rebooting your server. Because `winbind` is not installed automatically, you need to install it separately using `apt-get install winbind`. This adds the `winbind` script to `/etc/init.d` to ensure that the `winbind` service is started automatically after a reboot of your server.

Integrating CUPS with Samba

Printers can be shared in Samba as well, but you first need to set up your Linux printing environment. You read earlier how to do this with CUPS. After setting up the CUPS environment, you need the right parameters in the `smb.conf` file to make sure that your printers are shared. Listing 10-4 provides an example of a configuration that shares your CUPS printers automatically.

Listing 10-4. *You Need Some Specific Parameters in* `smb.conf` *to Make Sure That Your Printers Are Shared*

```
[global]
        printing = cups
        printcap name = cups
        printcap cache time = 750
        cups options = raw
[printers]
        comment = All Printers
```

```
        path = /var/tmp
        printable = Yes
        create mask = 0600
        browsable = No
[print$]
        comment = Printer Drivers
        path = /var/lib/samba/printers
        write list = @ntadmin root
        force group = ntadmin
        create mask = 0664
        directory mask = 0775
```

As you can see, the Samba printing environment consists of three different parts: [global], [printers], and [print$].

First, the [global] section contains four parameters to determine how to handle printing:

- printing = cups: This option sets CUPS as the default printing system. Alternatively, you could use the legacy LPD print system, but CUPS is so much more advanced that modern Linux systems don't use LPD anymore.

- printcap name = cups: This parameter indicates that the file containing printer definitions is not the legacy /etc/printcap that was used by LPD printing: it's the CUPS subsystem.

- printcap cache time = 750: This option specifies the number of seconds before Samba checks the CUPS configuration again to see if any new printers were defined.

- cups options = raw: This option specifies how print jobs offered to the CUPS server are handled. Because CUPS can't understand the data format generated by the Samba server, you should set this option to raw.

After the generic options in the [global] section, you must define two shares for the printers as well. The share [printers] sets up an environment in which all printers can store their temporary print jobs, and the [print$] share is used to store printer drivers. In both shares you refer to a directory in which the temporary files and printer drivers are stored. Make sure that you refer to an existing directory here.

In the example in Listing 10-4, all printers on the server are shared, but it's possible to share just one printer as well, as shown in Listing 10-5.

Listing 10-5. *Sharing Only One Printer*

```
[laserprinter]
    printable = yes
    printer = hl1430
    path = /var/tmp
```

Here, a share with the name laserprinter is defined, and this share needs just three options. The first option is printable = yes, which indicates that this is a printer and not a shared directory. The most important line is printer = hl1430, which refers to the queue as it is defined in the CUPS subsystem. Make sure that a queue with this name exists in CUPS, or it won't work. Finally, the path = /var/tmp option indicates what directory CUPS should use for the temporary spooling of printer jobs.

When sharing printers with your Samba server, you have to take care of the drivers as well. You can install the drivers at the Windows workstation locally, but the disadvantage of this approach is it forces you to maintain them on each individual workstation, which is not an ideal situation for centralized network administration. Therefore, it's easier to install printer drivers on the Samba server. To do this, you need the share [print$], as shown in the example in Listing 10-6.

Listing 10-6. *The* [print$] *Share Allows for Storage of Printer Drivers at the Samba Server*

```
[print$]
        comment = Printer Drivers
        path = /var/lib/samba/printers
        write list = @ntadmin root
        force group = ntadmin
        create mask = 0664
        directory mask = 0775
```

Some important options are used in this example. First, there's the name of the directory in which Samba stores the printer drivers. Next is the write list option that specifies which users are allowed to write to this directory; it should be write-accessible for root and members of the group ntadmin only. With these settings in place, you can set up the printer in your Windows environment, as described in the following procedure:

1. On Windows, start the Add Printer wizard.

2. Indicate that you want to add a network printer and then browse to the shared printer. When prompted, choose to install a new printer driver.

3. Select the printer model for which you want to install the drivers. This installs the drivers automatically in the /var/lib/samba/printers directory.

■**Tip** Make sure that you're installing the printer drivers from your Windows workstation as a user with sufficient permissions to the printer. By default, only the user root and members of the Linux group ntadmin have permissions to write new printer drivers to the /var/lib/samba/drivers directory.

Setting Up Samba As a Domain Controller

In a Windows environment, a domain is used to manage users for a group of computers. The only option to do this in a centralized way in Windows NT4 is by using domains. Windows 2000 introduced Active Directory as a system that sits above that. Because Samba Active Directory functionality still has some shortcomings, in this chapter I'll focus on configuring Samba as an NT4-style domain controller

Be aware that setting up a well-tuned scalable domain environment requires extensive knowledge of Microsoft networks, which goes far beyond the scope of this book. In this section, you'll learn only about the basic requirements needed to set up a Samba domain. Consider this section an introduction to the subject matter only; for more information, consult the man pages or the documentation at www.samba.org.

Modifying the Samba Configuration File

The first step in setting up a domain environment is to modify the Samba configuration file properly. Listing 10-7 reveals the settings required in the [global] section in /etc/samba/ smb.conf.

Listing 10-7. *Samba Domain Controller Settings*

```
[global]
    netbios name = STN
    workgroup = UK
    security = user
    passdb backend = ldapsam:ldap://HTR.mydomain.com
    logon script = %U.bat
    domain master = yes
    os level = 50
    local master = yes
    preferred master = yes
    domain logons = yes

[netlogon]
    path = /netlogin
```

Let's have a look at the different parameters that are used in this example. Table 10-4 summarizes all parameters that I didn't cover earlier.

Table 10-4. *Parameters Specifically for Domain Configuration*

Parameter	Meaning
netbios name	This is the name your server will have in the Microsoft network.
security	This option specifies how security should be handled. If you want to configure your server as a domain controller, set it to security = user.
passdb backend	Use this parameter to specify in what kind of database you want to store user and group information. The most common values for this parameter are smbpasswd, tdbsam, and ldapsam. The easiest way to configure your server is to use the tdbsam option, which creates a local database on your Samba server. The most flexible way to configure it is to use the ldapsam option. However, this option requires the configuration of an LDAP server as well and makes things more complicated. If you want to set up your Samba environment with PDCs as well as BDCs, make sure to use the ldapsam option and ensure that you have an LDAP server configured as a backend.

Parameter	Meaning
logon script	In a Windows environment, a user can have his own login script, which is a batch file that's executed automatically when the user logs in. In this example, the Samba server sees whether there is a script for your user that has the name of the user account, followed by .bat. You should put this script in the directory specified with the path parameter in the [netlogon] share.
domain master	This option tells the nmbd process that's responsible for name services that this server must be responsible for maintaining browse lists in the complete network. These browse lists allow others in the network to view a complete list of all members of the Windows network. A domain controller should always be the domain master for your network.
local master	A domain master browser communicates with local master browsers. These servers are responsible for maintaining browse lists on local network segments. Apart from being the domain master, your Samba servers should be local master browsers as well.
os level	Even if you specify that your server should be a local master and domain master, this doesn't really guarantee that it also will be the master browser. In a Windows network, the master browser is selected by election. To increase chances that your server will be the master browser, make sure that you use a value greater than 32 for the os level parameter. The highest value in the network is the most likely to win the browser elections.
preferred master	Normally, browser elections happen only occasionally. Use this option to immediately force a new browser election when the Samba server comes up.
domain logins	Set this parameter to yes to make the server a domain controller.

Creating Workstation Accounts

Now that you have your domain environment, you should add workstations to it. You need a workstation account on the Samba server for every workstation that is going to be a member of a domain, and this account gives the required permissions to the workstation in the domain. Setting up a workstation account is just like setting up a user account.

First, you add the account to the local user database on your server. Next, you add the workstation account as a workstation to the Samba user database. Notice that the name of the workstation should end with a dollar sign ($) to indicate that it is a workstation. To create a workstation with the name ws10, first use useradd ws10$ to create it in /etc/passwd. Next, add the workstation to the smbpasswd database by using the smbpasswd -a -m ws10 command. Notice that in the smbpasswd command, there's no need to use the $ to specify that it's a workstation; the -m option takes care of this.

Client Access to the Samba Server

Almost all operating systems can connect to your Samba server. In this subsection, you'll learn how to test your Samba server from a Linux workstation. Three different utilities can be used to test whether the server is working properly:

- Use the mount command to make a connection to a Samba share.

- Use the nmblookup utility to resolve NetBIOS names into IP addresses.

- Use the multipurpose smbclient utility to test many aspects of the Samba server.

Mounting Shares with the mount Command

The mount command is a fast and easy way to test whether your server is providing the services you expect it to. All you need to do is specify the cifs file system type and the options that are required to authenticate against the Samba share. You can use the following command to test access to a local share with the name share by connecting it to the /mnt directory temporarily:

```
mount -t cifs -o username=someone //localhost/share /mnt
```

Note that the only option that's really required in this command is the username option, which tells the Samba server what user you wish to be authenticated as. You can enter a password as well, but it's not a very good idea to provide that at the command line because everything entered at the command line is stored in your local history file.

As an alternative to the mount command followed by the -t cifs option, the smbmount command can be used as well. Basically, this command offers the same options; check its man page for more details.

Using nmblookup to Test Samba Naming

You can use the nmblookup command to test whether Samba name services are fully operational. For example, nmblookup lax searches the network for a host with the NetBIOS name lax and returns its IP address. To return the IP address of the given host name, the utility first uses a NetBIOS broadcast on the local network. If no WINS server is configured, it won't go any further. If NetBIOS nodes are present on other networks as well, a WINS server must be configured to manage the names for these hosts as well. Because WINS configurations aren't very common any more, I don't discuss them here.

Testing and Accessing the Samba Server with smbclient

The versatile smbclient utility can be used to test a Samba server. It can check availability of shares on a server, but with its FTP-like interface it can also move files to and from the Samba server. Probably the most useful check that you can perform with smbclient is listing the shares offered by a given server. For example, use smbclient -L //localhost to see what shares are offered by the localhost. Listing 10-8 is an example of this command's output.

Listing 10-8. *Example of* smbclient *Output*

```
 SFO:~ # smbclient -L //localhost
Password:
Domain=[SFO] OS=[Unix]

        Sharename       Type      Comment
        ---------       ----      -------
        profiles        Disk      Network Profiles Service
```

```
        users               Disk        All users
        share               Disk        my files
        groups              Disk        All groups
        print$              Disk        Printer Drivers
        IPC$                IPC         IPC Service
        ADMIN$              IPC         IPC Service
Domain=[SFO] OS=[Unix]

        Server              Comment
        ---------           -------


        Workgroup           Master
        ---------           -------
```

As you can see, the smbclient command first prompts for a password, which is required for privileged options only. Because only a list of available shares is requested in this example, no password is needed, so you can just press Enter. Next, smbclient displays a list of all available shares. This list shows the type of share, as well as the comment that was added to it.

You can also use the smbclient utility to upload and download files from a share. To do this, you'll use the same commands that are offered from an FTP client interface. The most important of these commands are ls (list files), cd (change directory), get (download files), and put (upload files). However, it's not the most practical way of working because the Samba file system is not integrated in the local file system at all.

Summary

In this chapter, you learned how to configure file and printer sharing on your server. You first read about the configuration of the CUPS print environment, which is used as the native way to share printers, especially in an environment in which only Linux or UNIX clients are used. Next, you read about the configuration of the NFS server, which is used to share files with other computers that can handle the NFS protocol. They typically are Linux and UNIX clients as well. In the last part of this chapter, you learned how to configure a Samba server to offer Windows-native file and print services. In the next chapter, you'll read how to configure Internet services such as FTP and web services.

■■■

## CHAPTER 11

Setting Up Web Services
Configuring Apache, MySQL, PHP, Squid, and FTP

The Internet is the environment in which Linux has its greatest popularity. Fortunately, Ubuntu Server makes a very good Internet server. In this chapter, you'll learn how to set up your server as an Apache web server, including support for PHP and MySQL. You'll also set Ubuntu up as an FTP server and learn how to configure Ubuntu as a Squid proxy server. Although the focus in this chapter is on Apache, you'll also learn how to enable the MySQL server so that the database administrator can create new databases in it and how Apache is integrated with PHP. Creating MySQL databases is a rather specialized job, however, so I won't go into great detail about that here.

Setting Up Apache

From a technical perspective, you could say that a web server is just a special kind of file server; all it does is offer files that are stored in a dedicated directory structure. The root of this structure is called the document root, and the file format that offers the files is HTML, the hypertext markup language. But a web server can provide more than just HTML files. In fact, the web server can serve just about anything, as long as it is specified in the HTML file. Therefore, a web server is a very good source for streaming audio and video, accessing databases, displaying animations, showing photos, and much more.

Apart from the web server in which the content is stored, the client also has to use a specific protocol to access this content as well, and this protocol is HTTP (the Hypertext Transfer Protocol). Typically, a client uses a web browser to generate HTTP commands that retrieve content, in the form of HTML and other files, from a web server.

You'll likely encounter two different versions of Apache web server. The most recent version is 2.x, and this is the one installed by default on Ubuntu Server. You might, however, encounter environments that still use the earlier version 1.3. This often happens if, for instance, custom scripts have been developed for use with 1.3, and those scripts aren't compatible with 2.x. As the 1.3 version is becoming increasingly rare, I won't cover it in this chapter.

To manage an Apache web server, you need to know—at the very least—exactly which Apache components are installed on your server. Therefore, in this section you'll first read about the Ubuntu Server components that contain Apache software. Next, you'll learn how to start, stop, and test the Apache web server. In the third part of this chapter, you'll explore the Apache configuration files to see what must be managed where. You'll also learn how easy it is to set up new virtual hosts in Apache.

Apache Components

Apache is a modular web server, which means that the core server (whose role is essentially to serve up HTML documents) can be extended by using a variety of optional modules. For example, the libapache2-mod-php5 module allows your Apache web server to work with scripts written in PHP 5. Likewise, many other modules are available for Apache. To give you an initial impression, I'll list some of the most useful modules:

- libapache2-mod-auth-mysqld: This module tells Apache how to handle user authentication against a MySQL database.

- libapache2-mod-auth-pam: This module instructs Apache how to authenticate users, using the Linux PAM mechanism.

- libapache-mod-frontpage: This module instructs Apache how to handle web pages using Microsoft FrontPage extensions.

- libapache2-mod-mono: This module tells Apache how to interpret ASP.NET code.

This is a short and incomplete list of all the modules you can use on the Apache web server; http://modules.apache.org currently lists more than 450 modules. It's important that you determine exactly which modules you need for your server so you can extend its functionality accordingly. Be careful when adding new modules, however. With every module you add, you also add to the potential security problems that could disturb your server's functionality. Now, let's move on to the configuration of the Apache web server itself.

Starting, Stopping, and Testing the Apache Web Server

Like almost all other services you can use on Ubuntu Server, the Apache web server is not installed automatically. The two packages that are available to install Apache are the apache package and the apache2 package. At present, apache2 is more common, and only in specific situations does it make sense to use the older apache package. Use dpkg -l | grep apache to check whether Apache has already been installed. If this command doesn't show an Apache server, install it using apt-get install apache2.

The most important part of the Apache web server is the Apache 2 daemon (apache2) process. This process is started from the script /etc/init.d/apache2; to run it from the command line, use /etc/init.d/apache2 start. If this command finishes without any errors, your web server is up and running, which you can check with the ps aux | grep apache command. As shown in Listing 11-1, this command shows that different instances of the Apache web server are ready and waiting for incoming connections.

Listing 11-1. *By Default, Several Instances of the* httpd *Process Are Started Automatically*

```
root@RNA:~# ps aux | grep apache
root      4535  0.0  1.1  20020  6012 ?    Ss 09:53   0:00 /usr/sbin/apache2 -k start
www-data  4581  0.0  0.6  20020  3212 ?    S  09:53   0:00 /usr/sbin/apache2 -k start
www-data  4582  0.0  0.6  20020  3212 ?    S  09:53   0:00 /usr/sbin/apache2 -k start
www-data  4583  0.0  0.6  20020  3212 ?    S  09:53   0:00 /usr/sbin/apache2 -k start
www-data  4584  0.0  0.6  20020  3212 ?    S  09:53   0:00 /usr/sbin/apache2 -k start
www-data  4585  0.0  0.6  20020  3212 ?    S  09:53   0:00 /usr/sbin/apache2 -k start
root      4824  0.0  0.1   2880   748 pts/1 R+ 09:58   0:00 grep apache
```

As you can see from the output of ps aux in Listing 11-1, the first Apache process started (the one with PID 4535) has root as its owner. This process, under control of the mod_prefork module, immediately forks five other processes that listen to incoming connections.

These child processes are automatically launched by the Apache parent process, as needed, so the right number of processes is always available for incoming connections. Later, in the section "Some Words on Apache Performance Tuning," you'll learn how to manage the minimum number of child processes that are always ready and waiting for new connections, as well as the maximum number of processes that can be started.

After starting the Apache web server, you can test its availability in several ways. The best way, however, is to just try to connect because a default web server is listening for incoming requests after being installed. So wait no longer; launch a browser and connect to HTTP port 80 on your local host. It should show you a page (see Figure 11-1). It doesn't look very nice, but that's only because you haven't configured anything yet.

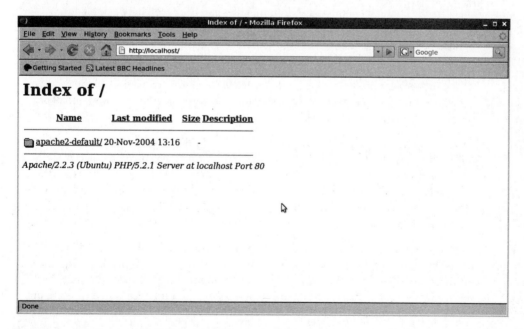

Figure 11-1. *To verify the working of the Apache server, just connect to it.*

Exploring the Configuration Files

On Ubuntu Server, the Apache server uses a few configuration files that define its operations (these files are in the /etc/apache2 directory). Let's start with a short overview:

- /etc/apache2/apache2.conf: This is the main configuration file for your Apache server. It contains the generic configuration for your server, such as the specification of the directory in which the server can find its configuration files (the so-called ServerRoot) and much more. If you want to tune the performance of your Apache server, this is the file that you should look in. From this file, Include directives are used to include all other configuration files.

- /etc/apache2/httpd.conf: This file is empty by default. If you want to create additional configuration parameters that by default are not in the apache2.conf file, put them here.

- /etc/apache2/envvars: You can place the environment variables to tune the operation of your Apache server in this file. It also contains some other important information about the way your Apache server is started, such as the user and group accounts used to run the Apache server.

- /etc/apache2/ports.conf: This file contains the port numbers that the Apache server will listen on. By default, the server listens on port 80.

- /etc/apache2/conf.d/: You can put additional Apache configuration files in this directory. After a default installation, the directory contains only the charset file, which specifies the character set to use. Additional files can be placed here as well. From /etc/apache2/apache2.conf, all files that are in this directory are included in the Apache configuration automatically.

- /etc/apache2/mods-available/: As stated before, you can extend the functionality of your Apache web server by using modules. In this directory, you'll find all the modules that are installed for your server. These are just the available modules, and not all of them are necessarily used by default.

- /etc/apache2/mods-enabled/: To enable a given module, you have to create a symbolic link in this directory that refers to the module file in /etc/apache2/mods-available. So, if you have a module by the name ldap.load in /etc/apache2/mods-available and you want to include it in your Apache configuration, create a symbolic link by first using cd /etc/apache2/mods-enabled and then ln -s ../mods-available/ldap.load ldap.load. This loads the module automatically the next time you restart your Apache web server.

- /etc/apache2/sites-available/: This directory stores all the configuration files for the web sites serviced by your Apache server. After a default installation, it contains just the file default that's used by the default web site. Configuration files for additional sites serviced by your Apache server are stored here as well, but the files stored here are not activated automatically.

- /etc/apache2/sites-enabled/: If you want to enable a web site for which you have created a configuration file in /etc/apache2/sites-available/, create a symbolic link in /etc/apache2/sites-enabled/ that refers to this configuration file:

  1. cd /etc/apache/sites-enabled

  2. ln ../sites-available/mysite mysite

- /etc/default/apache2: This file should contain the NO_START variable to manage automatic startup of the Apache server. By default, Ubuntu Server doesn't start the Apache server automatically. If you want to start the Apache server automatically when booting your server, use an editor to add this parameter and give it the value 1 (for instance, NO_START=1).

The Structure of the Apache Configuration Files

To tune the Apache web server, it's important that you understand the structure of its configuration files. The basic element of the configuration files is the directive that is used to group a set of options so they apply only to a specific item. As an example, Listing 11-2 includes the directive that's created to specify the options for the directory in which the web server starts looking for its documents, the so-called document root. This document root is very important because all other file names and directory names are relative to it. This configuration comes from the /etc/apache2/sites-available/default configuration file.

■Note To increase readability, I removed all comment lines from the example file.

Listing 11-2. *Specification of the Document Root in the Default Server Configuration File*

```
DocumentRoot "/var/www"
<Directory "/var/www">
        Options None
        AllowOverride None
        Order allow,deny
        Allow from all
</Directory>
```

This example first starts with the specification of the DocumentRoot. As you can see, it's in /var/www/ by default. Next, a directive is started for this directory to specify its options. Note that the directive starts with the line <Directory "/var/www/"> and ends with </Directory>. This is a generic rule for creating directives; if it starts with <Something>, it is closed with </Something>. When tuning directives by hand, don't forget this closing statement! Between the start and end of the directive are its options.

■**Tip** By default, the /var directory contains files that your server creates automatically, such as the log files. It's a rather dynamic directory, so there's always some risk of it being filled up very fast by some process that's gone crazy. To separate dynamic files such as log files from more static files such as the Apache document root, I think it's a good idea to use the /srv directory to store the Apache document root. Under /srv you can create a subdirectory with the name www for all web-related stuff. And if you start using an FTP server later, you can also put its configuration in /srv. If you want, you can keep it on a separate partition to further reduce the risk of some process that goes wild in /var trashing your precious web data in /srv.

The first option, Options None, indicates that no specific options are applied to this directory. Next, the AllowOverride None option makes sure that the settings made here can't be overwritten at a lower level in the directory structure. Without this option, a user can activate settings by creating a file with the name .htaccess in any subdirectory of the document root. If that file exists, and the AllowOverride None option doesn't, the settings from .htaccess will be applied.

Next, the Order allow,deny option indicates that allow statements must be evaluated first, and only then should the server check to see whether anything is denied. This is what you would typically want for an unsecured directory. The Allow from all statement confirms that this server is open to anyone; it grants access to this directory to all, which in most cases is reasonable for a document root. Directives for other directories do look very similar, although some directories might have specific options. For example, there's the cgi-bin directory, which is used to refer to the location of the CGI scripts that can be executed by your server. Because it contains scripts, this directory might require some additional options to make sure that no insecure scripts can be executed.

■**Note** Every instance of the Apache server has its own document root. If you want to run several virtual Apache servers (discussed later in this chapter), make sure that every virtual server has its own and unique document root.

Checking the Configuration

After tuning configuration files, you should make sure that they work. The first thing you need to do is run the apache2ctl command, which helps you test your configuration. To do this, run apache2ctl configtest. You'll be told whether everything is okay or not.

After verifying that everything is working as it should, you need to activate the changes by running the /etc/init.d/apache2 reload command. This command just activates the changes that you've made. That is, it does not unload and reload the Apache web server. Sometimes, however, this just isn't enough, and you need to restart the Apache server anyway. In this case, use /etc/init.d/apache2 restart.

Most scripts that run from /etc/init.d have a status option, but the apache2 script doesn't. To check the status of your Apache server, run the apache2ctl script with the status option or (even better) with the fullstatus option. The latter option gives an overview of all Apache processes by their PID and also mentions what the process is currently doing. Listing 11-3 shows an example of its output. In this example there's not much activity; the Apache server has sent a reply on one of its threads, and nothing else is happening.

Listing 11-3. *The Command Shows the Current Status of the Apache Server*

```
root@mel:~# apache2ctl fullstatus
Apache Server Status for localhost

Server Version: Apache/2.2.8 (Ubuntu) mod_perl/2.0.3 Perl/v5.8.8
Server Built: Feb 2 2008 03:59:12


_____

Current Time: Wednesday, 25-Jun-2008 09:57:24 EDT
Restart Time: Wednesday, 25-Jun-2008 09:51:36 EDT
Parent Server Generation: 0
Server uptime: 5 minutes 47 seconds
1 requests currently being processed, 49 idle workers

 _W_____.........................

Scoreboard Key:
"_" Waiting for Connection, "S" Starting up, "R" Reading Request,
"W" Sending Reply, "K" Keepalive (read), "D" DNS Lookup,
"C" Closing connection, "L" Logging, "G" Gracefully finishing,
"I" Idle cleanup of worker, "." Open slot with no current process

PID Key:

   5733 in state: _ ,    5733 in state: W ,    5733 in state: _
   5733 in state: _ ,    5733 in state: _ ,    5733 in state: _
   5733 in state: _ ,    5733 in state: _ ,    5733 in state: _
   5733 in state: _ ,    5733 in state: _ ,    5733 in state: _
   5733 in state: _ ,    5733 in state: _ ,    5733 in state: _
   5733 in state: _ ,    5733 in state: _ ,    5733 in state: _
   5733 in state: _ ,    5733 in state: _ ,    5733 in state: _
   5733 in state: _ ,    5733 in state: _ ,    5733 in state: _
   5733 in state: _ ,    5737 in state: _ ,    5737 in state: _
   5737 in state: _ ,    5737 in state: _ ,    5737 in state: _
   5737 in state: _ ,    5737 in state: _ ,    5737 in state: _
   5737 in state: _ ,    5737 in state: _ ,    5737 in state: _
   5737 in state: _ ,    5737 in state: _ ,    5737 in state: _
   5737 in state: _ ,    5737 in state: _ ,    5737 in state: _
```

```
5737 in state: _ ,    5737 in state: _ ,    5737 in state: _
5737 in state: _ ,    5737 in state: _ ,    5737 in state: _
5737 in state: _ ,    5737 in state: _ ,
```

```
To obtain a full report with current status information you\
 need to use the
ExtendedStatus On directive.
```

```
Apache/2.2.8 (Ubuntu) mod_perl/2.0.3 Perl/v5.8.8 Server at localhost Port 80
```

Working with Virtual Hosts

If you're installing the Apache web server to host several small web sites, the concept of the virtual host is very useful. Virtual hosts allow you to serve several sites from one instance of the Apache web server. For example, you could host www.mydomain.com, www.yourdomain.com, and www.someoneelsesdomain.com on the same machine. To make this work, you need to set up DNS, which we covered in Chapter 9.

When working with virtual hosts, the following process is what happens when a user accesses the virtual host through her browser:

1. The user enters the URL in her browser.

2. The DNS server redirects the user to your web server, based on the IP address that's assigned by the name of the server at the requested URL.

3. The request arrives at your server, which analyzes the port address the request is addressed to.

4. Based on the port information, the request is sent to the Apache server, which analyzes the request.

5. Apache matches the name used in the URL and forwards the packet to the right virtual server.

Configuring Virtual Hosts

To configure a virtual host, you need a configuration file for every virtual host in the /etc/apache2/sites-available directory and a link in /etc/apache2/sites-enabled to activate this configuration. To make it easier, I advise you to copy the default configuration file in /etc/apache2/sites-available and modify this copy. Make sure to include at least a unique document root for each virtual host; otherwise, all hosts will read the same HTML files.

If you know how to configure an Apache web server, you should be comfortable with configuring virtual hosts as well. Most of the directives in the default file speak for themselves, so all you need to do is give them the right value and restart Apache so that the virtual host can be accessed. Table 11-1 provides an overview of the most important of these directives.

Table 11-1. *Important Directives for Virtual Host Configuration*

Directive	Meaning
ServerAdmin	The mail address of the administrator of your virtual host.
ServerName	The host name of the virtual host. Make sure that it matches the host name as used in DNS. This is a very important directive because it allows your Apache process to find the right virtual server.
DocumentRoot	Every virtual host needs its own document root, and this is not the same as the document root used by your main Apache web server! It's a good idea to create a separate directory for every virtual server you're running. Don't create these directories under the document root of your main web server; instead, make a subdirectory for every virtual server that you want to run at the same level. Make sure that all files in the directory you're referring to are readable by the user www-data.
ErrorLog	The file where this virtual host logs its errors. Typically, this is a file in the /var/log/apache2 directory. Make sure that this file is writeable by the user www-data.
CustomLog	The file that's used for generic log messages.
HostnameLookups	This parameter has a default value of Off, which makes sure that your server does not try to resolve the host name for every IP address that comes in. This is very useful because the reverse name lookup normally takes a lot of time.
ScriptAlias	This sets the directory that contains the CGI script files. If your web server doesn't need to do any scripting, make sure that you disable this setting; allowing scripts to be executed by your server always carries a certain risk.

Apart from these important directives used in the virtual host file, other directives specify the options for the directories offered by your virtual hosts. These directives do not differ from directives with the same purpose on "real" Apache web servers. Listing 11-4 provides an example.

Listing 11-4. *Example of a Directive in a Virtual Host File*

```
<Directory "/var/www/vhosts/myvirtualhost/cgi-bin">
    AllowOverride None
    Options +ExecCGI -Includes
    Order allow,deny
    Allow from all
</Directory>
```

This example should be pretty clear; maybe the only new item is the Options +ExecCGI -Includes line. Its purpose is to allow the user to activate any script that is in the /var/www/ vhosts/ myvirtualhost/cgi-bin directory.

Managing Access to the Web Server

In most situations, a web server is publicly available so everyone can access all of its offered information. In some situations, though, you might need to add an extra layer of security and protect some directories on your web server. Without using additional modules, Apache offers two methods to restrict access: user-based and host-based. In this section, you'll learn how to configure both of them.

If you think these methods are too limited, you have to include other modules that offer more advanced user authentication (check http://modules.apache.org for a complete list of modules). To include other modules, first make sure that the module you want to use is installed. Make a symbolic link to activate the module, include it in the configuration of your (virtual) Apache server, and tune the specific configuration for that module.

Configuring Host-Based Access Restrictions

Apache offers three directives to configure host-based access restrictions:

- allow: Hosts or networks listed after this directive are allowed access to the web server.

- deny: Hosts or networks listed after this directive are denied access to the web server.

- order: This directive determines how allow and deny are applied.

The example in Listing 11-5 shows you how allow and deny can be set to protect a directory on a server. Note that the document root will always have its own settings, which can be overwritten at a lower level. Also note how the default access permissions for the document root are set.

Listing 11-5. *Default Access Restrictions for the Document Root*

```
<Directory "/var/www/documents">
    Order allow,deny
    Allow from all
</Directory>
```

In this example, you can see that the order in which access restrictions are evaluated is set first. In this case, it is set to allow,deny. With this setting, the allow directives are evaluated before the deny directives. Access is denied by default, which means that all clients that do not match either an allow directive or a deny directive are denied access. So in Listing 11-6, access is allowed only for hosts whose IP address starts with 192.168.

Listing 11-6. *Allow Access to Only Some Hosts*

```
<Directory "/var/www/documents">
    Order allow,deny
    Allow from 192.168.0.0/8
</Directory>
```

Instead of Order allow,deny, you can also use Order deny,allow. If you use this option, access is allowed by default, and deny directives are evaluated before the allow directives. Any client that doesn't match a deny directive or does match an allow directive is therefore allowed access. The example in Listing 11-6 can be rewritten using these directives as well, as shown in Listing 11-7.

Listing 11-7. *Allow Access to Only Some Hosts with* Order deny,allow

```
<Directory "/var/www/documents">
     Order deny,allow
     Deny from all
     Allow from 192.168.0.0/8
</Directory>
```

As you can see, the effect of the example in Listing 11-7 is the same as the result of the example in Listing 11-6; it just uses one more line of code. Also the idea of allowing access by default doesn't please everyone. Therefore, to make your web server really secure, it's better to choose the Order allow,deny directive.

As an alternative to Order allow,deny, you might also encounter the Order Mutual-failure option. This is an old option, and you shouldn't use it. The alternative options—Order allow,deny and Order deny,allow—do the same work, but better. You probably won't see it very often, but I mention it here in case you do.

Note that when allowing or denying access to directives, you have different options to specify the hosts you want to limit access for:

- all: Use this to apply an option to all hosts.

- *Complete IP addresses*: This speaks for itself—use it to allow or deny access to one specific host.

- *Partial IP addresses*: If this is used, the option applies to everything starting with the given partial IP address. For example, 192.168.0.0/16 can be rewritten as 192.168 as well.

- *A network in CIDR notation*: CIDR notation specifies the number of bits that should be used in the subnet mask. For example, 192.168.0.0/16 indicates that the setting applies to everything that matches the first two bytes of the IP address. This can be rewritten as 192.168.0.0/255.255.0.0.

- A network address and a subnet mask. This is a network address with the full subnet mask written out (for example 192.168.0.0 255.255.255.0).

Configuring User-Based Access Restrictions

Configuring access restrictions based on IP addresses might be useful if you want to grant access to an internal network and deny access to everyone else (although a firewall is a much better way to do this). For an access control mechanism that's more flexible, it's a good idea to work with user-based access restrictions. In this chapter, you'll learn how to configure simple user-based authentication.

Working with Simple Authentication

Working with basic authentication is the easiest solution. To use this, a simple password file needs to be created with the htpasswd command. Although this file can be located anywhere, make sure that it's not in a location where other users can read it. For example, storing the password file in the document root (or anywhere beneath that) is a very bad idea. The default location on Ubuntu Server is the /etc/apache2 directory, and that's a fine place for it. If you want to put it somewhere else, make sure that it's readable by the user www-data.

The first time you use the htpasswd command, make sure that you use the -c option with it to make sure that a new password file is created. For example, the following command can be used to do this:

```
htpasswd -c /etc/apache2/htpasswd linda
```

Next, the command prompts you to enter this user's password twice and it then creates an entry in the file you specified. Of course, a simple hashing algorithm is used to encrypt this password. When you add more users to the Apache password file, you won't have to use the -c option again: the file exists and you can just add new users to it. The htpasswd command also allows you to remove users from the password file; to do this, use it with the -D option. For example, htpasswd -D /etc/apache2/htpasswd stacey removes user stacey from the file.

Just creating a user isn't enough, however; you have to configure Apache to prompt for a password when a user tries to access restricted data. To do this, some code needs to be included in the directory that you want to protect, as shown in Listing 11-8.

Listing 11-8. *Protecting a Directory with Basic Authentication*

```
<Directory protected>
     Authtype Basic
     AuthName "Restricted directory"
     AuthUserFile /etc/apache2/htpasswd
     Require user linda
</Directory>
```

In this example, the directory protected is protected with a password. Because there's no absolute directory path, the directory is relative to the document root of this server. Also note that the authentication type Basic is enabled. Next, a label is given to this directory with the AuthName "Restricted directory" directive, after which the file containing the user information is declared. In the final line, one specific user is granted access to this directory. As an alternative, you can use the option Require user valid-user as well, which is useful if you just want to grant access to any user listed in the password file that you're using.

Enabling HTTPS

By default, Apache is insecure. This means that data sent from your Apache server to a client can be intercepted by others. You probably want to avoid that, especially if you want to send sensitive data from your Apache server to a user and back. To prevent unauthorized wire-tapping, you can enable Apache to use SSL. In such a configuration, your Apache server is configured with a public key and a private key.

When using public-private key encryption, the server hands out its public key to every user who wants to establish a secure connection. (This is an automatic procedure that end users aren't aware of.) End users use the public key to encrypt all data they send to the Apache server. This encrypted data can be decrypted only by using the private key used by the Apache server. (As you can imagine, the private key is stored in a very secure place at the Apache server.)

When using public-private key encryption, you normally also need a certificate authority (CA), which is a piece of software that guarantees that the public key handed out by the server is to be trusted. CAs are well known; for instance, VeriSign is a company that provides CA services, and all browsers know about VeriSign. So if an Apache server hands out a public key guaranteed by VeriSign, the end user knows that this certificate can be trusted.

The problem with commercial CA services such as the VeriSign service is that you have to pay for them. That's probably no problem if you want to mount a web shop, but if it's just for simple in-company use, you'll probably prefer using a CA that is free. Fortunately, it's not too hard to set it up for yourself.

In the following procedure, you'll learn how to create a *self-signed certificate*, which is a certificate used by your Apache server that's guaranteed by your server—and no one else.

Caution Using self-signed certificates might give awkward security warnings at the client computer. To avoid it, make sure that you don't use self-signed certificates; go online and buy a real certificate.

Creating a Self-Signed Certificate

Creating a self-signed certificate is a three-step procedure. First, you need to generate a certificate signing request, which is a public key that hasn't yet been guaranteed by anyone. Next, you'll sign this certificate; and in the third and final step, you'll install it at the right location. After you finish, you can configure your Apache server to use the self-signed certificate.

1. To generate the keys that you want to use, run the following command from a terminal prompt: `openssl genrsa -des3 -out server.key 1024`. To put the resulting key file in the right directory, run this command as root and make sure that you are in root's home directory. This command will generate a 1024-bit private key that is protected by a passphrase. Although using a passphrase is inconvenient, it's a very good idea to use it anyway because it's far more secure. Without a passphrase, anyone who steals your private key can pretend to be your server. You have to enter the passphrase every time you restart your server or Apache service manually, but how often do you really think you need to restart the server? So use a passphrase and enter it manually every time you restart your server.

2. Based on the private key that you just created, you now need to create the certificate signing request. You'll see a command that asks you to enter personal information such as your mailing address, your country, and the name of your company. This information makes it easier for users of the certificate to trace where the certificate comes from and alert you if anything is wrong with it. Enter the following command as root (make sure that you are in root's home directory before issuing this command):

   ```
   openssl req -new -key server.key -out server.csr
   ```

3. Now you can use the `server.csr` file that was generated in the preceding step as the input file to create a self-signed certificate. To do this, run the following command as root (make sure that you are in the home directory of user root before running it):

   ```
   openssl x509 -req -days 365 -in server.csr -signkey server.key -out server.crt
   ```

4. At this stage, you have created three different files:

- `server.key`: This file contains the private key of your server and must be kept secret at all times.

- `server.csr`: This file is the signing request for the key that you just created. You don't need it any more.

- `server.crt`: This file is the public key certificate of your server. It is the server's public key, including the signing information that you added in step 3 of this procedure. You now need to make sure that this information is transferred to users who want to establish an SSH connection with your server.

5. All files you have created so far are still in user root's home directory. You now need to copy them to the appropriate location. To do this, enter the following two commands as root:

```
cp ~/server.crt /etc/ssl/certs
cp ~/server.key /etc/ssl/private
```

Configuring Apache to Use the Self-Signed Certificate

The certificate and your server's private key are in place, and it's time for Apache to use SSL. After creating the certificate and the private key, this is not too difficult. Just follow these steps:

1. Install the SSL module. Ubuntu Server has a nice little utility to help you with that; run a2enmod `ssl` to enable the SSL module for Apache. You can also link the SSL module file from `/etc/apache2/mods-available` to `/etc/apache2/mods-enabled`, as described earlier in this chapter.

2. You need to tell Apache that it has to use the certificates by including four lines in the configuration file in `/etc/apache2/sites-available` for each server that you want to use SSL. Make sure to put these lines n the `VirtualHost` section under the `DocumentRoot` line:

```
SSLEngine on
SSLOptions +StrictRequire
SSLCertificateFile /etc/ssl/certs/server.crt
SSLCertificateKeyFile /etc/ssl/private/server.key
```

3. Restart your Apache server to enable the changes; use `/etc/init.d/apache2 restart` as root.

■Tip Because your server is now configured to use a private key that is protected by a passphrase, you probably don't want to start it automatically when your server boots. To ensure that it doesn't start automatically, enter the line NO_START=0 in `/etc/default/apache2`.

Some Words on Apache Performance Tuning

If you're running a very busy web server, it makes sense to do some performance tuning because the default settings are really for web servers with only an average workload. If you're hosting a very busy web server, the performance parameters might require some adjustment. You can find all performance-tuning parameters in the /etc/apache2/apache2.conf configuration file.

   To understand Apache performance tuning, you should know that Apache can run in two different modes. One of them is the prefork mode, in which a process is started for every incoming client. The alternative is the worker mode, which gives you a limited number of Apache processes, each of which creates threads for incoming user connections. To determine what mode your server starts in, you have to activate the corresponding modules: mpm_prefork_module for prefork mode and mpm_worker_module for worker mode. Listing 11-9 shows the code from /etc/apache2/apache2.conf that's used to tune the performance for either of these modes.

Listing 11-9. *Performance Optimizing Parameters in* apache2.conf

```
## Server-Pool Size Regulation (MPM specific)
##

# prefork MPM
# StartServers: number of server processes to start
# MinSpareServers: minimum number of server processes which are kept spare
# MaxSpareServers: maximum number of server processes which are kept spare
# MaxClients: maximum number of server processes allowed to start
# MaxRequestsPerChild: maximum number of requests a server process serves
<IfModule mpm_prefork_module>
    StartServers          5
    MinSpareServers       5
    MaxSpareServers      10
    MaxClients          150
    MaxRequestsPerChild   0
</IfModule>

# worker MPM
# StartServers: initial number of server processes to start
# MaxClients: maximum number of simultaneous client connections
# MinSpareThreads: minimum number of worker threads which are kept spare
# MaxSpareThreads: maximum number of worker threads which are kept spare
# ThreadsPerChild: constant number of worker threads in each server process
# MaxRequestsPerChild: maximum number of requests a server process serves
<IfModule mpm_worker_module>
    StartServers          2
    MaxClients          150
    MinSpareThreads      25
```

```
        MaxSpareThreads        75
        ThreadsPerChild        25
        MaxRequestsPerChild     0
</IfModule>
```

Let's have a look at some of the most important parameters.

- StartServers: This setting specifies the number of Apache processes that should always be started. The advantage of starting some processes in advance is that they are ready and listening for incoming clients and can thus respond quickly to new connections. Five servers are started by default. If you anticipate heavy use of your web server, it's a good idea to set this value higher.

- MinSpareServers: This is the minimum number of servers that should always be ready and waiting for new incoming connections. By default, five servers are always listening for new connections.

- MaxSpareServers: If too many server processes are waiting for new client connections that don't actually materialize, it might be reasonable to tune the MaxSpareServers setting. Its default value of 10 means that if more than 10 servers are waiting for new incoming connections, they should be closed down automatically.

- MaxClients: This is the maximum number of clients that Apache allows at the same time. The default is set to 150, which is reasonable for many web servers.

- MaxRequestPerChild: Use this parameter to specify the limit for the maximum number of requests that one instance (either a thread or a subprocess) of Apache can handle. The value of 0 indicates that there's no limit.

By now, you should know all that's needed to get an Apache web server up and running. The rest of its configuration is up to the web developers. Now let's have a look at how MySQL and PHP integrate with Apache.

Using PHP

PHP is one of the most popular programming languages used in a web environment. The language's most important advantage is that you can integrate it smoothly into an HTML page. PHP works together easily with MySQL to get and put data in a database. The only thing you have to do as an administrator to integrate PHP in your Apache web server is call the mod_php5 Apache module. Before you can do that, you need to install the module and make sure that the module is included in the Apache configuration. To install the PHP5 module for Apache, use the following command:

```
apt-get install php5 libapache2-mod-php5
```

In case you also want the PHP-MySQL integration, as well as the PHP5 command-line interface that allows you to run PHP scripts from the command line, use the following command as well:

```
apt-get install php5-cli php5-mysql
```

To confirm that PHP is properly installed on your server, write a simple script that includes the following line:

```
<?php phpinfo(); ?>
```

Write this text to a file with the name `test.php` and put the file in the document root of your web server. Next, open a web browser to `http://yourserver/test.php`. This should display a window with information about the current status of your PHP installation. Make sure that PHP is installed and responds properly to this page, as many current web pages include PHP code.

The biggest advantage of PHP is that you can use it to make your web pages dynamic. PHP is like Bash shell scripting; it can perform calculations based on certain conditions and execute a command only if a certain condition is true. If you're interested in learning how to code in PHP, I recommend the excellent book *Beginning PHP and MySQL 5: From Novice to Professional, Third Edition* by Jason Gilmore (Apress, 2008).

Setting Up MySQL

The combination of Apache, MySQL, and PHP is very popular with web developers. Apache serves pages that read scripts written in PHP, which query databases written in MySQL.

Setting up MySQL involves more than just enabling a module. MySQL is a service process on its own that you need to install and configure. If you already installed MySQL, your server starts it automatically. You can check whether it's there by using the command `ps aux | grep mysql`. If you can't see anything, use `dpkg -l | grep mysql` to check whether the MySQL packages are installed. If you don't see the `mysql-server` package in the output (check Listing 11-10 to see what it looks like if it is installed), install it by using `apt-get install mysql-server-5.0`.

Listing 11-10. *Use* `dpkg -l` *to See Whether MySQL Has Been Installed on Your Server*

```
root@RNA:~# dpkg -l | grep mysql
ii  libdbd-mysql-perl          3.0008-1build1              A Perl5\
    database interface to the MySQL data
ii  libmysqlclient15off        5.0.38-0ubuntu1             mysql\
    database client library
ii  mysql-client-5.0           5.0.38-0ubuntu1             mysql\
    database client binaries
ii  mysql-common               5.0.38-0ubuntu1             mysql\
    database common files (e.g. /etc/mysql
ii  mysql-server               5.0.38-0ubuntu1             mysql\
    database server (meta package dependin
ii  mysql-server-5.0           5.0.38-0ubuntu1             mysql\
    database server binaries
ii  php5-mysql                 5.2.1-0ubuntu1              MySQL\
    module for php5
```

Setting the MySQL Root Password

Because a database such as MySQL is typically managed by a database administrator (Linux admins generally don't care about databases), MySQL has its own root user. Before you can do anything with MySQL, however, you must set a password for this user, and you'll do this with the mysqladmin command:

```
mysqladmin -u root password secret
```

Now at least you can do something with your MySQL server. By the way, it's not a very secure idea to type the root password for your database server in clear text on the command line like this. You can also use the option -p to have mysqladmin prompt for a password:

```
mysqladmin -u root -p password
```

Next, your server will ask for you to input a password twice.

Creating a MySQL Database

Another task that a Linux administrator has to occasionally perform is to create a database. You will sometimes install applications that want to use a MySQL database, and you need to create that database first to use such applications. To do this, use the mysqladmin command again. In the following example, you'll create a database with the name DBASE1:

```
mysqladmin -p create DBASE1sudo
```

Normally, this is where your responsibilities as a Linux administrator end. The rest of the work on MySQL involves creating tables and populating the database with data, which is typical work for the database administrator, so it is not covered here.

Configuring a Squid Proxy Server

If your Internet connection is not so fast, you can benefit from using a proxy such as Squid. How does it work? The end user connects to the proxy, and the proxy fetches the requested information from the Internet. Using a proxy has two major benefits. First, it speeds things up. After the information is in the cache of the proxy server, the next user doesn't have to go fetch it somewhere far from the Internet. So there's a speed benefit.

There's also a security advantage. If the proxy server is the only way to connect to the Internet, you can set up authentication on the proxy, thus allowing only authorized users to access the Internet. Another security benefit is that you can work with ACLs to define which Internet sites are allowed and which are not. You'll learn more about Squid ACLs later in this chapter in the section "Configuring Squid Access Control List Policies."

When using a proxy, there is something to be aware of, however. A proxy works for the upper layers in the TCP/IP stack because typically it is application level–oriented. That means that some protocols are supported, whereas others are not. The most important protocols that are handled by Squid are HTTP and FTP. DNS requests can also be cached in the Squid proxy cache.

Installing a Squid Proxy Cache

If you're serious about running a proxy cache, you should use a dedicated machine with lots of memory. If no more RAM is available for caching, Squid will save the cache information to disk, which means that you have to pay a relatively high performance price for proxying. You can run Squid with other processes on the same server if you need to, but it is better to use a dedicated server. After all, you wouldn't implement a Squid proxy server in order to get better performance while wasting performance implementing it, would you?

Installing Squid is as easy as installing any other server on Ubuntu: run the following command as root:

```
apt-get install squid
```

Using this command installs a script that starts the proxy server in /etc/init.d/squid. All configuration is stored in the /etc/squid/squid.conf configuration file. As you will see when you open it with your preferred editor, it is a huge file that contains lots of comment lines that explain what certain options are used for. The next section discusses how to configure some of the most useful options.

Configuring Squid Access Control Policies

When configuring the Squid proxy, you need to determine the port on which it listens. By default, Squid uses port 3128, which also is the port address users have to configure in their browsers. The http_port parameter is used to change it to anything you like; for example, port 8080 is a rather popular choice for a proxy server. Don't forget to restart your Squid server using /etc/init.d/squid restart; otherwise, the changes are not activated.

When setting up a proxy server, you probably also want to configure ACLs to determine who can access what kind of information. The acl tag is used to specify a group to which access can be denied or allowed in an http_access tag (so you always need both of these tags to work together). The following shows a simple example of how these tags can be applied:

```
acl all src 0.0.0.0/0.0.0.0
acl allowed src 10.0.0.0/24
http_acccess allow allowed
http_access deny all
```

■**Caution** Before a Squid server can be used after installation, you need to modify the existing ACLs in the default file. By default, one ACL exists that denies access to all.

In the preceding example, two categories are defined in the ACLs. First is the category all, identified by the source address 0.0.0.0 with subnet mask 0.0.0.0. This notation refers to all IP addresses that exist. Then a category allowed is referred to. All nodes that have an IP address that starts with 10.0.0 belong to this category. Next, both categories are referred to in the http_access tags. The first rule grants access to all nodes belonging to the group of allowed hosts. For all these hosts, the procedure ends here because the first rule that matches will always be applied. Then the policy is applied for all other nodes. It is set to deny all.

■**Caution** When creating Squid access rules, you should never forget that when a rule applies, Squid executes it for the user in question, and other rules are not looked at any more. Therefore, always write your rules from very specific to more general rules.

In the previous example, the ACL was based on the source IP address. Many other criteria can also be used in an ACL:

- src: This type refers to the source address of a node. An individual IP address can be used, a range of IP addresses can be used, or a complete subnet mask can be used. An example of a range specified as the source address is 192.168.1.10–192.168.1.20/32. Note the 32-bit subnet mask, which is always needed if a range is specified.

- dst: This type refers to the destination IP address. It is not very useful to use this type to refer to addresses on the Internet because they can change without notice. If access has to be denied for users from the private network to a host in the DMZ, however, this type can be useful. An example is provided in the following listing:

```
acl protected_host dst 10.0.0.10/32
acl private_network src 10.0.10.0/24
http_access deny proteted_host private_network
```

- srcdomain: Like source, but refers to a DNS domain as source.

- dstdomain: Like dst, but based on a DNS domain name.

- time: This type refers to the time of day and day of the week when a tag should be used. (The day of the week can also be used, but it is not necessary.) The following are valid examples of using the time ACL type:

```
acl toolate time 20:00-6:00
acl weekend time A-S 0:01-24:00
acl notonfriday time F 16:00-24:00
```

If referring to the days of the week, the following can be used:

- Monday: M

- Tuesday: T

- Wednesday: W

- Thursday: H

- Friday: F

- Saturday: A

- Sunday: S

- url_regexp: This type looks for a regular expression in an URL. For example, you can use acl sex url_regex "sex" to deny access to all sites that have sex somewhere in the URL. This ACL often has unexpected results because other sites can be blocked. (For instance, it blocks access to www.essex.co.uk, which is a perfectly legitimate site.)

- port: This type blocks access on given ports.

- proto: This type blocks access to specified protocols only.

- reg_mime_type: This very useful type blocks access to specific file types. The type of file is determined by looking at the mime type. For example, think of an ACL as acl mp3 reg_mime_type "audio/mpeg".

After specifying the ACLs, it's time to define http_access tags that use the ACL. Although you can refer to one ACL in an http_access tag, more than one ACL can be referred to as well. (An example of this was shown in http_access deny protected_host private_network, which denied traffic coming from the private network and going to a protected host.) It's also possible to use exclusion in an ACL—for example in http_access deny protected_host !private_network—which denies access to the protected host to all hosts not coming from private network access.

Remember that no matter how complex the applied ACLs can be, you should always conclude the list of ACLs with a default policy. The policy defines what should happen if no specific match is found for a given package. In general, it is useful to conclude the list of http_access tags with http_access deny all to deny access to all packets that have not matched a specific http_access tag earlier in the chain.

Configuring User Authentication

Besides analyzing the packet (where it comes from and where it goes to), you can also use user authentication with Squid. The only thing necessary to make user authentication work is the use of a browser that supports user authentication (all current browsers do.) In a Squid environment, the browser and the proxy can exchange user name and password in three ways:

- Basic

- Digest

- NTLM

In the Basic method, the user name and password are sent in clear text to the proxy. The Digest method does not send the password in clear text; it uses a digest derived from the password instead. The advantage is that the password cannot be read while being sent from the browser of the user to the proxy. The NTLM method can also be used, but it is not a part of the HTTP protocol specifications. Therefore, you might encounter browsers in which this method is not supported.

Note Unfortunately, the Digest method was not implemented in the current version of Squid, so this section discusses only how the Basic authentication method is used.

When authentication is used to connect to the Squid proxy, it is not the proxy itself that handles authentication, but an external program. For example, the Linux PAM mechanism (refer to Chapter 5) can be used for proper authentication. The advantage of using PAM is that it can authenticate to any source you can think of. By default it will try to authenticate to the local files /etc/passwd and /etc/shadow to see whether the user that authenticates exists.

The communication between Squid and the authentication program will be plain text, which isn't an issue if the proxy server and the authentication service are used on the same server. If Squid needs to communicate to the authentication service over the network, you should use digest_pw_auth. The disadvantage of this method is that you need to maintain a text file on the Squid server that contains the user names and passwords unencrypted. Therefore, it is not considered a well-secured method, either.

If you want to configure Squid to authenticate to the PAM module, three tags are needed:

- auth_param: This tag refers to the program used for authentication. Other options are also used to specify how the authentication program should be used.

- acl: This tag defines groups of users.

- http_access: This tag specifies in what way users are granted access.

The following four lines specify how the PAM module can be used for Squid authentication:

```
auth_param basic program /usr/sbin/pam_auth
auth_param basic children 5
auth_param basic realm Squid proxy-caching web server
auth_param basic credentialsttl 4 hours
```

In the first line, the PAM module is specified as the program that should handle authentication requests. Next, there is a specification of the maximum number of authentication processes that might be started at the same time. More than five simultaneous processes are needed only on heavily used Squid servers; if users start to complain about the time it takes to log on, consider increasing this value. On the third line, you specify what to protect with authentication; this is the realm authentication. This parameter should always have the value of the Squid proxy-caching web server.

Finally, there is a line that specifies how long the credentials must be remembered; the default value is set to two hours, so users can connect to new resources without providing credentials for a period of two hours. After two hours, they have to provide a login name again. Because many companies consider this duration too short, I set this parameter to four hours in the example.

After you have specified that the PAM module should be used as the authentication mechanism, a PAM file must be created. There is no default file, so you have to create a Basic authentication file yourself. This file enables authentication to the local passwd-mechanism with the following two lines:

```
auth       required      pam_unix2.so
account    required      pam_unix2.so
```

Now that the authentication mechanism is specified, you have to create an ACL in which the user names you have defined are used. It might look like this:

```
acl allowed_users proxy_auth linda stephanie
```

In this example, only linda and stephanie are allowed users. There's often no need to limit access for a small number of users; you can just allow all authenticated users access to a resource. This can be accomplished by using REQUIRED instead of the name of one or more users, as shown in the following example:

```
acl all_users proxy_auth REQUIRED
```

Based on these two examples, you can create an environment in which only linda and stephanie are given access, whereas all other users are denied access by using the http_access tag:

```
http_access allow allowed_users
http_access deny all_users
```

While introducing user authentication, the entire list of access rules for your Squid proxy can become rather complex, especially because the first match is always applied. Therefore, the following does not work if you want to ensure that only allowed_users and users coming from trusted_net are granted access; all others are denied access:

```
http_access allow allowed_users
http_access allow trusted_net
http_access deny all
```

The goal of these rules was to grant access only to allowed users coming from trusted_net; in the previous rules, however, access is granted to a user who is not part of allowed_users, but is on trusted_net. To solve this problem, you should make combinations in the http_access rules, as in the following example:

```
http_access allow allowed_users trusted_net
http_access deny all
```

Setting Up FTP

FTP is another service that's quite popular on the web. It's popular because it makes sharing files so easy, and you can use several FTP servers on Ubuntu Server. One of the easiest and fastest of these is pure-ftpd. Let's have a look at how to set it up, but (as usual!) first make sure that it's installed: use the apt-get install pure-ftpd command, which also automatically starts the pure-ftpd server using its default settings.

Configuring the pure-ftpd Server

Running a pure-ftpd server is easy; it runs all by itself once you have installed it. By default, it uses PAM authentication to give authenticated users FTP access to your server. It has a few settings that you can change, though.

The first part of the pure-ftpd configuration is in the startup file in /etc/default/ pure-ftpd-common. In this script, you'll find a few parameters, which are explained in Table 11-2.

Table 11-2. *Configuration Parameters for* pure-ftpd

Parameter	Use
STANDALONE_OR_INETD	This parameter determines how you want to run the pure-ftpd process. It runs as a stand-alone process by default, but you can also run it from (x)inetd. For fast response, it's better to run it as a stand-alone process.
VIRTUALCHROOT	To secure the pure-ftpd server, you can start the process in a chroot jail, which means that the process is restricted to the contents of one directory instead of the complete file system of your server. By default, the pure-ftpd process runs without chroot restrictions. If you enable chroot restrictions by setting this parameter to true, all users who access the FTP process will see only their home directories.
UPLOADSCRIPT	When uploading files, you can determine how the uploading should take place by creating an upload script. For more information on how to format such a script, consult the man page for pure-uploadscript(8).
UPLOADUID, UPLOADGID	If you want to use an upload script, these parameters set the UID and GID that are used when running this script.

You can set other options besides the startup parameters in /etc/default/pure-ftpd-common. You'll find them in /etc/pure-ftpd/conf. The configuration is stored by default in six different configuration files, each of which sets one configuration parameter. Table 11-3 provides an overview.

Table 11-3. *Configuration Files for* pure-ftpd

File	Use
AltLog	Contains a complete path to the directory in which pure-ftpd logs its transfer data. The default value is set to /var/log/pure-ftpd/transfer.log.
MinUID	Indicates the minimal user ID used by pure-ftpd.
NoAnonymous	Specifies whether anonymous users are accepted. By default, the file contains the value yes, which means that anonymous users are not allowed. Change to no if you want to allow anonymous users. Notice that you can also enable anonymous user access via PAM.
PAMAuthentication	This file has the contents yes or no to indicate whether PAM authentication is used. If the value is set to yes (the default), the PAM configuration file /etc/pam.d/pure-ftpd is read to determine how the login procedure should proceed.
PureDB	Names the file that's used as the pure-ftpd authentication database. The default file is /etc/pure-ftpd/pureftpd.pdb, which you can use to authenticate users as an alternative to PAM-based authentication. Because PAM is a more versatile means of authentication, I recommend that you don't use the pureftpd.pdb file.
UnixAuthentication	Give this file the contents yes if you want to enable authentication based on /etc/passwd and /etc/shadow without using PAM.

As you can see, pure-ftpd offers a few options to handle authentication. Of these options, I recommend using the default value, which is set to PAM, because it gives you the most flexibility in setting up the way user authentication is handled. Listing 11-11 shows the default PAM configuration file that's used when PAM authentication is enabled.

Listing 11-11. *The Default* pure-ftpd *PAM Configuration File*

```
# PAM config for pure-ftpd

# allow anonymous users
auth    sufficient        pam_ftp.so
auth    required          pam_unix_auth.so shadow use_first_pass

# /etc/ftpusers contain user list with DENIED access
auth    required          pam_listfile.so item=user sense=deny\
# file=/etc/ftpusers onerr=succeed

# Uncomment next line to allow non-anonymous ftp access ONLY for users,
# listed in /etc/ftpallow
#auth    required          pam_listfile.so item=user\
#sense=allow file=/etc/ftpallow onerr=fail

# standard
auth    required          pam_shells.so
account required          pam_unix.so
session required          pam_unix.so
```

As you can see, the first thing handled by the pure-ftpd PAM configuration file is anonymous user authentication: the line auth sufficient pam_ftp.so specifies that anonymous users are welcome if the conditions defined in pam_ftp.so are met. This PAM module defines that a user who's mentioned in /etc/ftpusers will get access. So, you need to list the user anonymous in this file to enable anonymous user access. Next, in the /home/ftp directory, create a structure of all the files you want these users to have access to.

By using the sufficient statement in the PAM rule that allows users to come in via pam_ftp.so, you give user anonymous access without further restrictions. For all other users, the specifications in pam_unix_auth.so are used. This configuration file allows regular users to authenticate using their user name as it exists in /etc/passwd and /etc/shadow. The other lines in the PAM file are not as important for user authentication.

Summary

This chapter discussed how to create a basic web server environment on Ubuntu Server. You first learned how the Apache web server can be installed and configured. You also saw how to enhance Apache functionality by including modules that allow Apache to talk to MySQL and PHP. Finally, you learned how to install a Squid proxy server and an FTP server on Ubuntu Server.

Now that your server has some serious services to offer to the rest of the world, it's time to secure it. You certainly want to avoid unauthorized people coming in and doing nasty things to your server, so you'll learn how to configure the Netfilter firewall on Ubuntu Server in the next chapter.

CHAPTER 12

■■■

Setting Up the Netfilter Firewall with iptables and ufw

Most settings discussed so far involve security measures that make your server internally secure. You must also consider, however, that something or someone from the outside world will try to connect to your server, so you need some security at that level, too. The best way to achieve this security is with a firewall. If your server is connected to the Internet directly, you must have a firewall running on it. Netfilter, which is the default choice for all Linux distributions, is the firewall that is implemented in the Linux kernel. The iptables command gives you complete freedom to manipulate the Netfilter firewall. In day-to-day use, both names get confused frequently, but both refer to the same firewall. Ubuntu Server also offers a solution to make Netfilter administration easy: the uncomplicated firewall (ufw). In the second part of this chapter you'll learn how to use ufw.

■**Note** Having a firewall is important, but let's not exaggerate. If your server is on a network backbone with no way for external users to reach it directly, you can probably do with just a company firewall that provides security for the entire network. If the network firewall works well, it's not always necessary to implement a firewall on individual servers. If, however, you want to add an extra layer of protection, there's no problem in doing so.

All Linux distributions come with the Netfilter firewall available by default. As we mentioned, this firewall is implemented in the Linux kernel, which makes it very fast, and you manipulate the firewall with the iptables command. In this subsection I'll give you a short introduction to the inner workings of iptables.

Configuring a firewall without the proper preparation is a very bad idea. Before you start configuring, you should be very clear what exactly it is that you want and need your firewall to do. For a server that has a public as well as a private network card, you could make a table like the example in Table 12-1. You should mention on what network interface the service is offered and in what direction you want to allow this service (inbound or outbound).

Table 12-1. *Overview of Required Services for Your Firewall*

Interface	Service	Inbound/Outbound
private	SSH	outbound, inbound
public	HTTP	inbound
public, private	ping	outbound
public, private	DNS	outbound, inbound

Once you have a simple setup matrix like this, you can start configuring the firewall. But, before you start, you should know something about the way a Netfilter firewall is organized.

Netfilter Building Blocks

The most elementary building blocks for a Netfilter firewall are the chains, which are basically sets of rules that are applied to a certain traffic flow on your server. When setting up a Netfilter firewall, you start with three chains that by default are empty. To use these chains, you must add rules to them. Table 12-2 provides a short description of the three default chains.

Table 12-2. *Chains Are the Basic Building Blocks for a Netfilter Firewall*

Chain	Description
INPUT	This chain applies to all incoming traffic that is destined for the server itself. It does not apply to traffic that needs to be routed.
OUTPUT	This chain applies to all traffic that comes from a process on the server. It does not apply to traffic that comes from the routing process.
FORWARD	This chain applies to all traffic that comes in from a network interface, but is not destined for the local machine and has to be routed. You'll never use this chain on a server that doesn't provide routing functionality.

Figure 12-1 is a schematic that provides an overview of the place where the three default chains are functioning. The NIC positions in the figure indicate that the network interface card is involved. As you can see in the figure, the INPUT chain applies to incoming traffic before it encounters server processes, the OUTPUT chain involves outgoing traffic after it leaves the server processes, and the FORWARD chain involves traffic that goes from one network card directly to another.

The next requirement in a Netfilter configuration is a set of rules. In these rules, different packet types are defined, and a default action is defined for each of them as well. Three things may happen when a packet matches a rule: it can be accepted (ACCEPT), it can be dropped (DROP), and it can be logged (LOG). Note that, instead of DROP, which silently discards a packet, you can also use REJECT. In this case, a message is sent to the source of the packet. The rules are evaluated from top to bottom, and as soon as a rule matches a packet, the rule is applied and no other rules are evaluated. The one exception to this is if the packet matches a LOG rule, in which case it is logged and continues to go on to the next rule.

At the end of all rule sets, a policy must be defined. You must make sure that the default policy is always set to DROP so you can make sure that only packets that specifically match a rule are allowed and that everything else is dropped.

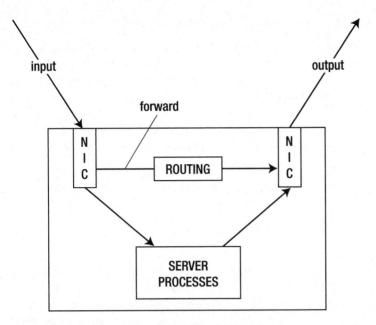

Figure 12-1. *Overview of the Use of Netfilter Chains*

To define the rules, you'll use the iptables command. Be aware that nothing you config-ure with iptables is stored automatically, so you need to store the rules that you create in a bash shell script so that they are executed automatically the next time your server boots. You can, for example, put them in /etc/init.d/boot.local to ensure that they are activated at the earliest possible stage in the boot process.

Using iptables to Create a Firewall

When creating your own firewall with iptables, the first thing you need to do is to set some default policies. Do note, however, that the policy will become effective immediately, so if you are configuring your firewall from an external connection, you will be locked out immediately. In this section, I'll assume that you are configuring iptables from the machine itself. (After all, you wouldn't connect an unsecured server to the network, would you?) So start by creating some policies, entering the following commands:

```
iptables -P FORWARD DROP
iptables -P INPUT DROP
iptables -P OUTPUT DROP
```

Your server is now completely secure; in fact, it is so secure that even your graphical envi-ronment won't come up anymore if it is installed, so don't save this configuration and reboot your server yet. Let's first do some additional tuning to allow for some minimal functionality.

Now that the default policy for every chain has been specified, you need to define the rules themselves. All rules must involve certain elements: the matching parts, the target, and the position in the chain. Basically, every iptables command uses the following generic structure:

```
iptables <position in the chain> <chain> <matching> <target>
```

The elements used in this example command are described as follows:

- `position in the chain`: This element indicates where in the chain the rule must be inserted. Netfilter uses an "exit on match" strategy, so if a rule is found that applies to a packet, it is applied, and the rest of the chain is not processed for that packet. So order does matter when writing `iptables` rules.

- `chain`: This element refers to the chain where the rule must be applied.

- `matching`: This element describes exactly what to look for. It refers to the packets you want to allow or disallow.

- `target`: This element determines what should happen when there is a match. For instance, you could decide to either drop or allow the packet.

The next subsections describe how these elements are used.

Defining Matching Rules

An important part of every rule is the matching part, and the following list comprises the most popular elements that can be used for matching. Note that you don't have to use them all in a rule: if one of these elements isn't specified, the rule is simply applied to all. For example, if you don't specify a source IP address, but you do specify a source port number, the rule applies to the source port number, regardless of the source IP address. The following elements can be used for matching in a rule:

- *Interface*: Use this element to specify the network interface to which the rule applies. The `-o` option is used to refer to an output interface, and `-i` is used for the input interface. It may not surprise you that `-o` isn't used in the INPUT chain (because it refers to incoming packets only), and `-i` isn't used in the OUTPUT chain (which refers to outgoing packets only).

- *Source/destination IP address*: You can use `-s` (source) or `-d` (destination) to refer to an IP address. Both IP addresses for individual hosts and IP addresses for complete networks can be used. For example, use `-s 192.168.0.1` to refer to one host only, or `-s 192.168.0.0/16` for all hosts that have a network address starting with 192.168.

- *Protocol*: Use this element to refer to protocols as defined in the file `/etc/protocols`. Protocol numbers as well as protocol names as used in this file can be used here. For example, `-p TCP` refers to all packets in which TCP is used.

- *Ports*: Another very popular method to filter, this one is based on TCP or UDP port numbers. You can use `--sport` to refer to a source port or `--dport` to refer to a destination port. Any port number can be used, so check `/etc/services` for a complete list of services and their default ports if you need more details. For example, use `--sport 1024:65535` if you want to refer to all ports above port 1024, or use `--dport 25` to refer to the SMTP port. Note that when using a port specification, you should always use a protocol specification as well. So don't just use `--dport 25`; use `-p TCP --dport 25`.

Specifying the Target

After specifying the matching criterion, a second part of all rules is the so-called target: the action that has to be performed when a rule matches a packet. All rules have a target, and the following targets are available:

- ACCEPT: The packet is accepted.

- REJECT: The packet is rejected, and a message is sent to its sender.

- DROP: The packet is discarded, and no message is sent to the sender.

- LOG: The packet is logged. Note that this is the only target that doesn't stop the packet from further evaluation.

Specifying the Position in the Chain

The very first thing you need to do is to specify where exactly in the chain you need to add a rule. Imagine, for example, that you want to disallow all traffic that has destination port 80, but you do want to allow all traffic coming from IP address 1.2.3.4. If you first create the rule that specifies the destination port and then create the rule for IP address 1.2.3.4, packets from 1.2.3.4 that have destination port 80 would be rejected as well. Order does matter. When creating a rule, the following options can be used to specify where in the chain you want the rule to appear:

- `-A`: Add the rule to the end of the chain.

- `-D`: Delete the rule from the chain.

- `-R`: Replace a rule.

- `-I`: Insert the rule at a specific position. For example, use `iptables -I INPUT 2` to place the rule on the second position in the INPUT chain.

Stateful Rules

When creating a rule to match packets that always use the same port numbers, everything is easy. Of course, this isn't always the case. For example, a user who connects to a web server will always connect to that web server on port 80, but the packets sent back from the web server use a randomly chosen port number above 1024. You could create a rule in which outgoing packets on all ports above 1024 are opened, but that's not ideal for security reasons.

A smart way of dealing with this problem is by using stateful packet filters. A stateful packet filter analyzes whether a packet that goes out is part of an already established connection; if it is, it allows the answer to go out. Stateful packet filters are useful for replies that are sent by web servers and for FTP servers as well because in the case of an FTP server, the connection is established on port 21, and once the session is established, data is sent over port 20 to the client.

By using the --state option you can indicate what state a rule should look at. This functionality, however, is not a part of the core Netfilter modules, and an additional module has to be loaded to allow for state checking. (This will happen automatically with the -m option.) Therefore, in every rule that wants to look at the state that a packet is in, the -m state option is used first, followed by the exact state the rule is looking at. For example, -m state --state RELATED,ESTABLISHED would look at packets that are part of related packets that are already allowed or packets that are a part of an established session.

The state module isn't the only module that can be used, and many other modules are available for more advanced configurations. For example, the nth module allows you to have a look at every nth packet (such as every tenth packet, for example). Using this module can be useful if you want to log information about (for example) every tenth HTTP packet that comes in to your web server. Further discussion of modules is out of the scope of this book, so check the documentation page of the Netfilter web site at www.netfilter.org/documentation for more in-depth information.

Creating the Rules

Based on this information, you should be able to create some basic rules. Let's assume that you have a server that has only one NIC. On this network card, you want to allow requests to the web server to come in and replies from it to go out. Also, you want to allow SSH traffic. For the rest, no other services are needed.

Like any other Netfilter configuration, you would start this configuration by creating some policies. Every chain needs its own policy. The following commands make sure that no packet comes in or out of your server by setting the policy for each chain to DROP:

```
iptables -P FORWARD DROP
iptables -P INPUT DROP
iptables -P OUTPUT DROP
```

Now that everything is blocked, you can start by allowing some packets to go in and out. First and foremost, you have to enable the loopback interface because the policies that you've just defined also disable all traffic on the loopback interface, and that's not good (because many services rely on the loopback interface). Without a loopback interface, for example, you have no way to start the graphical environment on your machine, and many other services will fail as well. Imagine that the login process queries an LDAP server that runs on the localhost. Now open the loopback interface using the following two rules:

```
iptables -A INPUT -i lo -j ACCEPT
iptables -A OUTPUT -o lo -j ACCEPT
```

In these two rules, the -A option is used to refer to the chain the rules have to be added to. You are using -A, so the rule is just appended to the INPUT and the OUTPUT chains. This would make the rule the last rule that is added to the chain, just before the policy that is always the last rule in a chain that is evaluated. Next, -i lo and -o lo are used to indicate that this rule matches to everything that happens on the loopback interface. As the third and last part of these two rules, the target is specified by using the -j option (which is short for "jump to target"). In this case, the target is to accept all matching packets. So now you have a server that allows nothing on the external network interfaces, but the loopback interface is completely open.

Next, it's time to do what you want to do on your server: allow incoming SSH and HTTP traffic and allow replies to the allowed incoming traffic to be returned. Note that these two requirements consist of two parts: a part that is configured in the INPUT chain and a part that is configured in the OUTPUT chain. Let's start with some nice rules that define the input chain:

```
iptables -A INPUT -m state --state ESTABLISHED,RELATED -j ACCEPT
iptables -A INPUT -p tcp --dport 22 -m state --state NEW -j ACCEPT
iptables -A INPUT -p tcp --dport 80 -m state --state NEW -j ACCEPT
iptables -A INPUT -j LOG --log-prefix "Dropped illegal incoming packet: "
```

The first rule in this INPUT chain tells Netfilter that all packets that are part of an already established or related session are allowed in. Next, for packets coming in on SSH port 22 that have a state NEW, the second rule indicates that they are allowed as well. Third, packets that are sent to TCP destination port 80 (notice the combination between -p tcp and --dport 80 in this rule) and have a state NEW are accepted as well. The last rule finally makes sure that all packets that didn't match any of the earlier rules are logged before they are dropped by the policy at the end of the rule. Note that logging all dropped packets as a default may cause big problems.

■**Caution** Use logging only if you need to troubleshoot your firewall. It's generally a bad idea to switch on logging by default because if not done properly, it can cause huge amounts of information to be written to your log files.

Now that you have defined the INPUT chain, let's do the OUTPUT chain as well. No specific services have to be allowed out, with the exception of the replies to incoming packets that were allowed, so creating the OUTPUT chain is rather simple and consists of just two rules:

```
iptables -A OUTPUT -m state RELATED,ESTABLISHED -j ACCEPT
iptables -A OUTPUT -j LOG --log-prefix "Dropped illegal outgoing packet: "
```

The use of these two rules should be clear from the explanation earlier in this section. Note that it is a good idea to turn on logging for the OUTPUT rule (unlike for the INPUT rule) because if an illegal packet should leave your server, that would indicate that some rogue service is active on your server, and you would absolutely need to know about it.

To make it a little easier to create your own Netfilter rules, Table 12-3 lists some of the port numbers that are commonly configured in a Netfilter firewall. For a complete list of all port numbers and the names of related services, check the contents of the /etc/services file, which lists all known services with their default ports.

Table 12-3. *Frequently Used Port Numbers*

Port	Service
20	FTP data
21	FTP commands
22	SSH
25	SMTP
53	DNS
80	WWW
88	Kerberos authentication
110	POP3
111	RPC (used by NFS)
118	SQL databases
123	NTP Time
137–139	NetBIOS ports (used by the Samba server)
143	IMAP
161	SNMP (network management)
389	Unsecure LDAP
443	HTTPS
524	NCP (used by some native Novell services like eDirectory)
636	Secure LDAP

Using Advanced Matches

You've just read about the option to use matches to add advanced criteria to check packets. The state match is without doubt the most important of all matches, but there are some others as well. Three of them are particularly useful:

- Multiport match

- Limit match

- Recent match

You can create rules for single ports or port ranges using the default firewall syntax, but it doesn't allow you to specify a list of ports such as 25, 80, and 110. Without the multiport match, you would have to create a different rule for each port. The *multiport match* allows you to create random lists. To specify a list of ports, use --dports for destination ports and --sports for source ports. The following example shows you how ports 25, 80, and 110 are allowed in one rule using the multiport match:

```
iptables -A INPUT -i eth0 -p tcp -m multiport --dports 25,80,110 -j ACCEPT
```

The *limit match* is also very useful. Using this match, you can define a threshold in a rule. The limit match is very useful for logging or preventing a port from being overloaded with packets. The following example shows how you would configure a limit of 5 packets to be logged per hour for packets coming in on any of the ports 135:137. Notice that it consists of two rules: the log rule that makes sure that ten packets per hour are logged and the rule that denies access to these ports:

```
iptables -A INPUT -p TCP --dport 135:137 -m limit --limit 5/hour\
    -j LOG --log-prefix "DROP-TCP"
iptables -A INPUT -p TCP --dport 135:137 -j REJECT --reject-with tcp-reset
```

The last match is the *recent match*, which you can enable to allow no more than a certain amount of packets coming from a certain host in a given period of time. Consider the following example lines:

```
iptables -A INPUT -p tcp --dport 22 -i eth0 -m state --state NEW -m recent\
    --update --seconds 60 --hitcount 2 -j DROP
iptables -A INPUT -p tcp --dport 22 -i eth0 -m state --state NEW -m recent --set
```

Now imagine the first SSH packet coming in. This packet does not give a match on the first rule because it is the first packet coming in. However, it does give a match on the second rule, which increases the counter related to recent matches in /proc/net/ipt_recent/DEFAULT. Because there is no target defined in this rule using the -j option, the packet travels further down the chain. When the second SSH packet comes in, the hit count is increased to 2, and the packet still can get through. When the third packet comes in within a minute, however, the first rule gives a match, so the packet will be denied. Using these two rules does allow a legitimate user to mistype his password twice per minute. At the same time, this rule would stop script kiddies who try a brute force password attack on your SSH process.

Working with User-Defined Chains

The last useful item in the advanced Netfilter options is the *user-defined chain*, which can reduce the number of rules to go through before a match occurs. A user-defined chain is used as a target instead of the default DROP, REJECT, or ACCEPT targets. So if a packet matches a certain condition, you'll send it down through the user-defined chain for further inspection. If the packet doesn't match that condition, it can just travel down the default INPUT, OUTPUT, or FORWARD chains.

When working with user-defined chains, the chain must exist before you can use it as a target in one of the default chains. For that reason, if you put all firewall rules in a script, you should first write all user-defined chains. At the end of the script, write only those default chains in which the user-defined chains are used as a target. To create a user-defined chain, you'll need the -N option. To add rules to that chain, you need -A. Following is an example in which user-defined chains are used:

```
iptables -N log_drop
iptables -A log_drop -p TCP --syn -j LOG --log-prefix "DROPPED-TCP-SYN"
iptables -A log_drop -p TCP --syn -m limit --limit 5/s -j\
 REJECT --reject-with tcp-reset
```

In this example, a user-defined chain with the name log_drop is created. I put just two example rules in this chain that handle TCP packets that have the SYN flag set. To make sure that this user-defined chain is used, you should specify it as a target in one of the normal chains. For example, the INPUT chain could redirect all nonmatching packets to this user-defined chain by using a rule like the following:

```
iptables -A INPUT -j log_drop
```

User-defined chains are important elements of complex iptables setups. You'll like them because using them allows you to get keep things organized and well-structured, which allows you to do easier troubleshooting if something goes wrong.

Let's stop talking about Netfilter. On a server that uses Netfilter as a kind of personal firewall, this is probably all you need to know. Notice, however, that much more can be done with iptables. But a discussion of all that goes beyond the scope of this book, so check www.netfilter.org/documentation for very complete and overwhelmingly in-depth information.

■**Tip** Were you looking for information on how to configure your server as a NAT firewall? Although that's also outside the scope of this book (most people use dedicated routers for this purpose), I'd like to share the rule to do that, anyway. Use iptables -t nat -A POSTROUTING -o eth0 -j SNAT --to-source yourserverspublicIPaddress to make your server a NAT router. Have a lot of fun with it!

Firewall Management Made Easy: Uncomplicated Firewall

Configuring your firewall with iptables (as described previously) works well, but it is rather complicated. Making a small error can have big results, such as no packet coming through at all. To make firewall management easier, you can also use the ufw solution, with the purpose of making firewall management as easy as possible. Like iptables, ufw also writes its configuration to the Netfilter firewall.

Before you start to work with ufw, you should know that it is not meant to be a replacement for iptables. It is not intended to provide a complete firewall solution, but you can use it to easily add and remove rules to your firewall configuration. Use ufw to configure a host-based firewall. That is, if you have a server and you want to protect that server by creating its own firewall, ufw is good. But if you want to configure a firewall on a server that is connected to multiple networks simultaneously, ufw is not the best solution you can use. In that case, use iptables.

Before being able to use it, you should enable the ufw packet. To do this, run the following command as root:

```
ufw enable
```

After enabling ufw, you'll automatically get a complete firewall configuration in which even SSH is disabled. So before being able to view your firewall configuration over an SSH session, you need to enable SSH. To do this, use the following command:

```
ufw allow 22
```

In this rule you haven't specified any information, such as which network card to allow SSH traffic to come in on; ufw opens port 22 on all interfaces. If you don't like it, use iptables instead.

You can use `ufw` to create rules and also to delete them. To delete the rule that allows SSH traffic to come in, use the following:

```
ufw delete allow 22
```

Notice that this rule didn't deny access to port 22; it just deleted the rule that allowed access to port 22, which is not the same thing. For example, if after the rule that specifically allows access to port 22, there had been a rule that allows traffic on all ports, deleting the rule that grants access to port 22 wouldn't automatically have disallowed access to port 22. To specifically deny access to port 22, use this:

```
ufw deny 22
```

Also very useful is the option to provide access to your server for complete networks. Let's say you want to allow all hosts that have an IP address that starts with 192.168 to any service offered by your host. You can accomplish it by using the following command:

```
ufw allow from 192.168.0.0/16
```

You can create more complex rules using `ufw` as well. But remember that the rules will never be as complex as when you are using `iptables`. Consider the following example:

```
ufw allow tcp from 192.168.1.100 to any
```

Using this rule, you would allow access to all IP addresses (hence any offered by this server for host 192.168.1.100) as long as it is using the TCP protocol. I advise you not to use `ufw` to create rules like this because the syntax tends to be more confusing if the complexity of the rules increases. In situations like these, use `iptables` instead.

Summary

In this chapter, you learned how to set up a firewall. Two different methods have been considered. First, you learned about the `iptables` command, which offers a complex interface that allows you to do anything with your firewall. Because it's versatile, it's also very complex. To make firewall management easier, Ubuntu Server also offers the `ufw` interface. Using this command, you can create firewall rules using a really simple and intuitive interface. Using `ufw` is great if you want to set up a firewall quickly and easily, but if you need to set up a complex and advanced firewall, it's not the best choice. In that case, use `iptables` because it has much more to offer.

In the 13th (and last) chapter of this book, you'll learn what Ubuntu Server has to offer with regard to virtualization.

CHAPTER 13

■ ■ ■

Multiplying Your Server Ubuntu Server and Virtualization

One of the hottest technologies for servers is virtualization, which allows you to install multiple instances of one or more operating systems on one machine. This is ideal especially for servers with a low average load because instead of configuring a separate physical box for every single instance of an operating system, you just run multiple instances of one or more operating systems on one machine. Unfortunately, it's a jungle out there: there are many different and competing virtualization options. This chapter will provide an overview of the possibilities that virtualization offers. You'll also learn how to set up Ubuntu Server for virtualization.

Understanding Virtualization

In this section you'll read about the different solutions that offer virtualization, and you'll explore its two main approaches: *full virtualization* and *paravirtualization*.

Virtualization Solutions

Many solutions are currently available to work with virtualization, but three of them are particularly important:

- VMware

- Xen

- KVM (Kernel-based Virtual Machine)

As for the other solutions, you won't often find them in a data center because of their considerable limitations, which include a lack of support, a limited selection of operating systems that can be installed as virtual machines, and a severe performance penalty when using them. For these reasons, I'll ignore them here, except for one. If you are interested in running Ubuntu Server in a virtualized environment from a desktop, you should consider installing

VirtualBox, which offers an excellent virtualization solution that runs from a graphical desktop.

Of the three important technologies, VMware is the current market leader. It offers a commercial solution to virtualize many different operating systems and is a well-established virtualization technology that has been available for more than 10 years. The most important VMware version in the data center is VMware ESX. You can use ESX as a virtualization host, on which you will install virtualized machines. ESX is made of a tuned Linux kernel that integrates the virtual machine manager, which is the process responsible for virtualization. However, if you want to use VMware ESX as a virtualization platform, you'll have to do it by running Ubuntu Server as a virtualized "guest" operating system within the VMware environment. There's currently no way to combine VMware ESX and Ubuntu Server as a virtualization "host" platform (and there will never be such a method). VMware ESX is a proprietary, well-tuned operating system environment that has virtualization as its only purpose. There is no need to replace it with anything open source.

■**Note** In the Xen community, the words *host* and *guest* are avoided when discussing operating systems. I'll explain why in "Installing Virtual Machines Using Xen," later in this chapter. However, for clarity's sake, I'll use these words anyway, but with the following definitions. In this chapter, the *host* is the physical machine that offers virtualization services. In some environments, the host takes care of handling all instructions that are generated by the virtualized operating system; in other environments, the host takes care of access to the drivers. The host may or may not run a specialized operating system to offer these services. A *guest* is a virtual machine without any management responsibilities with regard to virtualization.

The other important player in the field of virtualization is KVM, which offers virtualization support in the Linux kernel itself. KVM is currently the default virtualization technology used in Ubuntu Server. Other Linux vendors such as Red Hat also embrace it as their default. To use it, you'll need the kvm.ko kernel module for Linux, a CPU that has built-in virtualization support, and of course a kernel that supports KVM virtualization. (The 2.6.20 kernel is the first Linux kernel to do this.) To create virtual machines with KVM, you'll use the /dev/kvm interface, and this functionality requires a modified version of the QEMU program.

QEMU was originally developed as an open-source emulation product, but it never became very successful in the data center. And even though it was developed to be used as a virtualization solution, it never really made it. QEMU tools are still very useful, however, and QEMU tools and solutions are used in both KVM and Xen environments. Currently, most operating systems are supported on a KVM virtual host, provided that the operating system runs on the same processor architecture.

■Note *Emulation* means that software is used to simulate a hardware platform. An example is when you run a Sega Megadrive/Genesis emulator on your PC to run old games; the software runs all CPU instructions like the hardware does. The emulator behaves just like a software processor, a pure software virtual machine. You can run an i386 operating system on an i386-based CPU in two ways. First, you can use an i386 software emulator running on i386 (examples are Bochs and QEMU). In such a solution, the software behaves like a PC reproducing the complete hardware platform. Second, you can use a virtualization solution such as VMware Workstation. The virtualization solution does not provide a virtual CPU or any virtual base component of the basic PC hardware (IRQs controllers, hardware clock, and so on); it just puts the program to be virtualized on the real CPU and lets it execute the code. That solution needs complete hardware control, which is why it needs to run on privileged mode of the CPU and provides kernel modules for Linux to run in the kernel. Virtualization is not a next generation of emulation; it's a different way of executing an operating system.

The other major player in the Linux virtualization market is Xen, which began as a research project at the University of Cambridge (see http://www.cl.cam.ac.uk/research/srg/netos/xen). Its core component is its *hypervisor*, the layer that makes it possible to create virtual machines and to handle instructions generated by those virtual machines. When used on a virtual machine host, the hypervisor replaces the normal Linux kernel, which is loaded only after the Xen hypervisor. Xen is currently one of the best virtualization platforms available on Linux, mainly because of its strong developer community, which includes hardware vendors such as Intel, HP, and AMD; and software vendors such as Novell and Red Hat. You can use Xen on Ubuntu Server as well, but the default virtualization stack is KVM.

Approaches to Virtualization

Both Xen and KVM offer two approaches to virtualization: full virtualization and paravirtualization. Before starting to build a virtualization solution, you should understand the differences between the two.

Paravirtualization

Paravirtualization requires a modified version of the guest operating system, and this modified version generates instructions that are easier to handle for the hypervisor, which is the component that interprets virtualized instructions and passes them to the physical hardware. In paravirtualization, the operating system knows it is virtualized, so it can generate instructions that are optimized for use in a virtualized environment and don't have to be translated first. These modified instructions mean that the virtual machine manager doesn't need to change the normal instructions coming from the virtual machine to a format that works in a virtualized environment. Also, although paravirtualization doesn't require any specialized hardware, its big disadvantage is that it does require a specially modified version of the guest operating system. Some operating systems (such as Windows) just don't offer such a tuned version.

Full Virtualization

The alternative to paravirtualization is full virtualization, which lets you use an ordinary, unmodified, straight-out-of-the-box operating system as a guest. The downside is that it requires special hardware support, which is offered as a special feature in recent CPUs from both AMD and Intel. Because of this built-in support within the server's CPU, fully virtualized machines can work as efficiently as possible, despite the fact that the instructions coming from the virtualized operating system need to be translated by the virtual machine manager. Because the guest operating system has no idea that it is virtualized, it generates normal instructions. However, this can cause difficulties when there's a virtualization layer between the guest operating system and the hardware. Instructions addressed to the CPU are hard to virtualize, especially with the i386 architecture, so the CPU's hardware virtualization support makes sure that the performance penalty isn't too great.

Which Is Best for You?

After reading this, you may wonder which of the two approaches is best for your situation. Unfortunately, you can't always choose the ideal solution. If your operating system doesn't offer paravirtualization support, full virtualization is the only way to go. But if both your CPU and your operating system have virtualization support, it's always better to use paravirtualization because the virtualized operating system generates instructions that are optimized for a virtualized environment. In this way, the performance loss due to virtualization is kept to a bare minimum.

If you can't use paravirtualization because your operating system doesn't support it, you can see if paravirtualized drivers are available. Such drivers are supplied in some cases, and they can help increase the performance of particular devices such as your network interface card, hard drive, and other I/O devices. In other situations, however, you'll find that full virtualization is the only solution because the operating system you want to virtualize doesn't give you a choice or—as with KVM virtualization—paravirtualization for complete operating systems is not yet supported. Therefore, the hands-on parts of this chapter assume that you have a CPU with virtualization support.

■**Tip** Most modern Pentium IV and Xeon processors offer support for virtualization. If you're not sure about your CPU, just check the system's BIOS. If virtualization is supported, the BIOS will include a virtualization option. As an alternative, you can also check the `/proc/cpuinfo` file for the VMX flag for your CPU. If it's there, your CPU supports full virtualization.

Installing Virtual Machines with KVM

If your CPU supports virtualization, KVM-based virtualization is the easiest to use (although this is a very recent development). In this section, you'll read how to prepare your machine as a KVM virtualization host, and then you'll learn how to install Windows and Ubuntu as virtualized operating systems in the KVM-virtualized environment.

■**Caution** When using virtualization, it's a very good idea to differentiate between the host operating system and the others. The *host operating system* is the first operating system that your server boots. It also has some very specific responsibilities for the other operating systems, such as managing access to drivers and managing the virtual machines themselves. To make sure that it can perform these tasks in the most efficient way, don't run any services (other than virtualization services) in the host operating system!

Preparing Your Server for KVM Virtualization: Networking

On a server in which virtualization is used, you can have more virtual machines than you have network cards. Therefore, a solution needs to be implemented for the virtual machines to share network boards in your server.

To make this possible, you need to create a virtual network bridge by redefining the contents of the /etc/network/interface file (as shown in the example in Listing 13-1). This code is meant to replace all contents that you currently have in this file.

Listing 13-1. *A Network Bridge Provides Network Access for All Virtual Machines*

```
auto lo
iface lo inet loopback

auto br0
iface br0 inet static
     address 192.168.1.99
     network 192.168.1.0
     netmask 255.255.255.0
     broadcast 192.168.1.255
     gateway 192.168.1.254
     bridge_ports eth0
     bridge_fd 0
     bridge_hello 2
     bridge_maxage 12
     bridge_stop off
```

This configuration file makes sure that a device with the name br0 is created to replace the eth0 device when you reboot your server or restart your network. However, this device is meant to use eth0 as its physical back end, as specified by the line bridge ports eth0. After creating the configuration file in this way, use sudo /etc/init.d/networking restart to restart the network. Your network is now ready to handle KVM virtual machines.

Setting Up KVM on Ubuntu Server

Perform the following steps to set up your server for virtualization (the procedure described here is supported on Ubuntu Server version 8.04 and later):

1. Install all software necessary (the KVM and QEMU packages) for KVM virtualization. As root, use the command `apt-get install kvm qemu libvirt-bin`.

2. After installing these software packages, make sure that the `kvm` kernel module is loaded. Use `lsmod` to determine whether this is the case (`lsmod | grep kvm`). If the module is not loaded, install it using `modprobe kvm`.

■**Tip** Are you getting the "Operation is not supported" message while loading the kernel module? If so, this means that you have the wrong CPU. Either upgrade your CPU to one that offers virtualization support, or use Xen as your virtualization solution with an operating system that supports paravirtualization.

You have to do some additional preparation, which involves preparing the `libvirt` tools that you will use to create virtual machines. First, add the user account you want to use for KVM management purposes to the `libvirtd` group by using the `sudo adduser <username>` `libvirtd` command (replace `<username>` with the name of the user whose account you want to use).

■**Note** This command might appear strange because Linux has a `useradd` command that creates new user accounts. There is also the `adduser` account, which is used here (it adds an existing user to a group).

And that's it! Your Ubuntu Server is now ready for the installation and operation of guest operating systems. The next section describes how to install Windows as a guest operating system.

Installing Windows As a Guest Operating System on KVM

Before installing Windows as your first guest operating system, you should ask yourself exactly what you want to do with the virtualized machines. Is your server running in a data center, and are you accomplishing all tasks (including installation of the virtual machines) remotely? If so, you can run it without a graphical user interface (GUI), but, if you want to be able to manage the virtual machine(s) from the physical server itself, you'll need a GUI. (Refer to Chapter 3 to find out how to set up a GUI on your server.) I recommend not installing a GUI on your server, but instead use a graphical workstation to create and manage virtual machines. From the graphical workstation, establish an SSH session to your server; for example, `ssh -X myserver`. Don't forget the -X because it tells SSH to forward graphical screens. Next, from the SSH terminal you can launch any graphical management utility that is installed on your server.

The following procedure assumes that you have a graphical interface that can be used to display the Windows installation interface:

1. To install Windows as a virtualized operating system, you first need to set up storage. The simplest way of trying out virtualization is by using a disk image file. You can create it by using dd or qemu-img, as in the following command that creates an 8 GB disk image file with the name windows.img in the directory /var/lib/virt (make sure to create this directory before creating the image file):

```
dd if=/dev/zero of=/var/lib/virt/windows.img bs=1M count=8192
```

2. Now that you've created the disk image file, you can use the kvm command to install Windows. Make sure that the Windows installation CD is in the drive (or use an ISO file) and run the following command to start the installation, creating a Windows virtual machine with a total of 512 MB of RAM. This command uses the windows.img disk file that you just created. Want to use an ISO file instead of a physical CD-ROM? Just replace /dev/cdrom by a complete path to the ISO file. The -no-acpi option used in this example isn't really required, but it might be useful if you have problems using ACPI:

```
kvm -m 512 -cdrom /dev/cdrom -boot d windows.img
```

■**Tip** Is the kvm command complaining about the lack of support for virtualization on your CPU? You probably haven't switched virtualization support on in your system BIOS yet. Restart your machine, enter the system BIOS, and make sure that virtualization support is on (you typically find this in the Advanced section of your BIOS configuration). The option you're looking for has a name like *vm*, *vt*, or *virtualization*.

---

3. A QEMU window opens, in which you'll see the Windows installer loading (see Figure 13-1). Complete the Windows installation from this interface.

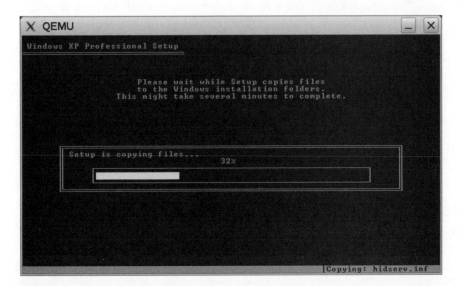

Figure 13-1. *With the required CPU support, KVM allows you to run virtual Windows machines.*

4. Once the installation of virtualized Windows is finished, you can run it in the same way you installed it. Use the kvm command again, but omit the -boot d option that ensures that you're booting from CD-ROM first. So the following command runs an installed instance of Windows that is on the windows.img file:

```
kvm  -m 512 -cdrom /dev/cdrom windows.img
```

You now have your virtualized Windows machine. That was easy, wasn't it? Next, you'll have a look at how to install Ubuntu as a guest on top of your Ubuntu Server virtualization host.

Installing Ubuntu Server As a Guest Operating System on KVM

After reading the previous section about installing Windows as a guest operating system in KVM, you probably can already guess how to install an instance of virtualized Ubuntu. Fundamentally there are no differences between installing Windows or Ubuntu: you create a virtual disk and install Ubuntu Server on it. Assuming that the installation CD is in an ISO image with the name ubuntu.iso, you can use the following procedure:

1. Create the disk file:

```
dd if=/dev/zero of=/var/lib/virt/ubuntu.img bs=1M count=4096
```

2. Use the kvm command to start the installation from the Ubuntu ISO file:

```
kvm  -m 256 -cdrom /isos/ubuntu.iso -boot d /var/lib/virt/ubuntu.img
```

■**Tip** Are you having problems installing Ubuntu or another Linux distribution as a guest operating system? The graphical menu that most boot loaders display before starting the installation might be the reason. Try a nongraphical installation program such as the Ubuntu netboot mini.iso file instead. This will help you install any Linux distribution without problems.

---

3. Install Ubuntu Server as if it were a "normal" server.

4. Boot the virtual Ubuntu Server you just installed with the following command and you're done:

```
kvm -m 256 ubuntu.img
```

Managing Virtual Machines with Virtual Manager

If you don't like starting and installing your virtual machines using the kvm command (or even with an enhancement to this command such as virt-install), virt-manager might be the solution for you. This graphical utility provides an easy solution to creating and managing virtual machines. It does have a disadvantage however: it needs an X server to run. You don't have to install the graphical environment locally on your server; you can run virt-manager from a workstation as well. For instance, establish an SSH session with your server from a workstation and start virt-manager that way. This procedure gives you all the benefits of the graphical virtual machine management tools without the hassle of installing a GUI on your server.

As an alternative, you can also use a boot parameter to tell virt-manager it has to get its information from another machine. For instance, the following command would connect to somenode.example.com and allow you to manage virtual machines on that node:

```
virt-manager -c qemu+ssh://somenode.example.com/system
```

In case you want to start virt-manager to create virtual machines on the local host, use the following:

```
virt-manager -c qemu:///system
```

The following procedure creates a virtual machine using virt-manager:

1. Start virt-manager. In this example, I'll assume you have established an SSH session with a remote server, so you can type virt-manager -c qemu:///system to start the virt-manager session. You'll see an interface like that in Figure 13-2.

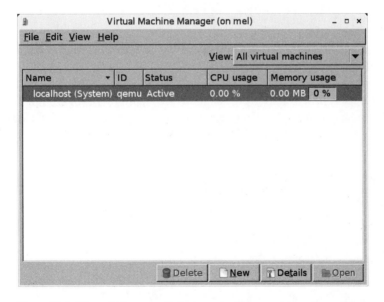

Figure 13-2. *Virtual Manager helps you easily create virtual machines.*

2. Select the localhost line and click New to start creating a new virtual machine. This brings you to the first step of a wizard interface; click Forward.

3. Enter the name of the system that you want to create. For instance, if you want to install a Windows XP test machine, **WinXP** might be a good idea. Click Forward to proceed.

4. The utility asks you what kind of virtualization you want to use (see Figure 13-3). Depending on the operating system that you want to install, Fully Virtualized might be the only option available.

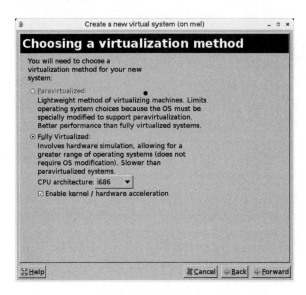

Figure 13-3. *Depending on the operating system that you want to virtualize, full virtualization might be the only option available.*

5. You need to specify how to start the installation (see Figure 13-4). For example, if you have an ISO image to install from, browse to the path where the installer can find the ISO image. Make sure to select the OS Type and OS Variant you want to install.

Figure 13-4. *To allow for an easy installation, install from an ISO image.*

6. Indicate what you want to install to (see Figure 13-5). For best performance, it is a good idea to give every virtual machine a dedicated partition or LVM logical volume. If you can't do that, you can install to a file instead. The installation interface creates this virtual disk file automatically for you.

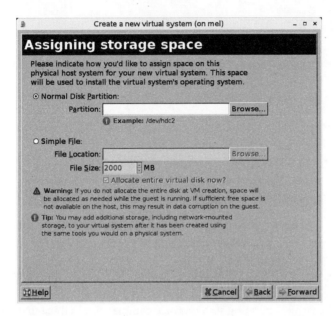

Figure 13-5. *For best performance, use a partition or LVM logical volume as the storage backend.*

7. Select the networking method that you want to use. The most flexible way is to create a virtual network. In this configuration, a network bridge is created in the network. If your server has a fixed IP address, you can also choose to assign a second IP address to the network interface by selecting the Shared physical device option. After making your choice, click Forward to proceed.

8. Enter the amount of RAM and CPUs you want to give to your virtual machine (see Figure 13-6); click Forward. Notice the difference that the utility makes between a logical CPU and a virtual CPU. A *logical CPU* is present on your physical hardware, either as a real CPU or as a CPU core on a multicore processor. A *virtual CPU* is present in the virtual machine. It can use any type of logical CPU.

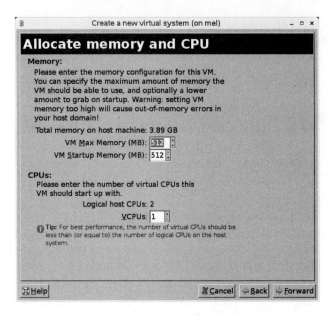

Figure 13-6. *Each virtual machine gets its own amount of RAM and virtual CPUs.*

9. In the last screen of the wizard, you see an overview of the installation settings that will be used. Are you happy with them? Click Forward to start the installation and complete the installation of the virtual operating system. Once completed, you'll see that the new virtual machine is added to the `virt-manager` interface; you'll be able to manage it from there.

Managing Virtual Machines with `libvirt` Tools

Even if `virt-manager` provides an easy way to set up and manage virtual machines, it is not the only way. The `libvirt` tools allow you to create and manage virtual machines without the need to run any graphical tools. It offers VNC access, so after you set up the virtual machine, you can make a VNC connection to it.

Creating Virtual Machines with `virt-install`

To create virtual machines, you can use the `virt-install` command. By default it is not present on your server, so first make sure to run the `apt-get install python-virtinst` command as root. Next, you can create a virtual machine from the command line, with a command such as the following:

```
virt-install -n testserver -r 512 -f /dev/system/testserver -s 10\
 -c jeos.iso --accelerate --vnc --noautoconsole
```

In this command, a number of options are being used to define the virtual machine:

- `-n testserver`: This option sets the name of the virtual machine to `testserver`. You'll need this name to start the virtual server again later.

- `-r 512`: This option grants 512 MB of RAM to the virtual server.

- `-f /dev/system/testserver`: This option specifies what to use as the virtual hard disk for your virtual machine. I like creating an LVM logical volume for each of my virtual machines, but you don't have to do that. Instead, you can refer to a disk image file that you have created earlier. Make sure that the device or disk file that you are referring to exists before copying over the virtual machine!

- `-s 10`: This option specifies the size in gigabytes for the virtual disk.

- `-c jeos.iso`: This option tells the installer from which device to start the installation.

- `--accelerate`: This option uses the kernel acceleration features to make it faster.

- `--vnc`: This option enables VNC access.

- `--noautoconsole`: Use this option to not attach automatically to the console of the virtual machine. It makes sense if you are using `virt-install` on a server that doesn't have a GUI. If you use it in a graphical environment, however, omit this option, which will automatically give you access to the console of the virtual machine.

After launching `virt-install` this way, you can connect to the console of the virtual machine locally if you have a GUI on your server, or you can connect remotely using the `virt-viewer` utility.

Using `virt-viewer` to Access the Virtual Machine Console

After starting the installation, you can use `virt-viewer` to access the console of your virtual machines. Make sure to install it first using `apt-get install virt-viewer` as root. After installing it, there are two ways to access it: locally or remotely. To access a virtual machine console locally, run the following command:

```
virt-viewer qemu:///system testserver
```

To access the console of a virtual machine that is running somewhere else, you need to set up SSH key–based authentication (see Chapter 8 for information on how to do that). Assuming that you set it up, the following command gives access to the console of a virtual machine that is running on the host with the IP address 192.168.1.200:

```
virt-viewer -c qemu+ssh:///192.168.1.200 testserver
```

Cloning Virtual Machines using `virt-clone`

Another useful command that comes from the `libvirt` package is `virt-clone`, which you can use to clone virtual machines. This command doesn't just copy the files of your virtual machine over; it also makes sure that the database that contains all information about your virtual machines is updated (which doesn't happen if you use `dd` to copy a disk image to somewhere else). The following line shows how to clone the virtual machine `testserver` created earlier to a new machine with the name `newserver`:

```
virt-clone -o testserver -n newserver -f /dev/system/newserver\
 --connect=qemu:///system
```

In this command, the -o testserver option is used to refer to the name of the original server. Next, -n newserver tells the KVM environment that the name of the new machine should be newserver. You need to specify what is used as the storage back end for the new machine. In this case, it will be an LVM logical volume with the name /dev/system/newserver. (Make sure that you use lvcreate to create this logical volume before entering this command!)

Instead of using an LVM logical volume, you can also copy the virtual machine to an image file. Finally, the --connect=qemu:///system option tells virt-clone where it can find the hypervisor that it should use for the copying.

Managing Virtual Machines with `virsh`

To manage virtual machines, libvirt offers virsh, which is a command-line utility that takes all-important management commands as its argument. The following list gives an overview of the most important management actions you can perform using virsh:

- virsh -c qemu:///system list: Provides an overview of all known virtual machines on the local system.

- virsh -c qemu:///system start testserver: Starts the virtual machine testserver.

- virsh -c qemu:///system autostart testserver: Sets testserver to autostart. It will automatically be started when the host server starts.

- visrh -c qemu:///system reboot testserver: Restarts testserver.

- virsh -c qemu:///system shutdown testserver: Shuts down testserver.

- virsh -c qemu:///system save testserver testserver-080208.state: Saves the current state of testserver to a file with the name testserver-080208.state.

- virsh -c qemu:///system restore testserver-080208.state: Restores the state of testserver as saved in testserver-080208.state to the current testserver.

- virsh -c qemu:///system attach-disk testserver /dev/cdrom /media/cdrom: Mounts the physical CD-ROM device to the /media/cdrom directory in testserver.

Installing Virtual Machines Using Xen

A second way of using Ubuntu Server as a virtualization host is to configure Xen. Since version 7.10, Ubuntu Server has drastically improved support for Xen, but Canonical made the decision to go with KVM as the default solution for virtualization in version 8.04. In this section, you'll see how to set up Ubuntu Server as a host for Xen virtualization. You'll also learn how to install Windows and another instance of Ubuntu Server as guests in a Xen environment.

Before starting the hands-on part of this section, you should know a bit about Xen terminology. In Xen, there's no difference between a host and a guest operating system. This is because the words *host* and *guest* suggest a hierarchical relation that doesn't exist. Instead, Xen talks about the domain 0 operating system and the other operating systems. These other operating systems are referred to as domain U machines. The domain 0 (or just dom0) is the first operating system that loads on a physical machine, and it has some specific responsibilities in the Xen environment, including driver management. In other environments, the dom0 machine would be referred to as the host operating system.

The domain U (or just domU) machines are virtualized machines that do not have a special responsibility with regard to virtualization. In other virtualized environments, these machines would be referred to as guest operating systems.

Setting Up Xen on Ubuntu Server

You need to install a few packages to configure Ubuntu Server as a Xen host. All are installed automatically when using the `ubuntu-xen-server` package, so simply issue the following command to start using Xen:

```
apt-get install ubuntu-xen-server
```

Because Xen uses a special kernel that's loaded before the normal Linux kernel, you have to check the `/boot/grub/menu.lst` file to make sure that the Grub boot configuration is changed to boot the Xen kernel as its default. To make sure that you're running a Xen kernel, use the `uname -r` command. Its result gives a kernel name such as `2.6.22-12-xen`, indicating that you're using a Xen kernel. Now reboot your server to load this specific Xen kernel.

After booting this kernel, the normal Linux kernel is booted; then your Ubuntu Server installation loads. By installing Xen, the Ubuntu Server instance technically becomes a virtual machine—but it's a special virtual machine that has specific management tasks in the Xen environment. To make sure that it can perform all of them in the most optimal way, make sure that no regular services (such as web or file servers) are started from your Ubuntu installation.

After installing the Xen packages, you need to configure Xen networking, and you'll do this by editing the generic Xen configuration file `/etc/xen/xend-config.sxp`. Xen offers different methods to create the virtualized network, but the network bridge is currently the most stable. To enable the network bridge, you need to change three lines in `/etc/xen/xend-config.sxp` so that they look like the lines in Listing 13-2.

Listing 13-2. *Enabling Networking in* `/etc/xen/xend-config.sxp`

```
...
(network-script network-bridge)
(vif-script vif-bridge)
#(network-script network-dummy)
```

These lines ensure that the dummy network device (which is on by default) is disabled, and it enables the network-bridge script. This script creates a device `br0` and several other network devices as well, as you can see in Listing 13-3.

Listing 13-3. *Networking in a Xen Environment*

```
root@lor:~# ifconfig
eth0      Link encap:Ethernet  HWaddr 00:14:22:FA:6F:22
          inet addr:192.168.1.82  Bcast:192.168.1.255  Mask:255.255.255.0
          inet6 addr: fe80::214:22ff:fefa:6f22/64 Scope:Link
```

```
          UP BROADCAST RUNNING MULTICAST  MTU:1500  Metric:1
          RX packets:310 errors:0 dropped:0 overruns:0 frame:0
          TX packets:59 errors:0 dropped:0 overruns:0 carrier:0
          collisions:0 txqueuelen:0
          RX bytes:27634 (26.9 KB)  TX bytes:7812 (7.6 KB)

lo        Link encap:Local Loopback
          inet addr:127.0.0.1  Mask:255.0.0.0
          inet6 addr: ::1/128 Scope:Host
          UP LOOPBACK RUNNING  MTU:16436  Metric:1
          RX packets:0 errors:0 dropped:0 overruns:0 frame:0
          TX packets:0 errors:0 dropped:0 overruns:0 carrier:0
          collisions:0 txqueuelen:0
          RX bytes:0 (0.0 b)  TX bytes:0 (0.0 b)

peth0     Link encap:Ethernet  HWaddr FE:FF:FF:FF:FF:FF
          inet6 addr: fe80::fcff:ffff:feff:ffff/64 Scope:Link
          UP BROADCAST RUNNING NOARP  MTU:1500  Metric:1
          RX packets:308 errors:0 dropped:0 overruns:0 frame:0
          TX packets:61 errors:0 dropped:0 overruns:0 carrier:0
          collisions:0 txqueuelen:1000
          RX bytes:28822 (28.1 KB)  TX bytes:8298 (8.1 KB)
          Interrupt:18

vif0.0    Link encap:Ethernet  HWaddr FE:FF:FF:FF:FF:FF
          inet6 addr: fe80::fcff:ffff:feff:ffff/64 Scope:Link
          UP BROADCAST RUNNING NOARP  MTU:1500  Metric:1
          RX packets:59 errors:0 dropped:0 overruns:0 frame:0
          TX packets:311 errors:0 dropped:0 overruns:0 carrier:0
          collisions:0 txqueuelen:0
          RX bytes:7812 (7.6 KB)  TX bytes:27704 (27.0 KB)

xenbr0    Link encap:Ethernet  HWaddr FE:FF:FF:FF:FF:FF
          UP BROADCAST RUNNING NOARP  MTU:1500  Metric:1
          RX packets:266 errors:0 dropped:0 overruns:0 frame:0
          TX packets:1 errors:0 dropped:0 overruns:0 carrier:0
          collisions:0 txqueuelen:0
          RX bytes:19042 (18.5 KB)  TX bytes:70 (70.0 b)
```

After modifying this script, use the following command as root to restart the xend process, which is responsible for management of the virtual network infrastructure:

```
/etc/init.d/xend restart
```

If after restarting the xend process, the ifconfig command doesn't show you all the network interfaces that you see in Listing 13-3, you should restart the entire machine.

In the Xen network environment, all virtualized operating systems (including the domain 0 virtualization host) use a virtualized driver to address the network card. This driver can be recognized as eth0 in the virtualized operating system. This eth0 is represented in the domain 0 operating system by an interface with the name vifx.y. In this name, x represents the ID of the virtualized operating system, and y represents the number of the virtualized network board. For example, the eth0 network card in domain 0 (which has ID 0) is represented as vif0.0; likewise, if a virtualized Windows server that has ID 4 (use the xm list command to learn the ID of a virtualized operating system) has four virtualized network cards, the second of them would be represented by vif4.1 in domain 0.

Now in the domain 0 system, all vif interfaces are attached to the virtual bridge, which is thus behaving like a real bridge or switch. This bridge in turn communicates with the representation of the physical network card, which is peth0 and talks directly to the network board in your server. Check Figure 13-7 for a graphical representation of how all this is organized.

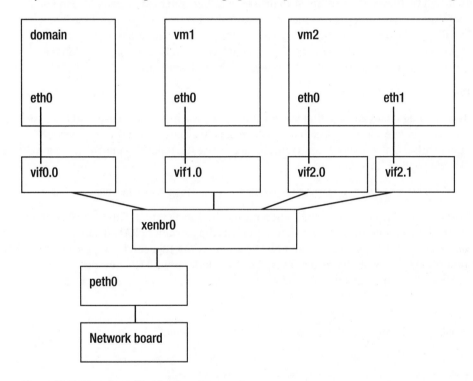

Figure 13-7. *The virtual bridge in a Xen environment*

After creating the virtual network, you have a bit more preparation work: edit the /etc/modules file and add the line loop max_loop=64. This is necessary to ensure that you can create enough virtual disks for your virtual machines. To confirm that this new setting works, reboot your machine before starting to create virtual machines.

Installing Windows as a Guest Operating System on Xen

To install Windows as a guest operating system in a Xen environment, you need a CPU that supports virtualization because Windows itself doesn't exist in a version that understands paravirtualization. So the only way to virtualize it is to use a CPU that has hardware virtualization support. To check your CPU, use the xm dmesg command to see an overview of all features that are relevant for Xen virtualization:

```
root@lor:~# xm dmesg | grep VMX
(XEN) HVM: VMX enabled
(XEN) VMX: MSR intercept bitmap enabled
```

If you see a result such as this one, you can continue creating your instance of virtualized Windows. If you don't get a result, your CPU doesn't support virtualization, which means that you can't virtualize Windows. Sorry!

So, if your processor has VMX, let's start virtualizing Windows.

1. To install Windows or any other virtualized operating system, it's a good idea to enable a VNC server. This lets you connect to the console of the virtualized machine while installing it. Without this VNC server, your only option is headless installation, which isn't easy at all. So make sure that the /etc/xen/xend-config.sxp configuration file includes the following line. After changing it, restart the xend process:

   ```
   (vnc-listen '0.0.0.0')
   ```

2. Now you need to make sure that the guest system has a hard disk to use, and the easiest way to create such a disk is to use disk image files. The /var/lib/xend/storage directory is a convenient place to put such a file. Use the following line to create a 4 GB disk image file in this directory:

   ```
   dd if=/dev/zero of=/var/lib/xend/storage/windows.img bs=1024 count=4000000
   ```

3. Next, you need to create a configuration file for the guest system. This file will contain all the settings used by the guest system, such as the amount of RAM it can use, the hard disk, and so on. The configuration shown in Listing 13-4 can be used to create a Windows XP virtual machine that uses 512 MB of RAM and a 4 GB hard disk, and accesses the optical disk in /dev/cdrom as the optical drive. Create this file with the name /etc/xen/windowsxp.

Listing 13-4. *Example Configuration File to Create a Windows XP Virtual Machine*

```
kernel = '/usr/lib/xen-ioemu-3.0/boot/hvmloader'
device_mode1 = '/usr/lib/xen-ioemu-3.0/bin/qemu-0dm'
builder = 'hvm'
memory = '512'
disk = [ 'file:/var/lib/xend/storage/windows.img,ioemu:hda,w'\
  , 'phy:/dev/cdrom,ioemu:hdc,r']
name = 'winxp'
vif = [ 'type=ioemu, bridge=xenbr0' ]
boot='d' # use boot='c' to boot from harddisk
vnc=1
vncviewer=1
sd1=0
```

4. Now it's time to run the virtual machine and start its installation process. To do that, use the following command:

```
xm create -c /etc/xen/windowsxp
```

Installing Ubuntu Server As a Guest Operating System on Xen

A different way of creating Xen images is to use the Xen-tools option. This solution consists of two elements: the xen-create-image command and the xen-tools.conf configuration file. You can use xen-create-imag with lots of command-line options, but an easier solution is to tell it to read the configuration file /etc/xen-tools/xen-tools.conf. Your result is a Xen virtual machine configuration file, just like the one you created manually based on the information from the preceding section.

In this section, you'll read how to install a Xen virtual machine using Xen tools. Before you start building this solution, think carefully about where you want to manage settings. The xen-tools.conf file functions as a template file that contains default settings, but these settings can also be specified as command-line options using xen-create-image. In this section, I'll show you how to apply both solutions.

1. Open the /etc/xen-tools/xen-tools.conf file with an editor and include the following settings:

```
dir = /home/xen # directory where the virtual disk files are created
install-method = debootstrap # specifies how to boot the virtual machine
dist = etch # specifies what distribution to install, check the
configuration file for information about supported distributions.
dhcp = 1 # use this to set up networking via DHCP
passwd = 1 # you need this to set the root password interactively
kernel = /boot/vmlinuz-`uname -r` # the kernel to use
initrd = /boot/initrd.img-`uname -r` # the initrd to use
boot = 1 # this allows the new virtual machine to boot after installation
mirror = http://de.archive.ubuntu.com/ubuntu/ # the mirror site
to perform the installation
```

2. Now that some of the basic settings for installing the virtual machine are in place, use the xen-create-image command to create the virtual machine. Because many options are already in the /etc/xen-tools/xen-tools.conf file, the xen-create-image command needs relatively few options:

```
xen-create-image --hostname=ubuntu.example.com --size=4Gb --swap=256Mb\
    --ide --memory=128Mb --debootstrap
```

3. The installation procedure now starts. Go have a cup of coffee; it takes some time to copy all the files to the virtual machine to perform the installation.

Because you told the installer to prompt for a password, after copying all files to the virtual machines, the installer asks for one. Once you've entered it, you'll see the "All done" message, indicating that the virtual machine is now installed. You'll also see that the installer created a log file with details about this virtual machine. This file is in the /var/log/xen-tools directory. The installer also created the configuration file that's used by the virtual machine.

This configuration file performs the same function as the virtual machine configuration file that you created manually for the Windows virtual machine in the previous section.

Now that the installation is finished, it's time to launch the virtual machine. To do this, use the following command:

```
xm create /etc/xen/ubuntu.example.com.cfg
```

Once the virtual machine has launched successfully, you can attach to its console using the following:

```
xm console ubuntu.example.com
```

This command brings you to the console of the virtual machine. Want to go back to the console of the host machine? Use the Ctrl+] shortcut. From the console of the host machine, you can use the xm command to perform virtual machine management tasks. The next section provides an overview of the important management commands.

Using Xen Management Commands

After starting the installation of your virtual machines, you also need some minimal knowledge of how to manage these machines. You can use the xm command, which is a very versatile command that uses subcommands to specify exactly what you want to do. Table 13-1 is an overview of some of the most useful xm commands.

Table 13-1. *Overview of the Most Important Xen Management Commands*

Command	Explanation
xm create -c /path/to/configfile	Runs a virtual machine. To run it, you need a configuration file like those created in the two subsections dealing with installation of Windows and Ubuntu virtual machines.
xm list	Gives a list of all virtual machines.
xm console <name>	Starts a console for the virtual machine <name>. Use xm list to find out what name to use. Without this command, you can't view information about your virtual machine.
xm shutdown <name>	Shuts down a virtual machine in a clean way.
xm destroy <name>	Kills a virtual machine instantaneously without shutting it down properly. This can lead to destruction of virtual machine configuration files.
xm top	Gives an overview that allows you to monitor performance of virtual machines.
xm help	Gives an overview of all xm subcommands that you can use.

Ubuntu Server in a VMware Environment

VMware offers several virtualization products that you can use with Ubuntu Server. The most important of these, from the point of view of a data center, is VMware ESX. Although para-virtualization can also be used in VMware ESX, to benefit from this solution, the virtualized operating system must be aware that it's being used in a paravirtualized environment. This is realized by the VMI support that Ubuntu Server has offered since version 7.04.

The VMI support ensures that the Linux kernel knows that it's being used in a paravirtualized environment. So Ubuntu Server generates instructions that are easier to handle in a virtualized environment. The good news is that this support comes out of the box. Immediately upon installation of Ubuntu Server, the installer detects that it's installed in a virtualized environment, and VMI support is activated automatically.

Ubuntu JeOS

Ubuntu offers a specific version of the server operating system that was made and tuned to be used in a virtualized environment: Ubuntu Server JeOS (pronounced as *juice* and stands for Just Enough Operating System). Ubuntu Server JeOS is specifically developed to make it easy for you to create virtual appliances. That means its kernel is stripped down to contain only those options that you need for your virtual appliance. Because of this, Ubuntu Server JeOS runs far more efficiently than any normal instance of Ubuntu Server.

To install a virtual machine using JeOS, start by downloading it from http://cdimage.ubuntu.com/jeos/releases/8.04/release/.

Browse to this Ubuntu download page and get the most current release of Ubuntu Server JeOS. Next, install it in VMware ESX, VMware Server, or in a KVM environment. Other virtualization platforms might work, but are not supported. The installation itself is straightforward: just install JeOS in the way you would install a normal instance of Ubuntu Server. You can then set up your appliance in it, which provides you with a perfectly optimized Ubuntu Server virtual machine.

The interesting part of configuring JeOS as an appliance comes after the installation is complete and the application is installed. Again just follow the standard procedure. When you hand out your JeOS virtual appliance, you probably want to start a setup program that allows users to configure the appliance according to their own needs.

Listing 13-5 shows how you can do that to perform an initial configuration of the SSH server. The example provides a blueprint of how to do this for any application:

1. To start the initial configuration, it's a good idea to create a script in /etc/bash.bashrc. The following code checks whether a check file is already present. This check file is created after successful configuration of the appliance. If the check file is present, no work has to be done. If it's not, this script makes sure that a configuration script is launched.

Listing 13-5. *Launch the Initial Configuration by Adding Some Code*

```
if [ ! -e /etc/opt/sshserver/config_done ]; then
  /opt/sshserver/bin/config
  sudo touch /etc/opt/sshserver/config_done
fi
```

2. The script from Listing 13-5 calls a configuration script with the name /opt/sshserrver/bin/config. Change the name of this script and its directory to match the application that you want to configure. Listing 13-6 gives an example of the contents of this configuration script. This is a very simple script, ensuring that the SSH server is reconfigured; change it to match the requirements of your application.

Listing 13-6. *Create a Configuration Script that Performs the Initial Configuration of Your Application*

```
#Perform the reinstall of openssh so that the key is regenerated
echo "Removing the openssh-server and installing it again."
echo "This makes sure that your SSH-keys are generated for your server."
sudo apt-get --purge -y remove openssh-server
sudo apt-get install -y openssh-server
# Add any other configuration lines that you need
```

3. This completes the example application configuration. Your JeOS virtual appliance is now ready for use.

Summary

Virtualization is one of the most dynamic areas of interest in the modern data center. In this chapter, you learned how virtualization is used in current versions of Ubuntu Server. But be aware that the available options may change fast. New versions of Ubuntu Server can be expected to offer enhanced support for virtualization, with more-advanced and user-friendly management tools, too.

Index

You Need the Companion eBook

Your purchase of this book entitles you to buy the companion PDF-version eBook for only $10. Take the weightless companion with you anywhere.

We believe this Apress title will prove so indispensable that you'll want to carry it with you everywhere, which is why we are offering the companion eBook (in PDF format) for $10 to customers who purchase this book now. Convenient and fully searchable, the PDF version of any content-rich, page-heavy Apress book makes a valuable addition to your programming library. You can easily find and copy code—or perform examples by quickly toggling between instructions and the application. Even simultaneously tackling a donut, diet soda, and complex code becomes simplified with hands-free eBooks!

Once you purchase your book, getting the $10 companion eBook is simple:

❶ Visit **www.apress.com/promo/tendollars/**.

❷ Complete a basic registration form to receive a randomly generated question about this title.

❸ Answer the question correctly in 60 seconds, and you will receive a promotional code to redeem for the $10.00 eBook.

THE EXPERT'S VOICE™

233 Spring Street, New York, NY 10013

Offer valid through 4/10.